*Genesis*

THE
CROSSWAY CLASSIC
COMMENTARIES

# Genesis

## JOHN CALVIN

SERIES EDITORS

*ALISTER MCGRATH*

*J. I. PACKER*

WHEATON, ILLINOIS

*Genesis*

Copyright © 2001 by Watermark

Published by Crossway
1300 Crescent Street
Wheaton, Illinois 60187

Scripture taken from *The Holy Bible: New International Version*®.
Copyright © 1973, 1978, 1984 by International Bible Society.
Used by permission of Zondervan Publishing House. All rights reserved.

The "NIV" and "New International Version" trademarks are registered in the United States Patent and Trademark Office by International Bible Society. Use of either trademark requires the permission of International Bible Society.

Cover design: Jordan Singer

First printing, 2001

Printed in the United States of America

ISBN-13: 978-1-58134-301-4
ISBN-10: 1-58134-301-9
PDF ISBN: 978-1-4335-0518-8
Mobipocket ISBN: 978-1-4335-0517-1
ePub ISBN: 978-1-4335-1739-6

**Library of Congress Cataloging-in-Publication Data**
Calvin, Jean, 1509-1564.
    Genesis / John Calvin.
      p.    cm. — (The Crossway classic commentaries)
    ISBN 13: 978-1-58134-301-4
    ISBN 10: 1-58134-301-9 (trade pbk. : alk. paper)
    1. Bible. O.T. Genesis—Commentaries. I. Title. II. Series.
BS1235.53.C35        2001
222'.11077—dc21                                    2001003932

Crossway is a publishing ministry of Good News Publishers.

CH      25    24    23    22    21    20    19    18    17    16

First British edition 2001

Production and Printing in the UK by 4edge for
CROSSWAY BOOKS
Norton Street, Nottingham, England NG7 3HR

ISBN 978-1-85684-209-9

# Contents

# Series Preface

The purpose of the Crossway Classic Commentaries is to make some of the most valuable commentaries on the books of the Bible, by some of the greatest Bible teachers and theologians in the last 500 years, available to a new generation. These books will help today's readers learn truth, wisdom, and devotion from such authors as J. C. Ryle, Martin Luther, John Calvin, J. B. Lightfoot, John Owen, Charles Spurgeon, Charles Hodge, and Matthew Henry.

We do not apologize for the age of some of the items chosen. In the realm of practical exposition promoting godliness, the old is often better than the new. Spiritual vision and authority, based on an accurate handling of the biblical text, are the qualities that have been primarily sought in deciding what to include.

So far as is possible, everything is tailored to the needs and enrichment of thoughtful readers—lay Christians, students, and those in the ministry. The originals, some of which were written at a high technical level, have been abridged as needed, simplified stylistically, and unburdened of foreign words. However, the intention of this series is never to change any thoughts of the original authors, but to faithfully convey them in an understandable fashion.

The publishers are grateful to Dr. Alister McGrath of Wycliffe Hall, Oxford, Dr. J. I. Packer of Regent College, Vancouver, and Watermark of Norfolk, England, for the work of selecting and editing that now brings this project to fruition.

THE PUBLISHERS
Crossway Books
Wheaton, Illinois

# Introduction

Calvin's commentary on Genesis, begun in 1550 and published in 1554, with a dedication to France's future Henry IV, is classic indeed. It was, and remains, a milestone in the interpreting of what we may still warrantably describe as Moses' first book.

As always in his handling of Scripture, Calvin looks for the theological content and the divine didactic purpose in the human writer's words, and he finds what he seeks in four themes.

The first is God's self-display to us in the world-order he has created.

The second is God's goodness in making humans in his own image, able to discern his glory in his works, to worship and adore him, to trust and hope in him, and to find freedom, fulfillment, and joy in obeying him.

The third is the ruinous guilt, pervasive perversity, and radical alienation from God that came on us all through the sin of Adam and Eve.

The fourth is the redeeming love of God the Father in initiating restoration, promulgating the promise and the bond of grace, creating, preserving, and providentially protecting the infant covenant community, and thereby adumbrating the new life and lifestyle that would later find its full shape and substance in personal discipleship to Jesus Christ, his only Son, our Lord.

If you want to get properly into Genesis, says Calvin, you must fix your mind on these things throughout. That is a word of wisdom if ever there was one!

Calvin knows that God's purpose in the opening book of the Bible is to acquaint us with these aspects of the knowledge of God and (not just of some historically distant humans but) of ourselves as those whom God calls on to abandon Adamic ways and learn to live in, through, with, and under Jesus Christ. To have projected the thrust of God so forcefully in an exposition extending over fifty chapters, while meticulously weighing every detail of the text, is the measure of Calvin's achievement, and it is this twofold excellence that gives his exposition classic status today. One may query details, but one cannot deny the magnificence of the work as a whole.

In a book that is four and a half centuries old one expects to find details that seem quaint and naive, but there are few such here. What we find instead is the outflow of a mind that is full of God and is constantly probing, practical, strong, clear, commonsensical, down-to-earth, and thorough in testing alternatives; a mind, in short, that it is a delight to be with as it digs into the text. Calvin's reflections on how God communicated with individuals and accommodated the book to simple readers, and his nose for the providential and miraculous, plus his elucidations of the anthropomorphic, plus his correlations of Genesis with other Scriptures, plus his insight in reconstructing events, discerning character and motivation from clues in the text, and understanding the past from his reading and his experience of the present, are all endlessly illuminating and suggestive.

I can, and do, assure you that if you care for the Bible at all, you will certainly like this reverent, alert, faith-full, thought-provoking exploration of one of its key books. Read on then! A feast awaits you.

J. I. PACKER

# Preface
## By John Calvin

Since the infinite wisdom of God is displayed in the wonderful structure of heaven and earth, it is absolutely impossible to display the history of the creation of the world in terms that equal its dignity. Just as our finite minds cannot comprehend things of such magnitude, so our tongues are incapable of giving a full account of them. If my readers wish to profit with me in meditating on the works of God, they must bring with them a sober, docile, mild, and humble spirit. We see, indeed, the world with our eyes, we tread the earth with our feet, we touch innumerable kinds of God's works with our hands, we inhale a sweet and pleasant fragrance from herbs and flowers, we enjoy boundless benefits; but in those very things of which we attain some knowledge, there dwells such an immensity of divine power, goodness, and wisdom as absorbs all our senses. Therefore, let men be satisfied if they obtain only a moderate taste of them, suited to their capacity.

The intention of Moses in beginning his book about the creation of the world is to show God, as it were, to us in a visible way in his works. Moses does not here give his own godly thoughts, since he is the instrument of the Holy Spirit to make known those things that it was important for all men to know. Those who think it absurd that the order of the creation, which had been previously unknown, should at length have been described and explained by Moses are greatly mistaken. For Moses does not mention things previously unheard of, but writes down for the first time facts that the fathers had communicated, as from hand to hand, over many generations to their children. Can we imagine that humankind was placed on the earth in such a way so that they were ignorant of their own origin? No sane person doubts that Adam was well-instructed about all these things. Was he really dumb afterwards? Were the holy patriarchs so ungrateful that they suppressed all such instruction? Did Noah, warned by a divine judgment in such a memorable way, neglect to transmit it to posterity? And we know that long before Moses' time all the people were acquainted with the covenant that God had entered into with their fathers. Therefore, we should not doubt that the creation of the world as it is described here was already known through the ancient and constant tradition of the fathers. Yet since it is so easy for God's truth to be corrupted by men, it pleased the Lord to commit the history to writing, so that its purity would be preserved. Moses, therefore, has established the credibility of that doctrine that is contained in his writings and that, by the carelessness of men, might otherwise have been lost.

I now return to the purpose of Moses, or rather the purpose of the Holy Spirit, who has spoken through Moses. We know God, who is invisible, only through his works. For his eternal power and godhead (as Paul says) are exhibited in the fabric of heaven and earth (Romans 1:20). David's declaration is true: The heavens, though without a tongue, are yet eloquent heralds of the glory of God, and this most beautiful order of nature silently proclaims his admirable wisdom (Psalm 19:1). This is to be diligently observed because so few pursue the right method of knowing God, and the majority of people look at the creatures without any consideration of the Creator himself. For people are commonly subject to these two extremes. Namely, some, forgetful of God, devote their minds to the consideration of nature; and others, overlooking the *works* of God, aspire with a foolish and insane curiosity to inquire into his *essence*. Both labor in vain. To be so occupied in the investigation of the secrets of nature as never to turn the eyes to its Author is a most perverted study; and to enjoy everything in nature without acknowledging the Author of the benefit is the basest ingratitude. Therefore, those who assume to be philosophers without religion and who, by speculating, remove God and all sense of piety far from them will one day feel the force of the expression of Paul, related by Luke that God has never left himself "without testimony" (Acts 14:17). They will not escape with impunity because they have been deaf and insensible to such illustrious testimonies.

In truth, it is the part of culpable ignorance never to see God, who everywhere gives signs of his presence. But if mockers now escape by their trivial objections, hereafter their terrible destruction will bear witness that they were ignorant of God only because they were willingly and maliciously blinded. As for those who proudly soar above the world to seek God in his unveiled essence, it is impossible but that at length they should entangle themselves in a multitude of absurd figments. For God—who is normally invisible (as we have already said)—clothes himself, so to speak, with the image of the world in which he would present himself to our contemplation. Those who will not deign to behold him thus magnificently arrayed in the incomparable vesture of the heavens and the earth afterwards suffer the just punishment of their proud contempt in their own ravings. Therefore, as soon as the name of God sounds in our ears or the thought of him occurs to our minds, let us also clothe him with this most beautiful ornament; let the world become our school if we desire rightly to know God.

Here also the impiety of those is refuted who cavil against Moses for relating that so short a space of time had elapsed since the creation of the world. For they inquire why it had come so suddenly into the mind of God to create the world or why he had so long remained inactive in heaven; and thus by sporting with sacred things they exercise their ingenuity to their own destruction. In the *Tripartite History* an answer is given by a pious man with which I have always been pleased. For when a certain impure dog was in this manner pouring ridicule upon God, the man retorted that God had been at that time by no means inactive because he had been preparing hell for the censorious. But by what reasonings can you restrain the arrogance of those men to whom sobriety is professedly contemptible and odious? Certainly those who now so freely exult in finding fault with the inactivity of God will find to their own great cost that his power has been infinite in preparing hell for them. As for ourselves, it should not seem so very absurd that God who, being satisfied in himself and therefore not needing the world, should create it only when he thought good. Moreover, since his will is the rule of all wisdom, we ought to be contented with that alone. For Augustine rightly affirms that injustice is done to God by the Manichaeans because they demand a cause superior to his will; and he prudently warns his readers not to push their inquiries respecting the infinity of time, any more than respecting the infinity of space. We indeed are not unaware that the circuit of the heavens is finite and that the earth, like a little globe, is in a sense placed in the center. Those who complain that the world was not created sooner may as well expostulate with God for not having made innumerable worlds. Yea, since they deem it absurd that many ages should have passed away without any world at all, they may as well acknowledge it to be a proof of the great corruption of their own nature that in comparison with the boundless waste that remains empty, the heaven and earth occupy but a small space. But since both the eternity of God's existence and the infinity of his glory would prove a twofold labyrinth, let us content ourselves with modestly desiring to proceed no further in our inquiries than the Lord, by the guidance and instruction of his own works, invites us.

Now, in describing the world as a mirror in which we ought to behold God, I do not want to be understood as asserting either that our eyes are sufficiently clear-sighted to discern what the fabric of heaven and earth represents or that the knowledge to be hence attained is sufficient for salvation. And whereas the Lord invites us to himself by the means of created things, with no other effect than that of thereby rendering us inexcusable, he has added (as was necessary) a new remedy; or at least by a new aid he has assisted in the ignorance of our mind. For by the Scripture as our guide and teacher, he not only makes those things plain that would otherwise escape our notice, but he almost compels us to behold them, as if he had assisted our dull sight with spectacles. As we have already observed, Moses insists on this point. For if the mute instruction of the heaven and the earth were sufficient, the teaching of Moses would have been superfluous. This herald therefore approaches and arrests our attention, so that we may perceive ourselves to be placed in this scene for the purpose of beholding the glory of God; not indeed to observe it all as mere witnesses, but to enjoy all the riches that are here exhibited as the Lord has ordained and subjected them to our use. And Moses not only declares generally that God is the architect of the world, but through the whole chain of history he shows how wonderful is his power, his wisdom, his goodness, and especially his tender concern for the human race. And thus the assertion of the apostle is verified—namely, that through no other means than faith can it be understood that the worlds were made by the word of God (Hebrews 11:3). For faith correctly flows from this so that we, being taught by the ministry of Moses, do not now wander into foolish and trifling speculations but contemplate the true and only God in his genuine image.

It may, however, be objected that this seems at variance with what Paul declares in 1 Corinthians 1:21, where he intimates that God is sought in vain under the guidance of visible things, and that nothing remains for us but to take ourselves immediately to Christ, and that we must not therefore commence with the elements of this world but with the Gospel, which sets Christ alone before us with his cross and holds us to this one point. I answer this objection: It is in vain for any to reason as philosophers on the work of creation except those who, having been first humbled by the preaching of the Gospel, have learned to submit the whole of their intellectual wisdom (as Paul expresses it) to the foolishness of the cross (1 Corinthians 1:21). We will find nothing, I say, above or below that can raise us up to God until Christ has instructed us in his own school. Yet this cannot be done unless we, having emerged out of the lowest depths, are borne up above all heavens in the chariot of his cross, that there we may by faith apprehend those things that the eye has never seen, the ear never heard, and that far surpass our hearts and minds. For the earth, with its supply of fruits for our daily nourishment, is not there set before us; but Christ offers himself to us for life eternal. Nor does heaven, through the shining of the sun and stars, enlighten our physical eyes; but the same Christ, the Light of the World and the Sun of Righteousness, shines into our souls. Neither does the air stretch out its empty space for us to breathe in, but the Spirit of God himself quickens us and causes us to live. There, in short, the invisible kingdom of Christ fills all things, and his spiritual grace is diffused through all. Yet this does not prevent us from applying our senses to the consideration of heaven and earth, that we may thence seek confirmation in the true knowledge of God.

For Christ is that image in which God presents to our view not only his heart, but also his hands and his feet. By *heart* I mean that secret love with which God embraces us in Christ; by his *hands* and *feet* I understand those works of his that are displayed before our eyes. As soon as we depart from Christ, there is nothing, be it ever so great or insignificant in itself, about which we are not necessarily deceived.

And in fact, though Moses begins in this book of Genesis with the creation of the world, he does not confine us to this subject. For these things ought to be linked—that the world was founded by God, and that man, after he had been endued with the light of intelligence and adorned with so many privileges, fell by his own fault and was thus deprived of all the benefits he had obtained. Afterwards, by the compassion of God, he was restored to the life he had forfeited, through the loving-kindness of Christ, so that there should always be some group of people on earth who, being adopted into the hope of the heavenly life, might in this confidence worship God. The end to which the whole scope of history tends is to this point: The human race has been preserved by God in such a manner as to manifest his special care for his church. This is the argument of the book of Genesis: After the world had been created, man was placed in it as in a theater that he, beholding above him and beneath him the wonderful works of God, might reverently adore their Author.

Second, all things were ordained for the use of man that he, being under deeper obligation, might devote and dedicate himself entirely to obeying God. Third, man was endued with understanding and reason, that being differentiated from brute animals he might meditate on a better life and respond directly to God, whose image he bore engraved on his own person. Afterwards followed the fall of Adam, whereby he alienated himself from God, as a result of which he was deprived of all rectitude. Thus Moses presents man as devoid of all good, blinded in understanding, perverse in heart, impaired in every part, and under sentence of eternal death. But he soon adds the history of man's restorations, where Christ shines forth with the benefit of redemption. From this point Moses not only relates continuously the singular providence of God in governing and preserving the church but also commends to us the true worship of God, teaches us where the salvation of man is placed, and exhorts us, from the example of the fathers, to perseverance in enduring the cross. Whoever, therefore, wishes to benefit from this book must devote his mind to these main topics. But especially let him observe that as Adam had by his own desperate fall ruined himself and all his posterity, the basis of our salvation, the origin of the church, is that we, being rescued out of profound darkness, have obtained a new life by the sheer grace of God; that the fathers (according to the offer made to them through the word of God) were by faith made partakers of this life; that this word itself was founded on Christ; and that all the pious who have since lived were sustained by the very same promise of salvation by which Adam was first raised from the Fall.

Therefore, the perpetual succession of the church has flowed from this fountain: The holy fathers, one after another, having by faith embraced the offered promise, were collected together into the family of God, in order that they might have a common life in Christ. Thus we should note this book carefully, that we might know the membership of the true church and the communion of faith among the children of God. Whereas Moses was ordained the teacher of the Israelites, there is no doubt that he made special reference to them in order that they might acknowledge themselves to be a people elected and chosen by God, and that they might seek the certainty of this adoption from the covenant that the Lord had ratified with their fathers and might know that there was no other God and no other genuine faith. But it was also his will to testify to all ages that whoever desired to worship God correctly and to be counted as members of the church must pursue no other course than that which is here prescribed. But as knowing that there is only one true God whom we worship is the commencement of faith, so it is confirmation of this faith that we are companions of the patriarchs; for since they possessed Christ as the pledge of their salvation when he had not yet appeared, so we retain faith in the God who formerly manifested himself to them. Hence we may infer the difference between the pure and lawful worship of God and all those adulterated services that have since been fabricated by the fraud of Satan and the perverse audacity of men. Further, the government of the church is to be considered, that the reader may come to the conclusion that God has been its perpetual Guard and Ruler, yet in such a way as to exercise its government in the warfare of the cross. Here, truly, the peculiar conflicts of the church present themselves to view; or rather the course is set as in a mirror before our eyes. So we must with the holy fathers press toward the mark of a happy immortality.

Let us now listen to Moses.

# Genesis
# Chapter 1

**1. In the beginning.** To expound the term **beginning** of Christ is altogether frivolous. Moses simply intends to assert that the world was not complete at its commencement, as it now is, but that it was created an empty chaos of **heavens** and **earth**. His language therefore may be explained in this way: When God in the beginning created **the heavens and the earth**, the earth was empty and waste. He moreover teaches by the word **created** that what before did not exist was now made; he did not use the term *yatsar*, which signifies "to frame or form," but *bara*, which signifies "to create." Therefore, his meaning is that the world was made out of nothing. Thus he refutes the folly of those who imagine that unformed matter existed from eternity and who gather nothing else from the narration of Moses than that the world was furnished with new ornaments and received a form of which it was before destitute. This indeed was formerly a common fable among heathens, who had received only an obscure report of the creation and who, according to custom, adulterated the truth of God with strange figments. But for Christian men to labor in maintaining this gross error is absurd and intolerable. Let this then be maintained in the first place—that the world is not eternal but was created by God. There is no doubt that Moses gives the name of **heavens** and **earth** to that confused mass that he shortly afterwards (verse 2) calls **waters**. The reason for this is that this matter was to be the seed of the whole world. Besides, this is the generally recognized division of the world.

**God.** Moses used the word *Elohim*, a plural noun. From this the inference is drawn that the three Persons of the Godhead are here noted; but since, as a proof of so great a matter, it appears to me to have little solidity, I will not insist upon this but rather caution readers to beware of uncertain interpretations of this kind. Some think they have testimony against the Arians here, to prove the deity of the Son and of the Spirit, but in the meantime they involve themselves in the error of Sabellius because Moses afterwards says that *Elohim* had spoken and that the *Spirit of the Elohim* rested upon the waters. If we suppose three persons are here denoted, there will be no distinction between them. For it will follow both that the Son is begotten by himself and that the Spirit is not of the Father, but of himself. For me it is sufficient that the plural number expresses those powers that God exercised in creating the world. Moreover, I acknowledge that the Scripture, although it recites many powers of the Godhead, yet always recalls us to the Father, and his Word, and his Spirit, as we will shortly see. But those absurdities to which I have alluded forbid us to distort with subtlety what Moses simply declares concerning God himself by applying it to the separate Persons of the Godhead. This, however, I regard as beyond controversy—that from the peculiar circumstance of the passage itself, a title is here ascribed to God, expressing that power that was previously in some way included in his eternal essence.

**2. Now the earth was formless and empty.** The Hebrews use *tohu* and *bohu* when they designate anything empty and confused, or vain and worth nothing. Undoubtedly Moses placed them both in opposition to all created objects that pertain to the form, the ornament, and the perfection of the world. Were we now to take away from the earth all that God added after the time alluded to here, we would have this rude and unpolished, or rather shapeless, chaos. Therefore I regard what he immediately adds—that **darkness was over the surface of the deep**—as a part of that confused emptiness: The light began to give some external appearance to the world. For the same reason he calls it the **deep** and **waters**, since in that mass of matter nothing was solid or stable, nothing distinct.

**And the Spirit of God was hovering over the waters.** Interpreters have misinterpreted this passage in various ways. The opinion of some that **Spirit** here means the wind is too weak to require refutation. Those who understand it to mean the Eternal Spirit of God are correct. I now state, in the first place, what (in my judgment) Moses intended. We have already heard that before God had perfected the world, it was a formless mass; he now teaches that the power of the Spirit was necessary in order to sustain it. There are two meanings of the Hebrew word for **hovering over** that suit the present place—either that the Spirit moved and agitated over **the waters** in order to change them, or that he brooded over them to cherish them. It makes little difference which of these explanations is preferred; so the reader is left to judge for himself. But if that chaos required the secret work of God to prevent its speedy dissolution, how could this order, so fair and distinct, subsist by itself unless it derived strength from somewhere else? Therefore, the following Scripture was fulfilled: "When you send your Spirit, they are created, and you renew the face of the earth" (Psalm 104:30). On the other hand, as soon as the Lord takes away his Spirit, all things return to dust and vanish away (Psalm 104:29).

**3. And God said.** Moses now, for the first time, introduces God in the act of *speaking*, as if he had created the mass of heaven and earth without a word. Yet John testifies that "without him nothing was made that has been made" (John 1:3). It is certain that the world had been *begun* by the same efficacy of the word by which it was *completed*. God, however, did not put forth his word until he proceeded to originate light; in the act of distinguishing between light and darkness, his wisdom begins to be conspicuous.

**"Let there be light."** It was proper that the light, by means of which the world was to be adorned with such excellent beauty, should be first created. It was not, however, by thoughtlessness or accident that the light preceded the sun and the moon. To nothing are we more prone than to tie down the power of God to those instruments that he uses. The sun and moon supply us with light. And according to our thinking we say that they give light, so that if they were taken away from the world, it would be impossible for any light to remain. But the Lord, by the very order of the creation, bears witness that he holds in his hand the light, which he is able to impart to us without the sun and moon.

**4. God saw that the light was good.** Here God is introduced by Moses as surveying his work, that he might take pleasure in it. But Moses does this for our sake, to teach us that God has made nothing without a certain reason and design. We should not understand the words of Moses as if God did not know that his work was **good** until it was finished. Rather, the meaning of the passage is that the work, such as we now see it, was approved by God. Therefore, nothing remains for us but to acquiesce in this judgment of God. This admonition is very useful, for while man ought to apply all his senses in admiring contemplation of the deeds of God, we see what license he allows himself in detracting from them.

**5. God called the light "day," and the darkness he called "night."** That is, God willed that there should be a regular vicissitude of days and nights; this followed immediately when the first day ended. God removed the light from view, that night might be the start of another day. What Moses says, however, admits a double interpretation; either this was the evening and morning belonging to the first day, or the first day consisted of the evening and the morning. Whichever interpretation is chosen, it makes no difference in the sense, for he simply understands the day to have been made up of two parts. Further, he begins the day, according to the custom of his nation, with the evening.

**The first day.** Here the error of those who maintain that the world was made in a moment is manifestly refuted. For it is too violent a cavil to contend that Moses distributes the work that God perfected at once into six days for the mere purpose of conveying instruction. Let us rather conclude that God himself took the space of six days for the purpose of accommodating his works to the capacity of men. God distributed the creation of the world into successive portions, that he might fix our attention and compel us, as if he had laid his hand upon us, to pause and to reflect.

**6. And God said, "Let there be an expanse between the waters to separate water from water."** The work of the second day was to provide an empty space around the circumference of the earth, that heaven and earth might not be mixed together. The proverb, "to mingle heaven and earth" denotes extreme disorder, and this distinction ought to be regarded as of great importance. If anyone should inquire whether this vacuity did not previously exist, I answer: However true it may be that all parts of the earth were not overflowed by the waters, yet now, for the first time, a separation was ordained, and it replaced the previous confused mixture. Moses describes the special use of this expanse: to divide water from water. This appears to contradict common sense, for it seems quite incredible that there should be water above the heavens. So some people resort to allegory. But to my mind this is a certain principle—namely, that nothing is here mentioned that is not visible in the world. We see the clouds suspended in the air, threatening to fall upon our heads, yet leaving us space to breathe. Those who deny that this is effected by the wonderful providence of God are vainly inflated with the folly of their own minds. We know, indeed, that the rain is naturally produced; but the Great Flood sufficiently shows how speedily we could be overwhelmed by the bursting of the clouds unless the cataracts of heaven were closed by the hand of God. Since, therefore, God created the clouds and placed them above us, we should not forgot that they are restrained by the power of God.

**9. And God said, "Let the water under the sky be gathered to one place, and let dry ground appear." And it was so.** It also is an illustrious miracle that the waters by their departure have given place for people to live. Let us, therefore, know that we are dwelling on dry ground because God, by his command, has removed the waters, so they do not flood the whole earth.

**11. "Let the land produce vegetation."** Hitherto the earth was naked and barren; now the Lord fructifies it by his word. For though it was already destined to bring forth fruit, yet until new virtue proceeded from the mouth of God, it remained dry and empty. Neither was it naturally fit to produce anything, nor had it a germinating principle from any other source until the mouth of the Lord was opened. What David declares concerning the heavens ought also to be extended to the earth: "By the word of the LORD were the heavens made" (Psalm 33:6). Moreover, it did not happen by chance that herbs and trees were created before the sun and moon. We now see, indeed, that the earth is quickened by the sun to enable it to bring forth its fruits, and God was not ignorant of this law of nature that he has since ordained. But in order that we might learn to refer all things to him, he did not then make use of the sun or moon. He permits us to perceive the efficacy that he infuses into them, so far as he uses their instrumentality; but because we tend to regard as part of their nature properties that they derive from elsewhere, it was necessary that the vigor that they now seem to impart to the earth should be manifest before they were created. We know that the First Cause is self-sufficient, and that intermediate and secondary causes have only what they borrow from this First Cause; but in practice we picture God as poor or imperfect unless he is assisted by second causes. What therefore we declare God to have done by design was indispensably necessary, so that we should learn from the order of the creation itself that God acts through the creatures not as if he needed external help but because it was his pleasure.

When Moses tells us that God said, **"Let the land produce vegetation: seed-bearing plants and trees on the land that bear fruit with seed in it, according to their various kinds,"** he signifies not only that herbs and trees were then created, but that at the same time both were endued with the power of propagation, in order that their several species might be perpetuated. Since, therefore, we daily see the earth pouring forth to us such riches from its lap, since we see the herbs producing seed, and this seed received and cherished in the heart of the earth until it springs forth, and since we see trees shooting from other trees—all this flows from the same word. If therefore we inquire how it happens that the earth is fruitful, that the germ is produced from the seed, that fruits come to maturity, and that their various kinds are annually reproduced, no other cause will be found but that God has once spoken—that is, has issued his eternal decree—and that the earth and all things proceeding from it are obedient to God's command, which they always hear.

**14. And God said, "Let there be lights in the expanse of the sky."** Moses passes on to the fourth day, on which the stars were made. God had before created the light, but he now institutes a new order in nature— that the sun should be the dispenser of daytime light, and that the moon and stars should shine by night. And he assigns them this office: to teach us that all creatures are subject to his will and must do what he tells them.

**"To separate the day from the night."** He means the artificial day, which begins at the rising of the sun and ends at its setting, for the natural day (which Moses mentions earlier) includes in itself the night. From this we infer that the interchange of days and nights will be continual because the Word of God, who determined that the days should be distinct from the nights, directs the course of the sun to this end.

**"Let them serve as signs to mark seasons and days and years."** It must be remembered that Moses does not speak with philosophical acuteness on hidden mysteries but relates those things that are everywhere observed, even by the uneducated, and that are in common use. A twofold advantage is chiefly perceived from the course of the sun and moon. The one is natural; the other applies to civil institutions. Under the term *nature*, I also comprise agriculture. For although sowing and reaping require human art and industry, it is, nevertheless, natural that the sun, by its nearer approach, warms our earth, introduces the vernal season, and is the cause of summer and autumn. But for the sake of assisting their memory, men number among themselves years and months; this is peculiar to civil polity. Both of these are mentioned here. I must, however, in a few words, state the reason why Moses calls the sun and moon **signs**, because certain inquisitive persons abuse this passage to give color to their frivolous predictions. I call those men Chaldeans and fanatics who divine everything from the aspects of the stars. Because Moses declares that the sun and moon were appointed for **signs**, they think themselves entitled to elicit from them anything they please. But this is easy to refute, for they are called **signs** of certain things, not signs to denote whatever is according to our fancy. What indeed does Moses assert they denote except things belonging to the order of nature? Finally, Moses commemorates the unbounded goodness of God in causing the sun and moon not only to enlighten us, but to provide us with various other advantages for our daily lives. It is obvious that we, simply enjoying the countless bounties of God, should learn not to profane such excellent gifts by our preposterous abuse of them. In the meantime, let us admire this wonderful Artificer who has so beautifully arranged all things above and beneath that they may respond to each other in most harmonious concert.

15. **"Let them be lights in the expanse of the sky to give light on the earth."** I repeat what I said before: This is not a philosophical discussion about how great the sun is in the heaven and how great, or how small, the moon is. Rather, we are told how much light comes to us from them. Moses here addresses himself to our senses, that the knowledge of the gifts of God that we enjoy may not glide away. Therefore, to understand Moses' meaning, there is no point in soaring above the heavens; let us only open our eyes to behold this **light** that God gives us **on the earth**. In this way (as I have before observed) the dishonesty of those men who censure Moses for not speaking with greater exactness is sufficiently rebuked. For he had concern for us rather than for the stars. Nor, in truth, was he ignorant of the fact that the moon did not have sufficient brightness to give light to the earth unless it borrowed from the sun; he deemed it enough to declare what we all may plainly perceive—that the moon is a dispenser of light to us.

16. **God made two great lights—the greater light to govern the day and the lesser light to govern the night. He also made the stars.** Regarding **the greater light**, Moses is not analyzing acutely, like the philosophers, the secrets of nature, and these words show that. First he sets the planets and stars in the expanse of the heaven. Astronomers distinguish a number of spheres in the firmament and teach that the fixed stars have their own places in it. Moses mentions two great luminaries.

The astronomers prove with strong arguments that the star Saturn, which seems small because of its distance, is larger than the moon.

All this shows that Moses described in popular style what all ordinary men without training and education perceive with their ordinary senses. Astronomers, on the other hand, investigate with great labor whatever the keenness of man's intellect is able to discover. Such study is certainly not to be disapproved, nor science condemned with the insolence of some fanatics who habitually reject whatever is unknown to them. The study of astronomy not only gives pleasure but is also extremely useful. And no one can deny that it admirably reveals the wisdom of God. Therefore, clever men who expend their labor upon it are to be praised, and those who have ability and leisure ought not to neglect work of that kind.

Moses did not wish to keep us from such study when he omitted the scientific details. But since he had been appointed a guide of unlearned men rather than of the learned, he could not fulfill his duty except by coming down to their level. If he had spoken of matters unknown to the crowd, the unlearned could say that his teaching was over their heads. In fact, when the Spirit of God opens a common school for all, it is not strange that he chooses to teach especially what can be understood by all.

When the astronomer seeks the true size of stars and finds the moon smaller than Saturn, he gives us specialized knowledge. But the eye sees things differently, and Moses adapts himself to the ordinary view.

God has stretched out his hand to us to give us the splendor of the sun and moon to enjoy. Great would be our ingratitude if we shut our eyes to this experience of beauty! There is no reason why clever men should jeer at Moses' ignorance. He is not explaining the heavens to us but is describing what is before our eyes. Let the astronomers possess their own deeper knowledge. Meanwhile, those who see the nightly splendor of the moon are possessed by perverse ingratitude if they do not recognize the goodness of God.

**20. And God said, "Let the water teem with living creatures, and let birds fly above the earth across the expanse of the sky."** On the fifth day the **birds** and fishes were created. The blessing of God is added, so that they themselves may produce offspring. Here is a different kind of propagation from that of herbs and trees. There the power of fructifying is in the plants, and that of germinating is in the seed; but here generation takes place. It seems unreasonable that Moses declares birds to have come from the waters [Editor's note: This verse in the *King James Version* reads: "Let the waters bring forth abundantly the moving creature that hath life, and fowl that may fly above the earth in the open firmament of heaven"]; and therefore this is seized upon by skeptical men who desire to slander the Scripture. But although there should appear no other reason but that it pleased God, would it not be becoming for us to acquiesce in his judgment? Why should not God, who created the world out of nothing, bring the birds out of water? And what greater absurdity has the origin of birds from the water than that of the light from darkness? Therefore, those who so arrogantly assail their Creator will face the Judge who will reduce them to nothing. Moses ought to be listened to as our teacher who would transport us with admiration of God through the consideration of his works. And truly the Lord, although he is the Author of nature, yet by no means has followed nature as his guide in the creation of the world but has rather chosen to put forth such demonstrations of his power as would make us have awe before him.

**21. So God created.** A question here arises concerning the word **created.** We have before contended that because the world was created, it was made out of nothing; but now Moses says that things formed from other matter were **created** (see verse 20 [KJV]). Those who assert that the fishes were created from nothing because the waters were in no way sufficient or suitable for their production are nevertheless resorting to rationalization, for the fact would remain that the material of which they were made existed before, which, strictly speaking, the word **created** does not admit. I therefore do not restrict the creation here spoken of to the work of the fifth day but rather suppose it to refer to that shapeless and confused mass that was in effect the fountain of the whole world.

God, then, it is said, **created the great creatures of the sea** (*balaenas*) and other fishes—not that the beginning of their creation is to be reckoned from the moment in which they received their form but because of the universal matter that was made out of nothing. So with respect to species, form only was added to them; but creation is nevertheless a term truly used respecting both the whole and the parts.

**22. God blessed them.** God quickly shows the meaning of this benediction. For God does not, like men, just pray that we may be blessed but, by the mere intimation of his purpose, effects what men seek by earnest entreaty. He therefore blesses his creatures when he commands them to increase and grow; that is, he infuses into them fecundity by his word. But it seems futile for God to address fishes and reptiles. I answer: This way of speaking was one that could easily be understood.

**24. And God said, "Let the land produce living creatures according to their kinds."** Moses comes to the sixth day, on which the animals were created, and then man. **"Let the land,"** he says, **"produce living creatures according to their kinds."** From where does a dead element gain life? This is in this respect a miracle as great as if God had begun to create out of nothing those things that he commanded to proceed from the earth. And he does not take his material from the earth because he needed it, but in order that he might combine the separate parts of the world with the universe itself. Yet it may be inquired: Why does God not here also add his benediction? I answer: What Moses previously expressed on a similar occasion is here also to be understood, although he does not repeat it word for word.

**26. Then God said, "Let us make man."** Although the tense here used is the future, all must acknowledge that this is the language of one apparently deliberating. Hitherto God has been introduced simply as *commanding*; now when he approaches the most excellent of all his deeds, he enters into *consultation*. God certainly might here command by his bare word what he wished to be done. But he chose to give this tribute to the excellency of man—that he would, in a manner, enter into consultation concerning his creation. This is the highest honor with which he has dignified us. Moses uses this language in order to draw our attention to this. For God is not now first beginning to consider what form he will give to man and with what endowments it would be fitting to adorn him; nor is he pausing as over a work of difficulty. But just as the creation of the world was spread over six days for our sake, so that our minds might more easily concentrate on God's deeds, now, for the purpose of commending to our attention the dignity of our nature, he, in taking counsel concerning the creation of man, testifies that he is about to undertake something great and wonderful. Truly there are many things in corrupted nature that may induce contempt; but if you correctly weigh all circumstances, man is among other creatures a preeminent specimen of divine wisdom, justice, and goodness, so that he is deservedly called by the ancients "a world in miniature." But note: Since the Lord needs no other counselor, there can be no doubt that he consulted with himself. The Jews are ridiculous to suggest that God consulted with the earth or with angels. God summons no foreign counselor; hence we infer that he finds within himself something distinct. As with truth, his eternal wisdom and power reside within him.

**". . . in our image, in our likeness, and let them rule over the fish of the sea and the birds of the air, over the livestock, over all the earth, and over all the creatures that move along the ground."** Interpreters do not agree concerning the meaning of these words. Nearly all of them think that the word **image** is to be distinguished from **likeness**. And the common distinction is, **image** exists in the substance, and **likeness** in the nonessential qualities of anything. Those who comment on this say that in the **image** are contained those endowments that God has conferred on human nature at large, while they expound **likeness** to mean gratuitous gifts. But Augustine, more than all the other commentators, speculates with excessive refinement in order to fabricate a trinity in man. In laying hold of the three faculties of the soul enumerated by Aristotle—the intellect, the memory, and the will—he derives from one trinity many such faculties. If any reader, having leisure, wishes to enjoy such speculations, let him read the tenth and fourteenth books on *The Trinity*, and also the eleventh book of the *City of God*. I have no difficulty in admitting the above distinction of the faculties of the soul, although the simpler division

25

into two parts, which is more often used in Scripture, is better suited to the sound doctrine of piety. But a definition of the image of God ought to rest on a firmer basis than such subtleties. As for myself, before I define the **image** of God, I would deny that it differs from his **likeness**. For when Moses afterwards repeats the same things (verse 27) he passes over the likeness and contents himself with only mentioning the **image**. We also know that it was customary for the Hebrews to repeat the same thing in different words. Besides, the phrase itself shows that the second term was added for the sake of explanation.

Although we have set aside all difference between the two words, we have not yet ascertained what this **image** or **likeness** is. But it must include the perfection of our whole nature as it appeared when Adam was endued with a right judgment, had affections in harmony with reason, had all his senses sound and well-regulated, and truly excelled in everything good. Thus the chief seat of the divine image was in his mind and heart; yet there was no part of him in which some scintillations of it did not shine out. In the mind perfect intelligence flourished and reigned, uprightness attended as its companion, and all the senses were prepared and molded for due obedience to reason; and in the body there was a suitable correspondence with this internal order. But now, although some obscure lineaments of that image are found remaining in us, yet they are so vitiated and maimed that they may be said to be destroyed. For besides the unsightly deformity that everywhere appears, this evil also is added—no part is free from the infection of sin. It is correctly stated that Christ is the only image of the Father, and yet the words of Moses do not bear the interpretation that "in the image" means "in Christ."

**"Let them rule over the fish of the sea."** Here God commemorates that part of dignity with which he decreed to honor man—namely, that he should have authority over all living creatures. He appointed man, it is true, lord of the world; but he specifically subjected the animals to him because they, having an inclination or instinct of their own, seem to be less under outside authority. The use of the plural (**them**) intimates that this authority was not given to Adam only but to all his posterity as well. And hence we infer what was the end for which all things were created—namely, that men might lack none of the conveniences and necessities of life. In the very order of the creation the paternal solicitude of God for man is conspicuous, because he furnished the world with all things needful, and even with an immense profusion of wealth, before he formed man. Thus man was rich before he was created. Since God had such care for us before we existed, he will by no means leave us destitute of food and other necessities of life now that we are placed in the world. The fact that he often keeps his hand as if closed is to be imputed to our sins.

**27. So God created man in his own image.** The repeating of **in his own image** is not a vain repetition. It is a remarkable instance of divine goodness that can never be sufficiently proclaimed. And at the same time he admonishes us as to the excellence from which we have fallen, that he may excite in us the desire of its recovery. When Moses adds a little later that God created them **male and female**, he commends to us that conjugal bond by which the society of mankind is cherished. For this way of speaking, **male and female he created them**, is of the same force as if he had said that the man himself was incomplete. Under these circumstances, the woman was added to him as a companion, that they both might be one, as he more clearly expresses in Genesis 2.

**28. God blessed them.** This blessing of God may be regarded as the source from which the human race has flowed. And we must view it in this way not only with reference to the whole but also in every particular instance. For we are fruitful or barren in respect of offspring as God imparts his power to some and withholds it from others. But here Moses would simply declare that Adam with his wife was formed for the production of offspring, in order that men might replenish the earth. God could himself indeed have covered the earth with a multitude of people; but it was his will that we should proceed from one fountain, in order that our desire of mutual concord might be the greater, and that each might more freely embrace the other as his own flesh.

**Subdue it.** God confirms what he had previously said about dominion. Man had already been created with this role of subjecting the earth to himself; but now, at length, he is put in possession of his right when he hears what has been given to him by the Lord. Moses expresses this more fully in the next verse, when he introduces God as granting to man the herbs and the fruits. It is very important that we do not touch any of God's bounty except what we know he has permitted us to; we cannot enjoy anything with a good conscience unless we receive it as from the hand of God. Therefore, Paul teaches us that in eating and drinking we always sin unless faith is present (see Romans 14:23). Thus we are instructed to seek from God alone whatever we need, and in the very use of his gifts we are to exercise ourselves in meditating on his goodness and paternal care.

Some infer from this passage that men were content with herbs and fruits until the Flood, and that it was even unlawful for them to eat flesh. This appears probable because God confines, in some way, the food of mankind within certain limits. Then after the Flood he specifically allows them to eat flesh. This argument, however, is not sufficiently strong; for it may be adduced on the opposite side that the first men offered sacrifices from their flocks. Moreover, it is the law of sacrificing in the right way not to offer to God anything except what he has granted to our use. And finally, men were clothed in skins; therefore it was lawful for them to kill animals. For these reasons I think it will be better for us to assert nothing concerning this matter. Let it suffice for us that herbs and the fruits of trees were given them as their common food; yet it is not to be doubted that this was abundantly sufficient for their highest gratification. They judge prudently who maintain that the earth was so marred by the Flood that we retain scarcely a moderate portion of the original blessing. Even immediately after the fall of man, it had already begun to bring forth degenerate and noxious fruits; but at the Flood the change became still greater. However this may be, God certainly did not intend that man should be sparingly sustained; rather, by these words he promises great abundance and provides for a sweet and pleasant life. Moses relates how beneficent the Lord had been to Adam and Eve in bestowing on them all things they could desire, that their ingratitude might have the less excuse.

**31. God saw all that he had made, and it was very good.** Once more, at the conclusion of the creation, Moses declares that God approved of everything that he had made. In saying that God **saw**, he means in a human way; for the Lord planned his judgment to be a rule and example to us, that no one should dare to think or speak otherwise of his deeds. It is not lawful for us to dispute whether what God has already approved ought to be approved or not; it rather becomes us to acquiesce without controversy. The repetition also denotes how wanton is the foolish contempt of man; otherwise it would have been enough to have said once for all that God approved of his deeds. But God six times inculcates the same thing, that he may restrain, as with so many bridles, our restless audacity. But Moses expresses more than before, for he adds *meod*—that is, **very**. On each of the days, simple approbation was given. But now, after the workmanship of the world was complete and had received, if I may so speak, the last finishing touch, God pronounces it perfectly good, that we might know there is in the symmetry of God's deeds the highest perfection, to which nothing can be added.

# Genesis
# Chapter 2

**1. Thus the heavens and the earth were completed in all their vast array.** Moses summarily repeats that in six days the fabric of the heaven and the earth was completed. The general division of the world is made into these two parts, as has been stated at the commencement of the first chapter. But he now adds **all their vast array,** by which he signifies that the world was furnished with all its embellishments. This epilogue, moreover, with sufficient clearness entirely refutes the error of those who imagine that the world was formed in a moment. For Moses declares that this world was in every sense completed, as if the whole house were well supplied and filled with its furniture. The heavens without the sun, moon, and stars would be an empty palace. If the earth were destitute of animals, trees, and plants, that barren waste would have the appearance of a poor and deserted house. God, therefore, did not cease from the work of the creation of the world until he had completed it in every part, so that nothing should be lacking.

 **2. By the seventh day God had finished the work he had been doing; so on the seventh day he rested from all his work.** We must not improperly ask what kind of rest this was. For it is certain that since God sustains the world by his power, governs it by his providence, and cherishes and even propagates all creatures, he is constantly at work. If God should but withdraw his hand a little, all things would immediately perish and dissolve into nothing, as is declared in Psalm 104:29. So why does Moses say God **rested?** The solution to the difficulty is well known: God ceased from all his **work** when he desisted from the creation of new kinds of things. But to make the sense clearer, understand that the last touch of God had been done in order that the world might be perfect. This is the meaning of the words of Moses, **finished the work he had been doing;** he points out the actual state of the **work** as God wanted it, as if he said, "Then was completed what God had proposed to himself." On the whole this language is intended merely to express the perfection of the fabric of the world; therefore we must not infer that God so ceased from his deeds as to desert them, since they only flourish and subsist in him. Besides, it is to be observed that in the deeds of the six days we see only those things that tend to the lawful and genuine adorning of the world. Many things that are now seen in the world are corruptions of the world rather than any part of its proper furniture. For ever since man declined from his high original state, the world necessarily and gradually degenerated from its nature. We must come to this conclusion with respect to the present existence and nature of fleas, caterpillars, and other noxious insects. In all these, I say, there is some deformity of the world that ought by no means to be regarded as within the order of nature since it proceeds from the sin of man rather than from the hand of God. Truly these things were created by God, but by God as an avenger. In this place, however, Moses is not considering God as armed for the punishment of the sins of men, but as the Artificer, the Architect, the bountiful Father of a family who has omitted nothing essential for the perfection of his edifice. At the present time when we look at the corrupt world, let Paul's words come to mind: "For the creation was subjected to frustration, not by its own choice, but by the will of the one who subjected it, in hope" (Romans 8:20). Thus let us mourn as we are admonished for our just condemnation.

**3. And God blessed the seventh day.** It appears that God is here said to bless according to the manner of men, because they bless the one whom they highly extol. Nevertheless, even in this sense it would not be inappropriate to God's character because his blessing sometimes means the favor that he bestows upon his people. The Hebrews call that man blessed by God who, by a certain special favor, has power with God (see Genesis 24:31). I have no doubt that Moses, by adding the words **made it holy**, wished to explain immediately what he had said, and thus all ambiguity is removed. The second word explains the first word, for *kadesh*, with the Hebrews, is separate from the common number. God therefore sanctifies **the seventh day** when he renders it illustrious, that by a special law it may be distinguished from the rest. From this it is also seen that God always respected the welfare of men. I have said above that six days were employed in the formation of the world. God, to whom one moment is as a thousand years, had no need of this succession of time, but he wanted to engage us in the consideration of his deeds. He had the same end in view in the appointment of his own rest, for he set apart a day selected out of the remainder for this special use. Therefore, that benediction is nothing other than a solemn consecration by which God claims for himself the meditations and activities of people on the seventh day. This is, indeed, the proper business of the whole of life—to consider the infinite goodness, justice, power, and wisdom of God in this magnificent theater of heaven and earth. But in case men should be inattentive to this, every seventh day has been especially selected for the purpose of supplying what was lacking in daily meditation. First, therefore, God **rested**; then he **blessed** this rest, that in all ages it might be held sacred among men. Or to put it another way, he dedicated every seventh day to rest, that his own example might be a perpetual rule. The design of the institution must be always kept in mind, for God did not command men simply to have a holiday every seventh day, as if he delighted in their indolence; rather, being released from all other business, they are to more readily apply their minds to the Creator of the world. Lastly, this is a sacred rest that draws men aside from the impediments of the world, that they may be dedicated entirely to God. For God cannot either more gently allure or more effectually incite us to obedience than by inviting and exhorting us to imitate himself.

Furthermore, we must know that this is to be the common employment not of one age or people only, but of the whole human race. Afterwards, in the law, a new precept concerning the Sabbath was given that was to be peculiar to the Jews for a season, because it was a legal ceremony showing a spiritual rest, the truth of which was manifested in Christ. Therefore the Lord frequently testifies that he had given, in the Sabbath, a symbol of sanctification to his ancient people. Therefore, when we hear that the Sabbath was abrogated by the coming of Christ, we must distinguish between what belongs to the perpetual government of human life and what properly belongs to ancient figures, the use of which was abolished when the truth was fulfilled. Spiritual rest is the mortification of the flesh, so that the children of God should no longer live for themselves or indulge their own inclinations. So far as the Sabbath was a figure of this rest, I say, it was but for a season; but in that it commanded men from the beginning to employ themselves in the worship of God, it is right that it should continue to the end of the world.

**4. This is the account of the heavens and the earth when they were created.** Moses' aim was to impress deeply on our minds the *origin* of the heavens and the earth. For there have always been ungrateful and malignant men who either by feigning that the world was eternal or by obliterating the memory of creation would attempt to obscure the glory of God. Thus the devil by his guile turns away from God those who are more ingenious than others in order that each may become a god to himself. Therefore, it is not a superfluous repetition that inculcates the necessary fact that the world existed only from the time when it was created since such knowledge directs us to its Architect and Author. Under the names of **the heavens and the earth**, the whole is, by a synecdoche, included.

**5. No shrub of the field had yet appeared on the earth.** This verse follows on from the preceding one and must be read in continuation with it. For Moses links the plants and shrubs to the earth as the garment with which the Lord has adorned it, lest its nakedness should appear as a deformity. When Moses says, **the LORD God had not sent rain on the earth,**

he intimates that it is God who opens and shuts the heavens, and that rain and drought are in his hand.

**7. The LORD God formed man.** Moses now explains what he had before omitted in the creation of man—namely, that his body was taken out of the earth: **The LORD God formed man from the dust of the ground.** He had said that man was formed in the image of God. This is incomparably the highest nobility; but lest men should use it as an occasion of pride, they are reminded of their origin. Adam's body was formed from clay and destitute of sense, so that no one can boast about his body. Only an excessively stupid person does not learn humility from this.

**And breathed into his nostrils the breath of life.** Whatever most commentators might think, I do not hesitate to subscribe to the opinion of those who explain this passage as meaning the animal life of man; and thus I expound what they call the vital spirits by the word **breath.** Should anyone object that if this is so, no distinction can be made between man and other living creatures since here Moses relates only what is common to all, I answer: Though the lower faculty of the soul is only mentioned here, imparting breath to the body and giving it vigor and motion, this does not prevent the human soul from having its proper rank, and therefore it ought to be distinguished from others. First of all Moses speaks about the **breath;** he then adds that a soul was given to man by which he might live and be endued with sense and motion [verse 7, KJV: **man became a living soul**]. We know that the powers of the human mind are many and various. So there is nothing absurd in supposing that Moses here alludes to one of them but omits the intellectual part, of which mention has been made in the first chapter. Three gradations, indeed, are to be noted in the creation of man: His dead body was formed out of the dust of the earth; it was endued with a soul, whence it should receive vital motion; and on this soul God engraved his own image, to which immortality is annexed.

**And the man became a living being.** I take *nepesh* to mean the very essence of the soul; but the epithet **living** suits only the present place and does not embrace generally the powers of the soul. For Moses intended nothing more than to explain the animating of the clay figure, whereby it came to pass that man began to live. In 1 Corinthians 15:45 Paul makes an antithesis between this living soul and the quickening spirit that Christ confers upon the faithful, for no other purpose than to teach us that the state of man was not perfected in the person of Adam but only through a peculiar benefit conferred by Christ.

**8. Now the LORD God had planted a garden in the east.** Moses now adds the condition and rule of living that were given to man. First, he narrates in which part of the world the man was placed, and what a happy and pleasant habitation was given to him. Moses says that God had **planted** a place for man to live, accommodating himself by a simple and uncultivated style to the understanding of the ordinary person. For since the majesty of God, as it really is, cannot be expressed, the Scripture often describes it in human terms. God, then, **planted** Paradise in a place that he had especially embellished with every variety of delights, with abundant fruits, and with all other most excellent gifts. It is called a **garden** on account of the elegance of its situation and the beauty of its form. The ancient interpreter did not improperly translate it Paradise because the Jews call the more highly cultivated gardens *Pardaisim*, and Xenophon pronounces the word to be Persian when he mentions the magnificent and sumptuous gardens of kings. That region that the Lord assigned to Adam as the firstborn of mankind was one selected out of the whole world.

**In Eden.** If the earth had not been cursed on account of the sin of man, the whole—as it had been blessed from the beginning—would have remained the fairest scene both of fruitfulness and of delight. It would have been, in short, not dissimilar to Paradise when compared with that scene of deformity that we now view. But when Moses describes here the situation of the region, commentators are wrong to transfer what Moses said of a certain particular place to the whole world. It is not indeed doubtful (as I just now hinted) that God would choose the most fertile and pleasant place, the firstfruits (so to speak) of the earth, as his gift to Adam, whom he had dignified with the honor of primogeniture among men, as a token of his special favor. Again, we infer that this garden was situated on the earth, not as some dream in the air; for unless it had been a region of our world, it would not have been placed opposite to Judea, toward the east. We must, however, entirely reject the allegories of Origin and of others like him that Satan, with the deepest subtlety, has endeavored to introduce into the church for the purpose of rendering the doctrine of Scripture ambiguous and destitute of all certainty and firmness. It may be, indeed, that some, impelled by a supposed necessity, have resorted to an allegorical sense because they never found in the world such a place as is described by Moses; but we see that the greater part, through a foolish affectation of subtleties, have been too much addicted to allegories. As it concerns the present passage, they speculate in vain by departing from the literal sense. For Moses has no other design than to teach man that he was formed by God with this condition—that he should have dominion over the earth, from which he might gather fruit, and thus learn by daily experience that the world was subject to him. What advantage is it to fly in the air and to leave the earth, where God has given proof of his benevolence toward the human race? But someone may say that to interpret this of celestial bliss is more skillful. I answer, since the eternal inheritance of man is in heaven, it is truly right that we should tend thither; yet we must fix our feet on earth long enough to enable us to consider the abode that God requires man to use for a time. For we are now conversant with that history that teaches us that Adam was, by divine appointment, an inhabitant of the earth in order that he might, in passing through his earthly life, meditate on heavenly glory, and that he had been bountifully enriched by the Lord with innumerable benefits, from the enjoyment of which he might infer the paternal benevolence of God.

**9. And the** LORD **God made all kinds of trees grow out of the ground.** The production here spoken of belongs to the third day of the creation. But Moses expressly declares the place to have been richly replenished with all kinds of fruitful **trees,** that there might be a full and happy abundance of all things. This was purposely done by the Lord, so that the cupidity of man might have less excuse if, instead of being contented with such remarkable affluence, sweetness, and variety, it should (as really happened) precipitate itself against the commandment of God. The Holy Spirit also relates through Moses the greatness of Adam's happiness, so that his vile intemperance might be more apparent; such superfluity was unable to restrain from breaking forth with the forbidden fruit. Certainly it was shameful ingratitude that he could not rest in a state so happy and desirable. It was certainly more than brutal lust that so great a bounty was not able to satisfy. No corner of the earth was then barren, nor was there even any that was not exceedingly rich and fertile. God's blessing, which was elsewhere comparatively moderate, had in this place especially poured itself wonderfully forth. Not only was there an abundant supply of food, but with it was added sweetness for the gratification of the palate and beauty to feast the eyes. Therefore, from such kindly provision, it is more than sufficiently evident how inexplicable has been the greed of man.

**The tree of life and the tree of the knowledge of good and evil.** It is uncertain whether Moses means two individual trees or two kinds of trees. Either opinion is possible, and the point is not worth arguing over. There is more importance in the epithets that were applied to each tree from its effect, and that not by the will of man but of God. He gave **the tree of life** its name not because it could confer on man that life with which he had been previously endued, but in order that it might be a symbol and memorial of the life he had received from God. We know it to be by no means unusual that God attests his grace by external symbols. He does not transfer his power into outward signs, but by them he stretches out his hand to us because without assistance we cannot ascend to him. He intended, therefore, that man, as often as he tasted the fruit of that tree, should remember from where he received his life, so that he might acknowledge that he lives not by his own power, but by the kindness of God alone, and that life is not (as men commonly say) an intrinsic good but proceeds from God.

Finally, in that tree there was a visible testimony to the declaration that in God "we live and move and have our being" (Acts 17:28). If Adam had been so far innocent, having an upright nature, and needed signs to lead him to knowledge of divine grace, how much more necessary are signs now since we have fallen from the true light? Yet I am not dissatisfied with what has been handed down by some of the fathers, such as Augustine and Eucherius, who say that the tree of life was a figure of Christ, inasmuch as he is the eternal Word of God. It could not indeed be other than a symbol of life, representing him in figure. We must maintain what is declared in John 1:1-3 that the life of all things was included in the Word, but especially the life of men, which is conjoined with reason and intelligence. Wherefore, by this sign Adam was admonished that he could claim nothing for himself as if it were his own, in order that he might depend wholly upon the Son of God and might not seek life anywhere but in him. Let us know, therefore, that when we have departed from Christ, nothing remains for us but death.

Concerning **the tree of the knowledge of good and evil**, we must hold that it was prohibited to man not because God would have him stray like a sheep, without judgment and without choice, but that he might not seek to be wiser than became him or trust to his own understanding. He must not throw aside God's yoke and constitute himself an arbiter and judge of good and evil. His sin came from an evil conscience. From this it follows that a judgment had been given him by which he might discriminate between virtues and vices. We now understand what is meant by abstaining from **the tree of the knowledge of good and evil**—namely, that Adam might not, in attempting one thing or another, rely upon his own prudence but rather, cleaving to God alone, become wise only by his obedience. **Knowledge** is here, therefore, taken disparagingly, in a bad sense, for that wretched experience that man, when he departed from the only fountain of perfect wisdom, began to acquire for himself. This is the origin of free will misused—that Adam wished to be independent and dared to try what he was able to do.

**10. A river watering the garden flowed from Eden.** Moses says that one **river** flowed to water the garden but later divided into **four headwaters.** Two of these **headwaters** are the **Euphrates** and the **Tigris** (verse 14), but there is a great controversy about the other two. Many think that **Pishon** (verse 11) and **Gihon** (verse 13) are the Ganges and the Nile; this error, however, is abundantly refuted by the distance of the positions of these rivers. Some people have even suggested that the River Danube is meant here, as if the habitation of one man stretched from the most remote part of Asia to the extremity of Europe. But since many other celebrated rivers flow through the region we are speaking about, it is more probable that the names of these two rivers has now been lost. Moses simply means that **the garden** that Adam lived in was well watered from the channel of a river passing that way, which later divided into **four headwaters.**

**15. The LORD God took the man and put him in the Garden of Eden to work it and take care of it.** Moses now adds that the earth was given to man with this condition—that he should cultivate it. From this it follows that men were created to work, and not to be inactive and indolent. This labor truly was pleasant and full of delight, entirely free from all trouble and weariness. So nothing is more contrary to the order of nature than to spend all one's life in eating, drinking, and sleeping.

16. **And the Lord God commanded the man, "You are free to eat from any tree in the garden."** Moses now teaches that man was the ruler of the world, though he was still subject to God. A law was imposed upon him as a sign of his subjection, for it would have made no difference to God if he had eaten indiscriminately of any fruit he pleased. Therefore the prohibition of one tree was a test of obedience. And in this way God designed that the whole human race should be accustomed from the beginning to reverence his deity. Doubtless, it was necessary that man, adorned and enriched with so many excellent gifts, should be held under restraint lest he break forth into licentiousness. Therefore, abstinence from the fruit of one tree was a kind of first lesson in obedience, that man might know he had a Director and Lord of his life, on whose will he ought to depend and in whose commands he ought to acquiesce. It seems, however, to some as if this did not accord with the judgment of Paul when he teaches that the law was not made for the righteous (1 Timothy 1:9). If this was the case, then when Adam was yet innocent and upright, he had no need of a law. But the solution is at hand. Paul is not writing controversially; rather, from the common practice of life he declares that those who are free do not need to be compelled by the necessity of law; as it is said in the common proverb, "Good laws spring from bad manners." In the meantime, he does not deny that God, from the beginning, imposed a law upon man, for the purpose of maintaining the right due to himself.

**"From any tree."** So that Adam might willingly comply with God's instructions, God commended his own liberality. "Behold," he says in essence, "I give into your hand whatever fruits the earth may produce, whatever fruits every kind of tree may yield. From this immense profusion and variety I except only one tree." Then by denouncing punishment, he struck terror for the purpose of confirming the authority of the law. So much the greater, then, is the wickedness of man, whom neither that kind commemoration of the gifts of God nor the dread of punishment was able to retain in his duty.

17. **"For when you eat of it you will surely die."** What kind of death does God mean here? It seems to me that the definition of this death is to be sought from its opposite; we must, I say, remember from what kind of life man fell. He was, in every respect, happy. Since in his soul a right judgment and a proper control of the affections prevailed, there also life reigned; in his body there was no defect, and so he was wholly free from death. His earthly life truly would have been temporal; yet he would have passed into heaven without death and without injury. Death, therefore, is

now a terror to us—first, because there is a kind of annihilation as far as the body is concerned, then because the soul feels the curse of God.

We must also see what is the cause of death—namely, alienation from God. From this it follows that under the name of death is included all those miseries in which Adam involved himself by his defection; for as soon as he revolted from God, the fountain of life, he was thrown down from his former state, in order that he might perceive the life of man without God to be wretched and lost and therefore no different from death. Hence the condition of man after his sin is not improperly called both the privation of life and death. The miseries and evils both of soul and body that beset man so long as he is on earth are a kind of entrance into death, until death itself entirely absorbs him. Scripture everywhere calls those dead who, being oppressed by the tyranny of sin and Satan, breathe nothing but their own destruction. Therefore the question of how God threatened death to Adam on the day in which he should touch the fruit, yet long deferred the punishment is superfluous. For Adam was consigned to death, and death began its reign in him until supervening grace should bring a remedy.

**18. The Lord God said, "It is not good for the man to be alone."** Moses now explains God's purpose in creating women—namely, that there should be human beings on the earth who might support each other. Yet a doubt may arise whether this design ought to be extended to progeny, for the words simply mean that since it was not expedient for man to be alone, a wife must be created to be his helper. I, however, take the meaning to be that God begins, indeed, at the first step of human society, yet designs to include others, each in his or her proper place. The commencement, therefore, involves a general principle: Man was formed to be a social animal. Now, the human race could not exist without the woman; and, therefore, in the conjunction of human beings, that sacred bond is especially conspicuous by which the husband and the wife are combined in one body and one soul, as nature itself taught Plato and some of the other better philosophers. But although God pronounced concerning Adam that it would not be profitable for him to be **alone,** I do not restrict the declaration to his person alone but rather regard it as a common law of man's vocation, so that everyone ought to receive it as if it were addressed to him. Solitude is not good except for those people whom God exempts by a special privilege.

Many think that celibacy is to their advantage and therefore abstain from marriage, in case they should be miserable. Not only have heathen writers defined that to be a happy life that is passed without a wife, but the first book of Jerome, against Jovinian, is stuffed with petulant reproaches by which he attempts to render hallowed wedlock both hateful and infamous. To these wicked suggestions of Satan let the faithful learn to oppose this declaration of God by which he ordains the conjugal life for man not to his destruction, but to his salvation.

**"I will make a helper."** It cannot be denied that the woman was created in the image of God. From this it follows that what was said in the creation of the man belongs to the female sex. Now, since God assigns the woman as a help to the man, he not only prescribes to wives the rule of their vocation to instruct them in their duty, but he also pronounces that marriage will really prove to be the best support of life for men. We may therefore conclude that the order of nature implies that the woman should be the **helper** of the man. The common proverb, indeed, is that she is a necessary evil; but the voice of God should be heard instead, declaring that woman is given as a companion and an associate to the man, to assist him to live well. Women, being instructed in their duty of helping their husbands, should be diligent to keep this divinely appointed order. It is also the part of men to consider what they owe in return to the other half of their kind, for the obligation of both sexes is mutual, and the woman is assigned as a help to the man, that he might fill the place of her head and leader.

**"Suitable for him."** Moses intended to note some equality. This refutes the error of some who think that the woman was formed only for the sake of propagation. They do not think that a wife was personally necessary for Adam because he was hitherto free from lust, as if she had been given to him only for the companion of his bedroom, and not rather that she might be the inseparable associate of his life.

**19. Now the LORD God had formed out of the ground all the beasts of the field . . .** This and the succeeding verse expand the exposition of the preceding sentence, for Moses says that of all the animals, when they had been placed in order, not one was found that might be conferred upon and adapted to Adam; nor was there such an affinity of nature that Adam could choose for himself a companion for life out of any one species. Therefore, unless a wife had been given him of the same kind with himself, he would have remained destitute of a suitable and proper help.

**21. So the LORD God caused the man to fall into a deep sleep; and while he was sleeping, he took one of the man's ribs and closed up the place with flesh.** Although to profane people this method of forming woman may seem ridiculous, and some of these may say that Moses is dealing in fables, yet to us the wonderful providence of God here shines forth. So that the human race might be the more sacred, God chose that both males and females should spring from one and the same origin. Therefore he created human nature in the person of Adam and thence formed Eve, that the woman should be only a portion of the whole human race. In this way Adam was taught to recognize himself in his wife, as in a mirror, and Eve, in her turn, to submit herself willingly to her husband, as being taken out of him. But if the two sexes had proceeded from different sources, there would have been occasion either of mutual contempt or envy or contentions.

**22. And he brought her to the man.** Moses now relates that marriage was divinely instituted, which is especially useful to know; for since Adam did not take a wife to himself at his own will but received her as offered and appropriated to him by God, the sanctity of marriage is seen more clearly because we recognize God as its Author. The more Satan has endeavored to dishonor marriage, the more should we vindicate it from all reproach and abuse, that it may receive its due reverence. Thence it will follow that the children of God may embrace a conjugal life with a good and tranquil conscience, and husbands and wives may live together in chastity and honor. The work of Satan in attempting the defamation of marriage was twofold: first, that by means of the odium attached to it he might introduce the pestilential law of celibacy; and, second, that married people might indulge themselves in whatever license they pleased. Therefore, by showing the dignity of marriage, we must remove superstition, lest it should in the slightest degree hinder the faithful from chastely using the lawful and pure ordinance of God; and further, we must oppose the lasciviousness of the flesh, in order that men may live modestly with their wives. If no other reason influenced us, this alone ought to be sufficient, that unless we think and speak honorably of marriage, reproach is attached to its Author and Patron, for this is how God is here described by Moses.

**23. The man said, "This is now bone of my bones and flesh of my flesh."** Some ask how Adam derived this knowledge since he was in deep sleep. We should not doubt that God would make the whole matter clear to him, either by secret revelation or by his word. For it was not from any necessity on God's part that he borrowed from man the rib out of which he might form the woman; and he designed that they should be more closely joined together by this bond, which could not have been effected unless he informed them of the fact.

**24. For this reason a man will leave his father and mother and be united to his wife.** It is unclear if Moses here introduces God as speaking or continues Adam's discourse or, indeed, has added this, in virtue of his office as teacher, in his own person. I incline to the last option. Therefore, after he has related historically what God had done, he also demonstrates the purpose of the divine institution. The sum of the whole is: Among the offices pertaining to human society, this is the principal one and, as it were, the most sacred—that a man should cleave unto his wife. And Moses amplifies this by adding that the husband ought to prefer his wife to his father. But the father is said to be left not because marriage severs sons from their fathers or dispenses with other ties of nature, for in this way God would be acting contrary to himself. While, however, the piety of the son toward his father is to be most assiduously cultivated and ought in itself to be deemed inviolable and sacred, yet Moses speaks of marriage to show that it is less lawful to desert a wife than parents. Therefore, they who for slight causes rashly allow divorces violate, in one single particular, all the laws of nature and reduce them to nothing. If we should make it a point of conscience not to separate a father from his son, it is a greater wickedness to dissolve the bond that God has preferred to all others.

**They will become one flesh.** Although the ancient Latin interpreter has translated the passage "in one flesh," yet the Greek interpreters have expressed it more forcibly: "They two will be *into* one flesh," and thus Christ cites the place in Matthew 19:5. But though here no mention is made of "two," yet there is no ambiguity in the sense; for Moses did not say that God has assigned many wives, but only one to one man, and in the general direction given, the wife is in the singular. It remains, therefore, that the conjugal bond subsists between two persons only, from which it is easy to see that nothing is less in line with the divine institution than polygamy. Now, when Christ, in censuring the voluntary divorces of the Jews, adduces as his reason for doing it that it was not so in the beginning (see Matthew 19:1-12), he certainly commands this institution to be observed as a perpetual rule of conduct. See also Malachi 2:15. So there is no doubt that polygamy is a corruption of legitimate marriage.

**25. The man and his wife were both naked, and they felt no shame.** That the nakedness of men should be deemed indecorous and unsightly while that of cattle has nothing disgraceful is heartily in agreement with the dignity of human nature. We cannot behold a naked man without a sense of shame; yet at the sight of a donkey, a dog, or an ox, no such feeling will be produced. In our uncorrupted nature, there was nothing but what was honorable; from which it follows that whatsoever is opprobrious in us must be our own fault, since our parents had nothing in themselves that was unbecoming until they were defiled with sin.

# Genesis
# Chapter 3

**1. Now the serpent was more crafty than any of the wild animals the LORD God had made.** In this chapter Moses explains that man, after he had been deceived by Satan and revolted from his Maker, became entirely changed and so degenerate that the image of God, in which he had been formed, was obliterated. He then declares that the whole world, which had been created for the sake of man, fell together with him, and thus much of its original excellence was destroyed.

But here many difficult questions arise. When Moses says that **the serpent was more crafty than any of the wild animals**, he seems to intimate that it had been induced to deceive man not by the instigation of Satan, but by its own malevolence. I answer that the innate subtlety of the serpent did not prevent Satan from making use of the animal to destroy man. Since he required an instrument, he chose the most suitable animal for his purpose.

Interpreters disagree in what sense the **serpent** is said to be **crafty**. Some would take this in a good, others in a bad sense. I think, however, that Moses does not so much point out a fault as praise nature because God had endued this beast with such singular skill, which made him the most quick-thinking animal. But Satan perverted to his own deceitful purposes the gift that had been divinely imparted to the serpent. I understand **serpent** not allegorically, as some foolishly do, but in its genuine sense.

Many people are surprised that Moses simply, and apparently abruptly, relates that men fell by the impulse of Satan into eternal destruction and yet never by a single word explains how the tempter himself had rebelled against God. And hence it has arisen that fanatical men have dreamed that Satan was created evil and wicked as he is here described. But the revolt of Satan is proved by other passages of Scripture; and it is an impious madness to ascribe to God the creation of any evil and corrupt nature, for when he had completed the world he himself gave this testimony to all his deeds—that they were **very good.** But Moses here passes over Satan's fall because his object is briefly to narrate the corruption of human nature and to teach us that Adam was not created to experience those multiplied miseries under which all his posterity suffer, but that he fell into them by his own fault.

We must now face that question by which vain and inconstant minds are greatly agitated—namely, why God permitted Adam to be tempted, seeing that the sad result was by no means hidden from him. When I say that Adam did not fall without the ordination and will of God, I do not mean that sin was ever pleasing to God. It offends the ears of some when it is said God *willed* this fall; but what else, I pray, is the *permission* of him who has the power of preventing and in whose hand the whole matter is placed but his will? I wish that men would rather suffer themselves to be judged by God than that, with profane temerity, they should pass judgment upon him; but it is the arrogance of the flesh to subject God to its own test. I hold it as a settled axiom that nothing is more unsuitable to God's character than for us to say that man was created by him for the purpose of being placed in a condition of suspense and doubt. Wherefore I conclude that, as it became the Creator, he had before determined with himself what would be man's future condition. Hence the foolish rashly infer that man did not sin by free choice, for he himself perceives, being convicted by the testimony of his own conscience, that he has been too free in sinning.

**He said to the woman, "Did God really say, 'You must not eat from any tree in the garden'?"** The impious assail this passage with their sneers because Moses ascribes eloquence to an animal that only faintly hisses with its forked tongue. They ask at what time animals began to be mute, if they at that time had a distinct language by which they could communicate with humans. The answer is this: The serpent was not eloquent by nature, but when Satan, by divine permission, procured it as a fit instrument for his use, he uttered words also by its tongue, which God also permitted. Nor do I doubt that Eve perceived it to be extraordinary and on that account received greedily what she admired.

**4. "You will not surely die," the serpent said to the woman.** Satan now sprang more boldly forward; because he saw a breach open before him, he broke through in a direct assault, for he never engages in open war until we voluntarily expose ourselves to him, naked and unarmed. He cautiously approaches us at first with allurements; but when he has stolen in upon us, he dares to exalt himself petulantly and with proud confidence against God, just as he now seized upon Eve's doubt, that he might turn it into a direct negative. We are instructed by many examples to beware of his snares and, by making timely resistance, to keep him far from us, that he may not be allowed access to us. He now, therefore, did not question, as before, whether or not the command of God, which he opposed, was true but openly accused God of falsehood, asserting that the word by which death was warned against was false and delusive. Fatal temptation! When God is threatening us with death, we not only securely sleep but hold God himself in derision!

**5. "For God knows that when you eat of it your eyes will be opened."** Now Satan attempted to prove what he had recently asserted. "God," he said in essence, "has forbidden you to eat from the tree, so that he may not allow you to take part in his glory; therefore the fear of punishment is quite needless." In short, the tempter denied that a fruit that is useful and salutary can be harmful. When he said, **"God knows,"** he censured God as being moved by jealousy and as having given the command concerning the tree for the purpose of keeping man in an inferior rank.

**"And you will be like God, knowing good and evil."** I have no doubt that Satan promised them divinity.

**6. When the woman saw that the fruit of the tree was good for food and pleasing to the eye . . .** Eve's look, infected with the poison of concupiscence, was both the messenger and the witness of an impure heart. She could previously look at the tree with such sincerity that no desire to eat of it affected her mind, for the faith she had in the word of God was the best guardian of her heart and of all her senses. But now, after her heart had declined from faith and from obedience to the word, she corrupted both herself and all her senses, and depravity was diffused through all parts of her soul as well as her body. It is, therefore, a sign of impious defection that the woman now judged the tree to be good for food, eagerly delighted herself in viewing it, and persuaded herself that it was desirable for the sake of acquiring wisdom, whereas before she had passed by it a hundred times with an unmoved and tranquil look.

**She also gave some to her husband.** From these words, some conjecture that Adam was present when his wife was tempted and persuaded by the serpent. This is not believable. Yet it might be that he soon joined her and that, even before the woman tasted the fruit of the tree, she related the conversation she'd had with the serpent and entangled him with the same fallacies by which she herself had been deceived.

The opinion of some of the ancients that Adam and Eve were allured by their appetite is puerile. For when there was such abundant choice fruit, what daintiness could there be about one particular kind? Augustine is nearer the mark when he says that pride was the beginning of all evils, and that by pride the human race was ruined. Yet a fuller definition of the sin may be drawn from the kind of temptation that Moses describes. First the woman was led away from the word of God by the wiles of Satan, through unbelief. So the beginning of the ruin by which the human race was overthrown was a defection from the command of God. But observe that men revolted from God when, having forsaken his word, they lent their ears to the falsehoods of Satan. From this we infer that God is to be

43

seen and adored in his word, and therefore that all reverence for him is shaken off when his word is despised.

A question is debated by some concerning the *time* of this fall, or rather ruin. The opinion has been generally received that they fell on the day they were created; and therefore Augustine writes that they stood only for six hours. The conjecture of others that the temptation was delayed by Satan until the Sabbath in order to profane that sacred day is a weak one. Certainly, by instances like these all pious people are admonished to indulge themselves sparingly in doubtful speculations. As for myself, since I have nothing to assert positively respecting the time, I think it may be gathered from the narration of Moses that they did not long retain the dignity they had received; for as soon as he has said they were created, he passes, without the mention of any other thing, to their fall. If Adam had lived but a moderate space of time with his wife, the blessing of God would not have been unfruitful in the production of offspring; but Moses intimates that they were deprived of God's benefits before they had become accustomed to use them. I therefore readily subscribe to the exclamation of Augustine: "O wretched free will, which, while yet entire, had so little stability!"

To say no more about the short length of time, the admonition of Bernard is worth remembering: "Since we read that a fall so dreadful took place in Paradise, what will we do on the dunghill?" Since the Scripture everywhere admonishes us about our nakedness and poverty and declares that we may recover in Christ what we have lost in Adam, let us, renouncing all self-confidence, offer ourselves empty to Christ, that he may fill us with his own riches.

**7. Then the eyes of both of them were opened.** It was necessary that the eyes of Eve should be veiled until her husband also was deceived; but now that both of them were bound by the chain of an unhappy consent, they began to be aware of their wretchedness, although they were not yet affected with a deep knowledge of their fault. **They realized they were naked.** They were ashamed of their nakedness; yet, though convinced, they did not humble themselves before God, nor feared his judgments as they ought; they did not even stop being evasive. Some progress, however, was made, for whereas recently they would, like giants, assault heaven by storm, now, confounded with a sense of their own ignominy, they fled and hid. And truly this opening of the eyes in our first parents to discern their baseness clearly proves them to have been condemned by their own judgment.

We see some good fruit daily springing from such a dreadful ruin in that God instructs us in humility through our miseries and then more clearly illustrates his own goodness; for his grace is now more abundantly poured forth through Christ upon the world than it was imparted to Adam in the beginning. If the reason this is so lies beyond our reach, it is not surprising that the secret counsel of God should be like a labyrinth to us.

**So they sewed fig leaves together and made coverings for themselves.** What I have already said—that they had not been brought either by true shame or by serious fear to repentance—is now even clearer. **They sewed fig leaves together and made coverings for themselves.** For what purpose? Was it to keep God at a distance, as by an invincible barrier? Their sense of evil was confused and combined with dullness, as is often the case. All of us smile at their folly since, certainly, it was ridiculous to place such a covering before God's eyes. In the meanwhile, we are all infected with the same disease. Indeed, we tremble and are covered with shame at the first pangs of conscience; but self-indulgence soon steals in and induces us to resort to vain trifles, as if it were easy to delude God.

**8. Then the man and his wife heard the sound of the Lord God as he was walking in the garden.** As soon as the voice of God sounded, Adam and Eve perceived that the leaves they used to cover themselves were of no avail. The things Moses relates here remain true in human nature and may be clearly discerned in the present day. The difference between good and evil is impressed on everyone's hearts, as Paul teaches (Romans 2:15); but all bury the disgrace of their vices under flimsy leaves until God, by his voice, strikes their inner consciences.

**9. But the Lord God called to the man, "Where are you?"** They had been already smitten by the voice of God, but they lay confounded under the trees until another voice penetrated their minds more effectively. Moses says that Adam was called by the Lord. Had he not been called before? The former, however, was a confused **sound** that did not have enough strength to press on his conscience. Therefore God now came closer. In the same way we also are alarmed at God's voice as soon as his law sounds in our ears; but we snatch at shadows until he, calling upon us more vehemently, compels us to come forward to stand before his tribunal.

**10. He answered, "I heard you in the garden."** Although this verse seems to be the confession of a dejected and humbled man, it will nevertheless soon appear that Adam had not yet come to repentance. He imputed his fear to the voice of God and to his own nakedness, as if he had never before heard God speaking without being alarmed and had not been even invigorated by his speech. His excessive stupidity appears in that he failed to recognize the reason for his shame, which was due to his sin.

**11. "Who told you that you were naked?"** This is an indirect reprimand to reprove the foolishness of Adam in not perceiving his fault in his punishment, as if it had been said not simply that Adam was afraid at the voice of God, but that the heavenly Judge's voice was formidable because Adam was a sinner. Let us remember that we will never benefit from prevaricating. God will always bind us through a just accusation touching the sin of Adam. The atrocious nature of sin is evident in this transgression and rebellion; for as nothing is more acceptable to God than obedience, so nothing is more intolerable than when men, having spurned his commandments, obey Satan and their own lust.

**12. The man said, "The woman you put here with me—she gave me some fruit from the tree, and I ate it."** Adam's boldness clearly showed itself; far from being subdued, he uttered coarse blasphemy. He had before been tacitly expostulating with God; now he began openly to contend with him and triumphed as one who has broken through all barriers.

"Each one," says James, "is tempted when, by his own evil desire, he is dragged away and enticed" (James 1:14). And Adam had deliberately set himself up as a rebel against God. Yet, as if he were not conscious of any evil, he laid the blame on his wife: **"She gave me some fruit from the tree, and I ate it."** Not content with this, he accused God of giving him the wife who had brought his ruin. We are trained in the same school of original sin and are all too ready to resort to subterfuges of the same kind, but to no purpose; for howsoever incitements and instigations from other quarters may impel us, yet the unbelief that seduces us away from obedience to God is within us; the pride within brings forth contempt.

**13. Then the Lord God said to the woman, "What is this you have done?"** The Judge now turned to the woman, so that after he had heard them both he could pronounce sentence. It is as if God said, "How was it possible that you should counsel your husband in such a perverse way?"

**The woman said, "The serpent deceived me, and I ate."** Eve should have been confounded at the grave wickedness about which she was admonished. Yet she was not struck dumb before the Judge but, like her husband, laid the blame on another, pointing accusingly to the serpent. In this way she foolishly and impiously thought she was absolved, for her answer came to this: "I received from the serpent what you have forbidden; the serpent, therefore, was the impostor." But who compelled Eve to listen to the serpent's fallacies and even to place confidence in them more readily than in the word of God?

**14. So the Lord God said to the serpent . . .** God did not question the serpent as he had the man and the woman, because in the animal itself there was no sense of sin and because he would hold out no hope of pardon to the devil. The Lord dealt with the serpent before he imposed punishment on man.

**"Cursed are you above all the livestock and all the wild animals!"** This divine curse made serpents despicable. They are not only the main enemy of the human race but, being separated from other animals, carry on a kind of war with nature. Before, it had been so gentle that the woman did not flee as it approached.

But what follows is difficult because what God denounced as a punishment seems to be natural—namely, that it should **crawl on [its] belly and . . . eat dust.** This objection has induced certain men of learning and ability to say that the serpent, before it was abused by Satan, had walked with an erect body. There is, however, no absurdity in supposing that the serpent was consigned to the former condition to which he was already naturally subject. Thus he who had exalted himself against the image of God was thrust back into his proper rank, as if God said, "You, a wretched and filthy animal, have dared to rise up against man, whom I appointed to the dominion of the whole world, as if you who are fixed to the earth had any right to penetrate into heaven. Therefore, I now throw you back again to the place from which you have attempted to emerge, that you may learn to be content with your lot and exalt yourself no more to reproach and injure humankind."

To **eat dust** is the sign of a vile and sordid nature. This (in my opinion) is the simple meaning of the passage, which is confirmed by Isaiah (see 65:25). For while Isaiah promises under the reign of Christ the complete restoration of a sound and well-constituted nature, he records among other things that dust will be the serpent's food.

**15. "And I will put enmity between you and the woman, and between your offspring and hers."** I interpret this to mean that there would always be hostile strife between the human race and serpents, which is now apparent, for man abhors them; and as often as the sight of a serpent inspires us with horrors, the memory of our fall is renewed. With this I combine in one continued discourse what immediately follows: **"He will crush your head, and you will strike his heel."** God declares that there will be such hatred that both sides will be troublesome to each other; the serpent will be vexatious toward men, and men will be intent on the destruction of serpents. Meanwhile, we see that the Lord acts mercifully in chastising man, whom he does not suffer Satan to touch except in the **heel,** while he subjects the **head** of the serpent to be wounded by him. For in the terms **head** and **heel** there is a distinction between the superior and the inferior. Thus God leaves some remains of dominion to man because he so places the mutual disposition to injure each other that their condition would not be equal, but man would be superior in the conflict.

We must now make a transition from the serpent to the author of this mischief himself, and that not only by way of comparison, for there truly is a literal analogy. God has not so vented his anger on the outward instrument in order to spare the devil, with whom lay all the blame. That this may be clearly seen by us, observe that the Lord spoke not for the sake of the serpent but for the sake of man. That God might revive the fainting minds of men and restore them when oppressed by despair, it became necessary to promise them, in their posterity, victory over Satan, through whose wiles they had been ruined. This, then, was the only salutary medicine that could recover the lost and restore life to the dead. I therefore conclude that God here chiefly assails Satan under the name of the serpent and hurls against him the lightning of his judgment. This he does for two reasons: first, that men may learn to beware of Satan as of a most deadly enemy; second, that they may contend against him with the assured confidence of victory.

God expressly says, **"between you and the woman, and between your offspring and hers"** and mentions **the woman** because as she had yielded to the subtlety of the devil and was first deceived and drew her husband into the participation of her ruin, so she had peculiar need of consolation.

**"He will crush your head, and you will strike his heel."** One exposition of this passage has been invented by applying to the mother of Christ what is said concerning her seed. There is, indeed, no ambiguity in the *words* here used by Moses, but I do not agree with others respecting their *meaning*. For other interpreters correctly take the woman's offspring for Christ, as if it were said that someone would arise from the seed of the woman who would wound the serpent's head. Gladly would I support this opinion, but I believe the word **offspring** is distorted by them, for who will concede that a collective noun is to be understood of one man only? Further, as the permanence of the contest is noted, so victory is promised to the human race through successive ages. I explain, therefore, that **offspring** means the posterity of the woman generally. But since experience teaches that not all the sons of Adam arise as conquerors of the devil, we must necessarily come to one head, that we may find to whom the victory belongs. So Paul, from the seed of Abraham, leads us to Christ. "The God of peace will soon crush Satan under your feet" (Romans 16:20). These words show that the power of bruising Satan is given to faithful men, and thus the blessing is the common property of the whole church.

**16. To the woman he said, "I will greatly increase your pains in childbearing; with pain you will give birth to children."** We must now consider the kind of punishment imposed on the woman. When God said, **"I will greatly increase your pains,"** he included all the trouble women sustain during pregnancy. It is credible that the woman would have given birth without pain or at least without such great suffering if she had stood in her original condition; but her rebellion against God subjected her to inconveniences of this kind.

The second punishment that God exacted is subjection. The words **"Your desire will be for your husband, and he will rule over you"** have the same force as if God had said that she would no longer be free and do as she wanted but would be subject to the authority of her husband and dependent upon his will, or as if he had said, "You will desire nothing but what your husband wishes" (cf. Genesis 4:7). Thus the woman, who had perversely exceeded her proper bounds, was forced back to her own position. She had, indeed, previously been subject to her husband, but that was a liberal and gentle subjection; now, however, she was made a servant.

**17. To Adam he said . . .** In the first place, it should be noted that punishment was not inflicted on the first members of our race to rest on them alone but was extended generally to all their posterity, in order that we might know that the human race was cursed in their person. We next observe that they were subjected only to temporal punishment, so that from the moderation of the divine anger they might entertain hope of pardon. After God had briefly spoken of Adam's sin, he announced that **the ground** would be **cursed** because of him. Now, as the blessing of the earth means, in the language of Scripture, that fertility that God infuses by his secret power, so the curse is nothing other than the opposite privation, when God withdraws his favor.

**18. "It will produce thorns and thistles for you, and you will eat the plants of the field."** The earth would not be the same as it had been before, producing perfect fruits, for God declared that the earth would degenerate from its fertility and bring forth briers and noxious plants. Therefore we know that whatever unwholesome things may be produced are not natural fruits of the earth but are corruptions that are the result of sin. These words were added for our consolation, as if God were saying, "Although the earth, which ought to be the mother of good fruits only, is covered with thorns and briers, it will yield sustenance by which you may be fed."

**19. "By the sweat of your brow."** By **sweat** is understood hard labor and weariness. This repeats the thought of an earlier sentence: **"Through painful toil you will eat of it"** (verse 17). From this passage, certain ignorant people would rashly force all men to engage in manual labor. But God was not here teaching as a master or legislator but is only announcing punishment as a judge. Truly God pronounced, as from his judgment-seat, that man's life would from now on be miserable, because Adam had proved himself unworthy of that tranquil, happy, and joyful state for which he had been created.

One question remains to be examined: God had previously shown himself propitious to Adam and his wife, giving them hope of pardon. So why did he exact punishment from them now? One may be naturally endued with such a gentle disposition that he does not disown the duty of submission to God; yet, having escaped from the hand of God after one allowed sin, he will soon relapse unless he is drawn back as by force. So this general axiom is to be maintained: All the sufferings to which our lives are subject are necessary exercises by which God partly invites us to repentance, partly instructs us in humility, and partly makes us more cautious and more attentive in guarding against the allurements of sin for the future.

**"For dust you are and to dust you will return."** God pronounced that the end of a miserable life would be death. Adam would at length come, through various and constant kinds of evil, to the last evil of all. This fulfills what we said before—that the death of Adam had commenced immediately from the day of his transgression. This accursed life of man could be nothing but the beginning of death. Some might object, "But where then is the victory over the serpent if death occupies the last place? For the words seem to have no other meaning than that man must be ultimately crushed by death. Therefore, since death left nothing to Adam, the promise recently given failed, to which may be added that the hope of being restored to a state of salvation was most slender and obscure."

Truly I do not doubt that these terrible words would grievously afflict minds already dejected from other causes. But since, though astonished by their sudden calamity, Adam and Eve were yet not deeply affected with the knowledge of sin, it is not surprising that God persisted in reminding them of their punishment, in order that he might beat them down as with reiterated blows. Although the consolation offered is itself obscure and feeble, God caused it to be sufficient for the support of their hope, lest the weight of their affliction should entirely overwhelm them. In the meantime it was necessary that they should be weighed down by a mass of many evils until God reduced them to true and serious repentance. Moreover, death is here put as the final issue because in Adam himself nothing but death would be found; yet, in this way he was urged to seek a remedy in Christ.

**"For dust you are."** Since what God declares here belongs to man's *nature*, not to his *crime* or *fault*, it might seem that death was now added as something not adventitious to him. And therefore some understand what was before said, **"you will die"** (verse 3), in a spiritual sense. The declaration of Paul is clear: "As in Adam all die, so in Christ all will be made alive" (1 Corinthians 15:22); this wound also was inflicted by sin. Nor truly is there a difficult solution to the question, "Why should God pronounce that he who was taken from the dust should return to it?" For as soon as he had been raised to a dignity so great that the glory of the divine image shone in him, the terrestrial origin of his body was seemingly almost obliterated. Now, however, after he had been despoiled of his divine and heavenly excellence, what remained but that by his very departure out of life he should recognize himself to be earth? Hence we dread death because dissolution, which is contrary to nature, cannot naturally be desired. Truly the first man would have passed to a better life had he remained upright; but there would have been no separation of the soul from the body, no corruption, no kind of destruction, and, in short, no violent change.

**20. Adam named his wife Eve.** As soon as Adam had escaped present death, being encouraged by a measure of consolation, he celebrated that divine benefit that, beyond all expectation, he had received, in the name he gave his wife.

**21. The LORD God made garments of skin for Adam and his wife and clothed them.** Moses here simply declares that the Lord undertook the labor of making garments of skins for Adam and his wife. It is not proper to understand his words as if God was a furrier or a servant to sew clothes. At the same time, it is not credible that skins were presented to them by chance; but since animals had before been destined for their use, being now impelled by a new necessity, they put some to death in order to cover themselves with their skins, having been divinely directed to adopt this counsel; therefore Moses calls God the Author of it. The reason the Lord clothed them with garments of skin appears to me to be this: Garments formed of this material would have a more degrading appearance than those made of linen or of wool. God therefore designed that our first parents should, in such a dress, behold their own vileness, just as they had before seen it in their nudity, and should thus be reminded of their sin.

**22. And the LORD God said, "The man has now become like one of us."** This was an ironical reproof by which God not only pricked the heart of man but pierced it through and through. He did not, however, cruelly triumph over the miserable and afflicted but, according to the necessity of the disease, applied a more drastic remedy. For though Adam was confounded and astonished at his calamity, yet he did not so deeply reflect on its cause as to become weary of his pride, that he might learn to embrace true humility. We may add that God inveighed by this irony not more against Adam himself than against his posterity, for the purpose of commending poverty of spirit to all ages.

**"Knowing good and evil"** describes the cause of so great a misery—namely, that Adam, not content with his condition, had tried to ascend higher than was lawful. It is as if God said, "See now where your ambition and perverse appetite for illicit knowledge have taken you." Yet the Lord did not even deign to hold a conversation with Adam but contemptuously drew him forth in order to expose him to greater infamy. Thus was it necessary for his iron pride to be beaten down, that he might at length descend into himself and become more and more displeased with himself.

**"He must not be allowed to reach out his hand and take also from the tree of life and eat, and live forever."** So that Adam might understand himself to be deprived of his former life, a solemn excommunication was added. Not that the Lord would cut him off from all hope of salvation; but by taking away what he had given, he would cause man to seek new assistance elsewhere. Now, there remained an expiation in sacrifices that could restore him to the life he had lost. Previously, direct communication with God was the source of life to Adam; but from the moment in which he became alienated from God, it was necessary that he should recover life by the death of Christ, by whose life he then lived. It is indeed certain that man would not have been able, had he even devoured the whole tree, to enjoy life against the will of God; but God, out of respect to his own institution, connected life with the external sign, until the promise should be taken away from it. For there never was any intrinsic efficacy in the tree, but God made it life-giving insofar as he had sealed his grace to man as he used it. In short, God resolved to wrest out of the hands of man what gave grounds for confidence, in case he should form for himself a vain hope of the perpetuity of the life that he had lost.

**23. So the LORD God banished him from the Garden of Eden.** Here Moses partly repeats what he had said concerning the punishment inflicted on man and partly celebrates the goodness of God, by which the rigor of his judgment was mitigated. God mercifully softened the exile of Adam by providing for him a remaining home on earth and by assigning to him a livelihood (**to work the ground from which he had been taken**). Moses, however, again speaks about punishment when he says that man was expelled and that **cherubim** had **a flaming sword flashing back and forth to guard the way to the tree of life.** This prevented Adam from returning to the garden.

# Genesis
# Chapter 4

**1. Adam lay with his wife Eve, and she became pregnant and gave birth to Cain.** Moses now begins to describe the propagation of mankind. Here it is important to notice that God's benediction to increase and multiply was not abolished by sin; furthermore, the heart of Adam was divinely confirmed so that he did not shrink with horror from the production of offspring.

**"With the help of the Lord I have brought forth a man."** Eve gave thanks to God for having begun to raise up a posterity through her, although she deserved perpetual barrenness and even utter destruction. While Eve congratulated herself on the birth of a son, she offered him to God as the firstfruits of his race. Eve called a newborn infant **a man** because she saw the human race renewed, which both she and her husband had ruined by their own fault.

**2. Later she gave birth to his brother Abel. Now Abel kept flocks, and Cain worked the soil.** Both Abel and Cain followed a kind of life in itself holy and laudable. For the cultivation of the earth was commanded by God; and the labor of feeding sheep was not less honorable than useful. In short, the whole of rustic life was innocent, simple, and accommodated to the true order of nature. Therefore, both exercised themselves in labors approved by God and necessary for human life. From this it is inferred that they had been well instructed by their father. The rite of sacrificing more fully confirms this because it proves that they had been accustomed to the worship of God. The life of Cain, therefore, was in appearance very well regulated, inasmuch as he cultivated the duties of piety toward God and sought to live by honest and just labor, as became a provident and sober father of a family.

This is a good moment to recall that the first men, though they had been deprived of the sacrament of divine love when they were prohibited from the tree of life, had yet been only so deprived of it that a hope of salvation was still left to them, of which they had the signs in sacrifices.

We must remember that the custom of sacrificing was not rashly devised by them but was divinely given to them. For since an apostle attributes the acceptance of Abel's sacrifice to faith, it follows, first, that he had not offered it without the command of God (see Hebrews 11:4). Second, it has been true from the beginning of the world that obedience is better than any sacrifices (see 1 Samuel 15:22) and is the parent of all virtues. Hence it also follows that man had been taught by God what was pleasing to him. Third, since God has been always the same, we may not say that he ever delighted in merely external worship. Yet he deemed those sacrifices of the first age acceptable. It follows further, therefore, that they had been spiritually offered to him; that is, the holy fathers did not mock him with empty ceremonies but comprehended something more sublime and secret, which they could not have done without divine instruction. It is interior truth alone that, in the external signs, distinguishes the genuine and rational worship of God from that which is gross and superstitious. We see then that God, when he took away the tree of life, in which he had first given the pledge of his grace, proved and declared himself to be propitious to man by other means.

**4. The Lord looked with favor on Abel and his offering.** Moses does not simply state that Abel's worship was pleasing to God, but he begins with the person of the offered. In this way Moses shows that God will not view with favor any deeds except those performed by someone who is already previously accepted and approved by him. And no wonder, for man sees things that are apparent, but God looks into the heart (1 Samuel 16:7).

Therefore, in the first place we must hold that all deeds done before faith, however righteous they may have appeared to be, were nothing but sins, being defiled from their roots and offensive to the Lord, whom no one can please without inward purity of heart. I wish those who imagine that men, by their own free will, are made fit to receive the grace of God would reflect on this. Certainly no controversy would then remain on the question of whether God justifies men gratuitously—by faith. For this must be received as a settled point—that in the judgment of God, no respect is given to deeds until man is received into favor with God.

Another point appears equally certain: Since the whole human race is hateful to God, there is no other way of reconciliation to divine favor than through faith. Moreover, since faith is a gratuitous gift of God, and a special illumination of the Spirit, it is easy to infer that we are *prevented* from another path solely by his grace, as if he had raised us from the dead. In this sense Peter says that it is God who purifies our hearts by faith. It can now be seen in what way purity is the effect of faith. It is a vapid and trifling philosophy to adduce as the cause of purity that men are not induced to seek God as their rewarder except by faith. Those who speak in this way entirely bury the grace of God, which his Spirit chiefly commends.

Others also speak coldly who teach that we are purified by faith only on account of the gift of regeneration in order that we may be accepted of God. Not only do they omit half the truth, but they build without a foundation since, on account of the curse on the human race, it became necessary that gratuitous reconciliation should precede. Again, since God never so regenerates his people in this world that they can worship him perfectly, no work of man can possibly be acceptable without expiation. And to this point the ceremony of legal washing belongs, in order that men may learn that as often as they wish to draw near unto God, purity must be sought elsewhere than themselves. God will then at length see our obedience when he looks upon us in Christ.

**5. But on Cain and his offering he did not look with favor. So Cain was very angry, and his face was downcast.** It is not to be doubted that Cain conducted himself as hypocrites are accustomed to do; namely, he wished to appease God, as one discharging a debt, by external sacrifices, without the least intention of dedicating himself to God. But in genuine worship we offer ourselves as spiritual sacrifices to God. When God sees such hypocrisy as Cain's, combined with gross and manifest mockery of himself, it is not surprising that he hates it and is unable to bear it; from which also it follows that he rejects with contempt the deeds of those who withdraw themselves from him.

For it is his will, first, to have us devoted to himself. Then he seeks our deeds in testimony of our obedience to him, but only in the second place. It is to be remarked that all the figments by which men mock both God and themselves are the fruits of unbelief. To this is added pride because unbelievers, despising the Mediator's grace, throw themselves fearlessly into the presence of God. The Jews foolishly imagine that the oblations of Cain were unacceptable because he defrauded God of the full ears of corn and meanly offered him only barren or half-filled ears. Deeper and more hidden was the actual evil—namely, that impurity of heart of which I have been speaking. On the other hand, the strong scent of burning fat did not procure divine favor for the sacrifices of Abel; rather, being pervaded by the good odor of faith, they had a sweet-smelling savor.

When Moses says that Cain was **downcast,** he means that not only was he seized with a sudden vehement anger but that, from a lingering sadness, he cherished a feeling so malignant that he was full of envy.

**6. Then the LORD said to Cain, "Why are you angry? Why is your face downcast?"** Moses does not specify how God spoke. Whether Cain was presented with a vision or heard an oracle from heaven or was warned by a secret inspiration, in any case he felt constrained by the judgment of God. To drag Adam into this, and to assume that as God's prophet and interpreter he inveighed against his son, is forced and vapid. I understand the aim of various good men, no less eminent for piety than for doctrine, when they play with such notions. They intend to glorify the visible ministry of the Word and to cut down Satan's sleights of hand that he passes off under the guise of revelation. I admit that nothing is more helpful to the church than to keep pious minds submissive to the authority of preaching so that they may not seek the word of God in erratic speculations. But in the beginning it is necessary to remember that the word of God was given in the form of oracles in order that later when administered by human hands it might be held in greater reverence.

I admit that Adam was given the duty of teaching, and I do not doubt that he carefully instructed his children. But the words of Moses are too arbitrarily limited by those who think that God spoke only by his ministers.

**7. "If you do what is right, will you not be accepted?"** In these words God reproved Cain for having been unjustly angry, since the cause of the whole evil lay in himself. Thus all wicked men, after they have been long and vehemently enraged against God, are at length so convicted by the divine judgment that they vainly desire to transfer to others the cause of their own evil. **"If you do what is right."** God will accept sacrifices when rightly offered. We now perceive how wrong Cain was to be angry that his sacrifices were not honored, seeing that God was ready to receive them with outstretched hands, provided they were not faulty. At the same time, we must remember that the main point of well-doing is, for pious people, relying on Christ the Mediator and on the gratuitous reconciliation procured by him, so that we can worship God sincerely and without dissimulation. Therefore, the faithful, as often as they enter into the presence of God, are commended by the grace of Christ alone, their sins being blotted out—provided they bring there true purity of heart.

**"But if you do not do what is right."** On the other hand, God pronounced a dreadful sentence against Cain if he hardened his heart in wickedness. It is as if God said, "Your obstinacy will not help you, for although you would have nothing to do with me, your sin will give you no rest but will drive you on, pursue you, urge you, and never allow you to escape." Hence it follows that Cain not only raged in vain but was held guilty by his own inner conviction, even though no one should accuse him; for the expression **sin is crouching at your door** relates to the inner judgment of the conscience, which presses upon the man convinced of his sin and besieges him on every side.

**"It desires to have you, but you must master it."** Nearly all commentators say this refers to sin and think that by this admonition those depraved hosts are restrained that solicit the mind of man. Therefore, according to their view, this sentence means, "If sin rises against you to subdue you, why do you indulge it rather than work to restrain and control it? For it is your part to subdue and bring into obedience those affections in your flesh that you perceive as opposing God's will and rebelling against him." But I believe Moses means something entirely different.

This seems to be a reproof by which God charged the impious man with ingratitude because he held in contempt the honor of being the firstborn. The greater the divine benefits with which any one of us is adorned, the more does he betray his impiety unless he endeavors earnestly to serve the Author of grace to whom he is under obligation. Though Abel was regarded as his brother's inferior, he was nevertheless a diligent worshiper of God. But the firstborn worshiped God negligently and perfunctorily. It is certain that only by the grace of the Holy Spirit can the affections of the flesh be so mortified that they will not prevail. Nor truly must we conclude that as often as God commands anything, we will have strength to perform it; rather, we must hold on to Augustine's saying, "Give what you command, and command what you will."

**8. Now Cain said to his brother Abel, "Let's go out to the field."** Some understand this conversation to have been general, as if Cain, perfidiously dissembling his anger, spoke in a fraternal manner. In my opinion the speech is obscure, and though something is to be understood, yet what it is remains uncertain. Nevertheless, I am not dissatisfied with the explanation that Moses concisely reprehends the wicked perfidy of the hypocrite, who by speaking familiarly presented the appearance of fraternal concord until the opportunity of perpetrating the horrid murder should be afforded. By this example we are taught that hypocrites are never to be more dreaded than when they stoop to converse under the pretext of friendship; when they are not permitted to injure by open hostility as much as they please, suddenly they assume a feigned appearance of peace. But it is not to be expected that those who are like savage beasts toward God should sincerely cultivate the confidence of friendship with men.

Yet let the reader consider whether Moses did not rather mean that although Cain was rebuked by God, he nevertheless contended with his brother, and thus this saying of his would depend on what had preceded. I certainly rather incline to the opinion that he did not keep his malignant feelings within his own breast, but that he broke forth in accusation against his brother and angrily declared to him the cause of his dejection.

**And while they were in the field Cain attacked his brother Abel and killed him.** From this we gather that although Cain had complained of his brother at home, he had yet so covered his diabolical anger that Abel suspected nothing. Moreover, this single deed of guilt clearly shows where Satan leads men when they harden their mind in wickedness, so that in the end their obstinacy is worthy of the most severe punishment.

**9. "Where is your brother Abel?"** God now speaks to us through the Scriptures, but he formerly manifested himself to the fathers through oracles. Thus the angel spoke to Hagar in the desert after she had fallen away from the church (see Genesis 16:8). It is indeed possible that God may have interrogated Cain through the silent examination of his conscience, and that he in return may have answered, inwardly fretting and murmuring. We must, however, conclude that he was examined not by the external voice of man but by a divine voice; so he felt he had to deal directly with God. Cain, in denying that he was his **brother's keeper**, attempted to repel God's judgment. He tried to escape by the foolish excuse that he was not required to give an account of his murdered brother because he had received no express command to take care of him.

**10. The LORD said, "What have you done? Listen!"** Moses shows that Cain gained nothing by his evasive argument. God first asked where his brother was; he then questioned him more closely, to exact an unwilling confession of his guilt. In no racks or tortures of any kind is there so much force to constrain evildoers as there was efficacy in the thunder of the divine voice to convict Cain.

**"Your brother's blood cries out to me from the ground."** God shows here, first, that he knows all about the actions of men; second, that he holds the life of man too dear to allow innocent blood to be shed with impunity; third, that he cares for the pious not only while they live but even after death. It is a wonderfully sweet consolation to good men who are unjustly harassed when they hear that their own sufferings, which they silently endure, go into the presence of God of their own accord to demand vengeance. Abel was speechless when his throat was being cut or in whatever other manner he lost his life; but after death the voice of his blood was more vehement than the eloquence of any orator.

Murderers often exult as if they have evaded punishment; but at length God will show that innocent blood has not been mute and that he has not said in vain, "Precious in the sight of the LORD is the death of his saints" (Psalm 116:15). This teaching brings relief to the faithful in case they should be too anxious concerning their life, over which they learn that God continually watches; it also thunders against the ungodly who have no scruples about harming those whom God has undertaken to preserve.

**11. "Now you are under a curse and driven from the ground."** Judgment was now pronounced on Cain. God appointed the earth to carry out his vengeance, since it had been polluted by the impious and horrible murder. It is as if God said, "You have just denied committing murder, but the senseless earth itself will demand your punishment." Because of the earth's abhorrence of the pollution, it had opened its mouth to cover the blood that had been shed by a brother's hand. This man's cruelty was most detestable as he did not shrink from pouring out his neighbor's blood into the heart of the earth.

**"Which opened its mouth to receive your brother's blood from your hand."** We must not imagine that any miracle took place here, as if the blood had been absorbed by any unusual opening of the earth. This is but a figurative way of speaking. It shows that there was more humanity in the earth than in man himself. Judgment was committed to the earth, so that Cain might understand that his judge did not have to be summoned from a distance. There was no need for an angel to descend from heaven since the earth voluntarily offered itself as the avenger.

**12. "When you work the ground."** This verse expounds the previous verse. It states more clearly what is meant by being cursed **"from the ground"** (verse 11); namely, **"it will no longer yield its crops for you."** The earth robs its cultivators of the fruit of their toil.

**"You will be a restless wanderer on the earth."** A second punishment is now inflicted—namely, that he would never be safe. Wherever Cain traveled, he would be unsettled and a fugitive.

**13. Cain said to the LORD, "My punishment is more than I can bear."** Nearly all commentators agree that this is the language of desperation, because Cain, confounded by God's judgment, had no hope of pardon. And, indeed, it is true that the reprobate are never conscious of their evils until they are overtaken by a calamity from which they cannot escape. Judas confessed his sin but, overwhelmed with fear, fled as far as possible from the presence of God. It is certainly true that when God's anger falls on reprobates, they are broken rather than corrected. Therefore their fear stuns them, so that they can think of nothing but hell and eternal destruction.

However, I am sure that the words here have another meaning as well. Cain, although he did not excuse his sin, complained about the intolerable severity of his judgment. In the same way the devils, although they feel they are justly tormented, constantly rage against God, their Judge, and accuse him of cruelty. It is as if Cain said, "If a safe place to live is denied me in the world, and you do not deign to care for me, what do you leave me? Would it not be better to die at once than to be constantly exposed to a thousand deaths?" From this we infer that reprobates, however clearly they may be convicted, never cease to complain as if they are able to stir up enmity against God on account of the severity of their own sufferings. How wretched, then, is the instability of the wicked, who know that God does not give them a foot of earth.

**14. "Whoever finds me will kill me."** Since Cain was no longer covered by God's protection, Cain concluded that he would be exposed to harm and violence from all men. And he reasoned correctly, for God's hand alone marvelously preserves us in the middle of many dangers. People have spoken prudently who said that our life hangs on a thread. Cain, however, considered himself deprived of God's protection and supposed all creatures to be divinely armed to take vengeance for his impious murder.

**15. But the LORD said to him, "Not so; if anyone kills Cain, he will suffer vengeance seven times over."** God said that he would prevent anyone from killing Cain with impunity. God did this not because he was granting the murderer a favor, but for the sake of posterity, in order to preserve human life. The Lord declared that if anyone imitated Cain, they would be punished even more severely.

**Then the LORD put a mark on Cain so that no one who found him**

would kill him. Moses said a mark was put on Cain that would strike terror into everyone, as they would see, as in a mirror, the tremendous judgment of God against bloody men. As Scripture does not describe what kind of mark it was, commentators have conjectured that his body shook with tremors. But it is enough for us to say that there was some visible token that would deter anyone from injuring Cain.

16. So Cain went out from the LORD's presence. Cain left God's presence as an exile.

17. Cain lay with his wife, and she became pregnant and gave birth to Enoch. From the context we may gather that Cain, before he killed his brother, had married; otherwise Moses would now have said something about his marriage. It is clear that many people, men as well as women, are not mentioned in this narrative, as it was Moses' aim only to follow one line of Cain's progeny, until he came to Lamech.

Cain was then building a city, and he named it after his son Enoch. This, at first sight, seems to contradict both God's judgment and the preceding verse. Adam and the rest of his family lived under the open heaven and sought protection under trees; but the exile Cain, whom God had commanded to wander as a fugitive, not content with a private house, built himself a city. It is, however, probable that the man, oppressed by an accusing conscience and not thinking himself safe within the walls of his own house, had contrived a new kind of defense. Therefore, it is a sign of an agitated and guilty mind that Cain wanted to build a city to separate himself from the rest of men.

19. Lamech married two women, one named Adah and the other Zillah. We have here the origin of polygamy in a perverse and degenerate race. Lamech violated the sacred law of marriage, which had been given by God. For God had planned that they will become one flesh (2:24), the they referring to two people. This was supposed to be followed forever. But Lamech, with utter contempt for God, corrupted nature's laws. The Lord, therefore, willed that the corruption of lawful marriage should come from Cain's family and from Lamech, in order that polygamists might be ashamed of whose example they were following.

20-22. Adah gave birth to Jabal; he was the father of those who live in tents and raise livestock. Moses now reminds us that some good was combined with the evils that came from the family of Cain. For the discovery of the arts and of whatever is useful and makes our common life more pleasant is a gift of God that is not to be despised and an achievement worthy of praise. It is indeed surprising that the race that had departed furthest from the right way surpassed the rest of Adam's descendants in serviceable endowments.

Indeed, I would suggest that Moses specifically enumerated the arts invented by the family of Cain to inform us that Cain was not so cursed by God that he had no gifts to distribute to his descendants. It is probable that others also were not lacking in talent and that there was among other sons of Adam no lack of industrious and clever men who busied themselves in inventing and developing the arts. Clearly, here Moses is celebrating what was left of God's blessing in a people whom we should otherwise regard as sterile and devoid of every other good.

We must therefore recognize that although the sons of Cain were deprived of the Spirit of regeneration, they were blessed with endowments far from negligible. In fact, the experience of all ages shows us how many rays of divine light have always gleamed among unbelieving nations and have contributed to the improvement of our present life. And today we see glorious gifts of the Spirit spread throughout the whole human race. The liberal and industrial arts and the sciences have come to us from profane men. Astronomy and the other branches of philosophy, medicine, political science—we must admit that we have learned all these from them.

No doubt God endowed them so liberally with his excellent favors to give them no excuse for their impiety. But while we are amazed at the riches of the grace that God pours upon them, we marvel much more at the grace of regeneration given to us, by which God sanctifies his elect to be his own.

Although the invention of musical instruments serves our enjoyment and our pleasures rather than our needs, it ought not on that account to be judged of no value; still less should it be condemned. Pleasure is to be condemned only when it is not combined with reverence for God and not related to the common welfare of society. But music by its nature is adapted to rouse our devotion to God and to aid the well-being of man; we need only avoid enticements to shame, and also empty entertainments that keep men from better employments and are simply a waste of time.

To conclude, in my opinion Moses here wished to show that the race of Cain excelled in many important endowments that at once made their impiety inexcusable and were shining witnesses to God's goodness.

**Jabal** is said to be the father of the people **who live in tents** because he invented that convenient shelter, and others afterwards imitated him.

**23. Lamech said to his wives, "Adah and Zillah, listen to me; wives of Lamech, hear my words. I have killed a man for wounding me, a young man for injuring me."** Moses describes the ferocity of **Lamech** to teach us that so far from being terrified by the example of divine judgment that he had seen in his ancestor, Cain, Lamech only hardened his heart. Lamech boasted that he had enough courage and strength to kill anyone who dared attack him. What he meant is, "I confidently take on my own head whatever danger there may be, for I am sure that I can escape."

The wickedness of Cain was indeed awful, but the cruelty of Lamech knew no bounds, for he spared no human blood. From this it follows that once people are imbued with blood, they go on to shed it and drink it without restraint.

**24. "If Cain is avenged seven times, then Lamech seventy-seven times."** God had intended that Cain's judgment should be a dreadful warning to others not to commit murder, and so had marked him with a shameful stigma. Yet in case anyone imitated his crime, God declared that whoever killed Cain would **"suffer vengeance seven times over"** (verse 15).

Lamech, ridiculing this divine declaration, also mocked its severity. He indulged in greater license to sin, as if God had granted some singular privilege to murderers. The number seven in Scripture means "many" and designates multitudes, and sevenfold, **"seventy-seven times,"** means an enormous number. This lay behind Christ's declaration, "I tell you, not seven times, but seventy-seven times" (Matthew 18:22).

**25.** Some infer from this verse that before Seth's birth our first parents were entirely deprived of their offspring, one of their sons having been killed, and the other banished. But it is utterly incredible that when God's blessing in the propagation of mankind was its strongest, Adam and Eve should have been unfruitful for so many years. Rather, before Abel was killed, Adam's family greatly increased.

What, therefore, does Moses mean? Moses ignores other members of Adam's family because he wants to trace the pious descendants through the line of Seth.

**"God has granted me another child in place of Abel, since Cain killed him."** Eve thought of herself as bereft of not one son only, but of all her other children in the person of **Abel**.

**26. At that time men began to call on the name of the LORD.** The verb **to call on** is a synecdoche, for it includes the whole worship of God. Religion is here correctly named by its principal part, for God prefers this service of piety and faith to all sacrifices (see Psalm 50:14). We may readily conclude that Seth was an upright and faithful servant of God. And after he fathered a son like himself and had a rightly constituted family, the church began to appear. The worship of God could now continue through successive generations. From this it is clear that men have a great propensity to reject God, and so Moses says it is a miracle that there was at that time a single family in which God was worshiped.

# Genesis
# Chapter 5

**1. This is the written account of Adam's line.** In this chapter Moses briefly recounts how much time elapsed between the creation of the world and the Flood, as well as mentioning part of the history of that period. While we may not understand the Spirit's purpose in leaving unrecorded great and memorable events, it is nevertheless our business to reflect on many things that are passed over in silence.

The book of Genesis, according to the Hebrew phrase, is a systematic enumeration and description of many events. **"Generations"** [KJV] signifies a continuous succession of a race, a continuous progeny. Further, the purpose of this catalog of events was to inform us that among the multitudes of men, there was always a number, though small, who worshiped God. This group of people was wonderfully preserved by heavenly protection, so God's name would never be entirely obliterated, and so the seed of the church would never become extinct.

**When God created man, he made him in the likeness of God.** God does not restrict **Adam's line** to the day of creation but only points to its beginning. Moses repeats that Adam was formed in the image of God, as the excellency and dignity of this favor could not be sufficiently celebrated. It was not possible for God to be more generous toward man than by stamping his own glory on him and thus making him, as it were, a living image of the divine wisdom and justice.

**2. He created them male and female and blessed them.** This clause commends the sacred bond of marriage and the inseparable union between husband and wife. At first (verse 1) Moses mentioned only one (**man**), but he immediately includes both under one name (**male and female**). The superficial inference of Jewish writers that only married people are called Adam (or man) is refuted by the history of the creation. Also in this verse the Spirit means that after the appointment of marriage, the husband and the wife were like one man.

**3. When Adam had lived 130 years, he had a son in his own like-**

ness, in his own image; and he named him Seth. In saying that Adam **had a son in his own likeness,** Moses is referring to the origin of our nature. But at the same time, he is alluding to its corruption and pollution, which because of Adam and the Fall has flowed down to all his posterity. Therefore, according to the flesh Seth was born a sinner; but later he was renewed by the grace of the Spirit. This sad example of the holy patriarch reminds us to deplore our own wretchedness.

**4. After Seth was born, Adam lived 800 years and had other sons and daughters.** The number of years recorded here indicates that the patriarchs lived for a long time. Through six successive generations, when the family of Seth had grown into a great people, the voice of Adam daily resounded to remind them about the creation, the Fall, man's punishment, and the hope of salvation.

**5. Altogether, Adam lived 930 years, and then he died.** The clause **and then he died,** which records the death of each patriarch, is by no means superfluous, for it warns us that we are now exposed to the curse of death.

**22. Enoch walked with God.** Undoubtedly **Enoch** was honored with special praise among the people of his own age, for it is said that he **walked with God.** Yet Seth and Mahalalel and Jared were then living, whose piety was celebrated in the earlier part of the chapter. From this we infer that this holy man, whom the Holy Spirit saved from the experience of death, was an exceptional person. The remarkable example of **Enoch** is given to teach us to pay more attention to God than to men. It is as if Moses said that Enoch, in case he should be diverted by corrupt men, had respect for God alone. So with a pure conscience he cultivated uprightness.

**24. Enoch walked with God; then he was no more, because God took him away.** Something extraordinary is pointed out here. Everyone ends this life by dying, but Moses clearly declares that Enoch was taken out of the world in an unusual manner and was received by the Lord in a miraculous way. Enoch, in the middle of his life, suddenly and uniquely vanished from the sight of men because the Lord **took him away.** We read later that this also happened to Elijah.

Enoch's translation was a visible representation of a blessed resurrection. This teaches all godly people that they should not keep their hope confined within the boundaries of this mortal life. Moses shows that this translation demonstrated God's love toward Enoch, linking it immediately with his pious and upright life. He was received into a heavenly country, as the epistle to the Hebrews (11:5) clearly teaches.

If you ask why Enoch was translated, and what his present condition is, I answer that his translation was a special privilege that other people would have experienced if they had remained in their original state. His translation was a placid and joyful departure out of the world.

**29. He named him Noah and said, "He will comfort us in the labor**

and painful toil of our hands caused by the ground the LORD has cursed." Lamech knew, through the inspiration of the Spirit, that Noah would **comfort** them. The Jews took Lamech's statement to be a prophecy. **"The labor and painful toil of our hands"** is a synecdoche because this one kind of **labor** represents the whole miserable state into which mankind had fallen.

**32. After Noah was 500 years old.** It is not easy to know if the fathers whom Moses had previously listed were all the firstborn in their families. Moses only wanted to trace the succession of the church. But as far as Noah is concerned, it is clear that he had no more than three sons. It is amazing that from the time he received the dreadful message about the destruction of the human race, he was not prevented by the greatness of his grief from intercourse with his wife, for this was necessary so that this family could restore the second world.

# Genesis
# Chapter 6

**1. When men began to increase in number on the earth and daughters were born to them.** Moses, having listed ten patriarchs who worshiped God faithfully, now relates that their families became corrupt. This account comes before the five hundredth year of Noah. For in order to make a transition to the history of the Flood, Moses prefaces it by declaring that the whole world was so corrupt that hardly anyone honored God. The world was then, as it were, divided into two parts: Seth's family worshiped God faithfully, but everyone else neglected God. This shows how ungrateful the descendants of Seth were when they mixed with the children of Cain and with other ungodly races (verse 2). In this way they voluntarily deprived themselves of the inestimable grace of God, for it was an ungodly act to go against God's instructions. At first sight it may seem that the sons of God were severely condemned for a minor wrongdoing—choosing beautiful wives from the daughters of men. But we must emphasize that it is not a small offense to break God's commands. Those who worship God must separate themselves from ungodly nations.

That old story about angels having sexual intercourse with women must be refuted, for it is absurd. Moses makes no distinction between **the sons of God** and **the daughters of men** because they were **the sons of God** by adoption. When Scripture speaks about **the sons of God**, it sometimes refers to eternal election, and sometimes to outward vocations among which many wolves may exist. By giving them this honorable title, Moses reproves their ingratitude because they deserted their heavenly Father.

**2. The daughters of men were beautiful.** Moses does not condemn **the sons of God** for choosing wives who were beautiful, but because they were ruled by lust. Marriage is too sacred an institution for men to enter it because of their lustful eyes. These words teach us that temperance is necessarily present in a holy marriage. The sons of the saints are not

67

condemned here for fornication, but for showing too much indulgence as they chose their wives.

**3. Then the LORD said.** Moses now introduces God himself as the speaker, for the declaration carries greater weight when it is pronounced by God's own mouth. To show that men have no grounds for complaining about God's judgment, God here pronounces the depravity of the world intolerable and beyond any remedy.

This passage has been expounded in different ways. Luther applies this verse to the external jurisdiction that God exercises by the ministry of the prophets, as if a patriarch had said in an assembly, "We must stop crying aloud because it is unbecoming that the Spirit of God, who speaks through us, should any longer weary himself in reproving the world." This is an ingenious interpretation, but because we must not seek the meaning of Scripture in uncertain conjectures, I interpret the words simply to mean that the Lord, as if wearied with the obstinate perverseness of the world, proclaimed that a vengeance was present that he had previously deferred. For as long as the Lord suspends punishment, he in a certain sense strives with men. In this way he had striven already for some centuries with the world, which nevertheless was constantly becoming worse. And now, as if he were worn-out, he declared that he had no desire to contend any longer. For when God, after inviting unbelievers to repent, had battled with them for a long time, he brought the controversy to a close with the Flood. However, I do not entirely reject Luther's opinion that God, having seen the deplorable wickedness of men, would not allow his prophets to spend their labor in vain. But the general declaration is not to be restricted to that particular case. When the Lord said, **"My Spirit will not contend with man forever,"** he demonstrated his patience. It is as if he said, "These battles will never end unless some unprecedented act of vengeance intervenes."

**"For he is mortal."** The reason is now given why there was no point in any further contention. The Lord here seemed to oppose man's human nature with his Spirit (see 1 Corinthians 2:14). Since man's soul is vitiated in every part, and man's reason is no less blind than his affections are perverse, we know that the whole man is naturally corrupt, until by the grace of regeneration he begins to be spiritual.

**4. The Nephilim were on the earth in those days.** Among the innumerable corruptions with which the earth was filled, Moses records one here—namely, that giants acted like tyrants. I do not, however, suppose that Moses is speaking of all people but of certain individuals who, being stronger than the rest and relying on their own might and power, exalted themselves without restraint.

**They were the heroes of old, men of renown.** It is as if Moses said that the world's first tyrants, who exercised excessive licentiousness and an unbridled lust for dominion, started from these people. Their first fault was pride; relying on their own strength, they arrogated to themselves more than was due to them. Pride produced contempt for God because, being swollen with arrogance, they began to shake off every yoke. At the same time, they were also disdainful and cruel toward men. It was impossible that these men, who would not obey God, should be tolerant toward men. Moses adds that they were **men of renown.** By this Moses means that they boasted about their wickedness and were what are called honorable robbers. Under the magnificent title of **heroes,** they cruelly exercised dominion and acquired power and fame for themselves by injuring and oppressing their brethren. This was the first nobility of the world. Having a well-known name is not in itself condemned, as those who are endowed with special gifts by the Lord are preeminent among others. But ambition is always harmful, especially in a tyrant, and this is seen as they insulted the weak with impunity.

**5. The Lord saw how great man's wickedness on the earth had become.** Moses ascribes human affections to God, and by using the word **saw,** he draws attention to God's great patience. It is as if he said that God did not pass the death sentence on men until he had observed them carefully. After a long time he **saw** that they would not recover. Moses also strongly emphasizes **how great man's wickedness on the earth had become.** Their iniquity had pervaded the whole earth. So the time for punishment had fully arrived. Wickedness reigned over the whole earth and covered it. From this we see that the world was not overwhelmed with a flood of waters until it had first been immersed in the pollution of wickedness.

**Every inclination of the thoughts of his heart was only evil all the time.** Moses traced the cause of the Flood to external acts of iniquity. He now declares that men were not only perverse by habit and were used to living in an evil way, but that wickedness was too deeply seated in their hearts to leave any hope of repentance. He could not have more forcibly asserted that man's depravity was such that no moderate remedy could cure it. Sometimes it may happen that men will plunge themselves into sin and retain a semblance of a sound mind. But Moses teaches us that the mind of those he is speaking about was so thoroughly imbued with iniquity that they could not but be condemned. He uses very emphatic language. It might have seemed enough to say that their heart was corrupt. But Moses was not content with this word. He specifically asserts, **every inclination of the thoughts of his heart** and adds the word **only—his heart was only evil**—as if to deny that there was a drop of good in it.

**All the time.** Some expound this to mean, commencing from infancy, as if to say that man's depravity is very great from the moment of birth. But the correct interpretation is that the world had then become completely hardened in its wickedness and only grew worse and worse. The inveterate depravity that the children had received, they transmitted to their descendants. Although Moses speaks of the wickedness that at that time prevailed in the world, the general doctrine is properly and consistently elicited from this. So it is correct to apply this passage to the whole human race. See Romans 3:12.

**6. The LORD was grieved that he had made man on the earth, and his heart was filled with pain.** The grief that is here ascribed to God does not properly belong to him but refers to our understanding of him. Since we cannot comprehend him as he is, he has to, in a certain sense, accommodate himself for our sake. God is not sorrowful or sad but remains forever like himself in his heavenly and happy repose. Yet, because it could not otherwise be known in any other way how much God detests sin, the Spirit accommodates himself to our human understanding. These words about God's grief teach us that from the time man was so greatly corrupted, God would not count him as one of his creatures. It is as if he says, "This is no part of my creation; this is not that man who was formed in my image, on whom I have lavished such excellent gifts. I do not now acknowledge this degenerate and defiled creature as mine." So unless we want to provoke God and to cause him to grieve, let us learn to abhor and flee from sin. Moreover, his paternal goodness and tenderness should in no small way subdue in us the love of sin, since God, in order to pierce our hearts effectually, clothes himself with our affections. So in this figure of speech God transfers to himself a characteristic of human nature.

**7. So the LORD said, "I will wipe mankind, whom I have created, from the face of the earth—men and animals, and creatures that move along the ground, and birds of the air—for I am grieved that I have made them."** Moses again introduces God as deliberating, so that we may know the world was not destroyed without God's careful consideration. The Spirit of the Lord designed that we should be diligently admonished about this, so that we would have no grounds for complaining about what was about to happen. The word **said** here means "decreed," because God says nothing without first carefully considering what he is going to do. Besides, he had no need for fresh counsel, as is the case when men make decisions, as if God were forming a judgment about something he had only just thought about. All this is said because of our spiritual sickness. It was said so that we might think about the Flood in the right way and realize that God's vengeance was just.

God, not content with the punishment of man, punishes **animals, and creatures that move along the ground, and birds of the air**. This seems to go beyond the bounds of moderation. God hates the impiety of men, but what is the purpose of being angry with unoffending animals? But is it not amazing that those animals, which were created for man's sake and lived for his purposes, should participate in his ruin? No donkeys or oxen or any other animal had done evil, but as they were subject to man when he fell, they were drawn with him into the same destruction. The earth was like a wealthy home, well stocked with every kind of provision. But now, since man has defiled the earth itself with his evil deeds and has corrupted all its riches, the Lord commanded that the whole house should be razed to the ground. This should fill us with a loathing for sin. We can now see clearly how terrible sin is since its punishment extends even to the brute beasts of creation.

**8. But Noah found favor in the eyes of the Lord.** This is a Hebrew expression that means God was propitious to Noah and favored him. The Hebrews often spoke in this way. They would say, "If I have found grace in your sight" instead of saying, "If I am acceptable to you" or "If you will grant me a favor." This phrase needs to be noted, because certain ignorant people infer with futile subtlety that if men find grace in God's sight, it is because they seek it through their own industry and merit. I acknowledge, indeed, that here Noah is declared to have been acceptable to God because by living uprightly he kept himself pure from the pollution of the world. But from where did he attain this integrity except from the preventing grace of God? The origin, therefore, of this favor was gratuitous mercy. Afterward the Lord, having once embraced him, retained him under his own hand, so that he would not perish with the rest of the world.

**9. This is the account of Noah. Noah was a righteous man, blameless among the people of his time, and he walked with God.** If we want to be approved by God and accounted righteous before him, we must not only regulate our hands, eyes, and feet to obey his law but, above everything else, have integrity of heart. This takes top priority in the true definition of righteousness. But remember that those who are called **righteous** and **blameless** are not perfect in every respect, as if they had no defects, but are those who cultivate righteousness in their hearts.

The clause **among the people of his time** is emphatic. Moses has already often said and will soon repeat that nothing was more corrupt than that age. Therefore, it was a case of remarkable constancy that Noah, being surrounded on every side with the filth of iniquity, should not have been contaminated himself. So let us remember that we are instructed on what we ought to do, even if the whole world is rushing to its own destruction. At the present time the morals of men are so vitiated and the whole way of life so confused that uprightness has become most rare, but Noah's day was even more vile and dreadful. He did not have one person to worship God with. If Noah could bear up against the evil tide of the whole world, we are left with no excuse. We must have the same strength of purpose as we pursue a right course through innumerable evils in the world.

The way in which Noah cultivated righteousness is explained in this verse. Noah **walked with God.** This excellent way to live was warmly commended in the holy father Enoch in the preceding chapter. Since the corruption of morals was so great in the earth, if Noah had followed the ways of other men he would have been completely entangled. Noah saw, therefore, that the only remedy was to disregard men, fix all his thoughts on God, and make God the sole Arbiter of his life.

**10.** Moses again mentions Noah's **three sons** to show that although he was surrounded by and nearly overwhelmed by the greatest sorrow, he was still able to have children, so that God would have a small remnant of people for himself.

**11. Now the earth was corrupt in God's sight and was full of violence.** In the first clause of this verse Moses describes an impious contempt of God that no longer left any religion in the world. Everyone was wallowing in sin. In the second clause Moses declares that the love of oppression, physical force, and all kinds of injustice prevailed. These are the fruits of impiety that grow everywhere when men have rebelled against God.

**God's sight.** God again declares that he had seen this, in order to commend his patience to us. **The earth** here stands for the inhabitants of the world. It is not meant here in a bad sense but stands for men and women; there is no hint of any rebuke in this phrase. This is the case in other places in Scripture as well (see Isaiah 40:5; Zechariah 2:13).

**13. So God said to Noah.** Moses begins to relate how Noah would be preserved. **"I am going to put an end to all people."** He starts by saying that the counsel of God about the destruction of the world was revealed to Noah. Second, he says Noah was ordered to build the ark. Third, Noah was promised that he would be kept safe as long as he obeyed God and took refuge in the ark. These main points need to be noted, as the apostle does when he proclaims the faith of Noah and links "holy fear" and obedience with confidence (see Hebrews 11:7).

In complete despair of help from any other quarter, Noah sought his safety, by faith, in the ark. For so long as life was promised to him on earth, he would never have been single-minded enough to build the ark. But being alarmed by the judgment of God, he earnestly embraced the promise of life given to him. He no longer depended upon the everyday things in life but relied solely on God's covenant, through which he was to be miraculously preserved. No work was now too much trouble or too difficult for him. He was not defeated by long periods of physical exertion. The spur of God's anger pierced him too sharply to allow him to be content with worldly delights or to give way under temptations. Rather, Noah stirred himself up, both to flee from sin and to search for a remedy. Hebrews teaches that it was not the least part of his faith that through the fear of those things that were not seen he prepared an ark. When faith is considered in a superficial way, only mercy and God's gracious promises are considered. But when we consider faith in all its aspects, holy fear must be taken into account as well. No one will ever seriously seek God's mercy unless he has been touched by God's warnings and so dreads the judgment of eternal death. It was, truly, a special privilege of grace that God warned Noah of the future flood. Indeed, God often issues his warnings to both the elect and reprobate. As he invites them both to repent, God humbles the former, and the latter are left with no excuse.

"**For the earth is filled with violence because of them. I am surely going to destroy both them and the earth.**" God intimated that men were to be taken away, because the earth had been polluted by the presence of such wicked people.

**14.** Now follows the command to build the ark, through which God wonderfully proved the faith and obedience of his servant.

**18. "But I will establish my covenant with you, and you will enter the ark—you and your sons and your wife and your sons' wives with you."** Since the construction of **the ark** was very difficult, and innumerable obstacles would constantly threaten the work, God encouraged his servant with this additional promise: "**I will establish my covenant with you.**" Thus was Noah encouraged to obey God as he relied on the divine promise and was confident that his labor would not be in vain. We gladly embrace God's commands when a promise is linked to them that teaches us we will not expend our strength for no purpose. So whenever we have no enthusiasm to do good deeds, let God's promises galvanize us into action. For according to the apostle Paul (see Colossians 1:5), love flourishes in the saints because of the hope laid up for them in heaven. It is particularly important that the faithful should be grounded in the Word of God, so they do not faint in the middle of their activities.

Now the essence of the **covenant** that Moses speaks about was that Noah would be safe, even though the whole world would perish in the Flood. There is an antithesis here between the whole world's being rejected and the Lord's establishing a special covenant with Noah alone.

**19. "You are to bring into the ark two of all living creatures, male and female, to keep them alive with you."** Here all living creatures is the name God gives to animals, regardless of what kind they are. He says Noah and his family were **to bring** animals, **male and female,** into the ark so that Noah might understand how the world would be replenished.

**22. Noah did everything just as God commanded him.** In a few words, but with great sublimity, Moses commends Noah's faith. The apostle says that Noah "became heir of the righteousness that comes by faith" (Hebrews 11:7). We should consider the assaults of temptation that constantly attacked Noah. First, the prodigious size of the ark might have so overwhelmed him that he never lifted a finger to start the work. Let the reader reflect on the great number of trees that needed to be felled, the great labor of moving the tree trunks, and the difficulty of making them suitable to build the ark. The work also took place over an extended length of time; the holy man worked on building the ark for more than a hundred years. Then there was all the opposition Noah had to suffer from the hands of evil men. They surely complained about Noah's felling so many trees. If these godless men had not been restrained by God's mighty hand, they would probably have stoned the holy man a hundred times. It is likely that they often scoffed and derided all his efforts. I even think they went as far as disturbing his work.

In addition to this, the work itself appeared to be impossible. It may be asked, from where were provisions for the year to be found? Where would food for so many animals be found? Noah was commanded to lay in enough stores to last for ten months—for his whole family, for cattle and wild beasts, and even for birds. Truly it seems absurd that after he had stopped farming in order to build the ark he should be commanded to collect a two-years' store of provisions. It would have been even more difficult to provide food for all the animals. He might have been tempted to think that God was mocking him.

Last of all, Noah had to collect all the different kinds of animals, as if he had all the beasts of the forest at his command or was able to tame them. Let us reflect on these conflicts of the holy man so that we may learn from his heroic courage as he carried out all that God had commanded him. Moses, indeed, says in a single word that he **did** it. But this was beyond all human power. It would have been better to die a hundred deaths than to undertake such a laborious task, unless he had looked to something beyond this present life. Moses shows that Noah obeyed God not in just one thing, but in **everything**.

# Genesis
# Chapter 7

**1. The LORD then said to Noah.** I have no doubt that Noah was encouraged, as he certainly needed to be, by God speaking to him frequently. Noah was commanded to forsake the world, that he might live in a sepulcher he had been laboriously building for himself for more than a hundred years. Why was this? Because in a little while the earth would be submerged in a flood of water. Yet nothing of the kind was apparent. Everyone around Noah continued to indulge in feasts, celebrate nuptials, and build sumptuous houses; in short, luxury was the order of the day everywhere. Christ himself testified that age was intoxicated with its own pleasures (see Luke 17:26-27). So there were good reasons for the Lord to continually encourage his servant. It was as if he were saying, "So far you have worked with fortitude in the middle of so many opposing forces, but now you need to take courage, so that you may reap the fruit of your labor. Do not, however, wait until the waters drench the earth, but while everything is still tranquil, enter the ark, and remain there until the seventh day. Then the flood will suddenly come." Although God no longer speaks to us directly from heaven, constant meditation on the Word is not ineffectual. For as new difficulties constantly arise in front of us, so God, through different promises, establishes our faith, so that our strength is renewed and we may, in due course, arrive at the goal. It is our duty to listen carefully to God. Here we note that it was God's intention to make one man a total contrast with the whole world, so that, in his person, he might condemn the unrighteousness of all men. God again testified that the punishment he was about to inflict on the world was just, since only one man was left, who then cultivated righteousness, and for whose sake God was propitious to his whole family.

Should anyone object that this passage teaches that God takes notice of the deeds of men in saving them, the solution is at hand. God accepts those gifts that he himself has conferred on his servants. We must observe in the first place that he loves men freely, in that he finds nothing in them

75

except what deserves to be hated since all men are born children of wrath and heirs of eternal malediction. He adopts them to himself in Christ and justifies them through his sheer mercy. After he has in this way reconciled them to himself, he also regenerates them by his Spirit to new life and righteousness. From this flow good deeds, which are pleasing to God himself. Thus he not only loves the faithful but also their deeds. We must again note that since our deeds are never perfect, it is not possible that they can be approved except as a matter of mercy. Christ's grace, therefore, and not any merit in the deeds themselves, is what makes our deeds worthy in God's sight. Nevertheless, we do not deny that God takes them into account, just as he here acknowledges and accepts the righteousness of Noah, which also came from God's own grace. It is in this way, as Augustine says, that God will crown his own gifts.

**"I have found you righteous."** Here God not only annihilates all hypocritical righteousness, which is devoid of inner holiness in the heart, but vindicates his own authority as he declares that he alone is competent to judge righteousness. The clause **in this generation** is added to emphasize the point. That age was completely depraved; but Noah would be free from the common infection.

**2. "Take with you seven of every kind of clean animal."** The Lord repeated what he had before said about animals, and he did so for a very good reason. It was a huge task to gather from woods, mountains, and caves such a great collection of wild beasts. Many of the species of these animals may not have been known. Most of them would have been dangerous. So God encouraged the holy man, so he was not dismayed by the difficulty that faced him.

At first sight there seems to be some kind of contradiction here. Previously God had spoken of pairs of animals, but now he speaks of **seven** of every kind of clean animal. But the solution is at hand. Previously Moses was not referring to the number of the animals but only said that females were to accompany the males. It was as if he had said Noah was told not to collect the animals randomly but to select pairs of them, so they could propagate the species. Now, however, the account focuses on the number of animals. In addition to this, **seven** does not refer to seven pairs of each kind of animals, but to three pairs of each kind, to which one animal was added, to be sacrificed.

**3. "To keep their various kinds alive."** In this way offspring would be born. Noah is mentioned here, although, strictly speaking, God alone gives life. But God had appointed Noah to do this work of collecting the animals so he could perpetuate the species. This is not an unusual way of speaking, since ministers of the Gospel are said, in a sense, to confer spiritual life.

In the next clause, **throughout the earth,** there are two consolations. The waters, after they had covered the earth for a time, would go down, so that the dry surface of the earth would reappear. Also, this clause implies that not only would Noah himself survive, but through God's blessing, the number of animals would increase in such a way that they would spread far and wide through the whole world. Thus in the middle of disaster, future restoration was promised to Noah. Moses is very particular to show that God took care to keep Noah obedient to his word. In this the holy man entirely acquiesced. This teaching is very valuable, especially when God either promises or threatens anything incredible, since men do not willingly receive what seems to them improbable. Nothing seemed as unlikely in the eyes of human beings than that the world should be destroyed by its Creator. So unless Noah had taken careful note of God's terrible judgment, he would never have believed it, perhaps thinking God would thus be acting against his own nature. The word *hayekom*, which Moses uses here, originally came from a word that meant "to stand"; but it is correct to say that it means whatever lives and flourishes and is **alive**.

**5.** This is not a mere repetition of 6:22. Moses is commending Noah's constant obedience to all of God's commandments. It is as if he says that in whatever particular way it pleased God to test his obedience, Noah always remained faithful. Certainly it is not right to pick and choose which of God's commandments we will obey. We must keep James's exhortation in mind: "He who said, 'Do not commit adultery,' also said, 'Do not murder.' If you do not commit adultery but do commit murder, you have become a lawbreaker" (James 2:11).

**6.** Moses mentions Noah's age—**six hundred years old**—for a purpose. Old age can make people more indolent and morose. So Noah's faith was the more remarkable because it did not fail him as he advanced in years.

Moses adds, **when the floodwaters came on the earth.** It is wrong to say that these words mean Noah entered the ark because of the floodwaters, as if he were compelled to do this by the rain. Rather, Noah was moved with fear through God's word. Noah perceived by faith that the flood that everyone else ridiculed was approaching. So his faith is commended again here because he did indeed raise his eyes above worldly concerns.

**8-10. Pairs of clean and unclean animals.** Moses now explains what had previously been unclear. He states how the animals were collected for the ark. He says that they came of their own accord—they **came to Noah** (verse 9). If this seems unlikely, remember that in the beginning every kind of animal presented itself to Adam so he could give them their names. We are frightened at the sight of wild beasts only because we have thrown off God's yoke and so have lost that authority over them that God had given to Adam. God's bringing those animals to Noah shows a kind of restoration of the former things. Those animals would be preserved through Noah's work and service. Noah kept the wild animals in his ark in exactly the same way in which hens and geese are housed in a coop. It is not an irrelevant detail to note that the animals **came** to Noah. This shows that God's blessing rested on the obedience of Noah, so that he did not labor in vain. It was impossible, humanly speaking, that such a great assembly of all the different types of animals should take place in so short a time. But Noah simply trusted God, and in return God supplied the means by which his own precept would come about. Strictly speaking, this was God's promise annexed to his commands. And therefore we must conclude that Noah's faith did more than any snares or nets could have done in capturing the animals. Through the same entrance into the ark came lions and wolves and tigers, along with oxen and lambs. The only way we can overcome difficulties is to be convinced that what is impossible for us is easy for God. We derive alacrity from this hope.

**11. On that day all the springs of the great deep burst forth, and the floodgates of the heavens were opened.** Moses makes us remember the first creation when the earth was originally covered with water. By the great kindness of God, they receded to make room for living creatures. Now, however, Moses states that when God resolved to destroy the earth through a flood, **the floodgates of the heavens were opened**. The element of water, which philosophers deem to be one of the principles of life, threatens us with death from above and from beneath unless it is restrained by God's hand.

**12. And rain fell on the earth forty days and forty nights.** Although the Lord burst open **the floodgates of the heavens,** he did not allow them to overwhelm the earth but made it rain for **forty days**. In this way Noah had a long time to reflect on what he had previously learned through the word. It also meant that the wicked, even before their death, realized that those warnings they had derided were not empty threats. Those who had for so long scorned God's patience deserved to feel that they were gradually perishing under his righteous judgment.

**13-15.** Through this repetition the Spirit focuses our minds on God's vengeance, which cannot be adequately described even if the most severe language is used. Everything related here is difficult to believe. These verses about the animals coming to Noah point to the fact that it was through the faith of holy Noah that they were drawn from their woods and caverns and were collected in one place, led by the hand of God. We see, therefore, that Moses deliberately emphasizes this point to teach us that each species of animals was preserved not by chance, not by human industry, but because the Lord reached out and offered to Noah himself whatever animal he intended to keep alive.

**16. Then the LORD shut him in.** This is not added for no purpose, nor should it be lightly passed over. That door must have been large enough to allow an elephant to walk through. Moses declares in one word that the ark was made secure from the Flood not by human work, but through a divine miracle. Doubtless Noah had been endued with new ability and wisdom so there would be nothing defective in the structure of the ark. But for this favor to be successful, something even greater was necessary. So, in order that we might not view the preservation of the ark according to mere human thinking, Moses teaches us that the waters were not restrained from breaking in upon the ark by pitch or bitumen only, but rather by the secret power of God and by the intervention of his hand.

**17. For forty days the flood kept coming on the earth, and as the waters increased they lifted the ark high above the earth.** Moses continues to insist on this fact, to show that the whole world was immersed in the Flood. It is the specific purpose of Moses' words that we should not ascribe the Flood by which the world perished to fortune. We must insist on this in the face of man's habit of drawing a veil over God's deeds in his vain attempt to obscure either God's goodness or God's judgments that are seen in them. As it is clearly declared that whatever was flourishing on the earth was destroyed, we infer that it is beyond dispute that this was God's remarkable judgment. It was the more remarkable because Noah and his family alone remained secure, because he had embraced by faith the word in which salvation was contained.

The two things that were diametrically opposed to each other—the destruction of the whole human race and Noah and his family escaping—Moses brings together. From this we learn how beneficial it was for Noah to disregard the world and to obey God alone. Moses states this not so much for the sake of praising Noah, but so that we might follow his example. In addition to this, in case the great number of sinners should draw us away from God, we must patiently bear it when the ungodly ridicule us. We have to be content to wait for them to be seen to triumph over us, until the Lord shows to everyone in the end that our obedience is approved by him. In this sense Peter teaches that Noah's deliverance from the universal flood was a figure of baptism (see 1 Peter 3:20-21). It is as if the apostle said, the salvation that we receive through baptism is similar to Noah's deliverance. At this time the world is also full of unbelievers, just as it was in Noah's day. Therefore, it is essential for us to separate ourselves from the great mass of sinners, that the Lord may snatch us from destruction.

In the same way, the church is rightly compared to the ark. And we must keep the similarity between these two things in our minds, for they come from the Word of God alone. Noah, believing the promise of God, gathered himself, his wife, and his children together in order that they might escape from what appeared to be certain death. In the same way it is right for us to renounce the world and die, in order that the Lord may make us alive through his Word. For in no other way is there salvation.

# Genesis
# Chapter 8

**1. But God remembered Noah.** Moses now moves on to the other part of his account, which shows that Noah was not disappointed in his hope concerning the salvation that had been promised to him by God. When Moses says that **God remembered Noah**, this refers not only to the external aspect of things, but also to the inner feeling of the holy man. It is certain that from the time when God welcomed Noah into his protection, he never forgot Noah. For it was indeed a great miracle that he did not suffocate in the ark or drown in the Flood. Moses had just said that by God's secret closing of the ark, the waters were prevented from penetrating into it. But as the ark was floating on the waters, the delay during which the Lord allowed his servant to endure must have made Noah most anxious. He might infer that his life had been prolonged so he might be more miserable than anyone else. For we know that we often imagine that God is absent unless we experience his presence with us in some way. While Noah held on tenaciously to the end to the promise he had embraced, it is still possible that he was attacked by various temptations. Without doubt, God deliberately tested Noah's faith and patience in this way. For why was the world not destroyed in three days? And why did the waters, after they had covered the highest mountains, cover the mountains to a depth of more than twenty feet (7:20)? It must have been so Noah and his family had more time to meditate on God's judgments, so that when the danger had passed they would acknowledge they had been rescued from a thousand deaths. Let us therefore learn from this example to rest in God's providence, even when he seems to have completely forgotten us. For in time, through helping us in some way, he will show that he has been mindful of us all the time. We must remember to say, "The Lord who has promised his help to the miserable will in due course be present with us, that we may indeed realize he takes care of us." We also note that it is stated that God remembered the **animals**. On account of the salvation God promised to man, his favor also extended to brute cattle and to wild beasts. So can we not imagine what his favor toward his own children will be, to whom he has so generously pledged his faithfulness?

**And he sent a wind over the earth, and the waters receded.** Here it is apparent that Moses is speaking about the effect of God's remembering Noah. We observe that this supplied sure proof for Noah to know that God cared for him. When God, through his secret power, desired to dry the earth, he made use of the wind. This is the same method he used to part the Red Sea. In this way he demonstrated that as he had the waters at his command, ready to carry out his judgment, so now he held the winds in his hand to bring relief. Although Moses records a remarkable account, we are also taught that the winds do not arise by chance but by God's command (see Psalm 104:4, where the winds are described as God's "messengers"). God, to restore the order he had originally appointed, recalled the waters to their previous boundaries.

**4. The ark came to rest on the mountains of Ararat.** As far as the name **Ararat** is concerned, I follow the generally accepted view. I do not see why some people deny it to be the Armenian mountains. But I am undecided about Josephus' claim that fragments of the ark were found there in his time, remnants of which, Jerome says, remained to his day.

**6. After forty days Noah opened the window he had made in the ark.** We can imagine how anxious the holy man Noah was at this moment. After he perceived that the ark had come to rest on solid ground, he still did not dare to open the window until the fortieth day. This was not because he was stunned or lethargic, but because God's vengeance had affected him so strongly. He was now full of fear and sorrow and devoid of all judgment; so he remained quietly in his ark.

At length he sent out a raven, from which he might find out about how dry the earth was. But the raven saw nothing but muddy marshes and immediately sought to be readmitted. I have no doubt that Noah deliberately chose the raven, which he knew might be allured by the odor of carcasses and so would fly away from the ark if the earth had animals on it that could be seen. But after flying around to survey the scene, the raven did not fly away. The dove, when it first emerged, behaved like the raven and flew back to the ark. Later, on its second flight from the ark, it brought back an olive branch in its beak. The third time it flew from the ark, it enjoyed the fresh air, as if it had been set free, and did not return.

Some writers give ingenious interpretations about the olive branch because among the ancients it was the emblem of peace, as the laurel was the emblem of victory. But I think that as the olive tree does not grow on mountainsides and because it is not a very tall tree, the Lord had given his servant some indication that pleasant regions, productive of good fruits, were now clear of the Flood. Because Jerome says it was a branch with green leaves, those who have thought that the Flood began in September take this as a confirmation of their opinion. But the words of Moses have no such meaning. And it might be that the Lord, willing to revive the spirit of Noah, offered some branch to the dove that had not yet altogether withered under the waters.

**15. Then God said to Noah.** Although Noah was frightened by God's judgment, his patience is commended in this respect: He now saw the earth beckoning him, but he did not leave the ark. Ungodly men may ascribe this to timidity or even to indolence; but holy is that timidity that is produced by the obedience of faith. Let us therefore know that Noah was restrained by a hallowed modesty from allowing himself to enjoy the bounty of nature until he heard God's voice directing him. Moses concludes this section in a few words, but it is right that we should take note of this event. Everyone should ponder Noah's great fortitude. After the incredible weariness of a whole year, when the Flood has ceased and new life was apparent on the earth, Noah did not move a foot out of his sepulcher without first receiving an instruction from God. From this we observe Noah's constant faith. The holy man was obedient to God. At God's command he entered the ark, and he remained there until God told him to leave. Even in minute details, Scripture commands us to attempt nothing without a clear conscience. In this way Moses relates that Noah went out of the ark as soon as he, relying on God's voice, was aware that a new place to live had been given to him on the earth.

**17. "So they can multiply on the earth and be fruitful and increase in number upon it."** With these words from the Lord, Noah took courage, for they inspired him with confidence. The seed that had been preserved in the ark would now increase until it replenished the whole earth. In short, the renovation of the earth was promised to Noah. From this Noah realized that the world itself was enclosed in the ark, and that the solitude and devastation that threatened to make him fainthearted would not last forever.

**20. Then Noah built an altar to the LORD.** As Noah had given many proofs of his obedience, he now presented us with an example of gratitude. This passage teaches us that sacrifices were instituted from the beginning so men would make use of them and through such spiritual exercises celebrate God's goodness as they give thanks to him. The bare confession of the tongue—yes, even the silent acknowledgment of the heart—might suffice for God. But we know how many stimulants our indolence requires. Therefore, when the holy fathers expressed their piety toward God by sacrifices, they were not using sacrifices in a superficial way. Besides, it was right that they should always have these symbols in their sight. These symbols admonished them and reminded them that they had no access to God except through a mediator. Now, however, the coming of Christ has replaced these ancient shadows. Therefore, let us use those things that the Lord has prescribed.

In addition to this, when I say that sacrifices were used by the holy fathers to celebrate God's bounty, I am referring to only one kind of sacrifice. Noah's offering was similar to the peace-offerings and the offerings of the firstfruits. We may now ask what made Noah offer an animal sacrifice to God, as he had received no command to do this. I answer: Although Moses does not specifically declare that God commanded him to do this, yet it is clear from what follows, and it may be deduced from the whole context, that Noah had relied on the word of God, and so he knew this kind of worship would be acceptable to the Lord. We have before said that one animal of every kind was preserved separately. But there was no point to set apart animals for sacrifice unless God had revealed this to holy Noah, who was to be the priest to offer up the victims. Besides, Moses says that sacrifices were chosen from among clean animals. But it is certain that Noah did not invent this distinction for himself since it does not depend on human choice. From this we conclude that Noah did nothing without first having received divine authority. Also, Moses immediately adds that the smell of the sacrifice was acceptable to God. This general rule, therefore, is to be observed: All religious services that are not perfumed with the odor of faith are not pleasing to God. Let us therefore know that Noah's altar was founded on the word of God. And the same word was as salt to his sacrifices, that they might not be insipid.

21. **The LORD smelled the pleasing aroma.** Moses calls what appeased God **the pleasing aroma.** It is as if he said that the sacrifice had been offered in the right manner. Yet nothing can be more absurd than to suppose that God should have been appeased by the smoke produced by the entrails and flesh of animals. But Moses here, according to his way of writing, invests God with a human character in order to accommodate himself to the understanding of ignorant people. For it is not to be supposed that the rite of sacrifice in itself was acceptable to God as a meritorious act. But we must take note of the purpose of the action, and not confine ourselves to the external form. For what else did Noah intend than to acknowledge that he had received his own life, and that of the animals, as the gift of God's mercy alone? This piety breathed a good and sweet odor before God (see Psalm 116:12).

**And said in his heart: "Never again will I curse the ground because of man."** This passage means that God decreed he would never again **curse** the earth. This type of expression has great weight. Although God never retracts what he has publicly said, yet we are more deeply moved when we hear that he has decided on something in his own **heart.** For an inner decree of this kind is in no way dependent on creatures. To sum up the whole matter, God certainly determined that he would never again destroy the world by a flood. Yet the expression, **"Never again will I curse"** is to be understood in a general way. We know how much the earth has lost of its fertility since it has been corrupted by man's sin, and we daily feel that it is cursed in various ways. The Lord explains this, as he says himself a little afterwards, **"And never again will I destroy all living creatures, as I have done."** In these words he does not allude to every kind of vengeance, but only to that which would destroy the world and bring ruin both on mankind and the rest of the animals. It is as if he says that he restored the earth with the stipulation that it would not again perish through a flood. So when the Lord declares in Isaiah 54:9 that he will be content with one captivity of his people, he compares it with the waters of Noah, through which he had resolved that the world should only once be overwhelmed.

**"Even though every inclination of his heart is evil from childhood."** This reasoning appears to be incongruous. For if the wickedness of man is so great that it never stops provoking God's anger, it must therefore bring down destruction on the world. So God seems to contradict himself by having previously declared that the world had to be destroyed because its iniquity was so desperate. We must ponder more deeply God's purpose here. It was God's will that men should live on earth. If, however, they were dealt with as they deserved, they required food to be provided for them every day. So God declares that in inflicting punishment on the second world he will do it in such a way that the external appearance of the earth will be preserved, and he will never again sweep away the creatures with which he has adorned it. Indeed, we ourselves may perceive such moderation to have been used, both in the public and special judgments of God, for the world still stands in its completeness, and nature yet retains its course. Moreover, since God here declares the kind of character men would have even to the end of the world, it is evident that the whole human race is under sentence of condemnation on account of its depravity and wickedness. This sentence does not refer only to corrupt morals; man's iniquity is said to be an innate iniquity, from which nothing but evil can come. I wonder, however, from where that false interpretation of this passage has crept in that the mind is not prone to evil. The corruption of human nature seemed a hard proposition to these people. They did not want to agree that man was subjected as a slave of the devil to sin. Therefore, by way of mitigation they have said that man had a propensity to vices. But when the celestial Judge thunders from heaven that **"every inclination of his heart is evil from childhood,"** how can one water down such a statement? It remains unalterable.

Let men therefore acknowledge that since they are born of Adam, they are depraved creatures and therefore can conceive only sinful thoughts until they are transformed by Christ's work and are remade by his Spirit into a new life. It should not be doubted that the Lord declares the very mind of man to be depraved and altogether infected with sin, so that all the thoughts that proceed from his mind are evil. If the fountain itself has such a defect, it follows that all man's affections are evil, and his deeds covered with the same pollution. God does not merely say that men sometimes think evil, for the language used knows no bounds, including the tree with its fruits. It is pointless to argue that ungodly men are often very generous. For since their mind is corrupted with contempt of God, pride, self-love, and ambitious hypocrisy, all their thoughts are contaminated with the same vices. All such seemingly good things in these kinds of people are like wine spoiled by the odor of the cask. The very affections of nature, which in themselves are laudable, are vitiated by original sin. The clause **from childhood** underlines the fact that men are born evil. It shows that as soon as they are old enough to think, they already have radically corrupt minds. Philosophers, by transferring to habit what God here ascribes to nature, betray their own ignorance.

In this way we please and flatter ourselves to such an extent that we do not perceive that the disease of sin is fatal. We fail to notice that depravity pervades all our senses. We must, therefore, acquiesce to God's judgment, which pronounces man to be so enslaved by sin that he can do nothing that is sound and sincere. At the same time, we must remember that God is not to be blamed for this. The origin of this disease stems from the defection of the first man, because of whom the order of the creation was subverted. And further, it must be noted that men are not exempt from guilt and condemnation, as if they could use this slavery as a pretext for indulging in evil. Although all rush to do evil acts, no one is forced into this except by the direct inclination of their own hearts. When they sin, they do so because they want to sin.

**22. "As long as the earth endures, seedtime and harvest, cold and heat, summer and winter, day and night will never cease."** Through these words the world is again completely restored. The confusion and disorder that had spread throughout the earth was so great that some renovation was necessary. This is why Peter speaks of the old world as having perished in the Flood (see 2 Peter 3:6).

# Genesis
# Chapter 9

1. **Then God blessed Noah and his sons, saying to them, "Be fruitful and increase in number and fill the earth."** From this we infer that Noah had been dejected by very great fear because God so often and at such length proceeded to encourage him. When Moses here says that **God blessed Noah and his sons,** he does not simply mean that the favor of fruitfulness was restored to them, but that at the same time God's purpose about the new restitution of the world was revealed unto them. To the blessing itself is added God's voice by which he addresses them. We know that brute animals produce offspring only by the blessing of God; but Moses here commemorates a privilege that belongs only to men. Therefore, in case those four men and their wives, seized with trepidation, had any doubts about why they had been delivered, the Lord laid before them their future way of life. Thus he not only renewed the world through the same word by which he had previously created it, but he directed his word to men in order that they might recover the correct use of marriage. In this way they would know that producing offspring is pleasing to God himself. They would also be assured that a progeny would spring from them that would spread around the whole world so that it was populated again, even though it had been laid waste and turned into a desert. Yet God did not permit promiscuous intercourse but sanctioned anew that law of marriage that he had previously ordained.

2. **"The fear and dread of you will fall upon all the beasts of the earth and all the birds of the air, upon every creature that moves along the ground, and upon all the fish of the sea; they are given into your hands."** This mainly refers to the restoration of the world, in order that the sovereignty over animals might remain with men. Although after the fall of man the **beasts** were endued with new ferocity, yet part of that dominion over them that God had conferred on man in the beginning was still left. God now promised that the same dominion would continue. We see that wild beasts attack men and tear many of them to pieces. If

God did not wonderfully restrain their fierceness, the human race would be utterly destroyed. It is little wonder that savage beasts indeed prevail and rage against men in various ways. Since we perversely exalt ourselves against God, why should not the beasts rise up against us? Nevertheless, the providence of God is a secret bridle to restrain their violence. For how is it that serpents spare us if it is not that God represses their virulence? Why is it that tigers, elephants, lions, bears, wolves, and other countless wild beasts do not tear and devour everything human unless they are withheld through this subjection to man as by a barrier? Therefore, we should acknowledge that we are kept safe through God's special protection and guardianship. If this was not the case, what could we expect since they seem to be born to destroy us and since they burn with a furious desire to harm us? Moreover, the bridle with which the Lord restrains the cruelty of wild beasts, to prevent them from falling upon men, is a definite fear and dread that God has implanted in them, so that they might reverence the presence of men. Daniel specifically states this about kings—namely, that they rule because the Lord has put the fear and the dread of them both on men and beasts.

**3. "Everything that lives and moves will be food for you. Just as I gave you the green plants, I now give you everything."** The Lord now goes further and gives animals to be food for men, so that they may eat their flesh. **"Everything that lives and moves will be food for you."** Because Moses now first relates that this right was given to men, nearly all commentators infer that it was unlawful for man to eat flesh before the Flood and that the natural fruits of the earth were his only food. But the argument is not a strong one. I hold to this principle: God here does not bestow on men more than he had previously given but only restores what had been taken away, that they might again possess the good things they had been excluded from. For since they had before offered sacrifices to God and were also permitted to kill wild beasts, from the hides and skins of which they might make for themselves garments and tents, I do not see what should prevent them from the eating of flesh. But since it is of little consequence what opinion is held, I affirm nothing on the subject.

What should be of much greater importance to us is that to eat the flesh of animals is granted to us by the kindness of God. So we should not indulge our appetites as robbers do, nor should we slaughter innocent cattle like tyrants, but only take what is offered to us by the hand of the Lord. Paul says we are free to eat what we please but must do so with a clear conscience, for if anyone thinks some food is unclean, to him it is unclean (see Romans 14:14). Paul also states that "the word of God" sanctifies the creatures so that we are allowed to eat them (see 1 Timothy 4:3-5). So we must utterly reject the saying that says, "No one can feed and refresh his body with a morsel of bread without at the same time defiling his soul." Therefore it should not be doubted that the Lord planned to strengthen our faith when he specifically declared through Moses that he gave to man the free use of flesh, so that we might not eat it with a doubtful and trembling conscience. At the same time, he invites us to be grateful to him. On this account also, Paul adds "prayer" to "the word of God" in 1 Timothy 4:5.

Now we must firmly retain the freedom the Lord has given to us. For through this word God addresses all the descendants of Noah and so makes this gift one for every age. And why is this done but so that the faithful may boldly assert their right to that which, they know, has God as its Author? It is an unsupportable tyranny when God, the Creator of all things, lavishes on us the earth and the air in order that we may take food from it, as from his storehouse, but these are shut up from us by mortal man, who is not able to create even a snail or a fly. I am referring to that atrocious insult done to God when we give such license to men as to allow them to pronounce that something is unlawful that God has planned should be lawful. In this terrible way consciences are bound with fictitious laws though the Word of God sets our consciences free. The fact that God prohibited his ancient people from using unclean animals, seeing that exception was but temporary, is passed over here by Moses.

**4. "But you must not eat meat that has its lifeblood still in it."** Some say that this passage means, "You may not eat any part that is cut off from a living animal." But this is a superficial interpretation. However, since there is no copulative conjunction between the two words **blood** and **life** [in KJV], I do not doubt that Moses, speaking of the life, added the word "blood" in an exegetical manner. It is as if he says that flesh is in some sense devoured with its life when it is eaten imbued with its own blood. Wherefore the life and the blood are not meant to indicate different things but the same thing. This is not because blood is in itself the life, but because vital elements mainly exist in the blood. It is a token that represents life. And this is specifically stated so that men may be totally put off from eating blood. Through this prohibition God intends to make men gentle by abstaining from the blood of animals. If they are not restrained and dare to eat wild animals, they will eventually not spare even human blood.

Yet we must remember that this restriction was part of the old law. Therefore, when Tertullian relates that in his time it was unlawful among Christians to taste the blood of cattle, this savors of superstition. The apostles, in commanding the Gentiles to observe this rite for a short time, did not intend to inject a scruple into their consciences but only to prevent the liberty that was otherwise sacred from offending the ignorant and the weak.

**5. "And for your lifeblood I will surely demand an accounting. I will demand an accounting from every animal. And from each man, too, I will demand an accounting for the life of his fellow man."** In these words the Lord more explicitly declares that he does not forbid the use of blood out of regard to animals themselves, but because he accounts the life of men precious. The sole purpose of his law is to support common humanity between man and man. This verse should be read in the following way: "And truly your blood, which is *in* your lives, or which is *as* your lives, that which vivifies and quickens you as it respects your body, will I require. From the hand of all animals I will require it; from the hand of man, from the hand, I say, of man, his brother, will I require the life of man." The distinction by which the Jews constitute four kinds of homicide is superficial. I have explained the simple and genuine sense—namely, that God so highly values our life that he will not allow murder to go unavenged. And he inculcates this in so many words so that he may make the cruelty of those who murder their neighbors the more detestable. In saying that he will exact punishment from animals for the violated life of men, he gives us this as an example. For if, on behalf of man, God is angry with brute creatures who are governed by a blind impulse to kill men for food, what, do we suppose, will become of the man who unjustly, cruelly, and contrary to nature murders his brother?

6. **"Whoever sheds the blood of man, by man shall his blood be shed."** This clause amplifies the previous one. This language expresses the atrocious nature of the crime. For whoever kills a man draws down upon himself the blood and life of his brother. On the whole, they are deceived (in my judgment) who think that a political law, for the punishment of homicides, is all that is meant here. I do not deny that the punishment that the laws ordain and that the judges execute are founded on this divine sentence; but I say that these words have a wider meaning and are more comprehensive. It is written, "Bloodthirsty and deceitful men will not live out half their days" (Psalm 55:23). We see some men die in fights and many in wars. Therefore, even if magistrates may ignore the crime, God sends executioners from other quarters who will give men their reward. God so threatens and denounces vengeance against the murderer that he even arms the magistrate with the sword for the avenging of slaughter, in order that the blood of men may not be shed with impunity.

**"For in the image of God has God made man."** To emphasize the above doctrines God declares that he does not respect human life without very good reason. Men will reject God's care of them if they only think about themselves. But since they bear God's image, stamped on them, God deems himself violated in their person. Thus although they have nothing of themselves with which they can obtain God's favor, God looks on his own gifts in them, and so loves and cares for them. This teaching must be carefully observed, for no one can harm his brother without in a sense wounding God himself. If this doctrine were deeply fixed in our minds, we would be much more reluctant than we are to inflict injuries. Should anyone object that this divine image has been obliterated, the solution is easy: First, there still exists some part of it, so that man possesses no small dignity; and, second, the heavenly Creator himself, no matter how corrupt man may be, still keeps in view the purpose of man's original creation. Following his example, we should consider why God created men and what excellent gifts he has bestowed on them that far exceed anything given to the rest of living beings.

**7. "As for you, be fruitful and increase in number; multiply on the earth and increase upon it."** God now spoke to Noah and his sons again, exhorting them to be fruitful. It is as if he said, "You see that I am intent upon cherishing and preserving mankind; so you must play your part in this." God commanded them to preserve the human seed and prohibited them from murder and from unruly acts of violence. Yet God's main purpose was to encourage their dejected minds, for these words contain no empty precept but a promise as well.

**8.** There is no doubt that it was God's plan to provide for all his posterity. This was not therefore a private **covenant** (verse 9) confirmed with one family only, but one that is common to all people and will flourish in all ages to the end of the world. Since at the present time impiety overflows no less than in Noah's time, it is especially necessary that the waters should be restrained by this word of God as by a thousand bolts and bars, so that they do not break in to destroy us. Wherefore, relying on this promise, let us look forward to the last day, in which the consuming fire will purify heaven and earth.

**10. "And with every living creature."** Although the favor that the Lord promises extends to animals, yet he speaks only to men, who through faith perceive this benefit. We enjoy the earth and the heavens in common with the beasts and draw the same vital breath, but it is no shared privilege when God directs his word to us. From this we learn that God pursues us with paternal love.

Three distinct steps can be traced here. First, God made a covenant with Noah and his family so that they themselves were not afraid of any flood. Second, God transmits his covenant to posterity. This is done in such a way that future generations can understand this by faith, and so conclude that the same thing that had been promised to the sons of Noah was promised to them. Third, God declares that he will be propitious also to brute animals, so that the effect of the covenant toward them might be the preservation of their lives. However, God did not give them sense and intelligence. From this the ignorance of the Anabaptists may be refuted, who deny that the covenant of God is common to infants because they are destitute of present faith.

All who withdraw their life from God's protection (since most men either despise or ridicule this divine covenant) deserve, by this single act of ingratitude, to be immersed in eternal fire. For although this is an earthly promise, yet God wants the faith of his people to be exercised, so that they may be assured that a definite place will, by his special goodness, be provided for them on earth until they are gathered together in heaven.

**12. A sign** was added to the promise, which expresses God's wonderful mercy. In order to strengthen our faith in his word, God does not disdain to use such helps. From these words of Moses we must remember that it is wrong to sever signs from the word of God. By the word I mean those things that strengthen our faith. Here the Lord speaks to holy Noah and his sons, and he then gives them a sign, to reassure them. So, if the sacrament is cut off from the word, it ceases to be what it is called. From this we also infer that from the beginning it was the special nature of sacraments to confirm faith. For in the covenant that promise is included to which faith should respond. It appears to some absurd that faith should be sustained by such helps. But those who speak in this way do not, in the first place, reflect on the great ignorance and imbecility of our minds; nor do they, second, ascribe to the secret power of the Spirit the praise that is due him. It is God's work alone to begin and to perfect faith; but he does it by such instruments as he sees fit, the free choice of which is in God's own power.

**13. "I have set my rainbow in the clouds, and it will be the sign of the covenant between me and the earth."** From these words certain eminent theologians have been induced to deny that there was any rainbow before the Flood. This is a superficial way to understand this verse. The words of Moses do not signify that a bow was then formed that did not previously exist, but that a mark was engraved on it that would give a sign of the divine favor to men. Some signs are natural, and some are preternatural, beyond nature. While there are many examples of this second class of signs in the Scriptures, they are still special and do not belong to the ordinary and constant use of the church. For as it pleases the Lord to employ earthly elements as vehicles for raising the minds of men on high, so I think the heavenly arch that had before existed naturally is here consecrated into a sign and pledge. The nature of the thing itself might indicate a different type of a sign, since it indicates more rain. This is what the words mean: "As often as the rain alarms you, look at the bow. For although it may seem to cause the rain to flood the earth, it will nevertheless be to you a pledge of returning dryness, and so you must stand with greater confidence, as if you stood under a clear and serene sky." So it is not for us to argue with philosophers about the rainbow; although its colors are the effect of natural causes, yet those who attempt to deprive God of the right and authority that he has over his creatures are behaving in a profane way.

**15-16.** Moses, by introducing God so frequently as the speaker, teaches us that his word holds the most important place, and that signs are to be evaluated by that word. God, however, speaks in human terms when he says that when he sees the rainbow he will remember his covenant. God speaks like this so that men may reflect that God, whenever he stretches out his arch over the clouds, is not unmindful of his covenant.

**18. The sons of Noah who came out of the ark were Shem, Ham and Japheth.** Moses lists the sons of Noah not only because he is about to speak about them but to illustrate God's promise to **"multiply on the earth"** (verse 7). We observe how effective God's blessing became as so many people grew from one family. One little family grew into many nations.

**20. Noah, a man of the soil, proceeded to plant a vineyard.** This does not mean that for the first time Noah began to cultivate the fields. Rather, in my opinion, Moses intimates that Noah, though now an old man, returned to the cultivation of the fields, to his former labors. It is, however, uncertain if he had tended vines or not. It is commonly believed that wine was not in use before that time. This opinion has been readily accepted because it is used to excuse Noah's sin. But it does not appear to me probable that the fruit of the vine, which excels all others, should have been neglected. Also, Moses does not say that Noah became drunk on the first day he tasted it. Therefore, leaving this as an open question, I believe that we are to learn from Noah's drunkenness and to see how detestable drunkenness is. The holy patriarch, although he had until then been a rare example of frugality and temperance, did then lose all self-respect and in a base and shameful manner prostrated himself naked on the ground, and so became a laughingstock to everyone. Therefore, with what care ought we to cultivate sobriety, in case anything like this, or even worse, should happen to us.

Previously a heathen philosopher said, "Wine is the blood of the earth; and, therefore, when men intemperately pour it down their throats, they are justly punished by their mother." Let us, however, rather remember that when men, by shameful abuse, profane this noble and precious gift of God, the Lord himself becomes the Avenger. And let us know that Noah, through God's judgment, remains a warning to others that they should not become intoxicated by excessive drinking. Some excuse might be made for the holy man who, having completed his labor and being exhilarated with wine, imagined that he was but taking his just reward. But God branded him with an eternal mark of disgrace.

**22. Ham, the father of Canaan, saw his father's nakedness and told his two brothers outside.** This detail is added to show how Noah became even more full of sorrow, for he was now mocked by his own son. We must always remember that this punishment was divinely inflicted on him. This was done partly because Noah's misconduct was no light matter and partly because through Noah God teaches the value of temperance for all ages. Drunkenness bequeaths its own reward. Those who deface the image of their heavenly Father in themselves become a laughingstock to their own children. Let us remember that if the Lord judged the single transgression of the holy man so strongly, he will be no less severe with those who are daily intoxicated. We constantly witness many such examples of drunkenness today.

In the meantime Ham, by laughing at his father, betrayed his own depraved and malignant disposition. We know that parents, next to God, are to be most deeply reverenced. Though there were no books or any sermons in that day, nature itself constantly teaches us this lesson. It is agreed by common consent that piety toward parents is the mother of all virtues. Ham, therefore, must have had a wicked, perverse, and crooked disposition since he not only took pleasure in his father's shame but wanted to expose him to his brothers. And this was no small offense. For, first, Noah, the minister of salvation to men and the chief restorer of the world, in extreme old age lay intoxicated in his house. God had selected eight souls as a sacred seed, thoroughly purged from all corruption, for the renovation of the church. But Ham, the son of Noah, shows how much men need to be restrained by God, as with a bridle, no matter how many privileges God showers on them. Ham's ungodliness proves how deeply rooted men's wickedness is. It continually produces shoots, except where the power of the Spirit defeats it. If in God's hallowed sanctuary, among such a small number of people, one fiend was preserved, we should not be surprised that today's church, in which there are many more people, has the wicked mingled with the good.

There is no doubt that Shem and Japheth were greatly upset when they saw such scorn in their own brother while their father was lying prostrate on the ground in such shame. Such a base mind existing in the prince of the new world and the state of the holy patriarch of the church could not less astonish them than if they had seen the ark itself broken, dashed in pieces and destroyed. Yet they overcame this offense through their magnanimity. Only Ham took the opportunity to ridicule and inveigh against his father. It is probable that Ham insulted his father so that he could himself sin with impunity. We see many such people today, who pry into the faults of holy and pious men so that they may indulge themselves in all iniquity. They even make the faults of other men opportunities to harden themselves in their contempt for God.

**23.** Here the piety, as well as the modesty, of the two brothers is commended. **Shem and Japheth,** so that the dignity of their father might not be lowered in their esteem, but that they might always cherish the reverence they owed him, turned their eyes away from looking at his nakedness. In this way they demonstrated that they honored their father, as they thought their own eyes would be polluted if they voluntarily looked upon the nakedness that disgraced him.

**24.** Moses does not here record Noah's reproaches as if they were uttered in rage and anger, but rather portrays him speaking in the spirit of prophecy. Therefore we should not doubt that the holy man was truly humbled (rightly so) as he honestly reflected on his own faults. But now, having been pardoned and having had his condemnation removed, he proceeded as the herald of divine judgment. It should not be doubted that the holy man, who was usually endued with a gentle disposition, and being one of the best of parents, would only pronounce this sentence on his son with a very heavy heart, for he saw him as one of the few who were miraculously preserved. Now, therefore, when with his own mouth Noah is compelled to separate him from the church of God, he undoubtedly bitterly regretted his son's malediction. But by this example God would admonish us that the constancy of our faith must be retained if at any time we see those fail who are most closely united to us, and that our spirits ought not to be broken. We must exercise the severity that God orders in such a way that we do not spare even those who are nearest and dearest to us. And since Noah does not pronounce such a harsh sentence except by divine inspiration, we must learn from the severity of this punishment how abominable in God's sight is contempt for parents, since it perverts the sacred order of nature and violates the majesty and authority of God in the person of those whom he has commanded to preside in his place.

**25. "Cursed be Canaan! The lowest of slaves will he be to his brothers."** It is asked in the first place why Noah, instead of pronouncing the curse upon his son, inflicts the severity of punishment that son had deserved on his innocent grandson. Does it not appear to conflict with God's justice to lay the crimes of parents upon their children? But the answer is well-known; namely, God, although he judges the sons and the grandchildren of the ungodly, yet in being angry with them is not angry with the innocent, because they themselves are found to be guilty. So there is nothing absurd in avenging the sins of the fathers on their reprobate children, for all those whom God has deprived of his Spirit are subject to his wrath. Yet it is surprising that Noah should curse his grandson and pass in silence over his son Ham, who committed the crime. The Jews imagine that the reason for this can be traced to God's special favor. They say that since the Lord had bestowed on Ham such a great honor, the curse was transferred from him to his son. But this conjecture is futile. To my mind, there is no doubt that the punishment was carried forward even to his posterity in order that the severity of it might be the more apparent. It was as if the Lord had openly proclaimed that the punishment of one man would not satisfy him but that he would attach the curse also to the posterity of the offender, so that it should extend through successive ages. In the meantime, Ham himself was so far from being exempt that God, by involving his son with him, aggravated his own condemnation.

Another question is also raised—namely, why from among the many sons of Ham, God chose only to punish one of them. But we must not indulge our curiosity here too freely. Remember that God's judgments are not called "a great deep" without good reason. It would be most degrading for God, before whose tribunal we all must one day stand, to be subjected to our judgments, or rather to our foolish temerity. God chooses whom he sees good that he may show in them an example of his grace and kindness. Other people God appoints for a different purpose—that they may be living proofs of his anger and severity. Here although the minds of men are blinded, let each one of us, conscious of his own infirmity, learn to ascribe praise to God's justice rather than plunge with insane audacity into the profound abyss. While God held the whole seed of Ham as deserving the curse, he mentioned the Canaanites by name, as those whom he would curse more than the others. From this we infer that this judgment came from God, proved by the event itself. Humanly speaking Noah could not know what the condition of the Canaanites would be. Therefore, in obscure and hidden things the Spirit directed Noah's tongue.

Another difficulty still remains. Scripture teaches that God avenges the sins of men on the third and fourth generation, which seems to give a limit to God's wrath. But the vengeance now mentioned extends to the tenth generation. I answer that these words of Scripture are not intended to prescribe a law for God that he is not allowed to set aside, since he has freedom to punish sins beyond four generations. The thing to be observed here is the comparison between punishment and grace. This teaches us that God, while he justly avenges crimes, is even more inclined to mercy. In the meantime, let his liberty remain unquestioned. God extends his vengeance as far as he pleases.

**26.** Noah now blessed his other children, but in a different way. He gave **Shem** the highest honor, and in blessing him, Noah also praised God. For the Hebrews, when speaking of any rare and transcendent excellence, raised their thoughts to God. Therefore the holy man, when he perceived that the most abundant grace of God was destined for his son Shem, gave thanks to God. From this we infer that he did not speak from a human point of view as he referred to the secret favors of God, which were to be deferred to a much later time. Finally, these words declare that the blessing given to Shem would be divine or heavenly.

**27.** Noah predicted there would be a temporary dissension between **Shem** and **Japheth**, although he retained both in his family and called both his lawful heirs. At a later time they would come back together in one body and have a common home. It is absolutely certain that Noah was giving a prophecy here. More than 2,000 years elapsed before the Gentiles and the Jews were gathered together in one faith. Then the sons of Shem, of whom the greater part had rebelled and cut themselves off from the holy family of God, were collected together and dwelt under one tabernacle. Also the Gentiles, the progeny of Japheth, who had for a long time been wanderers and fugitives, were received into the same tabernacle. God, by a new adoption, has formed a people out of those who were separated. This is done by the sweet and gentle voice of God, which he has uttered in the Gospel. This prophecy is still daily being fulfilled, since God invites the scattered sheep to join his flock and collects on every side those who will sit down with Abraham, Isaac, and Jacob in the kingdom of heaven. It is no ordinary matter that the calling of the Gentiles is not only decreed in the eternal counsel of God but is openly declared by the mouth of the patriarch. This prevents us from thinking that the inheritance of eternal life offered to all happened suddenly or by chance.

**"May Japheth live in the tents of Shem."** This expression reminds us that mutual support for each other should exist and be cherished among the faithful. For whereas God had chosen a church from the progeny of Shem, he later chose the Gentiles together with them, on the condition that they should join themselves to those who possessed the covenant of life.

**28.** Although Moses briefly states the age of the holy man and does not record his annals and the memorable events of his life, yet those things that are certain and that Scripture elsewhere commemorates ought to come to mind. Within 150 years, the offspring of Noah's three sons became so great that he had sufficient and even abundant proof of the efficacy of the divine blessing: "increase and multiply" (see verse 7). Noah sees not just one city filled with his grandchildren but many nations springing from one of his sons. This astonishing increase, since it was a visible representation of the divine favor toward him, would doubtless fill him with unbounded joy.

# Genesis
# Chapter 10

**1. This is the account of Shem, Ham and Japheth, Noah's sons, who themselves had sons after the flood.** I believe these genealogies were written by Moses for the following reasons. First, in these bare names we have some fragment of the history of the world. The next chapter will show how many years intervened between the Flood and the time when God made his covenant with Abraham. This second beginning for mankind should be especially noted. The ingratitude of those who, when they had heard from their fathers and grandfathers about the wonderful restoration of the world in so short a time and still deliberately ignored God's grace and salvation, is to be especially deplored. Most people even forgot about the Flood. Very few people cared by what means or for what purpose they had been preserved. Many ages afterwards, seeing that the wicked forgetfulness of men had made them callous to God's judgment and mercy, the door was opened to the lies of Satan. Through the wiles of Satan, heathen poets made up futile and even noxious fables that polluted the truth about God's deeds. The goodness of God, therefore, wonderfully triumphed over the wickedness of men when he granted such ungrateful, brutal, and barbarous people a prolonged life. Today, to censorious men (who do not think it absurd to refuse to acknowledge a Creator of the world) such a sudden increase of mankind seems incredible, and therefore they ridicule it.

I agree that if we use our own reason to judge what Moses recounts, it may appear to be a mere story. But people who do not take note of the purpose of the Holy Spirit act in a most high-handed way. For what else, I ask, did the Spirit mean than that the offspring of three men should be increased not by natural means or in a normal way but by the power of God, so that the earth would be replenished far and wide? Those who think that this miracle of God is unbelievable because of its magnitude would find it even more difficult to believe that Noah and his sons, with their wives, survived in the ark for nearly a whole year. So it is only madness to ridicule what is said about the restoration of the human race, for in this act the wonderful power of God was displayed. Would it not be much better to behold God, to admire his power, to celebrate his goodness, and to acknowledge his hand? God's restoration of the world is just as full of mystery as his creation of the world.

We must observe that in the three lists that Moses gives us, not all the heads of the families are enumerated; only Noah's grandsons are recorded, who were the princes of nations. As any one person in a family excelled in talent, valor, industry, or other endowments, he obtained for himself a name and power, so that others, resting under his shadow, freely conceded that he should lead the family. Therefore, among the sons of Japheth, Ham, and Shem, Moses enumerates only those who had become well-known. After the names of these individuals were the peoples called. It is not completely clear why Moses begins with Japheth and then goes on to Ham. But it is probable that the first place is given to the sons of Japheth because they, having wandered over many regions and having even crossed the sea, had traveled furthest from their country. Since these nations were less known to the Jews, Moses therefore alludes to them briefly. He assigns the second place to the sons of Ham. They were more well-known to the Jews because of where they lived. But since Moses planned to weave the history of the church in one continuous narrative, he delays mentioning the progeny of Shem, from which the church flowed, until the end. So these people are not mentioned according to their greatness. Moses puts first those whom he wished to pass over quickly. Besides, we must observe that the children of this world are exalted for a time, so that the whole earth seems as if it were made for their benefit; but their glory is transient and quickly vanishes away. But the church, in an ignoble and despised condition, as if creeping on the ground, is yet divinely preserved, until in God's own time God will lift up her head. I leave to others the meticulous investigation of the names mentioned here. Information about some of them is clear from the Scripture, such as Cush, Mizraim, Madai, Canaan, and the like. But information about some others can only be conjectured, while some are so obscure that it is impossible to reach any definite conclusion about them.

**8. Cush was the father of Nimrod, who grew to be a mighty warrior on the earth.** It is certain that Cush was the ruler of the Ethiopians. Moses relates the life of his son Nimrod because he became so eminent. I believe this passage means that men behaved in a reasonable way to each other. If one excelled more than the rest, he did not turn into a domineering tyrant. Justin, in *Trogus Pompeius*, declares this was normal in the ancient world.

**10. The first centers of his kingdom were Babylon, Erech, Akkad and Calneh, in Shinar.** Moses now designates the seat of Nimrod's empire. He also declares that four cities were subject to him: **Babylon,**

**Erech, Akkad and Calneh.** It is, however, uncertain whether he founded them or captured them.

**21. Sons were also born to Shem, whose older brother was Japheth; Shem was the ancestor of all the sons of Eber.** Moses, as he is about to speak about the sons of Shem, makes this brief introduction, as he had done about the others. He did this for a good reason. Since this was the race God chose, he wanted it to stand out in a special way from the other nations. This is also why Moses specifically labels him the father of **the sons of Eber** and the elder brother of **Japheth**. Shem's blessing did not fall on all his grandchildren indiscriminately but remained in one family. The grandchildren of Eber were not faithful in their worship of God, and so the Lord would have been justified in disinheriting them. Yet God's blessing remained on them and was only not visible for a season.

# Genesis
# Chapter 11

**1. Now the whole world had one language and a common speech.** Babylon had been mentioned (10:10) in a single word, but now Moses explains in detail how it came by its name. In this truly memorable account we perceive the greatness of men's obstinacy against God and the tiny benefit they derive from his judgments. At first sight the atrocity of the evil is not apparent. Yet the punishment that follows shows God was displeased with what these men attempted. Those who conjecture that the tower was built as a refuge from any future flood are guided by nothing other than their imagination, for the words of Moses signify no such thing. There is nothing here other than man's proud contempt for God. **"Come, let us build ourselves a city, with a tower that reaches to the heavens, so that we may make a name for ourselves and not be scattered over the face of the whole earth"** (verse 4). Here we see their motive in this undertaking. Whatever else might happen, they wanted their names to be immortalized on earth. So they built as if they were opposing God's will. Ambition not only harms men but stands in proud opposition to God. To erect a citadel was not in itself so great a crime. But to raise an eternal monument to themselves that might endure throughout all ages showed headstrong pride as well as contempt for God. And from this originated the stories of the giants who, as the poets have imagined, heaped mountains on mountains to drag God down from his heavenly throne. Such an allegory is not very different from the ungodly that Moses alludes to here. As soon as mortals forget who they are and inflate their own importance, they become like giants who wage war with God.

When Moses says, **the whole world had one language and a common speech,** he is alluding to God's peculiar kindness in that the sacred bond of society among men, although they lived far apart from each other, was maintained by their common language. The diversity of tongues is to be thought of as an extraordinary event not part of the original plan. This defect, therefore, since it is repugnant to nature, Moses declares to be a later consequence, and he pronounces that the division of tongues was a punishment divinely inflicted upon men because they impiously conspired against God.

**2.** It may be conjectured from these words that Moses speaks of Nimrod and of the people whom he had collected around him. If, however, we grant that Nimrod was the chief leader in the construction of so great a building, for the purpose of erecting a formidable monument of his tyranny, we must bear in mind that Moses specifically says that the work was undertaken not by the counsel or the will of one man only, but because they all conspired together. So blame should not attach itself exclusively to one person or even to just a few men.

**3. They said to each other.** That is, they exhorted each other. Not only did every man work, but he earnestly encouraged everyone else to do the same.

**"Come, let's make bricks and bake them thoroughly."** They used brick instead of stone, and tar for mortar. Moses intimates that they did not embark on this work because it could be easily accomplished. Rather, Moses shows that they were content to face great and arduous difficulties. On account of this, they were even more guilty of going against God. From this we are taught to what length men's desires carry them when they indulge their ambition.

**4. Then they said, "Come, let us build ourselves a city, with a tower that reaches to the heavens, so that we may make a name for ourselves and not be scattered over the face of the whole earth."** When Moses says they wanted to build **a tower that reaches to the heavens** he is using hyperbole. They also said, "Let us **make a name for ourselves.**" They intimated that their building would be celebrated everywhere, even in the most distant parts of the world. This is the perpetual infatuation of the world. Such people neglect heaven and seek immortality on earth, where everything is fading and transient. Therefore, their cares and pursuits have no other purpose than to acquire a name for themselves on earth. David, in the forty-ninth Psalm, rightly ridicules this blind cupidity. Juvenal's saying, "Death alone acknowledges how insignificant the bodies of men are," is well-known. Yet even the prospect of death does not correct our pride, nor does it force us to confess our miserable state. For pride is more often displayed in funerals than in nuptial pomp. This shows us how fitting it is that we should live and die humbly. And it is important to have death before our eyes in the middle of life, so that we become used to living in a sober way. Whoever wants to be great in the world starts by being contemptuous toward men and ends by being proud before God. So he is like one of the giants and fights against heaven.

**"Not be scattered over the face of the whole earth."** These men are devising a way to meet a danger they believe to be imminent. It is as if they said, "It cannot be that when our number increases, this region should always hold all men; therefore an edifice must be erected by which their name will be preserved in perpetuity, although they should themselves be dispersed in different regions." It is, however, asked how they derived the notion of their future dispersion. Some conjecture that they were warned about it by Noah who, perceiving that the world had relapsed into its former crimes and corruptions, foresaw, by the prophetic spirit, some terrible dispersion; and they think that the Babylonians, seeing they could not directly resist God, endeavored by indirect methods to avert the threatened judgment. Others suppose that these men, by a secret inspiration of the Spirit, uttered prophecies concerning their own punishment, which they did not themselves understand. But these expositions are forced; nor is there any reason to apply what they say here to the curse that was inflicted on them. They knew that the earth was formed to be inhabited and would everywhere supply its abundance for the sustenance of men; and the rapid multiplication of mankind proved to them that it was not possible for them to remain shut up for a long time within their present narrow limits. Wherefore, wherever it would be necessary for them to migrate, they wanted this tower to remain as a witness to their origin.

**5. But the Lord came down to see the city and the tower that the men were building.** In the remaining part of the account, Moses teaches us how easily the Lord overturned their insane attempts and scattered abroad all their preparations. There is no doubt that these men strenuously set out to do what they had presumptuously devised. But Moses first intimates that God, for a little while, seemed to take no notice of them, so that, suddenly breaking off their work at its commencement by the confusion of their tongues he might give the more decisive evidence of his judgment. He frequently bears with the wicked to such an extent that he not only suffers them to contrive many nefarious things, as if he were unconcerned or were taking repose, but even further allows their impious and perverse designs to succeed, in order that he may at length overthrow them. The descent of God that Moses records here is spoken of in reference to men rather than to God, who, as we know, does not move from place to place. But Moses intimates that God gradually appeared in the character of an Avenger. The Lord therefore descended that he might **see**; that is, he showed that he was not ignorant about what the Babylonians were attempting to make.

**6. The Lord said, "If as one people speaking the same language they have begun to do this, then nothing they plan to do will be impossible for them."** There seems to me to be here a suppressed irony, as if God would propose to himself a difficult work in subduing their audacity. So the sense might be, "This people have conspired against me, and since they can speak to one another in the same language, how can their plan be defeated?" Nevertheless, he ironically smiled at their foolish and hasty confidence because, when men rely on their own strength, there is nothing that they do not arrogate to themselves.

**7. "Come, let us go down and confuse their language so they will not understand each other."** God now declared that the work that men supposed could not be stopped would, without any difficulty, be destroyed. These words mean, "I will not use many instruments. I will only blow upon them, and they, through the confusion of tongues, will be contemptibly scattered." So as men, having collected a large group of people, were contriving how they might reach the clouds, God summoned his troops, by whose interposition he would ward off their fury. What troops did he intend to use? The Jews think he is speaking about the angels. But since no mention is made of angels, and God places those to whom he speaks in the same rank with himself, this exposition is deservedly rejected. This passage rather corresponds to the former, the account of man's creation, when the Lord said, **"Let us make man in our image"** (1:26). God wisely contrasts his own eternal wisdom and power with that of this great multitude. It is as if he said that he had no need of foreign auxiliaries but possessed within himself what was needed for their destruction. Therefore, this passage is not improperly adduced in proof that three people subsist in one essence of deity. Moreover, this example of divine vengeance holds true in all ages, for men are always full of desire to do what is unlawful. But this account shows that God always opposes such counsels and designs. We see here an example of what Solomon says: "There is no wisdom, no insight, no plan that can succeed against the LORD" (Proverbs 21:30).

**8.** Men had already been spread abroad before this, and that should not be thought of as a punishment, seeing that it flowed from the grace of God. But now those whom the Lord had previously distributed with honor in various places, he ignominiously scattered, driving them here and there. This scattering, therefore, was not a simple dispersion in order to replenish. It was a violent rout because the principal bond between these men and God had been cut asunder.

**9. That is why it was called Babel.** Behold what they gained by their foolish ambition to acquire a name! They hoped that an everlasting memorial of their origin would be engraved on the tower. God not only frustrated their vain expectation but branded them with eternal disgrace, to render them execrable to all posterity on account of the great mischief indicted on the human race through their fault. They gained, indeed, a name, but not the one they would have chosen. In this way God opprobriously throws down the pride of those who accrue honors to themselves when they do not deserve any title.

**10.** Concerning the descendants of **Shem**, Moses had said something in the previous chapter (10:1). But now Moses gives us more details so we can know the age of the world. **Two years after the flood, when Shem**

was 100 years old, he became the father of Arphaxad. Unless this brief description had been preserved, we would not know today how much time elapsed between the Flood and the day in which God made his covenant with Abraham. Moreover, it is to be observed that God reckons the years of the world from the progeny of Shem, as a mark of honor. Nevertheless, God has granted this not so much on account of the merits of the family of Shem as on account of God's own gratuitous adoption.

When Shem was 100 years old, he became the father of Arphaxad. Since Moses placed Arphaxad as the third of Shem's sons (10:22), it is asked how this tallies with his being born two years after the flood. The answer is easy. We cannot exactly ascertain from the lists that Moses gives the date of the birth of each person. Sometimes a person is mentioned before someone who was born after him.

27. Terah became the father of Abram, Nahor and Haran. And Haran became the father of Lot. Here also Abram is placed first among his brothers, not (as I suppose) because he was the firstborn, but because Moses, intent on the scope of his history, had no particular purpose in the arrangement of the sons of Terah. It is also possible that Terah had yet other sons. The reason Moses speaks especially of these sons is obvious— namely, on account of Lot and of the wives of Isaac and Jacob.

30. Now Sarai was barren; she had no children. Not only does Moses say that Abram had no children, but he states the reason—namely, the sterility of his wife. Moses does this to show that it was nothing short of an extraordinary miracle that she later bore Isaac. Thus was God pleased to humble his servant; and we cannot doubt that Abram suffered severe pain through this privation. He saw the wicked springing up everywhere, in great numbers, to cover the earth; he alone was deprived of children. Although he still did not know about his future vocation, God designed to make it evident in his person from what and in what way his church should arise. For at that time it lay hidden, as in a dry root under the earth.

31. Terah took his son Abram, his grandson Lot son of Haran, and his daughter-in-law Sarai, the wife of his son Abram, and together they set out from Ur of the Chaldeans to go to Canaan. But when they came to Haran, they settled there. The next chapter should begin at this point because Moses begins to treat of one of the principal subjects of his book—namely, the calling of Abram. He not only relates that Terah moved, but he also explains the purpose of his departure—he left his native land and embarked on his journey in order to come to the land of Canaan. Thus the inference is easily drawn that he was not so much the leader or author of the journey as the companion of his son.

# Genesis
# Chapter 12

1. **The Lord had said to Abram, "Leave your country, your people and your father's household and go to the land I will show you."** That an absurd division of these chapters may not trouble the readers, let them link this sentence with the last two verses of the previous chapter. Moses had previously said that Terah and Abram had left their country to live in the land of Canaan. He now explains that they had not been impelled by levity as rash and fickle men are wont to be; nor had they been drawn to other regions because they hated their own country, as morose people frequently are; nor were they fugitives on account of crime; nor were they led away by any foolish hope or by any allurements, as many are hurried hither and thither by their own desires. Abram had been divinely commanded to go forth and had not moved a foot except as he was guided by the word of God. In short, Moses records this oracle in order that we may know that this long journey was undertaken by Abram and his father Terah at the command of God. Whence it also appears that Terah was not so far deluded by superstitions as to be destitute of the fear of God. It was difficult for the old man, failing in health, to tear himself away from his own country. But some true religion, although smothered, remained in his mind. Therefore, when he knew that the place from which his son was commanded to depart was accursed, it was his wish not to perish there; so he joined himself as an associate with him whom the Lord was about to deliver. What a witness, I demand, will he prove in the last day to condemn our indolence!

"**Leave your country.**" This accumulation of words may seem to be superfluous. It may also be observed that Moses, who is so concise in other places, here expresses a plain and easy matter in three different forms of speech. But Moses does so deliberately. For since exile is in itself sorrowful, and the sweetness of their native land holds nearly all men bound to it, God strenuously persisted in his command to leave the country, for the purpose of thoroughly penetrating the mind of Abram. If he had said simply, "**Leave** your country," this indeed would not lightly have pained his mind; but Abram was still more deeply affected when he heard that he must renounce his kindred and his father's house. It is not to be supposed that God takes a cruel pleasure in the trouble of his servants; but he thus tries all their affections that he may not leave any places undiscovered in their hearts. We see many people zealous for a short time who afterwards become frozen. Whence is this but because they build without a foundation? Therefore God determined thoroughly to rouse all the senses of Abram, that he might undertake nothing rashly or inconsiderately, in case he should change his mind later on and return to his country of origin. Wherefore, if we desire to follow God with constancy, we must carefully meditate on all the inconveniences, all the difficulties, all the dangers that await us.

"Go to the land I will show you." This was another test to prove Abram's faith. For why did not God immediately point out the land except to keep his servant in suspense, that he might fully test his attachment to the word of God? It is as if God said, "I command you to go out with your eyes closed. You are not allowed to ask where I am about to lead you until, having renounced your country, you have given yourself wholly to me." It is the true proof of our obedience when we are not wise in our own eyes but commit ourselves entirely to the Lord. Whenever, therefore, he requires anything of us, we must not be so concerned about success as to allow fear and anxiety to hinder our course. For it is better, with closed eyes, to follow God as our guide than, by relying on our own prudence, to wander through those circuitous paths.

Should anyone object that this statement is at variance with the former sentence, in which Moses declared that Terah and Abram departed from their own country that they might come into the land of Canaan, the solution is easy, if we allow for a prolepsis (that is, an anticipation of something that is still in the future) in Moses' writing. Another example of this comes in this same chapter, in the use of the name Bethel. This figure of speech frequently occurs in the Scriptures. They did not know where they were going; but because they had resolved to go wherever God might call them, Moses, speaking in his own person, mentions the land, which, though hitherto unknown to them both, was later revealed to Abram alone. It is therefore true that they departed with the purpose of going to the land of Canaan because, having received the promise concerning a land that was to be shown them, they allowed themselves to be governed by God until he should actually bestow on them what he had promised. Nevertheless, it may be that God, having proved Abram's devotion, soon removed all doubt from his mind. For we do not know at what precise time God intimated to him what he would only conceal for a season. It is enough that Abram declared himself to be truly obedient to God when, having cast all his care on God's providence and having discharged, as it were, into God's heart whatever might have impeded him, he did not hesitate to leave his own country, uncertain where, at length, he might plant his foot. By this method the wisdom of the flesh was brought in line, and all his affections were at the same time subdued.

Yet it may be asked why God sent his servant into the land of Canaan rather than into the East, where he could have lived with some of the other holy fathers. The nations of Canaan, on account of their deplorable wickedness, were devoted to destruction. God required his servant to live among them for a time, that, by faith, he might perceive himself to be the heir of that land, the actual possession of which was reserved for his posterity a long time after his death. So he was commanded to cross over to that country for the sole reason that it was to be evacuated by its inhabitants for the purpose of being given to Abram's descendants for a possession. And it was very important that Abram, Isaac, and Jacob should be strangers in that land and should by faith embrace the dominion over it that had been divinely promised them, so that their posterity might with greater courage take possession of it.

**2. "I will make you into a great nation and I will bless you; I will make your name great, and you will be a blessing."** Hitherto Moses has related what Abram had been commanded to do; now he adds God's promise to the command. Because we are slothful to obey, the Lord commands in vain unless we are animated by his grace and benediction. For it is certain that faith cannot stand unless it is grounded on the promises of God. Faith alone produces obedience. Therefore, in order that our minds may be disposed to follow God, it is not sufficient for God to command what he pleases unless he also promises his blessing. We must mark the promise that Abram, whose wife was still barren, would become **a great nation**. This promise might have been very efficacious if God, by the actual state of things, had afforded ground of hope respecting its fulfillment; but now, seeing that the barrenness of Abram's wife meant he would never have any children, the bare promise itself would have been cold if Abram had not wholly depended upon the word of God. Wherefore, though he perceived the sterility of his wife, he yet apprehended, by hope, that great nation that was promised by the word of God.

**"I will bless you."** This is partly added to explain the preceding sentence. Lest Abram should despair, God offered his own blessing, which was able to effect more in the way of miracle than is seen to be effected in other cases by natural means. The benediction, however, pronounced here extends farther than to offspring and implies that he would have a prosperous and joyous issue of all his affairs, as appears from rest of the verse: **"I will make your name great, and you will be a blessing."** Abram was promised such happiness as would fill all men everywhere with wonder, so that they would introduce the name of Abram as an example into their pronouncements of benediction.

**3. "I will bless those who bless you, and whoever curses you I will**

curse." Here the extraordinary kindness of God manifests itself in that he makes a covenant with Abram as men do with their companions and equals. The usual form of covenants between kings and others are arranged so that they mutually promise to have the same enemies and the same friends. It is certainly an inestimable pledge of special love that God should so greatly condescend for our sake. For although he here addresses one man only, he elsewhere declares the same affection toward his faithful people. We may therefore infer the general teaching that God so embraced us with his favor that he will bless our friends and take vengeance on our enemies. We are, moreover, warned by this passage that however desirous the children of God may be for peace, they will never lack enemies. Certainly, of all people who ever conducted themselves so peaceably among men as to deserve the esteem of all, Abram might be reckoned among the chief; yet even he was not without enemies because he had the devil for his adversary, who holds the wicked in his hand, whom he incessantly impels to molest good people. There is, then, no reason why the ingratitude of the world should dishearten us, even though many hate us without any good reason and, when provoked by no injury, study to do us harm. But let us be content with the single consolation that God is on our side in the war. Besides, God exhorts his people to cultivate fidelity and humanity with all good men and, further, to abstain from harming anyone.

"All peoples on earth will be blessed through you." Should anyone choose to understand this passage in a restricted sense, as a proverbial way of speaking (those who will bless their children or their friends will be called after the name of Abram), let him enjoy his opinion; for the Hebrew phrase will bear the interpretation that Abram will be called a signal example of happiness.

But I extend the meaning further because I suppose the same thing to be promised in this place that God later repeats more clearly (see Genesis 22:18). And the authority of Paul brings me to this point as well, for he says that the promise to the seed of Abraham—that is, to Christ—was given 430 years before the law (see Galatians 3:17). To calculate this number of years we must understand that the blessing was promised to Abram in Christ, when he was coming into the land of Canaan. Therefore, God (in my judgment) pronounces that all nations should be blessed in his servant Abram because Christ was included in his body. In this manner, he not only intimates that Abram would be an *example*, but a *cause* of blessing. So an antithesis should be understood between Adam and Christ. For whereas from the time of the first man's alienation from God we were all born accursed, here a new remedy is offered to us. Nor is there anything contrary to this in the assertion that we must by no means seek a blessing in Abram himself, inasmuch as the expression is used in reference to Christ. For when it is said that the tribe of Levi will bless in the name of God, in such passages as Deuteronomy 10:8 and Isaiah 65:16, it is sufficiently evident that God is declared to be the fountain of all good, in order that Israel may not seek any portion of good elsewhere. Seeing, therefore, that the language is ambiguous, let men grant the necessity of choosing this or the other sense as may be most suitable to the subject and the occasion. Paul takes it as an axiom that is accepted by all pious people that the whole human race is offensive to God, and therefore holy people are blessed only through the grace of the Mediator. Thus he concludes that the covenant of salvation that God made with Abram is neither stable nor firm except in Christ. I therefore thus interpret the present place as saying that God promises to his servant Abram that blessing that will afterwards flow to all people.

**4. So Abram left, as the LORD had told him; and Lot went with him. Abram was seventy-five years old when he set out from Haran.** Abram was now the head of the family. He completed what his father had begun. It is certain that in this place the obedience of faith is commended, and not as one single act but as a constant way of life. Not everyone was commanded to leave their country. But generally it is God's will that everyone should be subject to God's word and should seek the law for the regulation of their life, so that they are not carried away by their own will or by the maxims of men. Therefore, by the example of Abram, entire self-renunciation is commanded, that we may live and die to God alone.

**5. He took his wife Sarai, his nephew Lot, all the possessions they had accumulated and the people they had acquired in Haran, and they set out for the land of Canaan, and they arrived there.**

**The people they had acquired in Haran** refers to servants. This is the first mention of servitude; thus it appears that not long after the Flood the wickedness of man made freedom, which by nature was common to all, disappear for much of mankind. In this way the order of nature was violently infringed because men were created for the purpose of cultivating mutual society between each other. Although it is advantageous that some should preside over others, yet an equality, as among brethren, ought to have been retained. However, though slavery is contrary to the right government that is most desirable and in its commencement was not without fault, it does not on this account follow that the use of it, which was afterwards received by custom and excused by necessity, is unlawful. Abram therefore might possess both servants bought with money and slaves born in his house. For that common saying, "What has not prevailed from the beginning cannot be rendered valid by length of time," admits (as is well-known) of some exceptions. Genesis 48:1-20 is an example of such an exception.

**6.** Here Moses shows that Abram did not immediately, on his entering the land, find a place to settle, a habitation in which he might rest. Wherefore it is just as Moses had said—the faith of Abram was again tried when God allowed him to travel through the whole land before he gave him anywhere to live.

**At that time the Canaanites were in the land.** This clause concerning

**the Canaanites** is not added without reason; it was no small temptation to be cast among that perfidious and wicked nation, destitute of all humanity. What could the holy man then think but that he had been betrayed into the hands of people who might murder him, or that he would have to spend a miserable life in the middle of constant troubles? But it was profitable for him to be accustomed, by such discipline, to cherish a better hope. For if he had been kindly and courteously received in the land of Canaan, he would have hoped for nothing more than to spend his life there as a guest. But now God raised his thoughts higher in order that Abram might conclude that at some future time, the inhabitants being destroyed, he would be the lord and heir of the land. Besides, he was admonished by the continual lack of rest to look up toward heaven. For since the inheritance of the land was specially promised to him and would only belong to his descendants, for his sake, it follows that the land in which he was so inhumanly treated was not set before him as his ultimate aim, but that heaven itself was proposed to him as his final resting-place.

**7.** Moses now relates that Abram was not left entirely destitute, but that God stretched forth his hand to help him. We must, however, note how God assisted him in his temptations. He offered him his bare word, and in such a way indeed that Abram might deem himself exposed to ridicule. For God declared he would give the land to his seed; but where was the seed, or where was the hope of seed, seeing that Abram was childless and old and his wife was barren? This was, therefore, an insipid consolation to the flesh. But faith has a different taste, the nature of which is to hold all the senses of the pious so bound by reverence to the word that a single promise of God is quite sufficient. Meanwhile, although God truly alleviates and mitigates the evils that his servants endure, he does it only so far as is expedient for them, without indulging the desire of the flesh. Let us hence learn that this single remedy ought to be sufficient for us in our sufferings.

This **altar** was a token of gratitude. As soon as God appeared to Abram, Abram raised an **altar**. To what end? That he might call on the name of the Lord. We see, therefore, that he was intent on giving thanks, and that **an altar** was built by him in memory of kindness received. Should anyone ask whether he could not worship God without an altar, I answer that the inward worship of the heart is not sufficient unless external profession before men is added. Religion truly has its appropriate seat in the heart; but from this root, public confession afterwards arises as its fruit. For we are created to this end, that we may offer soul and body unto God. The Canaanites had their religion; they too had altars for sacrifices. But Abram, that he might not involve himself in their superstitions, erected a private **altar** on which he could offer a sacrifice, as if he had resolved to place a royal throne for God within his house. But because the worship of God is spiritual, and because all ceremonies that have no right and lawful end are not only vain and worthless in themselves but also corrupt the true worship of God by their fallacious appearance, we must carefully observe what Moses says—namely, that the **altar** was erected for the purpose of calling on God. **So he built an altar there to the LORD, who had appeared to him.**

The altar then is the external *form* of divine worship; but *invocation* is its substance and truth. This mark easily distinguishes pure worshipers from hypocrites, who are far too liberal in outward pomp but wish their religion to terminate in bare ceremonies. Thus all their religion is vague, being directed to no certain end. On the whole, ceremonies are not acceptable to God unless they have reference to the spiritual worship of God.

**8. From there he went on toward the hills east of Bethel and pitched his tent, with Bethel on the west and Ai on the east.** When we read that Abram moved from the place where he had built **an altar** to God, we ought not to doubt that he was by some necessity compelled to do so. He there found the inhabitants unpropitious and therefore transferred his tabernacle elsewhere. Since Abram bore his continual wanderings patiently, our complaining spirit is utterly inexcusable when we murmur against God if he does not grant us a quiet nest. Certainly when Christ has opened heaven to us and daily invites us thither to dwell with himself, we should not take it amiss if he chooses that we should be strangers in the world. The sum of the passage is that Abram did not have a settled residence. Paul says of Christians that they are "homeless" (1 Corinthians 4:11). Moreover, there is a manifest prolepsis in the word **Bethel**, for Moses gives the place this name to accommodate his discourse to the men of his own age.

**There he built an altar to the LORD and called on the name of the LORD.** Moses commends Abram's unwearied devotedness to piety; by these words he intimates that whatever place Abram visited, he publicly worshiped God, both so he might have no religious rites in common with the wicked, and so he might keep his family in sincere piety. It is probable that for this reason he would be the object of no little enmity, because there is nothing that makes wicked people more angry than religion that is different from their own, in which they conceive themselves to be not only despised but altogether condemned as blind. And we know that the Canaanites were cruel and proud and too ready to avenge insults. This was perhaps the reason for Abram's constant moving. His neighbors regarded the altars that he built as reproachful to themselves. It was only through God's wonderful favor that Abram was not often stoned. Nevertheless, since the holy man knew that he was justly required to bear testimony that he had a God who was peculiarly his own, whom he must not by dissimulation virtually deny, he therefore did not hesitate to prefer the glory of God to his own life.

**9.** This was the third time the holy man moved within a short time after he seemed to have found some kind of abode. It is certain that he did not voluntarily and for his own gratification run hither and thither; rather, certain necessities drove him forth, in order to teach him that he was not only a stranger but a wretched wanderer in the land of which he was the lord. Yet no common fruit was the result of so many changes because he endeavored, as much as in him lay, to dedicate to God every part of the land to which he had access and perfumed it with the odor of his faith.

10. A much more severe temptation is now recorded by which the faith of Abram was tried to the utmost. He was not only led around the country but was driven into exile, away from the land that God had given to him and to his posterity. Being expelled by hunger from that land where in reliance on the word of God he had promised himself a happy life, supplied with all abundance of good things, what must have been his thoughts, had he not been well fortified against the devices of Satan? His faith would have been overturned a hundred times. We know that whenever our expectation is frustrated and things do not happen according to our wishes, our flesh soon insists, "God has deceived you." But Moses shows in a few words with what firmness Abram sustained this vehement assault. He did not indeed magnificently proclaim his constancy in verbose eulogies, but with just a few words Moses sufficiently demonstrates that the patriarch still trusted God, for he says that **Abram went down to Egypt to live there** *for a while* because the famine was severe.

Moses intimates that Abram did not forget about the land that had been promised to him. Let us be instructed by this example that the servants of God must contend against many obstacles, that they may complete their vocation. We must always remember that Abram is not to be regarded as an individual member of the body of the faithful, but as the common father of them all; and thus all should imitate his example. Since the condition of the present life is unstable and subject to many troubling changes, let us remember that wherever we may be driven by famine or by the rage of war or by other vicissitudes that occasionally happen beyond our expectation, we must yet hold our right course, and that though our bodies may be carried hither and thither, our faith ought to stand unshaken.

11. Moses now relates the counsel that Abram took for the preservation of his life when he was approaching Egypt. Since this place is like a rock on which many founder, it is proper that we should soberly and reverently consider how far Abram deserves to be blamed and how much he deserves to be excused. First, it seems that Abraham was deceitful in the action he persuaded his wife to take. Although afterwards he made the excuse that he had not lied or said anything that was untrue, he was definitely culpable in not looking after his wife, who could have been treated as a prostitute. For when he dissembled the fact that she was his wife, he deprived her chastity of its legitimate defense. In that he subjected his wife to the peril of adultery, his actions seem to be inexcusable. Hence it follows that Abram's end was right, but he erred in the method he followed. It often happens to us that even while we are approaching God, by our thoughtlessness in taking unlawful means, we swerve from his word. This is especially liable to take place in difficult matters. When there appears to be no way of escape, we are

easily led astray into various circuitous paths. Therefore, although they are rash judges who entirely condemn this deed of Abram, yet the special fault is not to be denied—namely, that he, trembling at the approach of death, did not commit the issue of the danger to God but instead sinfully betrayed the modesty of his wife. Wherefore, by this example we are admonished that in difficult and doubtful matters we must seek the spirit of counsel and of prudence from the Lord and must also cultivate sobriety, that we may not attempt anything rashly without the authority of his word.

**"I know what a beautiful woman you are."** It is asked how Sarai could be **beautiful** since she was an old woman. Though we grant that she previously had excelled in elegance of form, certainly years had detracted from her gracefulness; and we know how much the wrinkles of old age disfigure the best and most beautiful faces. In the first place I answer, there is no doubt that there was then greater vivacity in the human race than there is now; we also know that vigor sustains personal appearance. Again, her sterility availed to preserve her beauty and to keep her whole habit of body entire, for there is nothing that more debilitates females than frequent childbearing. I do not, however, doubt that the perfection of her form was a special gift of God; but why he would not allow the beauty of the holy woman to be worn down by age, we do not know.

**12.** It may seem that Abram was unfair to **the Egyptians** in suspecting them of evil, since they had not harmed him. And since charity truly is not suspicious, he may appear to deal unfairly in not only charging them with lust but also in suspecting them of murder. I answer that the holy man did, not without reason, fear for himself from that nation about which he had heard many unfavorable reports. And he had already, in other places, experienced so much of the wickedness of men that he might justly fear anyone who despised God. He did not, however, pronounce anything absolutely concerning the Egyptians; but wishing to bring his wife to his own opinion, he gave her timely warning of what might happen. God, while he commands us to abstain from malicious and sinister judgments, also allows us to be on our guard against unknown people; and this may take place without any injury to others. Yet I do not deny that this trepidation of Abram exceeded all bounds and that an unreasonable anxiety caused him to involve himself in another fault, as we have already stated.

**15.** Although Abram had sinned by fearing too much and too soon, yet the event teaches us that he had not feared without cause, for his wife was taken from him and was brought to the king. At first Moses speaks generally of the Egyptians; afterwards he mentions the courtiers, by which he intimates that the rumor of Sarai's beauty was everywhere spread abroad, but that it was more eagerly received by the courtiers who indulged themselves in greater license. He adds that they told the king; we hence infer how ancient is that corruption that now prevails immeasurably in the courts of kings. As everything there is full of flattery, so the nobles principally apply their minds to introduce, from time to time, what may be gratifying to royalty. Therefore we see that those who want to be promoted must not only be servile but must also pander to their master's lusts.

Since Sarai was carried off and lived for some time in the palace, many suppose that she was corrupted by the king. For it is not credible that a lustful man, when he had her in his power, should have spared her modesty. This, truly, Abram had richly deserved, who had neither relied upon the grace of God, nor had committed the chastity of his wife to God's faithfulness and care. But the **serious diseases** (verse 17) that immediately followed sufficiently proved that the Lord remembered her; and hence we may conclude that she remained uninjured. When Abram was in similar danger at another time (see Genesis 20:1), God did not allow her to be violated by the king of Gerar either. Will we suppose that she was on the occasion in Genesis 12 exposed to Pharaoh's lust? Moreover, when Moses adds, **he [Pharaoh] treated Abram well for her sake**, we conclude that she was honorably entertained by Pharaoh and was not dealt with as a harlot. When, therefore, Moses says she was brought into the king's palace (verse 15), I do not understand this to have been for any other purpose than that the king by a solemn rite might take her as his wife.

**17.** If Moses had simply related that God had punished the king for having committed adultery, it would be fairly clear that God had taken care of Sarai's chastity; but when he plainly declares that the house of the king was plagued because of Sarai, Abram's wife, all doubt is, in my judgment, removed because God, on behalf of his servant, interposed his mighty hand in time, lest Sarai should be violated. Here we have a remarkable instance of the careful concern with which God protects his servants by undertaking their cause against the most powerful monarchs. (See Psalm 105:12-15.) May we remember that we are covered by God's protection, in order that the violence of those who are more powerful may not oppress us.

Some ask whether Pharaoh was justly punished, seeing that he neither intended, by guile nor by force, to gain possession of another man's wife. I answer that the actions of men are not always to be estimated according to our judgment, but are rather to be weighed in the balances of God. For it often happens that the Lord will find in us what he may justly punish, while we seem to ourselves to be free from fault and absolve ourselves from all guilt. Let kings rather learn from this account to bridle their own power, to use their authority moderately, and to impose a voluntary law of moderation upon themselves.

**18.** Pharaoh justly expostulated with Abram, who was most at fault. No answer on the part of Abram is here recorded; perhaps he assented to the just and true reprehension.

**20.** Pharaoh commanded that Abram should have safe conduct out of the kingdom, lest he should be exposed to violence, for we know how proud and cruel the Egyptians were.

# Genesis
# Chapter 13

**1. So Abram went up from Egypt to the Negev, with his wife and everything he had, and Lot went with him.** At the beginning of this chapter, Moses commemorates God's goodness in protecting **Abram**; thus it came to pass that Abram not only returned in safety but took with him great wealth. Also note that when he was leaving **Egypt**, abounding in cattle and treasures, he was allowed to pursue his journey in peace. Moses then shows that riches proved no obstacle to Abram in pursing his goal. We know how much even a moderate amount of wealth hinders many from raising their heads toward heaven, while those who possess wealth in great abundance lie torpid in indolence. So Moses contrasts Abram with the common vice of others as he relates that the patriarch was not to be prevented by any impediments from seeking again the land of Canaan.

Two extremes, however, are to be guarded against concerning wealth. Many place angelical perfection in poverty, as if it were impossible to cultivate piety and to serve God unless riches are thrown away. Few indeed imitate Crates the Theban, who threw his treasures into the sea because he did not think he could be saved unless they were lost. Many fanatics deny rich men any hope of salvation, as if poverty were the only gate of heaven; yet this view sometimes involves men in more hindrances than riches. But Augustine wisely teaches us that the rich and poor are collected together in the same inheritance of life; poor Lazarus was received into the bosom of rich Abraham. On the other hand, we must beware of the opposite evil, lest riches should become a stumbling-block in our way or should so burden us that we should less readily advance toward the kingdom of heaven.

**3. From the Negev he went from place to place until he came to Bethel, to the place between Bethel and Ai where his tent had been earlier.** In these words Moses teaches us that Abram did not rest until he had returned to **Bethel**, for although he pitched his tent in many places, he did not stay there permanently.

**4.** Moses now adds that an **altar** had before been erected there by him and that he **called on the name of the** LORD **again.** From this we may learn that the holy man was always worshiping God and giving evidence of his piety. The explanation given by some that the inhabitants of the place had been brought to the pure worship of God is neither probable, nor to be deduced from the words of Moses. And we have stated elsewhere what is the force of the expression, "to invoke in the name of" or "to call upon the name of the Lord"—namely, to profess the true and pure worship of God. Abram did not invoke God only twelve times during the whole course of his life; whenever he publicly celebrated him and by a solemn rite made it manifest that he had nothing in common with the superstitions of the heathen, then he is also said to have called upon God. Therefore, although he always worshiped God and exercised himself in daily prayers, yet, because he did not daily testify his piety by outward profession before men, this virtue is here especially commended by Moses. It was therefore proper that invocation should be conjoined with the altar, because by the sacrifices offered, Abram plainly testified to the God he worshiped, in order that the Canaanites might know he was not addicted to their common idolatries.

**5. Now Lot, who was moving about with Abram, also had flocks and herds and tents.** Now follows an account of the trouble Abram suffered because of his wealth. Certainly he did not want to part from his nephew. If he had had a choice, he would have preferred the loss of his wealth to separation from Lot, whom he loved as if he were his own son. But Abram found no other remedy to stop the quarreling. Shall we ascribe this difficulty to his own stern temper or to his nephew's insolence? I think we would do better to consider the purpose of God.

There was danger that Abram might become too satisfied with his own good fortune, just as many men are blinded by lesser goods. Therefore, God seasoned the sweetness of wealth with vinegar and did not allow the mind of his servant to be too entranced with it. When a false sense of value leads us to seek riches more than is right, because we do not realize how many troubles they bring with them, this story should serve to limit our inordinate love. And whenever rich men fall into trouble because of their wealth, they should learn to use the pain it gives them as a medicine to purge their minds of too great a desire for the good things of this present life. Unless God in his wisdom tightened the reins wisely, men would leave the right road and would stumble badly in their pursuit of prosperity. On the other side, when we are hampered by poverty we should understand that God uses this also as a remedy for the secret vices of our flesh.

In conclusion, let those who have abundance remember that they are surrounded with thorns, and let them take great care not to be pricked by them. And let those who have little and are very much hemmed in know that God planned their poverty to keep them from evil and harmful snares.

Separation from Lot grieved Abram; but it could serve to correct much evil latent in him and prevent wealth from stifling the ardor of his devotion. If Abram needed such an antidote, we should not wonder that God employs painful checks against our lust for pleasure. He does not always wait until the faithful have actually slipped, but he looks ahead for them. He did not punish Abram, his servant, for avarice or pride; he gave him a preventive medicine to keep Satan from infecting his mind with such sentiments.

**7. And quarreling arose between Abram's herdsmen and the herdsmen of Lot.** What applies to wealth applies equally to large households. Yet we see how ambitiously many men seek to collect a great crowd of servants, as if they want to preside over a whole nation. But seeing that Abram's great establishment cost him so much, we should learn to be willingly satisfied with a small establishment or with none at all, if it so please God. It is almost impossible for a house to be filled with many people without its being in turmoil. Experience proves the truth of the proverb, "A crowd is the same as a tumult." If quiet tranquillity is an inestimable good, then we should see that our wisest course is to have a small house and to live unpretentiously within our family.

In this example, note carefully what we are advised to avoid if we are to keep Satan from drawing us into conflicts by circuitous devices. For when he cannot inflame us directly with mutual hate, he implicates us in the disputes of others. Lot and Abram agreed between themselves, but the quarrel that arose among the shepherds compelled them to separate.

There is no doubt that Abram had given strict orders to his servants to keep the peace; but his zeal and effort did not prevent his seeing the flame of discord, kept alight by small fans, blazing in his own home. So it is hardly surprising that disturbances arise in the church, which contains an even greater number of people. Abram had about 300 servants; Lot's household was certainly much smaller. What then will happen among 6,000, especially when those who quarrel are all free men?

We must not let ourselves be upset by these offenses, but equally we must be on guard in every way against the outbreak of fighting. For unless disagreements are completely stifled as they start, they will develop into harmful dissensions.

**The Canaanites and Perizzites were also living in the land at that time.** Moses adds this in order to highlight the evil. He declares the heat of the contention to have been so great that it could neither be extinguished nor assuaged, even by the fear of impending destruction. Abram and Lot were surrounded by as many enemies as they had neighbors. Nothing, therefore, was wanting in order to bring their destruction but a suitable occasion; and this they themselves were affording by their quarrels. To such a degree does blind fury infatuate men when once the vehemence of contention has prevailed that they carelessly despise death when placed before their eyes. Although we are not now continually surrounded by Canaanites, we are in the midst of enemies as long as we sojourn in the world. Wherefore, if we are influenced by any desire for the salvation of ourselves and of our brethren, let us beware of contentions that will deliver us over to Satan to be destroyed.

**8.** Moses first states that Abram no sooner perceived the strife that had arisen than he fulfilled the duty of a good householder by attempting to restore peace among his servants; and later, by his moderation, he endeavored to remedy the evil by removing it. Although the servants alone were contending, Abram yet did not say in vain, **"Let's not have any quarreling between you and me"** because it was hardly possible that the contagion of the strife would not transfer from the servants to their lords, although they were in other respects perfectly agreed. He also foresaw that their friendship could not remain intact for long unless he attempted, in time, to heal the insidious evil.

**9.** Here is that moderation of which I have spoken—namely, that Abram, for the sake of appeasing strife, voluntarily sacrificed his own right. For as ambition and the desire of victory is the mother of all contentions, so when everyone meekly and moderately gives up, in some degree, his just claim, the best remedy is found for the removal of all bitterness. Abram might indeed, with an honorable pretext, have more pertinaciously defended the right that he relinquished, but he shrank from nothing for the sake of restoring peace and therefore left the option to his nephew.

**10.** As the equity of Abram was worthy of no little praise, so the ill-advisedness of Lot, which Moses here describes, deserves censure. As if he were in every respect the superior, he took for himself the better portion and chose the region that seemed the most fertile and agreeable. It necessarily follows that whoever is too eagerly intent upon his own advantage is wanting in humanity toward others. There can be no doubt that this injustice would pierce the mind of Abram; but he silently bore it, lest by any means he should give occasion to new offense. We ought to behave like this whenever we perceive those with whom we are connected to be not sufficiently mindful of their duty; otherwise there will be no end of tumults.

**13.** Lot thought himself happy that so rich a habitation had fallen to his share. But he learned at length that the choice he had made with a rashness equal to his avarice had been unhappily granted to him, since he now had to deal with proud and perverse neighbors with whose conduct it was much harder to bear than it was to contend with the sterility of the earth. Therefore, seeing that he was led away solely by the pleasantness of the prospect, he paid the penalty of his foolish cupidity. Let us then learn by this example that our eyes are not to be trusted, but that we must rather be on our guard lest we be ensnared by them and be encircled, unawares, with many evils, just as Lot, when he fancied that he was dwelling in paradise, was nearly plunged into the depths of hell.

It seems amazing that Moses, when he wishes to condemn the men of Sodom for their extreme wickedness, should say that they **were sinning** greatly against the LORD and not rather before men. When we come to God's tribunal, every mouth will be stopped, and all the world will be subject to condemnation. Moses may be thought to be understating the situation. But the case is otherwise, for he means that they were not merely under the dominion of those common vices that everywhere prevail among men but were abandoned to most execrable crimes, the cry of which rose even to heaven and demanded vengeance from God. That God bore with them for a time, and not only so, but suffered them to inhabit a most fertile region though they were utterly unworthy of light and life affords, as we hence learn, the wicked no ground of self-congratulation. Though the wicked exult in their luxury, and even become outrageous against God, let the sons of God be admonished not to envy their fortune but to wait a little while, until God, arousing them from their intoxication, calls them to his dreadful judgment. Therefore Ezekiel, speaking of the men of Sodom, declares the cause of their destruction to their being saturated with bread and wine and filled with delicacies and exercising proud cruelty against the poor (16:49).

**14-15.** Moses now relates that after Abram was separated from his nephew, divine consolation was administered to comfort him. There is no doubt that the wound inflicted by that separation was very severe, since he was obliged to send away one who was not less dear to him than his own life. When it is said, therefore, that **the LORD said to Abram after Lot had parted from him,** the circumstances should be noted. It is as if Moses said that the medicine of God's word was now brought to alleviate Abram's pain. And thus he teaches us that the best remedy for sadness is in the word of God.

**"Lift up your eyes from where you are and look north and south, east and west."** Seeing that the Lord promised the land to the seed of Abram, we perceive the admirable design of God in the departure of Lot. He had assigned the land to Abram alone; if Lot had remained with him, the children of both would have been mixed together. The cause of their dissension was indeed culpable; but the Lord, according to his infinite wisdom, turned it to good, so that the posterity of Lot would possess no part of the inheritance. This is the reason why God says, **"All the land that you see I will give to you and your offspring forever."** Therefore, there was no reason why he, to whom a reward so excellent was hereafter to be given, should be excessively sorrowful and troubled on account of his solitude and privation. Although the same thing had been already promised to Abram, yet God now adapted his promise to the relief of the present sorrow. Thus it is to be remembered that not only was a promise here repeated that would cherish and confirm Abram's faith, but that a special oracle was given from which Abram might learn that the interests of his own seed were to be promoted by the separation of Lot from him.

In promising the land **forever,** God did not simply denote perpetuity, but that period that was brought to a close by the advent of Christ.

**16.** Omitting those subtleties by means of which others argue about nothing, I simply explain these words to signify that the seed of Abram was compared to the **dust** because of its immense multitude; and truly the sense of the term is to be sought for only in Moses' own words. It was, however, necessary to be here added that God would raise up for him a seed, of which he was hitherto destitute. Abram was commanded to look at the **dust**. But when he turned his eyes upon his own family, what similarity was there between his solitariness and the countless particles of **dust**? The Lord requires us to attribute authority to his own word, so that it alone will be sufficient for us. It may also appear to be an occasion for ridicule when God commanded Abram to travel until he had examined the whole land (verse 17). To what purpose would God do this, except that Abram might more clearly perceive himself to be a stranger, and that, being exhausted by continual and fruitless disquietude, he might despair of any stable and permanent possession? How would he persuade himself that he was lord of that land in which he was scarcely permitted to drink water, although he had with great labor dug the wells? But these are the exercises of faith, in order that it might perceive, in God's word, those things that are far off and that are hidden from carnal sense. For faith is the beholding of absent things (see Hebrews 11:1), and it holds God's word as a mirror in which it may discover the hidden grace of God. The condition of the pious at this time is not dissimilar. Though they are hated by all, are exposed to contempt and reproach, wander without a home, are sometimes driven hither and thither, and suffer from nakedness and poverty, it is nevertheless their duty to lay hold on the inheritance that is promised. Let us, therefore, walk through the world as people hindered from all repose, who have no other resource than the mirror of the word of God.

**18.** Here Moses relates that the holy man, animated by the renewed promise of God, traversed the land with great courage, as if by a look alone he could subdue it to himself. Thus we see how greatly the oracle had helped him—not that he had heard anything from the mouth of God to which he had been unaccustomed, but because he had obtained a medicine so seasonable and suitable to his present grief that he rose with collected energy toward heaven. At length Moses records that the holy man, having performed his circuit, returned to the **great trees** or valley of **Mamre**, to dwell there. And again Moses commends his piety in building **an altar** and calling upon God. I have already frequently explained what this means. Abram himself bore an altar in his heart; but seeing that the land was full of profane altars on which the Canaanites and other nations polluted the worship of God, Abram publicly professed that he worshiped the true God, and that not at random, but according to the method revealed to him by God's word. Hence we infer that the altar of which mention is made was not built rashly by his hand, but was consecrated by the same word of God.

# Genesis
# Chapter 14

**1-2. At this time Amraphel king of Shinar, Arioch king of Ellasar, Kedorlaomer king of Elam and Tidal king of Goiim went to war against Bera king of Sodom, Birsha king of Gomorrah, Shinab king of Admah, Shemeber king of Zeboiim, and the king of Bela (that is, Zoar).** The history related in this chapter is chiefly worthy of remembrance for three reasons: First, because Lot, with a gentle reproof, exhorted the men of Sodom to repentance. They had, however, become altogether unteachable and desperately perverse in their wickedness. But Lot was beaten with these scourges because, having been allured and deceived by the richness of the soil, he had mixed himself with unholy and wicked men.

Second, because God, out of compassion for him, raised up Abram as Lot's avenger and liberator, to rescue him, when a captive, from the hand of the enemy; in which act the incredible goodness and benevolence of God toward his own people is rendered conspicuous since, for the sake of one man, he preserved, for a time, many who were utterly unworthy.

Third, because Abram was divinely honored with a signal victory and was blessed by the mouth of Melchizedek, in whose person, as appears from other passages of Scripture, the kingdom and priesthood of Christ were foreshadowed. Respecting the sum of history, this is a horrible picture both of the avarice and pride of man.

The human race still had three progenitors—Shem, Ham, and Japheth—living among them, by the very sight of whom men were admonished that they had all sprung from one family and one ark. Moreover, the memory of their common origin was a sacred pledge of fraternal connection that should have bound them to assist each other by mutual good offices. Nevertheless, ambition so prevailed that they assailed one another on all sides with sword and armor, and each attempted to subdue the rest. Wherefore, while we see at the present day princes raging furiously and shaking the earth to the utmost of their power, let us remember that such evil is of ancient date since the lust of dominion has in all ages been too prevalent among men.

The ambition of **Kedorlaomer** was the torch of the whole war, for he, inflamed with the desire for conquest, drew three others into a hostile confederacy. Pride compelled the men of Sodom and their allies to take up arms for the purpose of shaking off the yoke.

That Moses, however, records the names of so many kings while Shem was yet living (although derided by profane men as a fable) will not appear absurd if we only reflect that this great propagation of the human race was a remarkable miracle of God. For when the Lord said to Noah and to his sons, "Increase and multiply," he intended to raise them to the hope of a far more excellent restoration than would have taken place in the ordinary course of nature. This benediction is indeed perpetual and will flourish even to the end of the world. But it was necessary that its extraordinary efficacy should then appear, in order that these earliest fathers might know that a new world had been divinely enclosed within the ark.

According to the poets, Deucalion with his wife allegedly sowed the race of men after the Flood by throwing stones behind him. The miserable minds of men were deluded with such trifles when they departed from the pure truth of God; and Satan has made use of such artifice to discredit the veracity of God's miracles. Since the memory of the Flood and the unwonted propagation of a new world could not be speedily obliterated, Satan scattered abroad clouds and smoke, introducing puerile conceits in order that what had before been held as certain truth might now be regarded as a fable. It is, however, to be observed that all are called kings by Moses who held the priority in any town or in any considerable assembly of men.

10. **Now the Valley of Siddim was full of tar pits, and when the kings of Sodom and Gomorrah fled, some of the men fell into them and the rest fled to the hills.** Some expound that the men of that region fell into **pits**; but this is not probable since they were by no means ignorant of the neighboring places. Such an event would rather have happened to foreign enemies. Others say they went down into them for the sake of preserving their lives. I, however, understand them to have exchanged one kind of death for another, as is common in the moment of desperation; as if Moses said that the swords of the enemy were so formidable to them that, without hesitation, they threw themselves headlong into the **pits**. For he immediately afterwards adds that they who escaped **fled to the hills.** Whence we infer that they who had rushed into the **pits** had perished. They **fell**, not so much deceived through ignorance of the place as disheartened by fear.

12. **They also carried off Abram's nephew Lot and his possessions, since he was living in Sodom.** It is uncertain whether Lot remained at home while others went to the battle and was there captured by the enemy, or whether he had been compelled to take up arms with the rest of the

people. As, however, Moses does not mention him until he speaks of the plundering of the city, the conjecture is probable that at the conclusion of the battle, he was taken at home, unarmed. We here see, first, that sufferings are common to the good and the evil; then that the more closely we are connected with the wicked and the ungodly, when God pours down his vengeance on them, the more quickly does the scourge come upon us.

**13.** This is the second part of the chapter, in which Moses shows that when God had respect to his servant Lot, he gave him Abram as his deliverer, to rescue him from the hands of the enemy. But here various questions arise—for example, whether it was lawful for Abram, a private person, to arm his family against kings and to undertake a public war. I do not, however, doubt that as he went to the war endued with the power of the Spirit, so also he was guarded by a heavenly command and so did not transgress the bounds of his vocation. And this ought not to be regarded as a new thing, but as his special calling; for he had already been made king of that land. And although the possession of it was deferred to a future time, yet God would give some remarkable proof of the power that he had granted him and that was hitherto unknown to men.

A similar prelude of what was to follow, we read in the case of Moses when he slew the Egyptian, before he openly presented himself as the avenger and deliverer of his nation. Some who wish to defend themselves by armed force whenever any force is used against them might from this passage frame a rule for themselves. However, we will hereafter see this same Abram bearing patiently and with a submissive mind injuries that had at least an equal tendency to provoke his spirit. Moreover, that Abram attempted nothing rashly but rather that his design was approved by God will appear presently from the commendation of Melchizedek. We may therefore conclude that this war was undertaken by him under the special direction of the Spirit. If anyone should object that he proceeded further than was lawful when he spoiled the victors of their prey and captives and restored them wholly to the men of Sodom, who had by no means been committed to his protection, I answer: Since it appears that God was his guide and ruler in this affair—as we infer from God's approbation—it is not for us to argue about God's secret judgment. God had destined the inhabitants of Sodom, when their neighbors were ruined and destroyed, to a still more severe judgment, because they were themselves the worst of all. He, therefore, raised up his servant Abram, after they had been admonished by a chastisement sufficiently severe, to deliver them in order that they might be rendered the more inexcusable. Therefore, this peculiar suggestion of the Holy Spirit ought no more to be drawn into a precedent than the whole war that Abram carried on.

With respect to the messenger who had related to Abram the slaughter at Sodom, I do not accept, as some suppose, that he was a pious man. We may rather conjecture that as a fugitive from home who had been deprived of all his goods, he came to Abram to elicit something from him. That Abram is called **Abram the Hebrew**, I do not explain from the fact of his having passed over the river, as is the opinion of some, but from his being of the progeny of Eber. It is a name of descent. And the Holy Spirit here again honorably announces that race as blessed by God.

**All of whom were allied with Abram.** It appears that in the course of time, Abram was freely permitted to enter into covenant and friendship with the princes of the land, for the heroic virtues of the man caused them to regard him as one who was not by any means to be despised. Rather, as he had so great a family, he might also have been numbered among kings if he had not been a stranger and a sojourner. But God purposed to provide for his peace by a covenant relating to temporal things in order that he might never be mingled with those nations. Moreover, that this whole transaction was divinely ordered we may readily conjecture from the fact that his associates did not hesitate, at great risk, to assail four kings who (according to the state of the times) were sufficiently strong and were flushed with the confidence of victory. Surely they would scarcely ever have been thus favorable to a stranger, except by a secret impulse of God.

**14.** Moses briefly explains the purpose of the war that was undertaken—namely, that Abram might rescue his **relative** from captivity. Meanwhile, what I have before said is to be remembered: He did not rashly fly to arms but took them as from the hand of God, who had constituted him lord of that land.

**15. During the night Abram divided his men to attack them and he routed them, pursuing them as far as Hobah, north of Damascus.** Some explain these words to mean that Abram alone, with his domestic troops, rushed upon the enemy, others that he and his three confederates divided their bands in order to strike greater terror into the foe. A third class suppose the phrase to be a Hebraism for making an invasion into the midst of the enemy. I rather embrace the first exposition—namely, that he invaded the enemy on different sides and suddenly inspired them with terror. The circumstance of time favors this view because he attacked them by night. Although examples of similar bravery occur in secular history, yet it ought to be ascribed to the faith of Abram that with a small band he dared to assail a large army elated with victory. But that he came off conqueror with little trouble and with fortitude pursued those who far exceeded him in number, we must ascribe to the favor of God.

**17.** Although **the king of Sodom** knew that Abram had taken arms only on account of his nephew, yet he went to meet him with due honor, in order to show his gratitude. It is a natural duty to acknowledge benefits conferred upon us even when not intentionally rendered, but only from unexpected circumstances and occasions or (as we say) by accident. Moreover, the whole affair yielded greater glory to God because the victory of Abram was celebrated in this manner.

Moses also identifies the place where the king of Sodom met Abram—namely, **the King's Valley**, which I think was so called rather after some particular king than because those kings met there for their pleasure.

**18. Then Melchizedek king of Salem brought out bread and wine. He was priest of God Most High.** This is the last of the three principal points of this history. **Melchizedek**, the chief father of the church, having entertained Abram at a feast, blessed him in virtue of his priesthood and received tithes from him. There is no doubt that by the coming of this **king** to meet him, God also designed to render the victory of Abram famous and memorable to posterity. But a more exalted and excellent mystery was at the same time shown: Seeing that the holy patriarch, whom God had raised to the highest rank of honor, submitted himself to Melchizedek, it is not to be doubted that God had constituted Melchizedek the only head of the whole church; for without controversy the solemn act of benediction that Melchizedek assumed to himself was a symbol of preeminent dignity. If anyone replies that he did this as a priest, I ask, was not Abram also a priest? Therefore God here commends to us something peculiar in Melchizedek, in preferring him before the father of all the faithful.

But it will be more satisfactory to examine the passage word by word, that we may thence better gather the import of the whole. Melchizedek's receiving Abram and his companions as guests belonged to his *royalty*; but the benediction pertained especially to his *sacerdotal office*. Therefore, the words of Moses ought to be thus connected: **Then Melchizedek king of Salem brought out bread and wine. He was priest of God Most High, and he blessed Abram.** Thus to each character is distinctly attributed what is its own. Melchizedek refreshed a wearied and famishing army with royal liberality; but because he was a priest, he blessed, by the rite of solemn prayer, the firstborn son of God and the father of the church—that is, Abram. Moreover, although I do not deny that it was the most ancient custom for those who were kings to fulfill also the office of the priesthood, yet this appears to have been, even in that age, extraordinary in Melchizedek. And truly he was honored with no common eulogy when the Spirit ratified his priesthood. We know that, at that time, religion was corrupt everywhere since Abram himself, who was descended from the sacred race of Shem and Eber, had been plunged into the profound vortex of superstitions with his father and grandfather.

Therefore, many imagine Melchizedek to have been Shem, an opinion, for many reasons, I am hindered from accepting. The Lord would not have designated a man worthy of eternal memory by a name so new and obscure that he must remain unknown. Second, it is not probable that Shem had migrated from the east into Judea; and nothing of the kind is to be gathered from Moses. Third, if Shem had dwelt in the land of Canaan, Abram would not have wandered by such winding courses as Moses has previously related before he went to salute his ancestor. But the declaration of the apostle is of the greatest weight—that this Melchizedek, whoever he was, is presented before us without any origin, as if he had dropped from the clouds, and without any mention of his death (see Hebrews 7:3).

But the admirable grace of God shines more clearly in a person unknown because, amid the corruptions of the world, he alone in that land was an upright and sincere cultivator and guardian of religion. I omit the absurdities that Jerome, in his *Epistle to Evagrius*, heaps together, lest, without any advantage, I should become troublesome and even offensive to the reader. I readily believe that **Salem** is to be taken for Jerusalem, and this is the generally received interpretation. If, however, anyone chooses rather to embrace a contrary opinion, seeing that the town was situated in a plain, I do not oppose it. On this point Jerome thinks differently; nevertheless, what he elsewhere relates—that in his own times some vestiges of the palace of Melchizedek were still extant in the ancient ruins—appears to me improbable.

It now remains to be seen how Melchizedek bore the image of Christ and became, as it were, his representative. These are the words of David: "The LORD has sworn and will not change his mind: 'You are a priest forever, in the order of Melchizedek'" (Psalm 110:4).

First, God placed him on a royal throne, and then he gave him the honor of the priesthood. But under the law, these two offices were so distinct that it was unlawful for kings to usurp the office of the priesthood. We may concede as true what Plato declares and what occasionally occurs in the poets—namely, that by the common custom of nations the same person could be both king and priest. But this was by no means the case with David and his posterity, whom the law peremptorily forbade to intrude on the priestly office. But it was right that what was divinely appointed under the old law was abrogated in the person of this priest. And the apostle does not contend without reason that a more excellent priesthood than that old and shadowy one was here pointed out, a priesthood confirmed by an oath. Moreover, we never find that king and priest who is to be preeminent over all until we come to Christ. And as no one has arisen except Christ who equaled Melchizedek in dignity, still less who excelled him, we hence infer that the image of Christ was presented to the fathers in his person. David, indeed, does not propose a similitude conceived by him but declares the reason for which the kingdom of Christ was divinely ordained, and even confirmed with an oath; and it is not to be doubted that the same truth had previously been traditionally handed down by the fathers.

The sum of the whole is that Christ would thus be the king next to God, and also that he would be anointed priest, and that forever. It is useful for us to know this, in order that we may learn that the royal power of Christ is combined with the office of priest. The same Person, therefore, who was constituted the only and eternal Priest in order that he might reconcile us to God and who, having made expiation, might intercede for us, is also a King of infinite power to secure our salvation and to protect us by his guardian care. Hence it follows that, relying on his advocacy, we may stand boldly in the presence of God, who will, we are assured, be propitious to us; and that trusting in his invincible arm, we may securely triumph over enemies of every kind. They who separate one office from the other rend Christ asunder and subvert their own faith, which is deprived of half its support.

It is also to be observed that Christ is called an eternal King, like Melchizedek. Since the Scripture, by assigning no end to Melchizedek's life, leaves him as if he were to survive through all ages, it certainly represents or foreshadows to us, in his person, a figure not of a temporal but of an eternal kingdom. But whereas Christ, by his death, has accomplished the office of priest, it follows that God was, by that one sacrifice, once appeased in such a manner that now reconciliation is to be sought in Christ alone. Therefore, they do him grievous wrong and wrest from him by abominable sacrilege the honor divinely conferred upon him by an oath who either institute other sacrifices for the expiation of sins or who make other priests.

I wish this had been prudently weighed by the ancient writers of the church. For then would they not so coolly, and even so ignorantly, have transferred to the bread and wine the similitude between Christ and Melchizedek, which consists in things very different. They have supposed that Melchizedek is the image of Christ because he offered bread and wine. They add that Christ offered his body, which is life-giving bread, and his blood, which is spiritual drink. But the apostle, though in his Epistle to the Hebrews he most accurately collects and specifically cites every point of similarity between Christ and Melchizedek, says not a word concerning the bread and wine. If the subtleties of Tertullian and others like him were true, it would have been a culpable negligence not to bestow a single syllable upon the principal point while discussing the separate parts, which were of comparatively trivial importance. And seeing that the apostle disputes at such great length and with such minuteness concerning the priesthood, how gross an instance of forgetfulness would it have been not to touch upon that memorable sacrifice in which the whole force of the priesthood was comprehended? He proves the honor of Melchizedek from the benediction given and tithes received; how much better it would have suited this argument to have said that he offered not lambs or calves, but the life of the world (that is, the body and blood of Christ) in a figure. By these arguments the fictions of the ancients are abundantly refuted.

Furthermore, from the very words of Moses a sufficiently lucid refutation may be taken. For we do not there read that *anything* was offered to God; rather, in one continued discourse it is stated, **Then Melchizedek king of Salem brought out bread and wine. He was priest of God Most High, and he blessed Abram** (verses 18-19). Abram was both refreshed with the wine and honored with the benediction. Utterly ridiculous are the Papists, who distort the offering of bread and wine to the sacrifice of their mass. For in order to bring Melchizedek into agreement with themselves, it will be necessary for them to concede that bread and wine are offered in the mass. With what audacity do they declare that the body of Christ is offered in their sacrifices? Under what pretext, since the Son of God is called the only successor of Melchizedek, do they substitute innumerable successors for him? We see, then, how foolishly they not only deprave this passage but babble without the color of reason.

**19. And he blessed Abram.** Unless these two parts of the sentence—**He was priest of God Most High** and **he blessed Abram**—cohere, Moses here relates nothing uncommon. For men mutually bless each other; that is, they wish well to each other. But here the priest of God is described who, according to the right of his office, sanctifies one inferior and subject to himself. He would never have dared to bless Abram unless he had known that in this respect he excelled him. In this manner the Levitical priests were commanded to bless the people; and God promised that the blessing would be efficacious and ratified (see Numbers 6:23ff.). So Christ, when about to ascend up to heaven, having lifted up his hands, blessed the apostles as a minister of the grace of God (see Luke 24:51), and then was exhibited the truth of this figure. He thus testified that the office of blessing the church, which had been foreshadowed in Melchizedek, was assigned to him by his Father.

**"Blessed be Abram by God Most High, Creator of heaven and earth."** Melchizedek's purpose was to confirm and ratify the grace of the divine vocation to holy Abram, for he pointed out the honor with which God had peculiarly dignified him by separating him from all others and adopting him as his own son. And he called God, by whom Abram had been chosen, the **Creator of heaven and earth** to distinguish him from the fictitious idols of the Gentiles. Afterwards, indeed, God invested himself with other titles, that by some peculiar mark he might make himself more clearly known to men, who because of the vanity of their mind, when they simply hear of God as the Framer of heaven and earth, never cease to wander until at length they are lost in their own speculations. But because God was already known to Abram, and his faith was founded upon many miracles, Melchizedek deemed it sufficient to declare him by the title of **Creator**. He whom Abram worshiped is the true and only God. And although Melchizedek himself maintained the sincere worship of the true God, he yet called Abram **blessed** of God in respect to the eternal covenant—as if he would say that, by a kind of hereditary right, the grace of God resided in one family and nation, because Abram alone had been chosen out of the whole world. Then is added a special congratulation on the victory obtained—not such as is wont to pass between profane men; rather, Melchizedek gave thanks unto God and regarded the victory that the holy man had gained as a seal of his gratuitous calling.

**20. "And blessed be God Most High, who delivered your enemies into your hand." Then Abram gave him a tenth of everything.** There are those who understand that the tithes were given to Abram; but the apostle speaks otherwise in declaring that Levi paid tithes in the body of Abram (see Hebrews 7:9) when Abram offered tithes to a more excellent priest. And truly what the expositors above-mentioned mean would be most absurd because if Melchizedek was the priest of God, he should *receive* tithes rather than give them. Nor is it to be doubted but that Abram offered the gift to God, in the person of Melchizedek, in order that by such firstfruits he might dedicate all his possessions to God. Abram therefore voluntarily gave tithes to Melchizedek to do honor to his priesthood. Moreover, since it appears that this was not done wrongfully nor rashly, the apostle properly infers that in this figure the Levitical priesthood is subordinate to the priest-hood of Christ. For other reasons, God afterwards commanded tithes to be given to Levi under the law; but in the time of Abram they were only a holy offering, given as a pledge and proof of gratitude. It is, however, uncertain whether he offered the tithe of the spoils or of the goods that he possessed at home. But since it is improbable that he would have been liberal with other people's goods and give a tenth part of the prey, of which he had resolved not to touch even a thread, I rather conjecture that these tithes were taken out of his own property. I do not, however, admit that they were paid annu-ally, as some imagine; rather, in my judgment, he dedicated this present to Melchizedek once, for the purpose of acknowledging him as the high priest of God. Nor could he at that time (as we say) hand it over; but there was a solemn stipulation, of which the effect shortly after followed.

21. Moses, having interrupted the course of his narrative concerning **the king of Sodom** by the mention of the **king of Salem**, now returns to it again and says that **the king of Sodom** came to meet **Abram**, not only for the sake of congratulating him but to give him a due reward. He makes over to Abram the whole prey, except the men; as if he said, "It is a great thing that I recover the men; let all the rest be given to you as a reward for this benefit." Thus to have shown himself grateful to man would truly have been worthy of commendation had he not been ungrateful to God, by whose severity and clemency he remained alike unmoved. It was even pos-sible that this man, when poor and deprived of all his goods, might, with a servile affectation of modesty, try to gain the favor of Abram by asking to have nothing but the captives and the empty city for himself. Certainly we will afterwards see that the men of Sodom were unmindful of the benefit received, for they proudly and contemptuously vexed righteous Lot.

22. But Abram said to the king of Sodom, "I have raised my hand to the LORD, God Most High, Creator of heaven and earth, and have taken an oath." This ancient ceremony was very appropriate to give expression to the force and nature of an oath. By raising the hand toward heaven, we show that we appeal to God as a witness, and also as an avenger if we fail to keep our oath. It may seem strange that Abram should so eas-ily have put himself forward to swear, for he knew that a degree of rever-ence was due to the name of God, which should constrain us to use it but

sparingly and only from necessity. I answer, there were two reasons for his swearing. First, since inconstant men are wont to measure others by their own standard, they seldom place confidence in bare assertions. The king of Sodom, therefore, would have thought that Abram did not seriously remit his right unless the name of God had been interposed. And, second, it was of great consequence to make it manifest to all that Abram had not carried on a mercenary war. The histories of all times sufficiently declare that even they who have had just causes of war have nevertheless been invited to it by the thirst of private gain. And as men are acute in devising pretexts, they are never at a loss to find plausible reasons for war, even though covetousness may be their only real stimulant. Therefore, unless Abram had resolutely refused the spoils of war, the rumor would immediately have spread that under the pretense of rescuing his nephew he had been intent upon grasping the prey. It was necessary for him carefully to guard against this, not so much for his own sake as for the glory of God, which would otherwise have received some mark of disparagement. Besides, Abram wished to arm himself with the name of God, as with a shield, against all the allurements of avarice. For the king of Sodom would not have desisted from tempting his mind by various methods if the occasion for using bland insinuations had not been promptly cut off.

**23. ". . . that I will accept nothing belonging to you, not even a thread or the thong of a sandal, so that you will never be able to say, 'I made Abram rich.'"** The Hebrews have an elliptical form of making an oath, in which the imprecation of punishment is understood. In some places the full expression of this occurs in the Scriptures: "May God deal with me, be it ever so severely . . ." (1 Samuel 14:44). Since, however, it is a dreadful thing to fall into the hands of the living God, in order that the obligation of oaths may be the more binding, this abrupt form of speech admonishes men to reflect on what they are doing, as if they should put a restraint upon themselves and stop suddenly in the midst of their discourse. This indeed is most certain—that men never rashly swear but they provoke the vengeance of God against them and make him their adversary.

**". . . so that you will never be able to say, 'I made Abram rich.'"** Although these words seem to denote a mind elated and too much addicted to fame, yet since Abram is on this point commended by the Spirit, we conclude that this was a truly holy magnanimity. But an exception is added—namely, that he will not allow his own liberality to be injurious to his allies, nor make them subject to his laws. For it is not the least part of virtue to act rightly, yet in such a manner that we do not bind others to our example as to a rule. Let everyone therefore regard what his own vocation demands and what pertains to his own duty, in order that men may not prejudge one another according to their own will. It is a moroseness too imperious to wish that what we ourselves follow as right and consonant with our duty should be prescribed as a law to others.

# Genesis
# Chapter 15

1. **After this, the word of the LORD came to Abram in a vision: "Do not be afraid, Abram. I am your shield, your very great reward."** Since Abram's affairs were prosperous and were proceeding according to his wish, this vision might seem to be superfluous, especially since the Lord commanded his servant, as one sorrowful and afflicted with fear, to be of good courage. Therefore, certain writers conjecture that Abram, having returned after the deliverance of his nephew, was subjected to some annoyance of which no mention is made by Moses—just as the Lord often humbles his people lest they should exult in their prosperity. These writers further suppose that when Abram had been dejected, he was again revived by a new oracle. But since there is no warrant for such conjecture in the words of Moses, I think the cause was something different. First, although he was on all sides applauded, it is not to be doubted that various surmises entered into Abram's mind. For though Kedorlaomer and his allies had been overcome in battle, yet Abram had so provoked them that they might with fresh troops and with renewed strength again attack the land of Canaan. Nor were the inhabitants of the land free from the fear of this danger.

Second, signal success commonly draws its companion envy along with it, and thus Abram began to be exposed to many disadvantageous remarks after he had dared to enter into conflict with an army that had conquered four kings. An unfavorable suspicion might also arise that perhaps by and by he would turn the strength that he had tried against foreign kings upon his neighbors and upon those who had hospitably received him. Therefore, as the victory was an honor to him, so it cannot be doubted that it rendered him formidable and an object of suspicion to many, while it inflamed the hatred of others, since each man would imagine some danger to himself from Abram's bravery and good success. It is, therefore, not strange that he should have been troubled and should anxiously have considered many things until God animated him anew by the confident expectation of his assistance.

There might be also another end to be answered by the oracle—namely, that God would meet and correct a contrary fault in his servant. It was possible that Abram might be so elated with victory as to forget his own calling and to seek the acquisition of dominion for himself as one who, wearied with a wandering course of life and with perpetual vexations, desired a better fortune and a quiet state of existence. We know how liable men are to be ensnared by the allurements of prosperous and smiling fortune. God anticipated the danger and, before this vanity took possession of the mind of the holy man, recalled to his memory the spiritual grace vouchsafed to him to the end that he, entirely acquiescing therein, might despise all other things. Yet because the expression **"Do not be afraid"** sounds as if God would soothe his sorrowing and anxious servant with some consolation, it is probable that Abram had need of such confirmation because he perceived that many malignantly stormed against his victory and that his old age would be exposed to severe annoyances. It might, however, be that God did not forbid him to fear because he was already afraid, but that he might learn courageously to despise and to account as nothing all the favor of the world and all earthly wealth, as if God said, "If only I am propitious to you, there is no reason why you should fear. Content with me alone in the world, pursue, as you have begun, your pilgrimage; rather depend on heaven than attach yourself to earth." However this might be, God recalled his servant to himself, showing that far greater blessings were treasured up for him in God, in order that Abram might not rest satisfied with his victory.

Moses says that God spoke to him **in a vision**, by which he intimates that some visible symbol of God's glory was added to the word, in order that greater authority might be given to the oracle. This was one of two ordinary methods by which the Lord was formerly wont to manifest himself to his prophets, as stated in the book of Numbers (12:6).

**"Do not be afraid, Abram. I am your shield, your very great reward."** Although the promise comes last in the text, it has precedence in order, because on it depends the confirmation by which God freed the heart of Abram from fear. God exhorted Abram to be of a tranquil mind. But what foundation is there for such security unless by faith we understand that God cares for us and learn to rest in his providence? The promise, therefore, that God would be Abram's **shield** and his **very great reward** held the first place, to which was added the exhortation that, relying upon such a guardian of his safety and such an author of his felicity, he should not fear. Therefore, to make the sense of the words more clear, the causal particle is to be inserted. "Fear not, Abram, because I am your shield." Moreover, by the use of the word **shield**, God signified that Abram would always be safe under his protection. And in calling himself Abram's **reward**, God taught Abram to be satisfied with himself alone. As this was, with respect to Abram, a general instruction given for the purpose of showing him that victory was not the chief and ultimate good that God had designed him to pursue, so let us know that the same blessing is promised to us all in the person of this one man. For by this voice God daily speaks to his faithful ones; having undertaken to defend us, he will take care to preserve us in safety under his hand and to protect us by his power. Since God ascribes to himself the office and property of a **shield,** for the purpose of rendering himself the protector of our salvation, we ought to regard this promise as a solid wall, so that we will not be excessively fearful in any dangers. Since men, surrounded with various and innumerable desires of the flesh, are at times unstable and are then too much addicted to the love of the present life, the other part of the sentence follows, in which God declares that he alone is sufficient for the perfection of a happy life for the faithful.

The word **reward** has the force of *inheritance* or *felicity*. Were it deeply engraved on our minds that in God alone we have the highest and complete perfection of all good things, we would easily fix bounds to those wicked desires by which we are miserably tormented. The meaning then of the passage is that we will be truly happy when God is propitious to us; for he not only pours upon us the abundance of his kindness, but offers himself to us so we may enjoy him. What more can men desire when they really enjoy God? David knew the force of this promise when he boasted that he had obtained "a delightful inheritance" because the Lord was his inheritance (see Psalm 16:6). But since nothing is more difficult than to curb the depraved appetites of the flesh, and since the ingratitude of man is so vile and impious that God scarcely ever satisfies those appetites, the Lord calls himself not simply "a reward" but **"your very great reward,"** with which we ought to be more than sufficiently contented. This truly furnishes most abundant material, and most solid support, for confidence. For whoever will be fully persuaded that his life is protected by the hand of God, and that he never can be miserable while God is gracious to him, and who consequently resorts to this haven in all his cares and troubles, will find the best remedy for all evil—not because the faithful are entirely free from fear and care as long as they are tossed by the tempests of contentions and miseries, but because the storm is hushed in their own breast. Because the defense of God is greater than all dangers, faith triumphs over fear.

**2. But Abram said, "O Sovereign LORD, what can you give me since I remain childless and the one who will inherit my estate is Eliezer of Damascus?"** The Hebrew text has *Adonai Jehovah*, from which name it is inferred that some special mark of divine glory was stamped upon the vision; and so Abram, having no doubt respecting its author, confidently broke out in this expression. Since Satan is adept at deceiving and deluding men with so many wiles, even in the name of God, it was necessary that some sure and notable distinction should appear in true and heavenly oracles that would not suffer the faith and the minds of the holy fathers to waver. Therefore, in this vision the majesty of the God of Abram was manifested, which would suffice for the confirmation of his faith. Not that God appeared as he really is, but only so far as he might be comprehended by the human mind. But Abram, in overlooking a promise so glorious, in complaining that he was childless, and in murmuring against God for having hitherto given him no seed, seemed to conduct himself with little modesty. What was more desirable than to be received under God's protection and to be happy in the enjoyment of him? The objection, therefore, that Abram raised when disparaging the incomparable benefit offered to him and refusing to rest contented until he received offspring appeared to be lacking in reverence. Yet the freedom that he took may be excused. First, because the Lord permits us to pour into his heart those cares by which we are tormented and those troubles with which we are oppressed. Second, the design of the complaint is to be considered, for Abram did not simply declare that he was solitary, but, seeing that the effect of all the promises depended upon his seed, he, not improperly, required that a pledge should be given him. If the benediction and salvation of the world was not to be hoped for except through his seed, when that principal point seemed to fail him, it is not to be wondered at that other things should seem to vanish from his sight or should at least not appease his mind or satisfy his wishes. This is the very reason God not only regarded with favor the complaint of his servant but immediately gave a propitious answer to his prayer.

Moses ascribes to Abram that affection that is naturally inherent in us all; but this is no proof that Abram did not look higher when he so earnestly desired to be the progenitor of an heir. And certainly these promises had not faded from his recollection: "To your seed will I give this land" and "In your seed will all nations be blessed," the former of which promises is so annexed to all the rest that if it be taken away, all confidence in them would perish, while the latter promise contains in it the whole gratuitous pledge of salvation. Therefore, Abram rightly included in it everything that God had promised.

**"I remain childless."** The language in this verse is metaphorical. We know that our life is like a race. Abram, seeing he was of advanced age, said that he has proceeded so far that little of his course still remained. "Now," he said, "I am near the goal; and the course of my life being finished, I will die childless." He added, for the sake of aggravating the indignity, that a foreigner would be his heir: **"The one who will inherit my estate is Eliezer of Damascus."** I do not doubt that **Damascus** was the name of that man's *country*, and not the proper name of his *mother*, as some falsely suppose. "Not one of my own relatives will be my heir, but rather a Syrian from Damascus." Perhaps Abram had bought him in Mesopotamia.

**4-5.** We hence infer that God had approved of Abram's wish. Whence also follows the point that Abram had not been impelled by any carnal affection to offer up this prayer, but by a pious and holy desire of enjoying the benediction promised to him. For God not only promised him a seed but a great people who in number would equal the stars of heaven. They who expound the passage allegorically, implying that a heavenly seed was promised him that might be compared with the **stars**, may enjoy their own opinion, but we maintain what is more solid—namely, that the faith of Abram was increased by the sight of the stars. For the Lord, in order more deeply to affect his own people and more efficaciously to penetrate their minds, after he reached their ears by his word also arrested their eyes by external symbols, that eyes and ears might consent together. Therefore the sight of the stars was not superfluous. God intended to strike the mind of Abram with this thought: "He who by his word alone suddenly produced a host so numerous by which he might adorn the previously vast and desolate heaven—will not he be able to replenish my desolate house with offspring?" It is, however, not necessary to imagine a nocturnal vision because the stars, which during the day escape our sight, would then appear. Since the whole was transacted in a vision, Abram had a wonderful scene set before him that would manifestly reveal hidden things to him. Therefore, though he perhaps might not move a step, it was yet possible for him in vision to be led forth out of his tent.

The question now occurs concerning what **offspring** is being referred to. It is certain that neither the posterity of Ishmael nor of Esau is seen in this account because the legitimate seed is to be reckoned by the promise, which God determined should remain in Isaac and Jacob. Yet, the same doubt arises respecting the posterity of Jacob because many who could trace their descent from him according to the flesh cut themselves off, as degenerate sons and aliens, from the faith of their fathers. I answer that this term **offspring** is indiscriminately extended to the whole people whom God has adopted to himself. Since many were alienated by their unbelief, we must come for information to Christ, who alone distinguishes true and genuine sons from such as are illegitimate. By pursuing this method, we find the posterity of Abram reduced to a small number, that afterwards it may be the more increased. For in Christ the Gentiles also are gathered together and are by faith ingrafted into the body of Abram, so as to have a place among his legitimate sons.

**6. Abram believed the LORD, and he credited it to him as righteousness.** None of us would guess, if Paul had not shown it to us, how rich and profound a doctrine this verse contains. It is a strange thing, extraordinary, that when the Spirit of God kindles so bright a light, most interpreters grope around with closed eyes as if in the darkness of night.

Even those who have in Paul a most lucid interpreter corrupt this passage. Indeed, in all ages Satan seems to have fought more violently against free justification by faith than against any other teaching, striving to extinguish it and smother it.

**Abram believed the LORD, and he credited it to him as righteousness.** First, Moses commends the faith of Abram, by which he embraced the promise of God. Second, he adds a eulogy about that faith, saying that because of it Abraham acquired **righteousness** before God, and that by imputation. For the verb *hashab*, which Moses uses, stands in relation to God's judgment; so also it is used in Psalm 106:31, where we read that the zeal of Phineas was counted to him for righteousness.

We know there are criminals before God to whom iniquity is imputed. Exactly in the same way, God approves as righteous those to whom he imputes righteousness. Therefore, Abram was received into the number and rank of the righteous by an imputation of righteousness. In order to show distinctly the force and nature of this righteousness, Paul brings us before the heavenly tribunal of God.

Those who twist this passage and interpret it as a description of righteousness, as if it says that Abram was a righteous and upright man, are talking insipid nonsense. The meaning of the text is corrupted no less by those who say ignorantly that Abram attributed to God the glory of righteousness and therefore dared confidently to credit God's promises, knowing him to be faithful and true. Although Moses does not expressly name God in the second clause, the usual mode of speaking in Scripture leaves no ambiguity. Certainly it is no less stupid than presumptuous to give to the words **credited it to him as righteousness** any other meaning than that Abram's faith was accepted by God instead of righteousness.

Yet it seems absurd that Abram was justified because he believed his offspring would be as numerous as the stars of heaven, for believing in one such promise could not make the whole man righteous. Besides, what earthly and temporal promise could be valid ground for eternal salvation? I answer that the faith that Moses records here is not restricted to one point but includes the whole promise of God. The promise of seed to Abram was not limited to this verse; it is given also in others where a special blessing is added. Hence we conclude that Abram did not hope merely for descendants, but for offspring through which the world would be blessed.

If anyone stubbornly insists that what was said of the children of Abram in general is distorted when applied to Christ, in the first place it cannot be denied that God's earlier promise to his servant was now repeated in answer to Abram's complaint. But we have said before, and the account as a whole plainly shows, that it was his knowledge of the promised blessing that led Abram to desire seed so greatly. Hence it follows that the promise in this passage cannot be taken by itself, separated from the other promises. To conclude the whole matter, I say that if we are to judge the faith of Abram properly, we must consider all that is involved in the accounts concerning Abram.

God does not promise to give this or that good thing to his servant in the way that he scatters benefits upon unbelievers who have no taste of his fatherly love. He assures Abram that he himself will be gracious to him, and he promises him the enjoyment of his own protection and grace and the confidence of salvation. A man whose heritage is God does not rejoice in flimsy pleasures; rather, as though already raised to heaven, he delights in the solid joy of eternal life. Certainly it must be held as self-evident that all God's promises, which are destined for the faithful, flow from God's gracious mercy and are proofs of his fatherly love and free adoption on which their safety is founded. Therefore we say that Abram was justified not because he snatched at one little word about producing offspring but because he embraced God the Father. Truly, faith justifies us for no other reason than that it reconciles us to God, and this not by its own merit, but only because as we receive the grace offered to us in the promises and are certainly persuaded that we are loved by God as children, we also come to possess the assurance of life eternal.

Therefore Paul argues further that he to whom faith is reckoned for righteousness is not justified by works. For the merits of all who seek justification by works are measured by God, before whom they are worthy of condemnation. We understand the meaning of justification by faith when we know that God reconciles us to himself freely. Hence it follows that concern with the merit of works ends when justification is sought through faith. For if anyone is to possess righteousness by faith, it must necessarily be given by God and proffered to us by his Word.

To make this more clearly understood, when Moses says that faith was **credited . . . to him [Abraham] as righteousness**, this does not mean faith was the first cause (what is called the efficient cause) of righteousness; it was only the formal cause. The words of Moses mean: "Abram was justified because, relying on the fatherly kindness of God, he had confidence in God's goodness alone, and not in himself and his merits." We need especially to understand that faith obtains from elsewhere a righteousness that we do not possess. Otherwise Paul would not put faith in opposition to works as a way of obtaining righteousness. And the mutual relation between free promise and faith leaves no room for doubt.

The sequence of time must now be noted. Abram was justified by faith many years after he had been called by God, after he had left his native land and had become a voluntary exile, after he had been a conspicuous mirror of endurance and self-control, after he had devoted himself wholly to holiness, after he had disciplined himself in the spiritual and the external worship of God and had led an almost angelic life. So it follows that even at the end of life we are brought into God's eternal kingdom by justification by faith.

At this point many are grossly deceived. They admit indeed that the righteousness that is given freely to sinners and offered to the undeserving is received by faith alone. But they limit this justification by faith to a moment of time, so that a man, having obtained righteousness by faith, is afterwards made righteous by good works. Faith is merely the beginning of righteousness, they think, but as life continues, righteousness consists in works. Those who so interpret the teaching must be insane. For if the angelic integrity of Abram, exercised faithfully and consistently for so many years, did not prevent the necessity of fleeing to faith to find righteousness, where in the world will be found a perfection that can meet God's scrutiny? Therefore, we conclude from the time sequence that justification by works is not to be substituted for justification by faith, as if the latter began and the former completed justification; rather, the saints, so long as they live in the world, are justified by faith. If anyone objects that Abram had formerly believed God when he followed his call and committed himself to his instruction and guardianship, the answer is easy. No statement is made as to when Abram first began to be justified by believing God; but this one passage does show in what way he was justified in his whole life. If Moses had spoken thus about Abram's first calling, the objection I have just mentioned (that initial righteousness, but not perpetual, is of faith) would have more support. But when Abram is said to become righteous by faith after having gone through so much, it easily appears that the saints are justified by grace until they die.

I agree that the mode of the justification of those who believe and are born again by God's Spirit differs somewhat from Abraham's justification. For those born of the flesh only, God reconciles to himself while they are empty of all good. When he finds in them nothing except a filthy heap of dreadful evils, he holds them righteous by imputation. But those to whom he has given the Spirit of holiness and righteousness, he clothes with his gifts. But even then, if their good works please God, this must be by his gracious imputation, because something of sin always remains in them.

This truth holds: Men are justified by believing, not by what they do. It is by faith that they receive grace; and grace cannot be earned as a payment for works. Since Abram, with all his preeminence in virtue, after a long life of exceptional service of God was yet justified by faith, the righteousness of each perfected man consists in faith alone. It is important to say plainly that what is here told of one man must be applied to all men. For Abram was called "father of the faithful" with good reason, and there are not diverse ways of seeking salvation. Paul rightly teaches that what is here described is not the righteousness of an individual man, but true righteousness as such.

**7.** Since it greatly concerns us to have God as our guide for our whole life, so that we may know we have not rashly entered on some doubtful way, the Lord confirmed Abram in the course of his vocation and recalled to his memory the original benefit of his deliverance. It is as if he said, "I, after I had stretched out my hand to you to lead you forth from the labyrinth of death, have carried my favor toward you thus far. You, therefore, ought to respond to me in turn by constantly advancing and steadfastly maintaining your faith, from the beginning even to the end." This indeed is said not with respect to Abram alone, in order that he, gathering together the promises of God made to him from the very commencement of his life of faith, should form them into one whole, but that all the pious may learn to regard the beginning of their vocation as flowing perpetually from Abram, their common father, and may thus securely boast with Paul that they know in whom they have believed (see 2 Timothy 1:12), and also so that God, who in the person of Abram had separated a church for himself, would be seen to be a faithful keeper of the salvation deposited with him. For this very end, the Lord declared himself to have been the deliverer of Abram, as seen hence: He connected the promise that he was about to give with the prior redemption. It is as if he said, "I do not now begin to promise you this land. For I brought you out of your own country to constitute you the heir of this land. Now, therefore, I covenant with you in the same form, lest you should deem yourself to have been deceived or fed with empty words; and I command you to be mindful of the first covenant, that the new promise, which after many years I now repeat, may be the more firmly supported."

**8.** It may appear absurd, first, that Abram, who before had placed confidence in the simple word of God without asking any question about the promises given to him, should now dispute whether what he heard from the mouth of God was true or not. And, second, that he ascribed but little honor to God, not merely by murmuring against him when he spoke, but by requiring some additional pledge to be given to him. Further, whence arises the knowledge that belongs to faith except from God's word? Therefore, Abram in vain desired to be assured of the future possession of the land while he ceased to depend upon the word of God.

I answer: The Lord sometimes concedes to his children, that they may freely express any objection that comes into their mind. For he does not act so strictly with them as not to suffer himself to be questioned. Indeed, the more certainly Abram was persuaded that God was true, and the more he was attached to his word, so much the more familiarly did he unburden his cares into God's heart. To this may be added that the prolonged delay was no small obstacle to Abram's faith. For after God had held him in suspense through a great part of his life, now when he was worn-out with age and had nothing to look forward to but death and the grave, God anew declared that Abram would be lord of the land. Abram did not reject, on account of its difficulty, what might have appeared to him incredible, but brought before God the anxiety by which he was inwardly oppressed. And therefore his questioning with God was rather a proof of faith than a sign of incredulity.

The wicked, because their minds are entangled with various conflicting thoughts, do not in any way receive the promises. But the pious, who feel the impediments in their flesh, endeavor to remove them, lest they should obstruct the way to God's word; and they seek a remedy for those evils of which they are conscious. It is, nevertheless, to be observed that there were some special impulses in the saints of old that it would not now be right to use as a precedent. Though Hezekiah and Gideon required certain miracles, this does not mean we should use such methods today; let it suffice us to seek for such confirmation only as the Lord himself according to his own pleasure will judge most appropriate.

**9.** The true purpose of sacrifice had so far been hidden from Abram. Therefore, by obeying God's command, of which no advantage was apparent, he proved the obedience of his faith; nor did his wish aim at any other end than reverently acquiescing in the word of the Lord. Let us, therefore, learn meekly to embrace those helps that God offers for the confirmation of our faith, although they may not accord with our judgment but rather may seem to be foolishness, until at length it becomes plain that God is in no way mocking us.

**10.** That no part of this sacrifice may be without mystery, certain interpreters weary themselves in the fabrication of subtleties; but it is our business, as I have often declared, to cultivate seriousness about the things of God. I confess I do not know why Abram was commanded to take **a heifer, a goat and a ram, each three years old, along with a dove and a young pigeon** (verse 9), unless this variety declared that all the posterity of Abram, of whatever rank, would be able to offer a sacrifice, so that the whole people, and each individual, would constitute one sacrifice. There are also other things here concerning which I will not be ashamed to acknowledge my ignorance, because I do not choose to wander in uncertain speculations.

This, in my opinion, is the sum of the whole: God, in commanding the animals to be killed, showed what would be the future condition of the church. Abram certainly wished to be assured of the promised inheritance of the land. Now he was taught that it would take its commencement from death; that is, he and his children would die before they would enjoy dominion over the land. In obeying the command to **cut in two** the slaughtered animals, it is probable that Abram followed the ancient rite in forming covenants, whether they were entering into an alliance or were mustering an army, a practice that also passed over to the Gentiles. The allies or soldiers passed between the severed parts, that, being enclosed together within the sacrifice, they might be the more sacredly united in one body. Jeremiah bears witness that this method was practiced by the Jews (Jeremiah 34:18-19), where he introduces God as saying, "The men who have violated my covenant and have not fulfilled the terms of the covenant they made before me, I will treat like the calf they cut in two and then walked between its pieces. The leaders of Judah and Jerusalem, the court officials, the priests and all the people of the land who walked between the pieces of the calf . . ." Nevertheless, there appears to me to have been this special reason for the act referred to: The Lord would admonish the race of Abram not only that it should be like a dead carcass, but even like one torn and dissected. For the servitude with which they were oppressed for a time was more intolerable than simple death. Yet because the sacrifice is offered to God, death itself is immediately turned into new life. This is the reason why Abram, placing the parts of the sacrifice opposite each other, fit them one to the other, because the people were again to be gathered together from their dispersion. But how difficult is the restoration of the church and what troubles are involved in it is shown by the horror with which Abram was seized. We see, therefore, that two things were illustrated—namely, the hard servitude with which the sons of Abram were to be pressed almost to destruction, and their redemption, which was to be the signal pledge of divine adoption. In the same mirror the general condition of the church is represented to us, for it is the peculiar province of God to create it out of nothing and to raise it from death.

**11.** Although the sacrifice was dedicated to God, yet it was not free from being attacked by birds. Neither are the faithful, after they are received into the protection of God, so covered with his hand as not to be assailed on every side; Satan and the world cease not to cause them trouble. Therefore, in order that the sacrifice we have once offered to God may not be violated but may remain pure and uninjured, contrary assaults must be repulsed with whatever inconvenience and toil.

**12-13.** The vision is now mingled with a dream. The Lord here joins those two kinds of communication together. **A thick and dreadful darkness** intervened, that Abram might know that the dream was not a common one but was divinely conducted; it nevertheless had a correspondence with the oracle then present, as God immediately afterward explained in his own words: **"Know for certain that your descendants will be strangers in a country not their own, and they will be enslaved and mistreated four hundred years."** God did not want to dazzle the eyes of his people with bare and empty specters; in visions, the principal parts always belonged to the word of God. Thus here not a mute apparition was presented to the eyes of Abram, but he was taught by an oracle what the external and visible symbol meant. It is, however, to be observed that before one son was given to Abram, he heard that his seed would be in captivity and slavery for a long time. Thus does the Lord deal with his own people; he always makes a beginning from death, so that by quickening the dead, he the more abundantly manifests his power. It was necessary, in part, on Abram's account that this should have been declared; but the Lord chiefly had regard to Abram's posterity, lest they should faint in their sufferings, of which, however, the Lord had promised a joyful and happy issue, especially since their long continuance would produce great weariness.

Three things are here, step by step, brought before them. First, it would be 400 years before the sons of Abram would attain the promised inheritance; second, they would be slaves; third, they would be inhumanly and tyrannically treated. The faith of Abram was admirable and singular, seeing that he acquiesced in an oracle so sorrowful and felt assured that God would be his deliverer after his miseries had proceeded to their greatest depth.

14. A consolation was now added, in which the first thing was: God would be the vindicator of his people. Whence it follows that he would take upon himself the care of the salvation of those he had embraced, and he would not suffer them to be harassed by the ungodly and the wicked with impunity. Although God here expressly announces that he would take vengeance on the Egyptians, all the enemies of the church are exposed to the same judgment, even as Moses in his song extended to all ages and nations the threat that the Lord will exact punishment for unjust persecutions. "It is mine to avenge; I will repay" (Deuteronomy 32:35).

Therefore, whenever we happen to be treated with inhumanity by tyrants (which is very usual with the church), let it be our consolation that after our faith will be sufficiently proved by bearing the cross, God, at whose pleasure we are thus humbled, will himself be the Judge who will repay to our enemies the due reward of the cruelty they now exercise. Although they now exult with intoxicated joy, it will at length appear by the event itself that our miseries are happy ones, but their triumphs wretched, because God, who cares for us, is their adversary. But let us remember that we must give place to the wrath of God, as Paul exhorts, in order that we may not be hurried headlong to seek revenge. Place also must be given to hope, that it may sustain us when oppressed and groaning under the burden of evils. To **punish** the nation means the same thing as to summon it to judgment, in order that God, when he has long reposed in silence, may openly manifest himself as the Judge.

15. Hitherto the Lord had respect to the posterity of Abram as well as to himself, that the consolation might be common to all; but now he turned his address to Abram alone because the patriarch needed special reassurance. The remedy proposed for alleviating his sorrow was that he would die in peace after he had attained the utmost limit of old age. The explanation given by some that he would die a natural death, exempt from violence, or an easy death, in which his vital spirits would spontaneously

and naturally fail, and his life itself would fall by its own maturity without any sense of pain, is in my opinion insipid. Moses wishes to express that Abram would have not only a long but a placid old age, with a corresponding joyful and peaceful death. The sense, therefore, is that although through his whole life Abram was to be deprived of the possession of the land, yet he would not be wanting in the essential materials of quietness and joy, so that having happily finished his life, he would cheerfully depart to his fathers. Certainly death makes the great distinction between the reprobate and the sons of God, though their condition in the present life is commonly one and the same, except that the sons of God have by far the worst of it. Wherefore peace in death ought justly to be regarded as a singular benefit, a proof of that distinction to which I have just alluded.

Even profane writers, feeling their way in the dark, have perceived this. Plato, in his book *The Republic*, cites a song of Pindar that says those who live justly are attended by a sweet hope, cherishing their hearts and nourishing their old age, which hope chiefly governs the fickle minds of men. Because men, conscious of guilt, must necessarily be miserably harassed by various torments, the poet, when he asserts that hope is the reward of a good conscience, calls it the nurse of old age. As young men, far removed from death, carelessly take their pleasure, the old are admonished by their own weakness seriously to reflect that they must depart. Unless the hope of a better life inspires them, nothing remains for them but miserable fears. Finally, as the reprobate indulge themselves during their whole life and stupidly sleep in their vices, it is necessary that their death should be full of trouble, while the faithful commit their souls into the hand of God without fear and sadness. Whence also Balaam was constrained to say, "Let me die the death of the righteous" (Numbers 23:10).

Moreover, since men have not the power to achieve such a desirable way of ending their lives, the Lord, in promising a placid and quiet death to his servant Abram, teaches us that it is his own gift. We see that even kings and others who deem themselves happy in this world are yet agitated in death because they are visited with secret compunctions for their sins and look for nothing in death but destruction. But Abram willingly and joyfully went forward to his death, seeing that he had in Isaac a certain pledge of the divine benediction and knew that a better life was laid up for him in heaven.

**16.** The reason here given is deemed absurd by some, for this verse seems to imply that the sons of Abram could not be saved except by the destruction of others. I answer that we must with modesty and humility yield to the secret counsel of God. Since he had given that land to **the Amorites** to be inhabited by them in perpetuity, he intimated that he would not, without just cause, transfer the possession of it to others. It is as if he said, "I grant the dominion of this land to your seed. The land at present is occupied by its lawful possessors, to whom I delivered it. Until, therefore, they deserve, by their sins, to be rightfully expelled, the dominion of it will not come to your posterity." Thus God taught Abram that the land had to be evacuated in order that it might lie open to new inhabitants. This passage is remarkable, showing that the abodes of men are so distributed in the world that though the Lord preserves people, each in their own stations, they will cast themselves out by their own wickedness. For by polluting the place of their habitation, they in a certain sense tear away the boundaries fixed by the hand of God that would otherwise have remained immovable.

Moreover, the Lord here commends his own long-suffering. Even then the Amorites had become unworthy to occupy the land; yet the Lord not only bore with them for a short time but granted them four centuries for repentance. Hence it appears that he does not without reason so frequently declare how slow he is to anger. But the more graciously he waits for men, if at length instead of repenting they remain obstinate, the more severely does he avenge such great ingratitude. Therefore, Paul says that those who indulge in sin while the goodness and clemency of God invite them to repentance heap up for themselves a treasure of wrath (see Romans 2:4). And in this way they reap no advantage from delay, seeing that the severity of the punishment is doubled, just as it happened to the Amorites, whom at length the Lord commanded to be so entirely cut off that not even infants were spared. Therefore, when we hear that God from heaven is silently waiting until iniquities reach their **full measure**, let us know that this is no time for torpor, but rather let each one of us stir himself up, that we may be prepared beforehand for the heavenly judgment. It has been said even by a heathen that God's anger proceeds with a slow step to avenge itself, but that it compensates for its tardiness by the severity of its punishment. Hence there is no reason why reprobates should flatter themselves when he seems to let them pass unobserved, since he does not so repose in heaven as to cease to be the Judge of the world; nor will he be unmindful of the execution of his office in due time. We infer, however, from Moses' words that though time for repentance is given to reprobates, they are still devoted to destruction.

**17.** Again a new vision was added, to confirm Abram's faith in God's oracle. At first he was horror-struck with the thick **darkness** (verse 12); now he saw **a smoking firepot with a blazing torch**. Many suppose that a sacrifice was consumed with this fire; but I rather interpret it as a symbol of future deliverance, which would well agree with the fact itself. For there are two contrasting things here—the obscurity of smoke and the shining of a lamp. Hence Abram knew that light would at length emerge out of darkness. An analogy is always to be sought between signs and the things signified, that there may be a mutual correspondence between them. Since the symbol in itself is but a lifeless carcass, reference ought always to be made to the word that is linked to it. Here by the word liberty was promised to Abram's seed in the middle of servitude. The condition of the church could not be more accurately painted than when God caused **a blazing torch** to proceed out of the smoke, in order that the darkness of afflictions may not overwhelm us, but that we may cherish a good hope of life even in death—because the Lord will at length shine upon us if only we offer up ourselves in sacrifice to him.

**18.** I willingly admit that the covenant was ratified by a solemn rite when the animals were divided into parts. For there seems to be a repetition in which Moses teaches what was the intent of the sacrifice that he has mentioned. Here also we may observe that the word is always accompanied with symbols, lest our eyes be fed with empty and fruitless ceremonies. God commanded animals to be offered to him; but he showed their end and use by a **covenant** appended to them. If, then, the Lord feeds us by sacraments, we infer that they are the evidences of his grace and the tokens of those spiritual blessings that flow from his grace.

God then enumerated the nations (verses 19-21) whose land he was about to give to the sons of Abram, in order that he might confirm what he before said concerning a numerous offspring. This was not to be a small band of men but an immense multitude, for which the Lord assigned a habitation of vast extent. God had before spoken only of the Amorites, among whom Abram then dwelt; but now, for the sake of amplifying his grace, he recounted all the others by name.

# Genesis
# Chapter 16

**1. Now Sarai, Abram's wife, had borne him no children. But she had an Egyptian maidservant named Hagar.** Moses here states that Sarai, through the impatience of long delay, resorted to a method of obtaining a child by her husband that was at variance with the word of God. She saw that she was barren and had passed the age of bearing children, and she inferred the necessity of a new remedy in order that Abram might obtain the promised blessing. Moses expressly relates that the idea of marrying a second wife did not originate with Abram himself but with Sarai, to teach us that the holy man was not impelled by lust, but that when he was thinking of no such thing, he was induced to act by the exhortation of his wife.

It is, however, asked, whether Sarai substituted her handmaid in her place through the mere desire of having offspring. So it seems to some; yet to me it is incredible that the pious matron should not have known about those promises that had been so often repeated to her husband. It ought to be fully taken for granted among all pious people that the mother of the people of God was a participator of the same grace with her husband. Sarai, therefore, did not desire offspring (as is usual) from a merely natural impulse but yielded her conjugal rights to another through a wish to obtain the benediction that she knew was divinely promised. She did not divorce her husband but assigned him another wife, from whom he might receive children. Certainly if she had desired offspring in the ordinary manner, it would have come into her mind to do it by the adoption of a son rather than giving way to a second wife, for we know the vehemence of female jealousy. Therefore, while contemplating the promise, she forgot her own right and thought of nothing but the bringing forth of children to Abram.

Sarai remains a memorable example from which no small profit accrues to us. For however laudable was Sarai's wish in regard to its end, nevertheless, in the pursuit of it she was guilty of no light sin, impatiently departing from the word of God for the purpose of enjoying the effect of that word. She rejected her own barrenness and old age and began to despair of offspring unless Abram should have children from some other quarter; in this there was already some fault. Yet, however desperate the affair might have been, still she ought not to have attempted anything at variance with the will of God and the legitimate order of nature. God designed that the human race should be propagated by sacred marriage. Sarai perverted the law of marriage by defiling the conjugal bed, which was appointed only for two people. Nor is her action justified by the excuse that she wished Abram to have a concubine and not a wife, since it ought to be regarded as a settled point that the woman is joined to the man, "that they two should be one flesh." And though polygamy had already prevailed among many, yet it was never left to the will of man to abrogate that divine law by which two people are mutually bound together. Nor was even Abram free from fault in following the foolish and preposterous counsel of his wife. Therefore, as the precipitancy of Sarai was culpable, so the facility with which Abram yielded to her wish was worthy of reprehension. The faith of both of them was defective—not indeed with regard to the substance of the promise, but with regard to the method in which they proceeded since they hastened to acquire the offspring that was to be expected from God without observing the legitimate ordinance of God.

From this we learn that God does not in vain command his people to be quiet and to wait with patience whenever he defers or suspends the accomplishment of their wishes. For they who hasten before the time not only anticipate the providence of God but, being discontented with his word, precipitate themselves beyond their proper bounds. But it seems that Sarai had something further in view, for she not only wished that Abram should become a father but wanted to acquire for herself maternal rights and honors. I answer: Since she knew that all nations were to be blessed in the seed of Abram, it is no wonder that she would be unwilling to be deprived of participation in his honor, lest she should be cut off as a putrid member from the body that had received the blessing and would also become an alien from the promised salvation.

**Had borne him no children.** This seems added as an excuse. Truly Moses intimates that she did not seek help from the womb of her maid before necessity compelled her to do so. Her own words also show that she had patiently and modestly waited to see what God would do until hope was entirely cut off, for she said she was restrained from childbearing by the Lord (see verse 2). What fault then will we find in her? Surely that she did not, as she should have, cast her care on God without binding his power to the order of nature or limiting it to her own understanding. And further, by neglecting to infer from the past what would take place in the future, she did not regard herself as in the hand of God, who could open the womb he had closed.

**2. So she said to Abram, "The LORD has kept me from having children.**

Go, sleep with my maidservant; perhaps I can build a family through her." The Hebrew phrase **build a family** signifies "to become a mother." Sarai claimed for herself by right of dominion the child that Hagar would bring forth, because maidservants do not bear children for themselves since they have no power over their own bodies. Sarai's desire proceeded from the zeal of faith; but because it was not so subjected to God as to wait for his time, she immediately had recourse to polygamy, which is nothing else than the corruption of lawful marriage. Moreover, since Sarai, that holy woman, fanned in her husband the same flame of impatience with which she burned, we learn how diligently we ought to be on our guard lest Satan should surprise us by any secret fraud. For not only does he induce wicked and ungodly men openly to oppose our faith, but sometimes, privately and by stealth, he assails us through the medium of good and simple men, that he may overcome us unawares. On every side, therefore, we must be on our guard against his wiles, lest by any means he should undermine us.

**Abram agreed to what Sarai said.** Truly Abram's faith wavered when he deviated from the word of God and allowed himself to be persuaded by his wife to seek a remedy that was divinely prohibited. He, however, retained the foundation because he did not doubt that he would at length perceive that God is true. By which example we are taught that there is no reason why we should become discouraged if at any time Satan should shake our faith, provided that the truth of God be not overthrown in our hearts. Meanwhile, when we see Abram, who through so many years had bravely contended like an invincible combatant and had surmounted so many obstacles, now yielding, in a single moment, to temptation, who among us will not fear for himself in similar danger? Therefore, although we may have stood long and firmly in the faith, we must daily pray that God would not lead us into temptation.

**3.** Moses states what was the design of Sarai, for neither did she intend to make her house a brothel, nor to betray the maid's chastity, nor to pander to her husband. Yet **Hagar** is improperly called a **wife**, because she was brought into another person's bed against the law of God. Wherefore, let us know that this connection was so far illicit as to be something between fornication and marriage. The same thing takes place with all those inventions that are appended to the word of God. For with whatever fair pretext they may be covered, there is an inherent corruption that degenerates from the purity of the word and vitiates the whole.

**4.** Here Moses relates that punishment for precipitancy quickly followed. The chief blame, indeed, rested with Sarai; yet because Abram had proved himself too credulous, God chastised both as they deserved. Sarai was grievously and bitterly tried by the proud contempt of her maidservant; Abram was harassed by unjust complaints. Thus we see that both paid the penalty for their levity, and that the contrivance devised by Sarai, and too eagerly embraced by Abram, was a failure. Meanwhile, in Hagar an instance of ingratitude is set before us because she, having been treated with singular kindness and honor, began to hold her mistress in contempt. Since, however, this is an exceedingly common disease of the mind, let the faithful accustom themselves to the endurance of it if at any time a return so unjust be made to them for their acts of kindness. But especially let the infirmity of Sarai move us thus to so endure since she was unable to bear the contempt of her maid.

**5.** It was also a part of Sarai's punishment that she was brought so low as to forget herself for a while and, being greatly upset, behaved with so much weakness. Certainly to the utmost of her power she had impelled her husband to act rashly; but now she petulantly insulted him, though she adduced nothing for which Abram was to be blamed. She reproached him with the fact that she had given her maid to him and complained that she was condemned by the maid without first ascertaining whether he intended to assist the bad cause or not. Blind is the assault of anger; it rushes impetuously hither and thither and condemns, without inquiry, those who may be entirely free from blame. If ever any woman had a meek and gentle spirit, Sarai excelled in that virtue. Seeing that her patience was violently shaken by a single offense, let each one of us so much the more resolve to govern his own passions.

**"May the LORD judge between you and me."** She made improper use of the name of God and almost forgot the due reverence that is so much a part of those who are godly. She made her appeal to the judgment of God. What else is this than calling down destruction on her own head? For if God had interposed as judge, he of necessity would have executed punishment upon one or the other of them. She must have felt the vengeance of God, whose anger she had so rashly brought upon herself. Had Moses spoken this of any heathen woman, it might have been passed over as a common thing. But now the Lord shows us, in the person of the mother of the faithful, first, how vehement is the flame of anger and to what lengths it will hurry men, then how greatly they are blinded who in their own affairs are too self-indulgent. From this we should learn to suspect ourselves whenever our own concerns are served.

Another thing must be noted here—namely, that the best ordered families are sometimes not free from contentions. Indeed, this evil reaches even to the church of God, for we know that the family of Abram, which was disturbed with strife, was the living representation of the church. As to domestic arguments, we know that the principal part of social life, which God hallowed among men, is spent in marriage; and yet various inconveniences intervene that defile that good state. The faithful must prepare themselves to cut off these occasions of trouble. For this end, it is of great importance to reflect on the origin of the evil; for all the troubles men find in marriage, they ought to impute to sin.

**6.** The greatness of Abram's humanity and modesty appears from his answer. He did not quarrel with his wife; and though he had the best cause, yet he did not pertinaciously defend it but voluntarily dismissed the wife who had been given to him. In short, for the sake of restoring peace, he did violence to his feelings, both as a husband and as a father. For in leaving Hagar to the will of her enraged mistress, he did not treat her as his wife; he also, in a certain way, undervalued that object of his hope that was conceived in her womb. It is not to be doubted that he was thus placid in bearing the vehemence of his wife because throughout her whole life he had found her to be obedient. Still it was a great excellence to restrain his temper under an indignity so great.

It may, however, be asked how it was that his care for the blessed seed had vanished from his mind. Hagar was pregnant; he hoped that the seed through which the salvation of the world was promised was about to proceed from her. Why, then, did he not set Sarai aside and turn his love and desire still more to Hagar? Truly we hence infer that all human contrivances pass away and vanish in smoke as soon as any grievous temptation is presented. Having taken a wife against the divine command, he thought the matter was succeeding well when he saw her pregnant and pleased himself in foolish confidence. But when contention suddenly arose, he was at his wit's end and rejected all hope, or at least forgot it. The same thing will necessarily happen to us as often as we attempt anything contrary to the word of God. Our minds will fail at the very first blast of temptation since our only ground of stability is to have the authority of God for what we do. In the meantime, God purified the faith of his servant from its rust. For by mixing his own and his wife's imagination with the word of God, Abram in a sense had stifled his faith; wherefore, to restore its brightness, that which was superfluous was cut off. God, by opposing himself in this manner to our sinful designs, recalls us from our stupidity to a sound mind.

**Then Sarai mistreated Hagar.** The word *anah*, **mistreated**, which Moses uses, signifies "to afflict" and "to humble." This reduced Hagar to submission. But it was difficult for an angry woman to keep within bounds in repressing the insolence of her maid. Wherefore, it is possible that Sarai became immoderately enraged against her, not so much considering her own duty as seeing the means of being avenged for the offenses committed. Since Moses brings no heavier charge, I confine myself to what is certain—that Sarai made use of her proper authority in restraining the insolence of her maid. And, doubtless, from the event we may conclude that Hagar was impelled to flee not so much by the cruelty of her mistress as by her own contempt for Sarai. Her own conscience accused her. Further, it is improbable that Sarai should have been so greatly incensed except by many and indeed atrocious offenses. Therefore, Hagar, being of servile temper and indomitable ferocity, chose rather to flee than to return to favor through the humble acknowledgment of her fault.

7. We are here taught with what clemency the Lord acts toward his

own people, although they deserve severe punishment. As he had previously mitigated the punishment of Abram and Sarai, so now he cast a paternal look upon Hagar, so that his favor was extended to the whole family. He did not indeed altogether spare them, lest he should cherish their vices; but he corrected them with gentle remedies. It is indeed probable that Hagar, in going to the desert of Sur, meditated a return to her own country. Yet mention seems to be made of the desert and the wilderness to show that she, being miserably afflicted, wandered from the presence of men until the angel met her. Although Moses does not describe the form of the vision, I do not doubt that this being was clothed in a human body, in which, nevertheless, manifest tokens of heavenly glory were conspicuous.

**8.** By the use of the epithet **Hagar, servant of Sarai**, the angel declares that Hagar still remained a **servant**, though she had escaped the hands of her mistress; for liberty is not to be obtained by stealth, nor by flight, but by being set free from slavery. Moreover, by this expression God shows that he approves of civil government and that the violation of it is inexcusable. The condition of servitude was then hard, and thanks are to be given to the Lord that this barbarity has been abolished; yet God has declared from heaven his pleasure that servants should bear the yoke, as stated also by the mouth of Paul, who does not give servants their freedom, nor deprive their masters of their use, but only commands them to be kindly and liberally treated (see Ephesians 6:5).

It is to be inferred also, from the circumstance of the time, not only that civil government is to be maintained as a matter of necessity, but that lawful authorities are to be obeyed for conscience's sake. Although the fugitive Hagar could no longer be compelled to obedience by force, yet her condition was not changed in the sight of God. By the same argument it is proved that if masters at any time deal too harshly with their servants or if rulers treat their subjects with unjust severity, their austerity is still to be endured, nor is there just cause for shaking off the yoke, although they exercise their power too imperiously. In short, whenever it comes into our mind to defraud anyone of his right or to seek exemption from our proper calling, let the voice of the angel sound in our ears, as if God would draw us back by putting his own hand upon us. Those who have proudly and tyrannically governed will one day render their account to God; meanwhile, their harshness is to be borne by their subjects until God, whose prerogative it is to raise the abject and to relieve the oppressed, will give them succor. If a comparison is made, the power of magistrates is far more tolerable than that ancient dominion was. The paternal authority is in its very nature amiable and worthy of regard. If the flight of Hagar was prohibited by the command of God, much less will he bear with the licentiousness of a people who rebel against their prince or with the stubbornness of children who withdraw themselves from obedience to their parents.

**"Where have you come from, and where are you going?"** The angel did not inquire, as concerning a doubtful matter; rather, knowing that no place for subterfuge was left to Hagar, he peremptorily reproved her for her flight, as if he said, "Having deserted your station, you will profit nothing by your wandering, since you cannot escape the hand of God that placed you there." It might also be that he censured her departure from the house that was then the earthly sanctuary of God. For she was not ignorant that God was worshiped there in a peculiar manner. And although she indirectly charged her mistress with cruelty by saying, **"I'm running away from my mistress Sarai,"** still the angel, to cut off all subterfuges, commanded her to return and to humble herself (verse 9).

**10.** To mitigate the offense and to alleviate what was severe in the precept by some consolation, **the angel** promised a blessing through the child that she would bear. God might indeed by his own authority have strictly enjoined what was right; but in order that Hagar might the more cheerfully do what she knew to be her duty, he allured her to obedience. To this point those promises tend by which he invites us to voluntary submission. For he would not draw us by servile methods, so that we obey his commands by constraint; therefore, he mingles mild and paternal invitations with his commands, dealing with us liberally, as with sons.

That the angel here promises to do what is peculiar to God alone involves no absurdity, for God invests the ministers whom he sends with his own character, that the authority of their word may appear the greater. I do not, however, disapprove the opinion of most of the ancients— namely, that Christ the Mediator was always present in all the oracles and that this is the cause why the majesty of God is ascribed to angels.

**11.** The angel explained what he had briefly said respecting her seed— namely, that it would not be capable of being numbered on account of its multitude. He commenced with **Ishmael,** who was to be its head and origin. Although we will afterward see that this man was a reprobate, yet an honorable name was granted to him, to mark the temporal benefit of which Ishmael became a partaker as being a son of Abram. I thus explain this passage: God intended that a monument of the paternal kindness with which he embraced the whole house of Abram should endure to his posterity. For although the covenant of eternal life did not belong to Ishmael, yet, that he might not be entirely without favor, God constituted him the father of a great and famous people. Thus we see that with respect to this present life, the goodness of God extended itself to the seed of Abram according to the flesh. But if God intended the name of Ishmael (which signifies "God will hear") to be a perpetual memorial of his *temporal* benefits, he will by no means bear with our ingratitude if we do not celebrate his *celestial* and *everlasting* mercies, even unto death.

"**For the** LORD **has heard of your misery.**" We do not read that Hagar, in her difficulties, had taken recourse in prayer; we are rather left to speculate from the words of Moses that when she was stupefied by her sufferings, the angel came of his own accord. It is, therefore, to be observed that there are two ways in which God looks down upon men for the purpose of helping them—either when they, as suppliants, implore his aid, or when he, even unasked, succors them in their afflictions. He is indeed especially said to hearken to those who by prayers invoke him as their Deliverer. Yet sometimes when men lie mute and because of their stupor do not direct their wishes to him, he is said to listen to their miseries. That this latter way of hearing was fulfilled toward Hagar is probable, because God freely met her as she wandered through the wilderness. Moreover, because God frequently deprives unbelievers of his help until they are worn-out as with a progressive illness or else suffers them to be suddenly destroyed, let none of us give way to our own sloth. Rather, being admonished by the sense of our evils, let us seek him without delay. In the meantime, it is of no small avail to the confirmation of our faith that our prayers will never be despised by the Lord, seeing that he anticipates even the slothful and the dull with his help. And if he is present to those who seek him not, much more will he be propitious to the pious desires of his own people.

12. The angel declared what kind of person Ishmael would be: "**He will be a wild donkey of a man.**" The simple meaning (in my judgment) is that he would be a warlike man and so formidable to his enemies that none would injure him with impunity.

"**He will live in hostility toward all his brothers**" [KJV: "**he shall dwell in the presence of all his brethren**"]. As this is correctly applied only to a nation, we hence the more easily perceive that those who restrict the passage to Ishmael are wrong. Again, others understand that the posterity of Ishmael was to have a fixed habitation in the presence of their brethren, who would be unwilling to allow it; as if it were said that they would forcibly occupy the land they inhabit, although their brethren might attempt to resist them. Others adduce a contrary opinion—namely, that the Ishmaelites, though living among a great number of enemies, would yet not be destitute of friends and brethren. I approve, however, of neither opinion, for the angel rather intimated that this people would be separate from others, as if he said, "They will not form a part or member of any one nation but will be a complete body, having a distinct and special name."

13. She gave this name to the LORD who spoke to her: "**You are the God who sees me,**" for she said, "**I have now seen the One who sees me.**" Moses, I have no doubt, implies that Hagar, after she was admonished by the angel, changed her mind and, being thus subdued, began to pray; unless, perhaps, the confession of the tongue rather than a change

of mind is here denoted. I rather incline, however, to the opinion that Hagar, who had before had a wild and intractable temper, began now to acknowledge the providence of God. Hagar now perceived and acknowledged that human affairs are under divine government. And whoever is persuaded that he is looked upon by God must of necessity walk as in his sight.

I willingly accept what some adduce—that Hagar wondered at the goodness of God, by whom she had been regarded even in the wilderness. But this, though something, is not the whole. In the first place, Hagar chided herself because, as she had before been too blind, she even now opened her eyes too slowly and indolently to perceive God. For she aggravated the guilt of her dullness by the circumstance both of place and time. She had frequently found by many proofs that she was regarded by the Lord; yet becoming blind, she had despised his providence, as if with closed eyes passing by him when he presented himself before her. She now accused herself for not having more quickly awakened when the angel appeared. The consideration of place is also of great weight because God, who had always testified that he was present with her in the house of Abram, now pursued her as a fugitive, even into the desert. Her being blind to the presence of God implied a base ingratitude on her part, so that even when she knew he was looking upon her, she did not, in return, raise her eyes to behold him. But it was a still more shameful blindness that she, being regarded by the Lord although a wanderer and an exile, paying the just penalty of her perverseness, still would not even acknowledge him as present.

We now see the point to which her self-reproach tended. She said in effect, "Hitherto I have not sought God, nor had respect for him except by constraint, though he had before deigned to look down upon me. Even now in the desert, where, being afflicted with evils, I ought immediately to have roused myself, I have, according to my custom, been stupefied; nor should I ever have raised my eyes toward heaven unless I had first been looked upon by the Lord."

**14. That is why the well was called Beer Lahai Roi.** I think this common appellation originated with Hagar, who, not content with one simple confession, wished that the mercy of God would be attested in time to come; therefore she transmitted her testimony as from hand to hand. Hence we infer how useful it is that they who do not freely humble themselves should be subdued by stripes. Hagar, who had always been wild and rebellious and who had at length entirely shaken off the yoke, now, when the hardness of her heart was broken by afflictions, appeared altogether another person. She was not, however, reduced to order by stripes only; a heavenly vision was also added that thoroughly arrested her. And the same thing is necessary for us—namely, that God, while chastising us with his hand, must bring us into a state of submissive meekness by his Spirit.

**15.** We may easily gather that Hagar, when she returned home, related the events that had occurred. Therefore, Abram showed himself to be obedient and grateful to God because he both named his son according to the command of the angel and celebrated the goodness of God in having listened to the miseries of Hagar.

# Genesis
# Chapter 17

1. **When Abram was ninety-nine years old, the LORD appeared to him and said, "I am God Almighty; walk before me and be blameless."** Moses passes over thirteen years of Abram's life not because nothing worthy of remembrance had in the meantime occurred, but because the Spirit of God, according to his own will, selects those things that are most important. He purposely points out the length of time that had elapsed from the birth of Ishmael to the period when Isaac was promised, for the purpose of teaching us that Abram long remained satisfied with that son who would at length be rejected, and that he was as one deluded by a fallacious appearance.

Abram, being contented with his only son, ceased to desire any other seed. The lack of offspring had previously moved him to constant prayers and sighings, for the promise of God was so fixed in his mind that he was ardently carried forward to seek its fulfillment. But now, falsely supposing that he had obtained his wish, he was led away by the presence of his son according to the flesh from the expectation of a spiritual seed. Again the wonderful goodness of God shows itself, in that Abram himself was raised, beyond his own expectation and desire, to a new hope, and he suddenly heard that what never came into his mind to ask was granted unto him. If he had been daily offering up importunate prayers for this blessing, we would not so plainly see that it was conferred upon him by the free gift of God as when it was given to him without his either thinking of it or desiring it. Before, however, we speak of Isaac, it will be worthwhile to notice the order and connection of the words.

First, Moses says that the Lord **appeared** to Abram, so that we may know that the oracle was not pronounced by secret revelation, but that a vision at the same time was added to it. Further, the vision was not speechless but had the word annexed, from which the faith of Abram might receive profit. God entered into covenant with Abram, then

161

unfolded the nature of the covenant itself, and finally put a seal upon it, with accompanying attestations.

"**I am God Almighty.**" The Hebrew noun *El*, which is derived from the word for power, is here used for **God**. The same remark applies to the accompanying word *shaddai*, **Almighty**, as if God would declare that he had sufficient power for Abram's protection. Our faith can only stand firm while we are certainly persuaded that the defense of God is alone sufficient for us and can sincerely despise everything in the world that is opposed to our salvation. God, therefore, does not boast of the power that lies concealed within himself, but of that which he manifests toward his children; and he did so on this occasion in order that Abram might hence derive materials for confidence. Thus, in these words a promise is included.

"**Walk before me.**" In making the covenant, God stipulated obedience on the part of his servant. Yet he did not in vain prefix the declaration that he is **God Almighty** and is furnished with power to help his own people, because it was necessary that Abram should be recalled from all other means of help, that he might entirely devote himself to God alone. For no one will ever take himself to God but he who keeps created things in their proper place and looks up to God alone. Where, indeed, the power of God has been once acknowledged, it ought so to transport us with admiration, and our minds ought so to be filled with reverence for him, that nothing will hinder us from worshiping him. Moreover, because the eyes of God look for faith and truth in the heart, Abram was commanded to be full of integrity ("**be blameless**"). The Jews call him a "man of perfections" who does not have a deceitful or double mind but sincerely cultivates rectitude. In short, the integrity here mentioned is opposed to hypocrisy. And surely when we have to deal with God, no place for dissimulation remains. From these words we learn for what end God gathers together for himself a church—namely, that they whom he has called may be holy. The foundation, indeed, of the divine calling is a gratuitous promise; but it follows immediately after that they whom he has chosen as a peculiar people to himself should devote themselves to the righteousness of God. On this condition he adopts children as his own, that he may in return obtain the place and the honor of a Father. And as he himself cannot lie, so he rightly demands mutual fidelity from his children. Wherefore, let us know that God manifests himself to the faithful in order that they may live as in his sight and may make him the arbiter not only of their deeds but of their thoughts. Whence also we infer that there is no other method of living piously and justly than by depending upon God.

**2. "I will confirm my covenant between me and you and will greatly increase your numbers."** God now began more fully and abundantly to explain what he had before alluded to briefly. His covenant with Abram had two parts (verse 1). The first was a declaration of gratuitous love, to which was annexed the promise of a happy life. But the other was an exhortation to a sincere endeavor to cultivate uprightness, since God had given in a single word only a slight taste of his grace and then immediately had descended to the design of this calling—namely, that Abram should be upright.

He now amplified the declaration of his grace, so Abram would endeavor more willingly to form his mind and his life both to reverence God and to cultivate uprightness, as if God said, "See how kindly I indulge you, for I do not require integrity from you simply on account of my authority, which I might justly do. Rather, whereas I owe you nothing, I condescend graciously to engage in a mutual covenant." He did not, however, speak of this as of a new thing but reminded him of the covenant he had previously made and now fully confirmed and established its certainty. For God is not wont to utter new oracles that may destroy the credit or obscure the light or weaken the efficacy of those that preceded; rather he continues, as in one perpetual tenor, those promises that he has already given. Wherefore, by these words he intended nothing else than that the covenant that Abram had heard before should be established and ratified. But he expressly introduced that principal point concerning the multiplication of seed, which he afterwards frequently repeated.

**3. Abram fell facedown.** We know that was the ancient rite of adoration. Moreover, Abram testified, first, that he acknowledged God, in whose presence all flesh ought to keep silence and to be humbled, and, second, that he reverently received and cordially embraced whatever God was about to speak.

**4.** God declared that he was the speaker in order that absolute authority might appear in his words. Since our faith can rest on no other foundation than his eternal veracity, it becomes, above all things, necessary for us to be informed that what is proposed to us has proceeded from his sacred mouth.

**"You will be the father of many nations."** What is this multitude of **nations**? It obviously appears that different nations had their origin from the holy patriarch. Ishmael grew to a great people; the Idumeans, from another branch, were spread far and wide; large families also sprung from other sons whom Abram had by Keturah. But Moses looked still further because, indeed, the Gentiles were to be, by faith, inserted into the stock of Abram, although not descended from him according to the flesh. Paul is a faithful interpreter and witness about this for us. He does not gather together the Arabians, Idumeans, and others for the purpose of making Abram **the father of many nations**; but he so extends the name of *father* as to make it applicable to the whole world, in order that the Gentiles, in other respects strangers and separated from each other, might from all sides combine in one family of Abram.

**7.** There is no doubt that the Lord distinguished the race of Abraham from the rest of the world. We must now see what people he intended. They are deceived who think that God's elect alone are here pointed out. On the contrary, the Scripture declares that the race of Abraham, by lineal descent, had been peculiarly accepted by God. And it is the evident doctrine of Paul concerning the natural descendants of Abraham that they are holy branches that have proceeded from a holy root (see Romans 11:16). Wherefore, nothing is more certain than that God made his covenant with those sons of Abraham who were naturally to be born of him. If anyone objects that this opinion by no means agrees with the former, in which we said that they are reckoned the children of Abraham who being by faith ingrafted into his body form one family, the difference is easily reconciled by laying down certain distinct degrees of adoption that may be collected from various passages of Scripture.

In the beginning, preceding this covenant, the condition of the whole world was one and the same. But as soon as it was said, "I will be a God to you and to your seed after you," the church was separated from other nations, just as in the creation of the world the light emerged out of the darkness. The people of Israel were received as the flock of God into their own fold; the other nations wandered, like wild beasts, through mountains, woods, and deserts. Since this dignity, in which the sons of Abraham excelled other nations, depended on the word of God alone, the gratuitous adoption of God belongs to them all in common. For if Paul deprives the Gentiles of God and of eternal life on the ground of their being aliens from the covenant (see Ephesians 4:18), it follows that all Israelites were of the household of the church and sons of God and heirs of eternal life. And although it was by the grace of God and not by nature that they excelled the Gentiles, and although the inheritance of the kingdom of God came to them by promise and not by carnal descent, yet they are sometimes said to differ by nature from the rest of the world.

In the epistle to the Galatians (see 2:15) and elsewhere, Paul calls them saints "by birth," because God was willing that his grace should descend, by a continual succession, to the whole seed. In this sense, those who were unbelievers among the Jews are still called the children of the heavenly kingdom by Christ (see Matthew 8:12). Nor does what St. Paul says contradict this—namely, that not all who are from Abraham are to be esteemed legitimate children, because they are not "the children of the promise" but only of the flesh (see Romans 9:8). For there the promise is not taken generally for that outward word by which God conferred his favor upon the reprobate as well as upon the elect but must be restricted to that efficacious calling that he inwardly seals by his Spirit. That this is the case is proved without difficulty, for the promise by which the Lord had adopted them all as children was common to all; and in that promise it cannot be denied that eternal salvation was offered to all. What, therefore, can be the meaning of Paul when he denies that certain people have any right to be reckoned among the children of God except that he is no longer reasoning about the externally offered grace but about that of which only the elect effectually partake? Here, then, a twofold class of sons presents itself to us in the church; for since the whole body of the people is gathered together into the fold of God by one and the same voice, all without exception are in this respect accounted children. The name of the church is applicable in common to them all; but in the innermost sanctuary of God, none others are reckoned the sons of God but they in whom the promise is ratified by faith. Although this difference flows from the fountain of gratuitous election, whence also faith itself springs, yet since the counsel of God is in itself hidden from us, we therefore distinguish the true from the spurious children by the respective marks of faith and of unbelief. This method and dispensation continued even to the promulgation of the Gospel; but then "the dividing wall of hostility" was broken down (see Ephesians 2:14), and God made the Gentiles equal to the natural descendants of Abraham. That was the renovation of the world by which they who had before been strangers began to be called sons. Yet whenever a comparison is made between Jews and Gentiles, the inheritance of life is assigned to the former as lawfully belonging to them; but to the latter, it is said to be adventitious.

Meanwhile, the oracle was fulfilled in which God promised that Abraham would be the father of many nations. Whereas previously the natural sons of Abraham were succeeded by their descendants in continual succession, and the benediction that began with him flowed down to his children, the coming of Christ, by inverting the original order, introduced into his family those who before were separated from his seed. At length the Jews were cast out (except that a hidden seed of the election remained among them), in order that the rest might be saved. It was necessary that these things concerning the seed of Abraham should once be stated, that they may open to us an easy introduction to what follows.

**"For the generations to come."** This succession of generations clearly proves that the posterity of Abraham was taken into the church in such a manner that sons might be born to them, who would be heirs of the same grace. In this way the covenant is called perpetual, lasting until the renovation of the world, which took place at the coming of Christ. I grant, indeed, that the covenant was without end and may with propriety be called eternal as far as the whole church is concerned. It must, however, always remain as a settled point that the regular succession of ages was partly broken and partly changed by the coming of Christ because, the dividing wall of hostility being broken down and the sons by nature being at length disinherited, Abraham began to have a race associated with himself from all regions of the world.

**"To be your God and the God of your descendants after you."** Here we are plainly taught that this was a spiritual covenant, not confirmed in reference to the present life only, but one from which Abraham might conceive the hope of eternal salvation so that, being raised to heaven, he might lay hold of solid and perfect bliss. For those whom God adopts to himself, seeing that he makes them partakers of his righteousness and of all good things, he also constitutes heirs of heavenly life. Let us then mark as the principal part of the covenant that he who is the God of the living, not of the dead, promises to be a God to the children of Abraham. It follows afterward, in the way of augmentation of the grant, that he promised to give them the land (verse 8). I confess, indeed, that something greater and more excellent than itself was foreshadowed by the land of Canaan; yet this is not at variance with the statement that the promise now made was an accession to that primary one, "I will be your God."

Although God affirmed, as before, that he would give the land to Abraham himself, we nevertheless know that Abraham never possessed dominion over it. But the holy man was contented with his title to it, although the possession of it was not granted him; and therefore he calmly passed from his earthly pilgrimage into heaven. God again repeated that he would be a God to the posterity of Abraham, in order that they might not settle upon earth but may regard themselves as trained for higher things.

**9-10.** Covenants were not only committed to public records but were also often engraved in brass or sculptured on stones, in order that the memory of them might be more fully recorded and more highly celebrated. So in the present instance God inscribed his **covenant** on the body of Abraham. Circumcision was a solemn memorial of that adoption by which the family of Abraham had been elected to be the peculiar people of God. The pious had previously possessed other ceremonies that confirmed to them the certainty of the grace of God; but now the Lord attested a new covenant with a new kind of symbol. The reason he suffered the human race to be without this testimony of his grace during so many ages is concealed from us; but we do see that it was instituted at the time when he chose a certain nation for himself, which itself depends on his secret counsel.

Since circumcision is called by Moses a **covenant** of God, we infer that the promise of grace was included in it. Had it been only a mark or token of external profession among men, the name *covenant* would not at all be suitable. For a covenant is not confirmed unless it is matched with faith. Further, it is common to all sacraments to have the word of God linked to them. This calls us to the hope of salvation. A sacrament is nothing other than a visible word or sculpture and image of God's grace.

**10. "Every male among you shall be circumcised."** Although God's promises extend to men and women alike, what he sanctioned by circumcision, he nevertheless conveyed to one sex; but he did so as if to both men and women. God's covenant was engraved on the bodies of the males with this condition linked to it—that the females also take part in that covenant.

**11.** This command at first sight appears to be very strange. But the subject under discussion is the sacred covenant in which righteousness, salvation, and happiness were promised. The descendants of Abraham had to be distinguished from other nations, so that they would be holy and blessed. But who can say it is reasonable for circumcision to be used for such a mysterious sign? But it was necessary for Abraham to become a fool in order to prove his obedience to God. Anyone who is wise will both soberly and reverently receive what God has commanded, even if it may appear to be foolish.

It is probable that the Lord commanded circumcision for two reasons: First, to show that every person who is born is polluted, and, second, that salvation would stem from the blessed seed of Abraham. In the first place, therefore, God made known in his appointment of circumcision the corruption of human nature. From this it follows that circumcision was a sign of repentance. We also learn, in the second place, how reconciliation between God and men, which was exhibited in Christ, was witnessed to by this sign. For this reason Paul calls circumcision "a seal of righteousness that he had by faith" (Romans 4:11).

**12. "For the generations to come every male among you who is eight days old must be circumcised."** God now prescribed that circumcision should take place with **every male . . . who is eight days old**. In this symbol God depicted the destruction of the old man and the restoration of men to life.

**"Including those born in your household or bought with money from a foreigner—those who are not your offspring."** When God commanded Abraham to circumcise everyone in his **household**, God's special love toward that holy man was clearly seen. God embraced Abraham's whole family in his grace. We know that previously slaves were hardly thought to be members of the human race. But God, out of regard for his servant Abraham, adopted them as his own sons.

**13. "My covenant in your flesh is to be an everlasting covenant."** This expression may mean one of two things—either that God promises that his grace, of which circumcision was a sign and pledge, should be eternal, or that he intended the sign itself to be observed forever. Indeed, I have no doubt that this perpetuity ought not to be referred to the visible sign. Those who say that circumcision should still be practiced by Jews today are (in my opinion) deceived. They do not follow the axiom that we ought to regard as fixed—that since Christ is the end of the law, the permanent nature of the ceremonies of the law was terminated as soon as Christ appeared. However, circumcision does not cease to be an everlasting covenant, so long as Christ is regarded as the Mediator. For although the sign has changed, the truth is confirmed. The coming of

Christ marked the end of external circumcision. This is clear from Paul's words, which teach us that we are circumcised by Christ spiritually. Paul also substitutes baptism for circumcision (see Colossians 2:11-12). If baptism replaces circumcision, circumcision is done away with. Therefore, in Colossians 3:11 Paul denies that there is any difference between circumcision and uncircumcision because at that time circumcision was of no importance. In this way we refute the error of those who think circumcision should still be retained by the Jews, as if it were a symbol of their nation and should never be abrogated. I acknowledge that for a time the Jews were allowed to be circumcised, until freedom in Christ became well-known. But even though it was permitted for a time, it did not retain its original force. For it would be absurd for a believer to be initiated into the church by two different signs, especially since one of them witnessed that Christ has already come and the other foreshadowed him.

14. **"Any uncircumcised male, who has not been circumcised in the flesh, will be cut off from his people; he has broken my covenant."** To make sure the people took circumcision seriously, God pronounced a severe punishment on anyone who neglected it. On the one hand, this shows God's great concern for the salvation of men; on the other hand, it rebukes man's neglect of salvation. This passage teaches us that contempt for circumcision will not pass unpunished. Since God threatened only to punish those who despised circumcision, we infer that any children who died before they were eight days old would come to no harm if they died uncircumcised. For the promise of God by itself was effective for their salvation. God did not affirm salvation through external signs in such a way that salvation was only effective if a person received these signs. Let us remember that the salvation of Abraham was included in the expression, "I will be a God to your descendants." Circumcision was added to confirm this, but it did not deprive the word of its force and efficacy. But because it is not in man's power to sever what God has joined, no one can despise or neglect the sign without at the same time being guilty of rejecting the word itself. In this way he deprives himself of the benefit that the sign offers. Therefore, the Lord punished neglect of circumcision with great severity. But again, if any infants did not receive the tokens of salvation before they died, God spared them, because they had not broken God's covenant.

The same reasoning is applied today about baptism. Whoever neglects baptism and pretends that he is content with God's promise on its own tramples on the blood of Christ, or at least does not allow it to wash his children. Therefore, the punishment that followed contempt for the sign of circumcision was just. But to consign to destruction those infants who die before they are presented for baptism is a cruel superstition. There is no doubt that God's promise belongs to such children. For what can be more absurd than that the symbol, which is given to confirm the promise, should in reality vitiate it? So the commonly held opinion that baptism is necessary for salvation ought to be moderated so that it does not bind God's grace or the power of the Spirit to external symbols.

**15-16.** God now promised Abraham a legitimate heir through Sarai. God also changed the name of Abraham's wife from **Sarai** to **Sarah.** The Hebrew letter *y* (*yod*) appears in the name **Sarai** but not in the name **Sarah.** In Hebrew the letter *yod* acts as the possessive pronoun. This was now taken away. So God planned that Sarah's influence would be everywhere, without exception. She would be celebrated as a sovereign and princess. This is also apparent from the context of the verse where God promised that he would give her a son, from whom eventually nations and kings would be born: **"I will bless her and will surely give you a son by her. I will bless her so that she will be the mother of nations; kings of peoples will come from her."**

**17. Abraham fell facedown.** This was a token not only of his reverence but also of his faith. Abraham not only adored God but in giving him thanks testified that he received and embraced what was promised concerning a son.

**He laughed.** We infer that **he laughed** not because he either despised or rejected God's promise but **laughed,** as often happens, when something least expected occurs.

**He laughed** partly out of joy and partly out of wonder. I do not follow the view that this laughter flowed only from joy. Rather, I think Abraham was totally astonished by this news. This is confirmed by his next question. He **said to himself, "Will a son be born to a man a hundred years old? Will Sarah bear a child at the age of ninety?"** Abraham did not reject out of hand what the angel had said, yet showed that he was deeply affected, like a person who receives some incredible news. For a short time he was confounded. Yet he humbled himself before God and with confused mind prostrated himself before God as he, by faith, acknowledged God's power. What Abraham said was not the language of someone who doubts. Paul, in his Epistle to the Romans, supports this interpretation: "Without weakening in his faith, he faced the fact that his body was as good as dead—since he was about a hundred years old—and that Sarah's womb was also dead. Yet he did not waver through unbelief regarding the promise of God, but was strengthened in his faith and gave glory to God, being fully persuaded that God had power to do what he had promised" (Romans 4:19-21).

**18.** Abraham did not now wonder silently within himself. He expressed his wish in prayer. But what he said betrayed a vacillating mind: **"If only Ishmael might live under your blessing!"** It was as if Abraham did not dare to hope for all that God promised, and so he fixed his mind on the son who had already been born. Abraham therefore asked the Lord to preserve the life he had given to Ishmael.

**19. Then God said, "Yes, but your wife Sarah will bear you a son, and you will call him Isaac."** God roused the slumbering mind of his servant. It is as if he said, "The sight of one favor prevents you from rising any higher. You confine your thoughts within too narrow limits. Therefore, enlarge your mind, so you can receive what I promise about Sarah. For the door of hope ought to be sufficiently open to admit the word in its full magnitude."

**"I will establish my covenant with him as an everlasting covenant for his descendants after him."** God confined the spiritual covenant to one family, so that Abraham would learn to hope for the blessing previously promised. As that man had entertained a false hope that was not founded on the word of God, it was necessary that this false hope should first be dislodged from his heart, so that he might rely completely upon the heavenly oracles. God called the covenant **an everlasting covenant,** then declared that it would not be confined to one person only but would go on down to his descendants.

**20-21.** Here God clearly chose between the two sons of Abraham. To one he promised wealth, status, and other things that belong to this present life. In this way he demonstrated that Ishmael was a son from a human viewpoint. But God made a special **covenant** with **Isaac,** which extended beyond the world and this frail life. God did this not to cut **Ishmael** off from the hope of eternal life but to teach him that salvation should be sought from the people of Isaac, where it really dwells.

We infer from this passage that the holy fathers were by no means kept down to earth by the promises of God but rather were borne upward to heaven. For God generously promised to Ishmael everything that is needed for this earthly life. And yet God accounts these gifts as nothing when compared with the covenant established in Isaac. It therefore follows that neither wealth, nor power, nor any other temporal gift is promised to the children of the Spirit. However, they *are* promised an eternal blessing that is possessed only by hope.

**22. When he had finished speaking with Abraham, God went up from him.** This expression contains useful teaching. Abraham certainly knew this vision was from God. It is important for the pious to be completely sure that what they hear comes from God, so that they may not be carried along here and there but will depend on heaven alone. And while God does not openly ascend to heaven before our eyes today, this should not affect our faith. For God has been fully seen in Christ, and it is right that we should be satisfied with this. Further, he gives sufficient authority to his word when he seals it on our hearts by his Spirit.

**23. On that very day Abraham took his son Ishmael and all those born in his household or bought with his money, every male in his household, and circumcised them, as God told him.** Moses now praises Abraham's obedience because he circumcised his whole household as he had been commanded. Two points are worth considering. First, Abraham was not deterred by the difficulty of the task from offering to God the sacrifice that he owed. We know that he had a great number of people **in his household**. And there was danger of stirring up a riot in a peaceful community. But relying on God, he began what was an impossible task. Second, we see how well-ordered **his household** was. Not only the slaves born in the house, but also foreigners bought with money quietly accepted the pain of circumcision. Obviously Abraham had made a great effort to train them in their duty. And since he had kept up a holy discipline, he now received the reward of the care he had taken. Discipline in easy things prepared the way for something hard.

Today when God wants his Gospel to be preached throughout the world, so the world may be restored from death to life, he seems to ask for the impossible. We see how we meet resistance. Satan works against us, so that all roads are closed by the rulers themselves. Yet each man must carry out his duty without yielding to any impediment. In the end our efforts will not fail; they will be successful, even though this is not apparent now.

# Genesis
# Chapter 18

**1. The LORD appeared to Abraham near the great trees of Mamre while he was sitting at the entrance to his tent in the heat of the day.** God strengthened the heart of his servant with a new vision, just as the faith of the saints requires, at intervals, renewed assistance. It is also possible that the promise was repeated for Sarah's sake. **Mamre** was probably a grove of oaks where Abraham lived.

**2.** Before Moses comes to his main subject, he describes the hospitality Abraham gave. He calls the angels **men** because, being clothed with human bodies, they appeared to be nothing else than men. This was done on purpose so Abraham's generosity would be seen. So Abraham's humanity deserves to be highly praised. He freely offered hospitality to total strangers, from whom he expected nothing in return. Why did Abraham do this? He did it to provide what his guests clearly needed. He saw that their journey had made them tired and was sure they were suffering from the **heat**. He knew it was not a good time of day for them to travel. It might be further asked if Abraham was in the habit of receiving all kinds of guests. I reply that he acted as he usually did and treated his guests in different ways. The invitation that Moses recounts here is quite unusual. Undoubtedly the angels' manner bore the marks of exceptional dignity; so Abraham realized they not only deserved food and drink but were also worthy of honor.

**Abraham . . . bowed low to the ground.** This token of respect was commonly practiced among oriental nations. He was just being civil to them.

**4.** It was a normal practice to wash the feet of travelers in that part of the world. People traveled with nothing on their feet, in the scorching sun. To wash feet burning with heat was most refreshing.

**5.** Abraham said they had come at an opportune moment. It was as if he said, "You have not slipped into this place by chance but have been led here by God's direction." Abraham spoke in a most sincere way. So we should follow his example and conclude that whenever our brethren who need our help meet us, they are sent to us by God.

**6-8.** The care Abraham took in entertaining his guests is here recorded. At the same time, Moses shows how well-ordered a house Abraham's home was. In short, he presents us in a few words with a beautiful picture of a well-run home.

Some people question Moses' assertion that the angels ate. Some have explained this by suggesting the angels only appeared to be eating. This fanciful reply only produces a further problem, since angels do not have real bodies. But in my judgment this is very wide of the mark. In the first place, this was no prophetic vision, in which the images of things that do not exist are brought before our eyes. The angels really came into Abraham's house. So I do not doubt that God—who created the whole world out of nothing and who daily proves himself to be a wonderful Creator—gave them bodies, for a time, so they could accomplish the task they had been given. And just as they walked and spoke, so I conclude that they also ate and drank. They did this not because they were hungry but to conceal their identity. Just as God later destroyed those bodies, which he had created for a temporary purpose, so there is nothing absurd in saying that the food itself was destroyed along with their bodies. While it is profitable briefly to touch on such questions, and since we are not forbidden to do so, we should be content with straightforward solutions to them.

**9.** God now began to reveal himself in his angels. We may infer that the question concerning Sarah was asked so that the promise about her having a son could be repeated, since Sarah had not been present at the former oracle.

**10.** God promised that he would return when Sarah gave birth to her son.

**11.** Moses includes this verse to inform us that what the angel was saying seemed very improbable to Sarah. It is unnatural for children to be promised to decrepit old men. It was scarcely possible for Abraham, now that his body was half dead, to have children. He had indeed fathered Ishmael in his old age, which was quite contrary to expectation. But now, twelve years later, it would scarcely be credible to become a father again with his elderly wife. However, Moses concentrates mainly on Sarah because child-bearing was no longer possible for her.

**12.** Abraham had laughed before (17:17). But Sarah's laughter and Abraham's laughter were not at all similar. Sarah was not full of joy and wonder as she received God's promise. She foolishly refused to accept the word of God on account of her husband's age and her own age. She only considered what could be accomplished by natural means. She did not raise her thoughts to consider God's power. In this way she discredited God and what he had said.

In this way we too often consider God's promises and deeds according to our own reason and the laws of nature. When we do this we are reproaching God, even if we do not intend to do this. While Sarah's incredulity was not to be excused, she, nevertheless, did not directly reject God's favor. So let us note that nothing was further from Sarah's mind than to make God appear to be a liar. We must here note the admonition that the apostle draws from this passage because Sarah here calls Abraham "her master" (see 1 Peter 3:6). Peter exhorts women to follow Sarah's example and to be obedient and well-behaved toward their own husbands.

**13. Then the LORD said to Abraham, "Why did Sarah laugh and say, 'Will I really have a child, now that I am old?'"** Because God's majesty had been manifested in the angels, Moses specifically mentions his name, **the LORD**. The word of the Lord is so precious to the Lord himself that he should be acknowledged as present whenever he speaks through his ministers. Also, whenever the Lord manifested himself to the fathers, Christ was the Mediator between him and them. Sarah's laughter had not been detected by any human—she laughed **to herself**. But Moses specifically declares that she was rebuked by God.

**14. "Is anything too hard for the LORD?"** Sarah's laughter was mixed with incredulity. **"Is anything too hard for the LORD?"** is a very weighty question. The angel chided Sarah because she limited God's power to her own understanding of what is possible. God's power should not be calculated according to human reason. We now see that Sarah sinned by not acknowledging the greatness of God's power. In the same way we attempt to rob God of his power whenever we distrust his word. In short, he who does not expect more from God than he is able to understand by his own reasoning commits a grave sin.

The angel again repeated the promise that he would return **"at the appointed time next year,"** that is, when the time for Sarah to give birth arrived.

**15.** Sarah sinned again when she tried to hide her laughter with a lie. Yet this excuse did not stem from obstinate wickedness. Though Sarah repented of her own folly, she was still so terrified that she denied what she had done, for she now perceived that it was displeasing to God. It is not enough that God's judgment should be reverently acknowledged unless we also confess our sins without any evasion. Seeing that God only gave a friendly reprehension, and that he did not punish Sarah's second offense more severely, we see how tenderly the Lord views his own people. Zacharias was treated more severely when he was struck dumb for nine months (see Luke 1:20). In Sarah, the Lord gives a wonderful example of his compassion. He freely forgave all her sins and still chose her to be the mother of the church. In the meantime, we must observe how much better it is to be brought before the Lord as a guilty person and, like convicted criminals, to be silent than to take delight in sin, as most of the world does.

**16.** Moses again calls these angels **men.** He is calling them by the name of the form they had assumed. We are not, however, to suppose that they were clothed with human bodies in the same way in which Christ clothed himself in our nature as well as with our flesh. God invested them with temporary bodies, so that they might be visible to Abraham. Abraham is said to have **walked along with them to see them on their way** as he showed them the honor that is due to angels.

**17-18. Then the LORD said, "Shall I hide from Abraham what I am about to do? Abraham will surely become a great and powerful nation, and all nations on earth will be blessed through him."** When God proposes something as if he is not sure about it, he does so out of kindness to men, for he has already decided what he will do. Here he intended to make Abraham pay close attention to the reasons he gave for the destruction of Sodom.

God gave two reasons for wanting to reveal his purpose before it was fulfilled: first, because Abraham was worthy of the privilege; second, because it would be useful and fruitful for his descendants' learning. This in brief is the scope and value of this revelation.

One reason, as I said, why God wished his servant to know beforehand about his terrible judgment on Sodom was to honor him with special gifts. God has always shown this same kindness to the faithful. What reason is there for the innumerable favors God constantly bestows on us except that he cannot refrain from expressing his fatherly love with which he has enfolded us? As he does this, he honors himself and his own gifts in us.

Moreover, we learn from this passage what experience also teaches us—that it is the special privilege of the church to know the meaning of the judgments of God. God proves himself a just judge of the world by inflicting punishment on evil men. But because everything seems to happen by accident, God enlightens his children by his word, so that they may not walk blindly like unbelievers. So in the past when he stretched out his hand to judge the whole world, he confined his holy oracle to Judea; that is, when he was ready to bring misfortune on the nations, he only revealed what he was doing to his prophets and to his chosen people.

Let us then remember that God, who has blessed us in every way, will complete our salvation. Having adopted us and enlightened our minds by his word, he keeps the torch of the word blazing before our eyes, that we may in faith keep our minds on the judgment and punishment of evil, which the impious confidently ignore.

Therefore, the faithful should be well informed about the history of all times, to be able to judge according to the Scriptures the various calamities that befall the wicked, both privately and in public. While Sodom was unharmed and enjoying its pleasant luxuries, the Lord announced to his servant Abraham that it would soon perish. There was then no doubt that it perished not by chance, but by God's actions.

We must accept the same conclusion in other cases, for although God does not tell us the future, he wants us to be eyewitnesses of his acts.

**19. "For I have chosen him, so that he will direct his children and his household after him to keep the way of the LORD by doing what is right and just, so that the LORD will bring about for Abraham what he has promised him."** The words **"He will direct his children"** reveal the second reason God wanted Abraham to share his counsel. He did not reveal it for no purpose. The plain meaning of the verse is that Abraham was told of God's plan because he was to act like a good father and teach his family. So we infer that Abraham was told of Sodom's coming destruction not for his own sake alone, but as a kindness to all his descendants.

Indeed, the scope of God's purpose must be carefully noted. His will, as made known to Abraham, bound all Abraham's descendants. Certainly God does not make his will known to us so that knowledge of him should die with us. He requires us to be his witnesses to the next generation, so that they in turn may hand on what they have received from us to their descendants. Therefore, it is a father's duty to teach his children what he himself has learned from God. In this way we must propagate God's truth. It was not given to us for our private enjoyment; we must mutually strengthen one another according to our calling and our faith.

There is no doubt that the gross ignorance that prevails in the world is the just punishment of men's indolence. While most people shut their eyes to the light shed by heavenly doctrine, many smother it by making no effort to transmit it to their children. God rightly withholds the precious treasures of his Word as punishment for the world's spiritual sloth.

We must consider particularly the phrase **after him**, which teaches us that God's care is not limited to our own lives—**"so that he will direct his children and his household after him."** He takes steps to ensure that his eternal truth will live and flourish after our death and that a godly way of living will continue on earth when we are dead. Hence we also conclude that accounts of events that strike terror in us are worth knowing about, since our carnal confidence needs sharp resistance so that we may be moved to fear God.

Let no one imagine that this kind of teaching does not apply to him, for when God mentions the sons of Abraham, he means the whole household of the church. Perverse and deluded interpreters insist that if they terrify consciences, they repel and discourage faith. However, nothing is more alien to faith than disrespect and sloth.

**"To keep the way of the LORD."** With these words Moses shows that the judgment of God is announced not only in order that those who in their stupidity are self-satisfied may be filled with dread and so be driven to long for the grace of Christ, but also so that the faithful, who are already endowed with the fear of God, may become more and more practiced in the pursuit of religion. God desires to have Sodom's destruction recounted not only to draw wicked men to himself by their fear of the same punishment, but also to give to those who have already begun to serve God a better understanding of true obedience. The law contributes not only to the beginning of repentance but also to our continuing perseverance in the Christian life.

When God adds **"by doing what is right and just,"** he is describing briefly his way that he has already mentioned. Although the definition is not complete, yet he briefly indicates by synecdoche the duties of the second table of the law and shows us what he especially requires of us. The Scripture often draws a description of a good and godly life from the second table of the law. This does not mean that love of neighbor is more important than the service of God, but that men can prove their loyalty to God only by living honestly and doing no injury to their neighbors. By the words **right and just,** God includes the kind of equity that gives to each man his due. If one wants to differentiate between the two words, **just** implies the honesty and kindness that we practice when we strive to help our brothers in every way and avoid hurting them in any way by fraud and violence. **Right** means that we stretch out our hands to the poor and oppressed, support good causes, and work hard to keep the weak from being unjustly hurt. These are the lawful tasks that the Lord orders his own to do.

**20-21.** The Lord now began to explain in more detail to Abraham his counsel concerning the destruction of the five cities, although he only named **Sodom and Gomorrah,** which were much more well-known than the rest. But before he mentioned their punishment, he stated their iniquities, to teach Abraham that they deserved to be destroyed. For when we perceive that God's anger is provoked by the sin of man, we are inspired with a dread of sinning. In saying that **the outcry against Sodom and Gomorrah is so great,** God indicated how serious their sins were. Therefore, this phrase signifies that all our deeds, even our hidden sins, are presented before the bar of God, and that they demand vengeance, even if there was nobody else to level any accusations against us.

**22.** Moses declares that **the men . . . went toward Sodom,** giving the impression that having finished their discourse, they took leave of Abraham, so that he might return home. Moses then adds, **but Abraham remained standing before the LORD**—in the way that people do who, though dismissed, do not leave immediately because something still remains to be said or done. Moses says that **men,** not angels, **went toward Sodom,** but that Abraham stood **before the LORD.** With his eyes Abraham saw men, but by faith he looked upon God. And his words show that he did not speak as he would have with a mortal man. From this we infer that we should not allow external symbols, by which God represents himself, to stop us from going directly to God.

Some people suppose that Abraham was more concerned about the safety of his nephew than for Sodom and the rest of the cities. But I do not doubt that he was so touched with compassion for the five cities that he drew near to God and interceded for them. But Abraham's prayers did not ask God not to scourge those cities, but only not to destroy them completely. It is as if he said "O Lord, whatever punishment you may inflict upon the guilty, will you not still leave some place for the righteous? Why should that region be completely destroyed as long as some people remain who can live in the area?" Abraham, therefore, did not desire that the wicked should escape from the hand of God, but only that God, in inflicting public punishment on a whole nation, would not destroy the good people as well.

**23.** It is clear that when God punishes a group of people, he often involves the good and the reprobate in the same punishment. Daniel, Ezekiel, Ezra, and others like them, who worshiped God in purity in their own country, were suddenly taken into exile. But when God seems to be angry with everybody all in common, we must remember that in the end, God will make a distinction between the wicked and the good. God's reply to Abraham (verse 26) should be understood in the following way: "If in Sodom I find fifty righteous people, I will spare the whole place for their sake." Yet God did not here bind himself by a perpetual rule, so that he cannot whenever he sees fit bring the wicked and the just together to punishment.

**25.** Abraham was not here teaching God his duty, as if anyone should say to a judge, "Remember what your office requires." But Abraham did reason from the nature of God that it is impossible for him to do anything that is unjust (see Romans 3:5-6).

**27. "I am nothing but dust and ashes."** Abraham spoke in this way in order to gain pardon. For what is mortal man when compared with God? He therefore confessed that he was too bold in the way he was interrogating God. But Abraham still wanted God to grant him this favor through divine indulgence. It should be noted that the nearer Abraham came to God, the more aware he became of the abject condition of men. For it is only the brightness of the glory of God that covers with shame and thoroughly humbles men, stripped of their foolish and intoxicated self-confidence. Whoever, therefore, seems to himself to be something, let him turn his eyes to God, and immediately he will acknowledge himself to be nothing.

Although Moses in the next chapter mentions the most vile crime that reigned in Sodom, we must nevertheless remember what Ezekiel teaches in Ezekiel 16:48-49 about Sodom. If we dread extreme inordinate passion, let us live in a temperate and frugal way.

# Genesis
# Chapter 19

**1. The two angels arrived at Sodom in the evening, and Lot was sitting in the gateway of the city. When he saw them, he got up to meet them and bowed down with his face to the ground.** The question arises, why has one of the three angels suddenly disappeared, so that only **two angels arrived at Sodom?** The Jews, with their traditional audacity, say that one came to destroy Sodom, the other to preserve Lot. But from Moses' discourse this appears to be frivolous, for we will see that they both helped free Lot. God gave Abraham a special favor. God not only sent him two angelic messengers but also revealed himself to him in his own Son.

**2.** The angels did not at once agree to Lot's invitation, so they could fully investigate the disposition of that holy man. For he was about to bring them to his own house not merely to give them supper, but to defend them from the citizens of Sodom. The angels replied to Lot in order to make apparent the great wickedness of the people.

**3.** Moses shows that the angels were more lavishly entertained than was usual. Moses says that the angels **ate.** They did not eat because they had to but because it was not yet time to reveal their heavenly nature.

**4.** By describing one evil act, Moses sets before us an instructive picture of Sodom. The greatness of their iniquity and wantonness is apparent from the fact that like a group of soldiers they laid siege to Lot's house. How blind and impetuous was their lust. Without any shame, they rushed together like brute animals! Paul describes such men accurately when he says, "God gave them over to shameful lusts" (Romans 1:26). When there is no sense of shame, and lust is given into, a vile barbarism follows, in which many kinds of sin are mixed together.

**Both young and old.** Moses passes over many things in silence that may come to the reader's mind. For instance, he does not mention who stirred up the multitude. But he intimates that any respect for others had been swept away, so that the order of nature was perverted as **young and old** came together from every part of the city.

**5.** They called to Lot, "Where are the men who came to you tonight? Bring them out to us so that we can have sex with them." As God called the men of Sodom to judgment, he showed, as it were, their extreme wickedness.

**6.** The fact that Lot went out and exposed himself to danger shows how faithfully he observed the sacred right of hospitality. It was a rare virtue that he put the safety and honor of the guests whom he had undertaken to protect above the safety of his own life. This kind of magnanimity is still required of God's children. Where duty and fidelity are concerned, they should not spare themselves. The brutal rage of these men of Sodom teaches us that reprobates, when they have been blinded by the just judgment of God, rush to engage in every kind of evil, until they make themselves altogether detestable to God and men.

**8.** Lot did not hesitate to make prostitutes of his own daughters in his desire to quell the indomitable fury of the people. But he should have endured a thousand deaths rather than have resorted to such a measure. I readily understand why some people excuse Lot; yet he is not free from blame, because he tried to ward off evil with evil. We are warned by this example that when the Lord has furnished us with the spirit of invincible fortitude, we must also pray that he may govern us by the spirit of prudence, and that he will never allow us to be deprived of sound judgment.

**9.** Every word these men spoke demonstrates that they were swollen with pride. They challenged Lot and, as it were, said, "By what right do you alone challenge the authority of the whole city?" Then they boasted that while they had always lived in Sodom, he was but a stranger. But, however many accusations the wicked bring against the righteous, and however little they submit to reason, let us know that they are exalted only for their own ruin.

**10.** Here Moses teaches that the Lord, although he may for a time appear to be indifferent to evil, while the faithful are engaged in fighting evil, yet never deserts his own but stretches out his hand at the critical moment. So in protecting Lot the Lord delayed his help until the last moment.

**11.** When Moses says that the men were **struck . . . with blindness**, we should not assume that they were totally deprived of sight, but that their vision became so blurred that they could not see anything with any clarity. This miracle was more stunning than if their eyes had been taken away or if they had been completely blinded. With open eyes they felt around everywhere, just like blind men; they saw, yet did not see.

**12.** At length the angels declared why they had come and what they were about to do. For so great was the indignity of the last act of this people that Lot certainly now saw how impossible it was for God to bear with the people there any longer. In the first place, the angels declared that they had come to destroy the city (verse 13). For the more sins men heap together, the higher their wickedness rises.

**13.** This verse teaches us that angels are the ministers of God's wrath as well as of his grace. This statement is not nullified just because the latter service is peculiarly ascribed to certain angels (see Hebrews 1:14; Psalm 91:11), for the Scriptures also declare that God judges people with his "destroying angels" (Psalm 78:49). Let us learn from this that it is not unknown for elect angels to descend armed for the purpose of carrying out God's vengeance and to inflict punishment. As the angel of the Lord destroyed, in one night, the army of Sennacherib that besieged Jerusalem (2 Kings 19:35), so also the angel of the Lord appeared to David with his drawn sword when the plague was raging against the people of Israel (2 Samuel 24:16). The angels now repeated what they had previously said, so that Lot would flee the city: **"The outcry to the LORD against its people is so great that he has sent us to destroy it."**

**14.** The faith of the holy man, Lot, is seen, first, in that he was completely awed and humbled at God's threat. Second, Lot's faith shone because in the middle of destruction, he still held on to the promise of salvation. In inviting his sons-in-law to join him, he showed the kind of diligence that should characterize the children of God. For they should use every means at their disposal to rescue their own families from destruction. But when Moses says, **But his sons-in-law thought he was joking**, he means that the pious old man was despised and derided because his sons-in-law thought he had gone mad in imagining danger. From this we learn how fatal an evil a false security is. While evil people are saying, "Peace and safety," they are overwhelmed by sudden ruin. Their indolence should make us alive to the fear of God, so that we may always be alert, especially when some token of the wrath of God presents itself to us.

**15.** Having praised the faith and piety of Lot, Moses shows that he still acted in a human way because the angels had to tell him to **"Hurry!"** as he was lingering.

**16.** The angels urged Lot to leave by speaking to him, but then they seized his hand and with apparent violence forced him to depart. What Moses says here must be carefully noted. It is often necessary for us to be forcibly drawn away from scenes that we do not willingly leave. If riches or honors or any other things of that kind prove an obstacle to anyone, let him realize that the Lord has taken hold of his hand, since words and exhortations were not sufficient to move him.

**17.** Moses adds these words to teach us that the Lord not only stretches out his hand to us for a moment, in order to begin our salvation, but keeps doing this right to the end. Let us also learn from this that God provides for our salvation when he banishes us from a pleasant plain to a desert mountain.

**18.** Lot is here censured for another fault. Rather than simply obeying God, he substituted his own plan for escaping from Sodom. God told Lot to take refuge in a mountain, but Lot preferred to go to a city (verse 20). Moses' aim is to teach us that Lot's faith was not entirely pure or free from all defects. Similarly, our prayers are faulty whenever they are not founded on the word of God. Lot not only moved away from the word but opposed it. Everyone vacillates in this way when they do not submit themselves to God.

**19.** Lot did not rage against God as the wicked do; yet because he did not rely on the word of God, he slid and almost fell away. Why did he fear destruction in the mountain, where he would be protected by the hand of God, and yet expect to find safety in a place that was close to Sodom? It is the nature of men to prefer to seek their safety in hell rather than in heaven. This happens whenever they follow their own reason.

**21.** Some people argue from this verse that Lot's prayer was pleasing to God because he assented to his request and gave him what he sought. But it is nothing new for the Lord to sometimes grant, by way of indulgence, what he does not approve of. And God now indulged Lot, but in such a way that he soon corrected his folly.

**22.** The angel had not only been sent to destroy Sodom but had received a command to preserve Lot. Therefore, he declared that he would not do the former unless the latter was done at the same time. But we must not conclude from this that God's power is limited when he deliberately seems to curb his authority in this way. From this it should be correctly said that God can do nothing except what he wills and promises. This is a true and profitable doctrine.

**24. Then the LORD rained down burning sulfur on Sodom and Gomorrah—from the LORD out of the heavens.** Moses here succinctly relates in very unostentatious language the destruction of Sodom and the other cities. It was not God's will that those cities should be simply swallowed up by an earthquake. They were to be a conspicuous example of his judgment; so he **rained down burning sulfur** on them from heaven.

It is often asked of this passage, "What had infants done to deserve being swallowed up in the same destruction as their parents?" The answer to this question is easy—namely, that the human race is in God's hand, so that he may destroy whomever he chooses and may have mercy on whomever he chooses. Whatever we are unable to grasp because of our limited understanding ought to be submitted to God's judgment. Furthermore, all of those people were accursed and condemned, and so God could not justly spare them, not even the least of them.

**26.** Moses here records God's awesome judgment by which Lot's wife was transformed into **a pillar of salt.** We can consider whether Moses' narrative contains anything absurd or incredible. First, I ask: Since God created men out of nothing, why may he not, if he sees fit, reduce them to nothing again? If this is granted, as it must be, why, if he should please, may he not turn them into stones? Philosophers who display their own cleverness in detracting from God's power see miracles as great as this in nature every day. How does the crystal acquire its hardness? How are birds produced from eggs? So why does a miracle seem ridiculous to them in this instance when they are obliged to acknowledge innumerable similar miracles? And how can those who say it is unbelievable that the body of a woman should be changed into a mass of **salt** believe that the resurrection will restore people to life? When, however, it is said that Lot's wife was changed into **a pillar of salt**, let us not imagine that her soul passed into the salt. For it should not be doubted that she lives and will take part in the same resurrection as we will.

It may now be asked why the Lord punished the imprudence of this unhappy woman so severely. Perhaps she doubted that Sodom would be destroyed and wanted to see definite evidence about this. Or she might have felt pity for people as they perished, and so she turned her eyes in that direction. Moses certainly does not say that she deliberately fought against God's will. But inasmuch as the deliverance of her and her husband was an incomparable instance of divine compassion, it was right that her ingratitude should be punished in this way. So if we weigh all the circumstances, it is clear that she was guilty of serious fault. First, the desire to look back stemmed from incredulity. No greater injury can be done to God than when credit is not given to his word. Second, we infer from the words of Christ that she was moved by some evil desire (see Luke 17:31-33) and so left Sodom reluctantly. Christ commands us to remember Lot's wife so that the allurements of the world will not draw us aside from concentrating on the heavenly life. Although it is not lawful to affirm anything about her eternal salvation, it is nevertheless probable that God, having inflicted temporal punishment, spared her soul.

**27.** Moses now returns to Abraham and shows that he had not neglected what he had heard from the angel, for he relates that Abraham came to a place where he could see God's judgment. We must not think, as we have just said about Lot's wife, that Abraham trusted his own thoughts more than the word of God. Rather we infer from the verse that Abraham, who was already fully persuaded the angel had not spoken in vain, sought confirmation by actually watching the event.

**29.** If anyone thinks it is absurd that the holy man Lot should be delivered because of someone else, I reply as follows: The Lord, since he helps his own people, cared for Lot, whom he had chosen and whom he ruled by his Spirit. But at the same time he would show, in the preservation of Lot's life, how greatly he loved Abraham, to whom he not only granted personal protection but also the deliverance of others. It is, however, right to observe that what the Lord does gratuitously—induced by no other reason than his own goodness—is ascribed to the piety or the prayers of men. This is done so that we may be stirred up in our worship of God and our prayers to him.

**30.** This part of the narrative proves what I have previously alluded to—the things that men strive after for themselves never prosper. This is especially true when men who are deluded by vain hope depart from the word of God (see Isaiah 30:1). When Lot was told to go to the mountain, he chose instead to live in Zoar. After this was granted to him, he soon regretted his own choice, **for he was afraid to stay in Zoar.**

**31.** Here Moses narrates an event that astonishes readers. How could unchaste thoughts come into the minds of the daughters of Lot while God's terrible punishment on the Sodomites was so fresh in their minds? It is true that they were not so much motivated by sensual lust as a foolish desire to procreate their family.

**"There is no man around here to lie with us."** They did not mean that all the nations were destroyed, as many expositors say, but that since they lived in a cave, leading a lonely life, they were cut off from any hope of marriage. Being separated from the rest of the nations, they lived as if they were sent away to some separated world.

Their first sin was that they, in their desire to propagate the human race, violated the holy law of nature. Next, it was wrong and wicked of them to not flee to the Creator of the world himself to cure them from that desolation about which they were worried. Third, they showed their negligence when their hearts were set only on this earthly life, and they were not concerned about the heavenly life. Without calling upon God or asking their father for advice, they were carried away by animal instinct. We see from this how quickly they forgot about their deliverance and the punishment of the Sodomites.

**33.** Although Lot did not consciously sin, yet, because his sin was caused by his drunkenness, his guilt, though diminished, was not annulled. It was wrong for Lot, being so much under the influence of wine, to pour out his lust in this way. As God has not spared the holy patriarch, how can we imagine we will be unpunished when we indulge in the same excessiveness? Let us learn from this example, so that we will act modestly and moderately.

Some people say, in order to reduce Lot's guilt, that he was not so much intoxicated through drink as depressed through sadness. But I maintain that he who was endowed with more splendid gifts also deserved greater punishment, and that therefore his reason was taken away from him, so that he, like an unreasonable beast, lost himself in sensual lust.

**37-38.** To their sons, or rather to two nations, the daughters gave names. From these names everybody would know that this was a family that originated in adultery and unchaste intercourse. This example of God's punishment is revealed to us so we will not tolerate any sin, and so we will not lose ourselves in licentiousness, but rather, through the fear of God, will be spurred on to penitence.

# Genesis
# Chapter 20

**1. Now Abraham moved on from there into the region of the Negev and lived between Kadesh and Shur.** Moses' account of the destruction of Sodom was a digression. He now returns to show what happened to Abraham. Moses shows how Abraham behaved and how the Lord protected him until the promised seed, the future source of the church, was born to him.

**2.** In this account, the Holy Spirit presents us with a remarkable instance, both of the infirmity of man and of the grace of God. It is a common proverb that even fools become wise through suffering evil. But Abraham, forgetting the great danger that he fell into in Egypt, once more struck his foot against the same stone. This happened despite the fact that the Lord had purposely chastised him in order to provide him with a useful warning for the rest of his life. Therefore, we see from the example of the holy patriarch how easily we become oblivious to both the chastisements and the favors of God. For it is impossible to excuse Abraham's great negligence in not remembering that he had previously sinned, and that he only had himself to blame if his wife became the property of another man.

We must note the nature of Abraham's sin. Abraham did not, for the sake of providing for his own safety, make his wife into a prostitute, as impious men claim. But just as he had previously been anxious to preserve his life until he should receive the seed divinely promised to him, so now, as his wife was pregnant, Abraham was so caught up in the hope of enjoying so great a blessing that he ignored his wife's danger. Therefore, if we carefully consider the matter we see that he sinned through unbelief, for he did not rely on God's providence. From this we are admonished concerning how dangerous it is to trust our own counsel.

**3.** Here Moses shows that the Lord acted with such gentleness that in punishing his servant, he yet, as a father, forgave him. He deals with us in the same way, so that while chastising us with his rod, his mercy and his goodness far exceed his severity. Hence also we infer that the Lord takes greater care of the pious than worldly people can appreciate, since he even watches over them while they sleep.

God reproved king **Abimelech** for Abraham's sake, whom he covered with his special protection. But God intended to show, generally, his great displeasure with adultery. Abraham is not mentioned by name in this verse, as a general announcement is made to promote faithfulness in marriage. **"You are as good as dead because of the woman you have taken; she is a married woman."** Let us therefore learn that a precept was given in these words to mankind that forbids anyone to touch his neighbor's wife. Since nothing in this life is more sacred than marriage, it comes as no surprise that the Lord requires mutual fidelity to be cherished between husbands and wives. God is speaking here only to one man, but the warning should ring in everyone's ears that adulterers—although they live with impunity for a time—will experience God's vengeance on them, for it is God who presides over marriage, and he will take vengeance on them (see Hebrews 13:4).

**4.** Although Abraham had neglected his wife, the Lord interposed in time to preserve her from being injured. When Moses previously related that Sarah was taken away by Pharaoh, he did not say whether her chastity was assailed or not; but since the Lord then also declared that he was the vindicator of her whom he now saved from dishonor, we should not doubt that her integrity was preserved on both occasions.

**Now Abimelech had not gone near her, so he said, "Lord, will you destroy an innocent nation?"** The explanation given by some that Abimelech here compared himself with the men of Sodom is perhaps too forced. The following meaning seems to me to be the correct one: "O Lord, although you do severely punish adultery, will your wrath pour itself out on innocent men who have rather fallen into error than sinned knowingly and willingly?" Moreover, Abimelech seemed to clear himself as if he were entirely free from blame. We must, however, note in what way and to what extent he boasted that his heart and hands were guiltless. He did not arrogate to himself a purity that was altogether spotless but only denied that he was led by lust to abuse another man's wife. We know the big difference between a crime and a fault. Thus Abimelech did not excuse himself from every kind of charge but only showed that he had been conscious of no wickedness that required this severe punishment.

**6.** We infer from God's reply that Abimelech did not testify falsely concerning his own integrity. Yet, while God agreed that his excuse was true, he nevertheless chastised him. Let us learn from this that even those who are pure in the judgment of men are not entirely free from blame. For it is not right for anyone to absolve himself by his own judgment; rather, let us learn to bring all our conduct to be judged by God's standard (see Proverbs 21:2). If even those who are unconscious of any evil in themselves do not escape censure, what will be our condition if we are held smitten by our own conscience?

**"I have kept you from sinning against me."** This declaration implies that God not only cared for Abraham but also for the king. Because Abimelech had no intention of defiling another man's wife, God had compassion on him. It frequently happens that the Spirit restrains, by his bridle, those who are gliding into error. As God brought to the heathen king, who had not been guilty of deliberate wickedness, a timely remedy in order that his guilt should not be increased, so God proves himself daily to be the faithful guardian of his own people, to prevent them from rushing forward from small faults into desperate crimes.

**7.** God did not now speak of Abraham as if he were an ordinary man but as one who was so especially dear to him that God defended the honor of his marriage. God called Abraham **a prophet** in order to honor him. Although the word *prophet* is the name of an office, I think it has here a wider meaning—a chosen man, one who is close to God. Since at that time no Scripture was in existence, God not only made himself known by dreams and visions but chose exceptional and excellent men to spread the seed of piety by which the world would be without excuse. Since Abraham was a prophet, he was constituted, as it were, a mediator between God and Abimelech. Christ, even then, was the only Mediator; but this did not mean that men should not pray for other people (see James 5:16). And today we should not neglect such intercession, provided it does not obscure the grace of Christ or lead us away from him.

**8.** Moses teaches how efficacious the oracle had been. For Abimelech, alarmed at the voice of God, arose in the morning, not only so that he himself might quickly obey God, but that he might exhort his people to do the same. This example of willing obedience is given us in a heathen king so that we may no longer make excuses for our torpor when we pay so little attention to divine remonstrances. God appeared to Abimelech in a dream, but since God daily cries aloud in ears—through Moses, through the prophets and apostles, and finally through his only-begotten Son—it is absurd to suppose that so many testimonies should be less effective than the vision of a single dream.

**9.** Some suppose that the king of Gerar did not complain to Abraham but rather declared his own repentance here. If, however, we weigh his words we find confession mixed with expostulation. Although he complained that Abraham had acted unjustly, he yet did not so much attach the blame to him as to free himself from all fault. And he was right to impute part of the blame to Abraham, provided he also acknowledged his own sin. Let us note that this king did not act like a hypocrite. No one, therefore, should exonerate himself from blame under the pretense that he had been induced by others to sin.

It is, however, to be noted that the king's adulterous intention is called

**great guilt** here because it bound not one man only but a whole people, as in a common crime. The king of Gerar could not have spoken in this way had he not acknowledged the sacred right of marriage. But at the present time Christians—at least those who boast of the name—are not ashamed to excuse great crimes of infidelity, from which even the heathen shrink with the greatest horror. Let us, however, realize that Abimelech was a true herald of that divine judgment that miserable men in vain endeavor to elude by their excuses. Let Paul's words from 1 Corinthians 5:9 and Ephesians 5:5-6 always be in our minds.

10. Abimelech, by his earnest question, showed that he wanted the evil action to be rectified. We know how fierce people are who think they themselves have been aggrieved. So greater praise should be given to Abimelech for the moderation he showed toward an unknown foreigner. Meanwhile, let us learn from his example that whenever we expostulate with our brethren who have done us wrong, we should allow them freely to answer us.

11. **Abraham replied, "I said to myself, 'There is surely no fear of God in this place, and they will kill me because of my wife.'"** Two points are contained in this answer. First, Abraham confessed that he had been induced by fear to conceal his marriage. He then denied that he had lied for the purpose of excusing himself. Although Abraham declared with truth that he had not concealed his marriage with any fraudulent intention, nor for the purpose of injuring anyone, yet he was worthy of censure because through fear he had allowed, so far as he was concerned, his wife to become a prostitute. So little can be said in Abraham's defense. He should have been more courageous and resolute in fulfilling the duty of a husband by vindicating the honor of his wife, whatever danger might threaten him. Besides, it was a sign of distrust to resort to unlawful subtlety. With regard to his suspicion, although he had perceived that a monstrous licentiousness prevailed in Gerar, it was nevertheless not right to form such an unfavorable judgment about a people he did not know. Abraham had assumed they were all murderers.

12. Some think that Sarah was Abraham's own sister, though not through the same mother but from a second wife. As, however, the name **sister** has a wider meaning among the Jews, I adopt a different conjecture. I think that Sarah was Abraham's **sister** in a lesser sense. They had a common father—that is, a grandfather. So although Abraham did not lie in words, yet with respect to actual fact, his dissimulation was a lie by implication.

13. These words taught Abimelech that Abraham was also free from malicious cunning and falsehood. Also, since they were living a nomadic and unsettled life, Sarah had agreed always to say the same thing she had said in Gerar. Abraham hoped his wretched anxiety would move Abimelech to have compassion on the holy man and cause his anger to abate.

14. Abraham had previously received possessions and gifts in Egypt.

But this was different. Whereas Pharaoh had commanded him to leave, Abimelech offered him a home in his kingdom (verse 15). It therefore appears that both kings were stricken with a great deal of fear. For when they perceived that they were reproved by the Lord because they had been troubling Abraham, they found no way to appease God except by acts of kindness for the harm they had done to the holy man.

**16.** When Abimelech had given **a thousand shekels of silver,** so that his generosity might not be in doubt, he declared that he had given them to Abraham. Since Abraham had been treated in this honorable way, his wife would not be thought of as a harlot.

**17-18. Then Abraham prayed to God, and God healed Abimelech, his wife and his slave girls so they could have children again, for the LORD had closed up every womb in Abimelech's household because of Abraham's wife Sarah.** God's wonderful favor to Abraham is seen here in two ways. First, as with an outstretched hand, God avenged the injury that had been done to him. Second, through Abraham's prayer, God was pacified toward the house of Abimelech. It was necessary to declare that the house of Abimelech had been healed in answer to Abraham's prayers, so that the inhabitants might be grateful to him.

A question may arise about the kind of punishment described by the words, **the LORD had closed up every womb in Abimelech's household.** If Abraham had gone into the land of Gerar after Sarah had conceived, and if all that Moses relates here was fulfilled before Isaac was born, how was it possible that in so short a time this sterility should be manifest? If we say that the judgment of God was made plain in a manner to us unknown, the answer would not be inappropriate. Yet I am not certain that events recorded here have not been inverted. The more probable supposition may be that Abraham had already been living in Gerar when Isaac was promised to him, but that events that had before been omitted are now inserted by Moses. Should anyone object that Abraham lived in Mamre until the destruction of Sodom, there would be nothing absurd in the belief that what Moses here relates had taken place previously. Yet, since the correct notation of time does little for the confirmation of our faith, I leave both opinions open.

# Genesis
# Chapter 21

**1.** In this chapter not only is the birth of Isaac recorded, but because in his very birth God has set before us a picture of his church, Moses also gives a detailed account of this matter. First, he says **the LORD did for Sarah what he had promised.** All children flow from the kindness of God (see Psalm 127:3). For although the fetus seems to be produced naturally, there is no procreation unless the Lord's power is present to fulfill his words, "Increase and multiply." In the propagation of the human race, God's special blessing is obvious. Therefore, the birth of every child is rightly said to be the result of a divine visitation.

Anyone who wants to rightly and prudently reflect on God's work in the birth of Isaac must begin with the promise. There is great emphasis in the words, **the LORD did for Sarah what he had promised.** Moses draws the attention of his readers to this fact so they may pause to reflect on so great a miracle. Meanwhile, Moses commends the faithfulness of God—God never feeds men with empty promises.

**2.** This is said according to the customary way because the woman is neither the head of a family, nor bears children by herself. What follows, however, should be noted carefully. **In his old age:** Abraham's **old age** emphasizes the magnitude of this miracle. And now Moses, for the third time, reminds us of the word of God—**at the very time God had promised him.** Although the time had been foretold to both Abraham and his wife, yet this honor is expressly attributed to the holy man, because the promise had been especially given on his account. Both, however, are specifically mentioned in this verse.

**3.** Moses does not mean that Abraham gave this name to his son, but that he kept to the name that had been previously given by the angel (see 17:19). This act of obedience, however, was worthy of commendation since he not only ratified the word of God but also executed his office as God's minister. For as a herald he proclaimed to all what the angel had committed to his trust.

**4.** Abraham continued to be obedient and did not spare his own son. Although it would be painful for him to wound the tender body of the infant, he set aside all human affection and obeyed the word of God, for Moses records that he did **as God commanded him**. Nothing is more important than to take the pure word of God for our rule. This submissive spirit is especially required in reference to sacraments, lest men should either invent anything for themselves or should transfer those things that are commanded by the Lord to be used in any way they please. We see, indeed, how inordinately the desires of men prevail, in that they have dared to devise innumerable sacraments. An example of this is that God gave only two sacraments to the Christian Church, but others boast that they have seven.

**5-6.** Moses again records the age of Abraham, to alert the minds of his readers to consider this miracle. Although only Abraham is mentioned [in verse 5], let us remember that he is in this place set before us not as a man of lust but as the husband of Sarah, and he obtained through her a lawful seed in extreme old age, when the strength of both had failed. The power of God was mainly seen in that when their marriage had been fruitless for more than sixty years, suddenly they had a child. Sarah, in order to make amends for the doubt to which she had given way, now exultingly proclaimed the kindness of God with becoming praises. **Sarah said, "God has brought me laughter, and everyone who hears about this will laugh with me."** By **"Everyone who hears about this will laugh with me"** Sarah meant, "They will congratulate me and rejoice with me."

**7.** Sarah linked the work of nurse with that of mother, for the Lord prepares nourishment for children in their mothers' breasts before they are born.

**8.** Moses now begins to relate how Ishmael was rejected by Abraham's family, in order that Isaac alone might be the lawful son and heir. It seems, indeed, at first sight that Sarah was being angry about nothing. But Paul teaches that a sublime mystery is being revealed here about the constant state of the church (see Galatians 4:21-31). If we consider carefully the people mentioned, we will see that it is no trivial matter that the father of all the faithful was divinely commanded to eject his firstborn son.

**On the day Isaac was weaned Abraham held a great feast.** It may be asked why Abraham did not choose the day of Isaac's birth or circumcision. The clever reasoning of Augustine that the day of Isaac's weaning was celebrated in order that we may learn from his example no more to be children in understanding is too strained. What others say has no greater consistency—namely, that Abraham chose a day that was not usually taken so that he might not imitate the customs of the Gentiles. Indeed, it is very possible that he may also have celebrated the birthday of his son with honor and joy. But special mention is made of this **feast** for another reason—namely, because Ishmael's mocking (verse 9) was then discovered. Moses does not speak in a disparaging way about the festivities of that **feast** but rather takes their lawfulness for granted. It is not his purpose to prevent holy men from inviting their friends to take part in a joyful occasion, so they can all give thanks to God, though temperance and sobriety should always be observed. I would only say that God does not treat us in such an austere way that he does not sometimes allow us to entertain our friends—for example, as we celebrate the birth of a child.

**9.** That Ishmael's **mocking** was not innocent teasing is apparent from Sarah's indignation. It was a malignant expression of scorn, by which the youth showed his contempt for his infant brother. Paul identifies Ishmael's **mocking** as persecution: "At that time the son born in the ordinary way persecuted the son born by the power of the Spirit" (Galatians 4:29). Was this done with sword or violence? No, but with the scorn of a venomous tongue, which does not injure the body but pierces into the very soul. Moses might indeed have emphasized his crime with a long description of it, but I think he spoke about it in this concise way on purpose—to show how detestable Ishmael's contempt was, for he ridiculed the word of God.

**10.** Not only was Sarah exasperated with the transgressor, but she acted in an unbecoming way toward her husband. The apostle Peter shows that on a previous occasion when Sarah "called him her master" (1 Peter 3:6), she did so in a respectful way. Although I do not deny that Sarah, moved by womanly feelings, exceeded the bounds of moderation, I do not doubt that both her tongue and mind were governed by a secret impulse of the Spirit and that this whole incident was directed by God's providence.

**11.** Although Abraham had already been assured by many oracles that the blessed seed would only come from Isaac, yet as a result of paternal affection he could not bear that Ishmael should be cut off. It may truly seem absurd that God's servant would be carried away by blind impulse. But God deprived him of judgment in this way, not only to humble him but also to testify to all ages that his grace depends on his own will alone. Moreover, in order that the holy man might bear with greater equanimity the departure of his son, he was promised a double consolation. First, God reminded him (verse 12) about the promise concerning Isaac. It was as if God said, "It is enough and more than enough that Isaac, in whom the spiritual benediction completely rests, is left." He then promised that he would take care of Ishmael, even though he would be exiled from his paternal home. Abraham was further promised that a whole nation would come from him.

**12.** I have just said that although God used the ministry of Sarah in so great a matter, it was yet possible that she might have acted in the wrong way. God now commanded Abraham to pay attention to his wife, not because God approved her disposition, but because God wanted the work that he authored accomplished. In this way God showed that his purposes are not subject to any human way of doing things, especially when the salvation of the church is concerned. For God purposely inverted the normal order of nature, so that he could show that he himself was the Author and Perfecter of Isaac's vocation. This event is considered in more detail by Paul, while just the summary of it is given here. Paul says that what is read here was written allegorically. However, Paul does not want historic events to be indiscriminately interpreted in an allegorical way so that the sense is mangled, as Origen does. For Origen hunts everywhere for allegories and so corrupts all of Scripture. Other people eagerly emulating his example have vitiated the simplicity of Scripture and have opened the door to many foolish ideas.

Paul's purpose was to raise the minds of the pious to consider the secret work of God in this event. It is as if he said, "What Moses relates concerning the house of Abraham belongs to the spiritual kingdom of Christ, since certainly that house was a strong image of the church." This, however, is the allegorical similitude that Paul commends: Whereas two sons were born to Abraham, one by a slave woman, the other by a free woman, Paul infers that there are two kinds of people born in the church—the faithful, whom God endues with the Spirit of adoption, that they may enjoy the inheritance, and hypocritical disciples who usurp for a time a name and place among the children of God.

Later on Paul uses another similitude in which he compares Hagar with Mount Sinai and Sarah with the heavenly Jerusalem. It is perfectly clear what Paul is teaching. We know that the true children of God are born of the incorruptible seed of the Word; but when the spirit that gives life to the doctrine of the law and the prophets is taken away, and the dead letter alone remains, that seed becomes corrupt. Spiritually adulterous children are born in a state of slavery; yet because they are apparently born of the Word of God, though corrupted, they are in a sense the children of God. Meanwhile, none are lawful heirs except those whom the church brings into freedom, as they are conceived by the incorruptible seed of the Gospel. These two people, Ishmael and Isaac, represent the constant condition of the church. For hypocrites not only mingle with the children of God in the church but despise them and proudly appropriate to themselves all the rights and honors of the church. As Ishmael, inflated with the vain title of firstborn, harassed his brother Isaac with his taunts, so these men, relying on their own splendor, reproachfully assail and ridicule true faith. They arrogate everything to themselves and leave nothing to the grace of God. Hence we are admonished that men are not assured of salvation unless they take note of the mercy of God as the basis for their spiritual life.

**14.** We can gather how painful Abraham found the wound that the ejection of his firstborn son inflicted on his mind from the double consolation God gave him to mitigate his grief: Abraham **sent** him into the desert as if he were tearing out his own heart. But as Abraham was used to obeying God, he overrode his paternal love, which he was not able to cast totally to one side. It is the true test of faith and piety when the faithful are compelled to deny themselves in such a way that they even submit the affections of their human nature to God's will, even though such affections are neither evil nor vicious in themselves.

Moses intimates not only that Abraham committed his son Ishmael to the care of his mother, but that he also relinquished his own paternal right over him. For it was necessary for this son to be alienated from him so that he might not later be considered the seed of Abraham. But what a meager provision he gave to his wife and her son. Abraham placed **some food and a skin of water** on her shoulders. Why did he not at least load up a donkey with more food? Why did he not assign one of his servants to them? Either God shut Abraham's mind to what was really necessary or Abraham gave only limited provisions on purpose, in order that Hagar might not go far from his house. Perhaps he preferred them to be near him so he could help them if the need arose. Meanwhile, God designed that Ishmael's banishment would be severe and sorrowful (see verses 15-16). In this way his example would strike terror into the proud who, intoxicated with present gifts, trample underfoot in their haughtiness the very grace to which they are indebted for all things.

**17.** Moses had said in verse 16 that Hagar wept. So why did God disregard her tears and only hear the voice of **the boy**? If we say that the mother did not deserve to have her prayers answered favorably, her son was no more worthy. As for the supposition that they were both brought to repentance by punishment, that is an uncertain conjecture. I leave their repentance, of which I can see no sign, to the judgment of God. The boy's cry was heard, as I understand it, not because he had prayed in faith but because God, mindful of his own promise, had compassion on them. For Moses does not say that their cries and sighs were directed toward heaven. Rather, it is to be believed that in bewailing their miseries, they did not resort to divine help. But God, in helping them, remembered not what they wanted from him, but what he had promised to Abraham concerning Ishmael. In this sense Moses seems to say that the voice of the boy was heard because he was the son of Abraham.

The angel reproved Hagar's ingratitude because when she was in great danger she did not reflect on God's former kindness to her and throw herself on his faithfulness. Nevertheless, the angel assured her that a way out had been provided if she would only seek it. We see from this example the truth in the saying that when father and mother forsake us, the Lord will look after us.

**18.** We must note carefully that when God leaves us destitute of his care and takes his grace away from us, we are deprived of all the assistance that is close to hand, as if it were taken very far away from us. Therefore, we must ask that God would not only give us the things that will be useful to us, but that he will also enable us to use them.

**20. God was with the boy as he grew up. He lived in the desert and became an archer.** There are many ways in which God is said to be present with men. He is present with his elect as he rules them with the special grace of his Spirit; he is present also sometimes, as far as external life is concerned, not only with his elect but with strangers when he grants them some special blessing. In the instance here Moses focuses on the extraordinary grace through which the Lord declared that his promise was not void, since he pursued Ishmael with favor because he was Abraham's son. From this, however, the general doctrine is inferred that when men grow up and enjoy the light and breath of heaven and feed on food from the earth, it is all from God's hand. But it must be remembered that Ishmael's prosperity flowed from God because this earthly blessing was promised him on account of his father Abraham.

**21.** In saying that Hagar **got a wife** for Ishmael, Moses is showing respect for the civil order, for marriage forms a principal part of human life. But as the wife came **from Egypt**, this was a kind of prelude to the future dissension between the Israelites and the Ishmaelites.

**22.** Moses recounts how Abraham and Abimelech entered into an agreement to show that after various agitations some rest was, at length, granted to the holy man. He had been living as a nomad, without any settled place to live, having to move his tent from place to place, for the past sixty years. Although God would make Abraham to be a traveler until he died, yet under King Abimelech he granted him some tranquillity.

Moses wants to show how it happened that Abraham stayed in this one place longer than he normally stayed anywhere else. It should be noted that this happened soon after he had sent his son away. It seems that his great sadness was immediately followed by this consolation. In this way he received some respite from traveling and was able to devote himself to bringing up his little son Isaac.

**23.** The Hebrew word for **kindness**, *chesed*, signifies "to deal gently or kindly" with someone. Abimelech did not come to implore compassion from Abraham but rather to assert his own royal authority, as is apparent from the context.

**24.** Abraham did not refuse to **swear**, because he knew it was lawful that covenants should be ratified between men in the sacred name of God. In short, we see Abraham willingly submitting himself to the laws of his vocation.

**25.** We see from this incident how severely the Lord exercised Abraham as soon as his life appeared to be more at ease. Certainly it was not a light trial to be compelled to argue over **a well of water** that he himself had dug.

**27.** From this it appears that the covenant Abraham and Abimelech made was not the usual one entered into between equals. For Abraham considered his own position and as a sign of being inferior to Abimelech offered a gift from his flocks to that king of Gerar. This was what the Romans call paying tax or tribute, and what we call doing homage, and what the Jews call offering gifts.

**28-30.** Moses recounts another major point of the covenant—namely, that Abraham made specific provision for himself concerning the well so he would be able to freely use its water. Abraham presented **seven ewe lambs** so that after the king had been presented with this honorary gift, he might approve and ratify the digging of the well.

**31.** Moses has already called the place by the name **Beersheba** (verse 14), but proleptically. Now, however, he declares when and for what reason the name was given. It was given because there both Abraham and Abimelech swore an oath. Therefore I translate **Beersheba** as "the well of swearing." Others translate it "the well of seven." But Moses plainly derives the word from swearing or oath. In fact, Moses does not restrict the etymology to the well but includes the whole covenant. I do not, however, deny that Moses might allude to the number "seven."

**33.** It seems from this that Abraham was granted more rest after he had made the covenant than he had previously enjoyed. He now began to plant **a tamarisk tree**, which is a sign of a tranquil and settled life, for we never read prior to this that he planted a single shrub.

The assertion that Abraham **called upon the name of the Lord, the Eternal God** I explain as follows: He instituted anew the solemn worship of God, to bear witness to his gratitude to God. We know that Abraham, wherever he went, never neglected this religious duty. Nor was he deterred by dangers from professing himself a worshiper of the true God, although on this account he was hated by his neighbors.

**34. And Abraham stayed in the land of the Philistines for a long time.** Abraham is here said to have settled in that land. But his mind was not so fixed on this time of repose to prevent him from considering what he had previously heard from God—that he with his posterity would be strangers until 400 years had elapsed.

# Genesis
# Chapter 22

**1. Some time later God tested Abraham. He said to him, "Abraham!"** **"Here I am," he replied.** This chapter contains a most memorable narrative. Although Abraham throughout his life gave astonishing witness to his faith and obedience, nothing can equal the sacrifice of his son. Other temptations with which the Lord had exercised him may have wounded him, but this inflicted a wound that was worse than death itself. Here, however, we must consider something greater and higher than paternal grief and anguish over the death of an only son, which pierced the heart of the holy man. It was sad for him to be deprived of his only son, sadder still that this son should be torn away by a violent death, but most grievous of all that Abraham himself should be appointed as executioner to kill him with his own hand. If we compare all the other spiritual conflicts Abraham engaged in with this one event, they are mere shadows. For the reason for his own sadness was not his own bereavement or that he was commanded to kill his only heir, but that in the person of this son, the whole salvation of the world seemed to perish. His struggle, too, was not with his carnal passions; as he wanted to devote himself wholly to God, his very piety and religion filled him with distracting thoughts. For God, as if engaging in a personal contest with him, required the death of the boy in whom God himself had linked the hope of eternal salvation. So that latter command was, in a certain sense, the destruction of faith. This foretaste of the story before us has been given to the readers so that they may reflect on how important it is for their meditation.

**Some time later God tested Abraham.** The expression **some time later** should not be restricted to Abraham's last vision. Rather, Moses intended to include in one phrase the various events in which Abraham had been tossed up and down, as well as the more settled state of life into which, in his old age, he had recently entered. He had lived through an unsettled life in constant exile up to his eightieth year. He had been harassed by many enemies; he had endured a miserable and anxious existence, in constant fear for his life; famine had driven him out of the land he had gone to by the command and under the auspices of God, into Egypt. Twice his wife had been torn from his heart; he had been separated from his nephew; he had delivered this nephew, when captured in war, at the peril of his own life. He had lived childless with his wife, with no hope of having any children. Having at length obtained a son, Ishmael, he was compelled to disinherit him and to drive him far from home.

Now Isaac alone remained, Abraham's special but only consolation. Abraham was enjoying peace at home. But now God suddenly thundered out of heaven, pronouncing the death sentence on this son. This passage means that by this test, Abraham's faith was far more severely tried than before.

**God tested Abraham.** James, in denying that anyone is tempted by God (James 1:13), refutes the profane suggestions of those who, to exonerate themselves from the blame of their sins, attempt to blame God when they are tempted. Therefore, James rightly argues that our sins, which are rooted in our own desires, should not be thought of as coming from elsewhere. Although Satan instills his poison and fans the flame of our corrupt desires within us, we are still not made to sin by any external force, since our own evil desires entice us and we willingly yield to their allurements. This, however, is no reason why God may not be said to test us in his own way, just as he **tested** Abraham, that he might try the faith of his servant.

**He said to him, "Abraham!"** Moses points out the kind of test Abraham was faced with. God would shake the faith that the holy man had placed in his word with an assault of the word itself. God addressed him by name—**"Abraham!"**—so there would be no doubt about who was issuing the command. For unless Abraham was totally convinced it was God's voice that commanded him to kill his son Isaac, he would have been quickly released from anxiety; relying on the certain promise of God, he would have rejected the suggestion as a trick from Satan. In this way and without any difficulty, the test would have been shrugged off. But now all reason for doubt was removed. Abraham had to acknowledge that the oracle that he heard was from God.

**"Here I am," he replied.** From this it appears that the holy man was in no way afraid of the wiles of Satan. The faithful are not in such a hurry to obey God that they allow a foolish credulity to carry them in whatever direction the breath of a doubtful vision may blow. But as soon as it was clear to Abraham that he was called by God, he testified by his answer that he was ready to obey. It was as if he said, "Whatever God is pleased to command, I am perfectly ready to do." Abraham did not wait until God specifically told him what he must do but promised that he would simply and without exception be obedient in all things. It certainly is true subjection when we are prepared to act before the will of God is made known to us. We find, indeed, that all men boast that they will do as Abraham did, but when it comes to the trial, they shrink from God's yoke. But the holy man soon proved by his actions that he, without delay and without any argument, subjected himself to God's hand.

**2. Then God said, "Take your son, your only son, Isaac, whom you love, and go to the region of Moriah. Sacrifice him there as a burnt offering on one of the mountains I will tell you about."** Abraham was commanded to offer his son as a sacrifice. If God had just said that his son would die, the message would have wounded Abraham's heart dreadfully. For whatever favor he could hope for from God was included in this single promise: "In Isaac will your seed be called." From this he correctly inferred that his own salvation, and that of the whole human race, would perish unless Isaac remained safe. For he was taught that God would not be propitious to man without a mediator. How could he have had this hope if it did not come from Isaac? The matter had come to this: It appeared that God had done nothing but mock him. Yet not only was the death of his son announced, but Abraham was commanded with his own hand to kill him, as if he were required not only to throw to one side but to cut in pieces or throw into the fire the charter of his salvation. In this way he would have nothing left for himself but death and hell.

It may be asked how, under the guidance of faith, he could be brought to sacrifice his son, seeing that what was proposed to him contradicted that word of God on which it is necessary for faith to rely? To this question the apostle answers that his confidence in the word of God remained unshaken. Abraham hoped that God would be able to make the promised blessing spring up, even out of the dead ashes of his son (see Hebrews 11:19). His mind, however, was crushed and agitated when the command and the promise of God seemed to contradict each other. But when he had come to the conclusion that the God whom he knew he had to obey could not be his adversary, although he did not at once know how the contradiction might be removed, he nevertheless, by hope, reconciled the command with the promise; being indubitably persuaded that God was faithful, he left the unknown issue to divine providence. Meanwhile, as if his eyes were closed, he went where he was directed.

**"Take your son, your only son, Isaac, whom you love."** As if it were not enough to command in one word the sacrifice of Abraham's son, God pierced, as with fresh strokes, the mind of the holy man. By calling **Isaac** Abraham's **only** son, the Lord aggravated the wound that had been recently inflicted by the banishment of the other son. As he looked into the future, Abraham saw that there was no hope of any offspring remaining. If the death of a firstborn son is unbearable, how severe Abraham's bereavement would certainly be. Each word that followed was emphasized and served to increase his grief. **"Sacrifice him,"** God said, **"Isaac, whom you love."**

Isaac was the mirror of eternal life, and the pledge of all good things. Therefore, God seemed not so much to assail the paternal love of Abraham as to trample upon his own benevolence. There is strong emphasis on the name **Isaac** through whom, Abraham had been taught, resided the only possibility of any joy for him. Certainly when he who had been given as the occasion of joy was taken away, it was as if God condemned Abraham to eternal torment. We must always remember that Isaac was not a son in any ordinary way, but one in whom the Mediator was promised.

**"Go to the region of Moriah."** The bitterness of Abraham's grief was greatly increased by this detail. For God did not require him to put his son to death at once but compelled him to think about this execution for the next three days. As he prepared to sacrifice his son, Abraham's senses were tortured all the more severely. Besides, God did not even state the exact place where he required the dire sacrifice to be offered. **"Sacrifice him there as a burnt offering on one of the mountains I will tell you about."** Before, when God commanded Abraham to leave his country, he kept him in suspense. But in this matter, the delay that most cruelly tormented the holy man, as if he had been stretched upon the rack, was even more unbearable. There were, however, two reasons for this suspense. There is nothing to which we are more prone than being wise beyond our capabilities. Therefore, in order that we may become docile and obedient to God, we benefit from being deprived of our own wisdom. Thus we are left with nothing to do but to resign ourselves to be led according to God's will. Second, this also tended to make Abraham persevere, so that he would not obey God just because he had a sudden impulse to do so.

Jerome explains that the land of **Moriah** is "the land of vision," as if the name had been derived from *rahah*. But all who know Hebrew do not agree with this opinion. I am no happier with the interpretation that suggests this refers to the "myrrh" of God. Most people agree that this word is derived from the word *yarah*, which comes from the word *yarai*, which signifies "fear." It is called the land of divine worship either because God had appointed it for the offering of the sacrifice, so that Abraham might not say that some other place should be chosen, or because this place had already been chosen as the site for the temple. I prefer this second explanation. And there is no doubt that this is the place where the temple was later built. God required his servant Abraham to worship him there because already in his secret counsel he had made up his mind that this was the place where he would be worshiped in the future. Also sacrifices are rightly associated with the word that means "fear" because they show reverence for God.

**3.** Abraham's prompt actions reveal the greatness of his faith. Innumerable thoughts must have come into the mind of the holy man. Each thought would have overwhelmed his spirit unless he had fortified it by faith. And there is no doubt that Satan, during the darkness of the night, heaped on him a vast weight of worry. Therefore, in a few words Moses highly extols the patriarch's faith, declaring that it surmounted in a short time all these temptations.

**4-6.** Abraham saw with his eyes the place that he had previously been shown in a secret vision. But when it is said **Abraham looked up,** Moses doubtless signifies that Abraham had been very anxious during the whole of the three days.

In commanding **his servants** to remain behind, Abraham ensured that they would not lay their hands upon Isaac. When, however, he said, **"we will come back to you,"** he appeared not to be free from dissimulation and falsehood. Some think he uttered this declaration prophetically; but since it is certain that he never lost sight of what had been promised concerning the raising up of seed in Isaac, it may be that he, trusting in the providence of God, thought of his son as surviving even in death itself. And seeing that he went, as with closed eyes, to slaughter his son, there is nothing improbable in the supposition that he spoke in an obscure way.

**7.** God produced here a new instrument of torture by which he might more and more torment Abraham's heart, which was already pierced with so many wounds. It should not be doubted that God purposely made Isaac ask a tender question: **"The fire and wood are here,"** Isaac said, **"but where is the lamb for the burnt offering?"** This only served to increase the extreme severity of Abraham's grief. Yet the holy man sustained even this attack with invincible courage; and far from being deflected from his proposed course, he showed himself to be entirely devoted to God. Abraham paid no attention to anything that might shake his confidence or hinder his obedience.

It is important to notice how Abraham untied this inextricable knot: He took refuge in divine providence. **"God himself will provide the lamb for the burnt offering, my son"** (verse 8). We should follow this example. We hardly honor God when we hope for nothing from him except what our senses can perceive. But we show him the highest honor when, in our great perplexity, we nevertheless entirely acquiesce to his will.

**8.** Here we see both Abraham's unwavering faith and the humility of his son. Abraham was not put off by this obstacle, and his son did not persist in questioning his father. For Isaac might easily have objected, "Why have we brought wood and the knife without a lamb if God has commanded sacrifices to be made to him?" But because he supposed that the victim had been omitted for some valid reason, and not through his father's forgetfulness, he acquiesced and was silent.

**9.** Moses deliberately passes over many things that, nevertheless, the reader should consider. After Moses mentions the building of **an altar,** he immediately adds that Isaac was **bound.** But we know that he might have been stronger than his father or at least would have been able to resist him. So I do not think force was used against the youth, as against one who struggles and is unwilling to die. Rather, Isaac voluntarily surrendered himself. It was, however, hardly possible that he would offer himself up to be killed unless he had already known about the divine oracle. But Moses, passing over this, only recounts that he was **bound**.

Should anyone object there was no need to bind one who willingly offered himself to be killed, I answer that the holy man anticipated in this way a possible danger, lest anything might happen to interrupt the sacrifice. The simplicity of Moses' narrative is wonderful. It is more powerful than the most detailed description. The whole event turns on this point: Abraham, when he had to kill his son, remained faithful to God. The strength of his mind made his aged hand equal to the task of offering a sacrifice, the very sight of which was enough to defeat his whole body.

**11.** The inner temptation had been already overcome when Abraham intrepidly raised his hand to slay his son, and it was by the special grace of God that he obtained such a special victory. But now Moses adds that suddenly, beyond all the bounds of hope, Abraham's sorrow was changed into joy. Poets in their fables, when affairs are desperate, introduce some god who unexpectedly appears at the critical moment. It is possible that Satan, through such devices, has tried to obscure God's wonderful interventions when the Lord has unexpectedly appeared to assist his servants. This event should be known and celebrated by everyone. We should consider how God, in the very moment of death, both brought Isaac back from death to life and restored to Abraham his son as one who had risen from the grave.

Moses also describes the voice of **the angel**, which rang out from heaven to assure Abraham that he had come from God in order that the holy man might withdraw his hand, directed by the same faith that had told him to stretch it out. For at such a momentous time it was not right for Abraham to do anything or refrain from doing anything unless it was directed by God. Let us, therefore, learn from his example not to follow what our earthly desires may dictate but rather to follow God's will.

**12.** Moses simply means that Abraham, by this very act, testified how reverently he feared God. It may, however, be asked whether he had not already on previous occasions given ample proof of his piety. I answer that when God had willed him to proceed this far, he had at length completed his true trial. In other people a much lighter trial might have been sufficient. As Abraham showed that he feared God by not sparing his own and only son, so all godly people should carry out acts of self-denial.

**13.** What the Jews imagine about this **ram**—that it was created on the sixth day of the world—is just a story. But we should not doubt that it came to be there in a miraculous way. It was a miracle whether it was created on the spot or whether it was brought there from some other place. For God intended to give it to his servant so that he could with joy offer up a sacrifice. Moreover, since a **ram** takes the place of Isaac,

God shows us, as in a mirror, what the purpose of our mortification is—namely, that by the Spirit of God living within us, we, though dead, may yet be living sacrifices.

**14.** Abraham, by this act of thanksgiving, acknowledged that God had at that moment, in a remarkable manner, provided for him. But Abraham also left a monument of his gratitude to posterity. **So Abraham called that place The LORD Will Provide. And to this day it is said, "On the mountain of the LORD it will be provided."**

**15.** What God had promised to Abraham before Isaac was born, he now again confirmed and ratified after Isaac was restored to life. Isaac rose from the altar—as if it had been from the grave—to illustrate God's complete triumph. **The angel** spoke in the person of God, so that those who bear his name may have greater authority.

**17.** Moses means that Abraham's offspring would be victorious over their enemies. While God has often allowed the enemies of the Jews to rule over them tyrannically, he so curbed their revenge that this promise always prevailed in the end. Further, we must remember that the victory is not promised indiscriminately to all children of Abraham but to those who are in Christ, those who belong to him. For unless we make a distinction between the legitimate and the degenerate sons of Abraham, this promise will be thought to include the Ishmaelites and Idumeans as well as the people of Israel.

**19-24.** Moses repeats that Abraham, having passed this severe and incredible test, **stayed in Beersheba**. This is inserted, together with what follows about Abraham's family increasing, to show that the holy man, when he had been delivered from the abyss of death, was made happy in many ways. God revived him, so that he became a new man.

Moses also records the progeny of **Nahor** for another reason—namely, because Isaac took his wife from this line. Women are rarely mentioned in Scripture. It is possible that many daughters were born to Nahor, of whom only one, Rebekah, is here introduced.

# Genesis
# Chapter 23

**1. Sarah lived to be a hundred and twenty-seven years old.** It is remarkable that Moses, who relates the death of Sarah in a single word (verse 2), uses so many words to describe her burial. But we will soon see that the latter record is not superfluous. Why he so briefly alludes to her death, I do not know, except that he leaves it to be reflected on by his readers. The holy fathers saw that they in common with reprobates were subject to death. Nevertheless, they were not deterred. While leading a life full of suffering, they advanced toward the goal. From this it follows that they were animated by the hope of a better life.

**2.** Why did Abraham **weep over** Sarah? If Abraham both privately wept over the death of his wife and mourned over the common curse of mankind, there is no fault in either of these. To feel no sadness at the contemplation of death is barbaric. Nevertheless, it might be that his grief was excessive. And yet Moses adds that **he rose from beside his dead wife** (verse 3). This witnesses to Abraham's showing moderation in his grief. From this Ambrose prudently infers that we are taught by this example how wrong it is to be preoccupied for a long time over mourning for the dead. If Abraham placed a limit on his grief and restrained his feelings when the doctrine of the resurrection was still obscure, we are without excuse, since we now have abundant consolation in the resurrection of Christ.

**3.** Moses is silent about the rite used by Abraham in burying his wife's body. But he describes at great length how Abraham purchased the tomb. Why he did this we will soon see. For now I will briefly touch on the custom of burial. How this has been observed in all ages and among all people is well known. Ceremonies have indeed been different, and men have endeavored to outdo each other in various superstitions. But to bury the dead has been common to all. And this practice has not arisen either from foolish curiosity or from the desire of fruitless consolation or from superstition, but from the natural sense with which God has imbued the minds of men. This sense he has never allowed to disappear, so that men might witness to themselves about a future life. It has not, I confess, always entered into the minds of heathens that their *souls* survived death and that the hope of a resurrection remained even for their *bodies*. Abraham, however, seeing he had the hope of a resurrection, deeply fixed in his heart its visible symbol.

The importance he attached to this is clear because he thought he would pollute Sarah's body if he buried it with the corpses of strangers. So Abraham bought a cave, that he might have for himself and his family a holy and pure tomb. He did not desire to have a foot of earth to pitch his tent. He only cared about his grave. And he particularly wanted to have his own family tomb in that land that had been promised to him for an inheritance. This would bear testimony to posterity that God's promise did not end with his own death or with the death of his family. For while the corpses themselves were silent and speechless, the tomb cried out that death was no obstacle to their taking possession of their inheritance. A thought like this would have been impossible unless Abraham by faith had looked up to heaven. And when he called the corpse of his wife *"my dead"* (verse 4), he intimated that though death is a kind of separation, some link still remains.

**4.** Abraham showed that he could possess no tomb unless he was granted permission to do so, for he was **an alien and a stranger** among the people whom he lived. Also, to avoid any ill will from those who lived in that land, Abraham said that he wanted to buy some land for his family tomb. It is as if he said, "I do not refuse to continue to live as a stranger among you, as I have done until now; I do not desire your possessions, in order that I may have something of my own, which may enable me to fight you as if I were your equal. It is enough for me to have a place where we may be buried."

**6.** The Hittites offered Abraham any tomb he wished; they would give it to him. They did this as a tribute to him. From this we see that some seeds of piety showed themselves in the Hittites.

**7.** Abraham declined the favor the Hittites offered because he did not want to be indebted to them in any way. Moses also commends the holy man's modesty when he says that Abraham **rose and bowed down before the people of the land, the Hittites**. This token of showing respect either by bowing the knee or in any other gesture of the body may be paid to men as well as to God, but for different purposes. Men either bend the knee or bow the head before each other for the sake of civil honor; but if the same thing is done in the name of religion, it is a profane gesture. For religion allows us only to worship the true God. Scripture, in general terms, forbids adoration to be given to men. But in case anyone should be surprised that Abraham acted in such a suppliant way and so submissively, we must be aware that it was done in line with the customs of that age. It is well known that the Orientals were immoderate in their use of ceremonies. If we compare the Greeks or Italians with ourselves, we are more sparing in our ceremonial actions than they are. So we must not compare the honor Abraham gave to the rulers of the land with our customs.

**8.** Abraham often declared that he was buying the field as a tomb. And Moses emphasizes this point so that we may learn to raise our minds to the hope of the resurrection with our father Abraham. Because he was certain that his wife was not cut off from the kingdom of God, he hid her dead body in the tomb until he and she should be gathered together.

**11.** Ephron insisted on giving his field to Abraham without charging him anything: **"I give you the field."** But the holy man continued to ask that the field be sold to him.

**16. Four hundred shekels of silver, according to the weight current among the merchants.** Moses speaks like this because this was the normal way in which merchandise was bought and sold. Moses says at the end of the chapter that **the field and the cave in it, and all the trees within the borders of the field . . . was deeded to Abraham as his property** (verses 17-18) by the Hittites, in the sense that the purchase was attested to publicly. Although it was a private sale, the people presented the contract between the two parties.

# Genesis
## Chapter 24

**1. Abraham was now old and well advanced in years, and the LORD had blessed him in every way.** Moses moves on to the subject of Isaac's marriage, for Abraham knew he was worn-out with old age. Abraham wanted to ensure that his son would not marry anyone in the land of Canaan. Moses specifically describes Abraham here as **old and well advanced in years**; he realized in his elderly state that a wife must be sought for his son. Old age itself, which is not far from death, ought to make us put our family affairs in order. Then when we die, our family will be at peace, and the fear of the Lord will flourish. When Abraham realized how old he was, he thought it was time to take action for the future welfare of his son. Irreligious men, partly because they do not hold marriage in honor, partly because they do not recognize how important Isaac's marriage would be, are surprised that Moses, or rather the Spirit of God, would relate this in such detail. But if we read the sacred Scriptures with reverence, we will readily understand that there is nothing superficial about this event. Most men do not think the providence of God extends to marriages. But Moses is most insistent that it does. His main aim, however, is to teach that God honored Abraham's family in a special way because the church would spring from it.

**2.** Abraham performed the normal duty of parents in being concerned about the choice of a wife for his son. Since God had separated him from the Canaanites by a sacred covenant, he was rightly concerned that Isaac should not join himself to them, as he might then shake off God's yoke. Abraham would not allow his own race to be mingled with that of the Canaanites, whom he knew God had already appointed for destruction.

**"Put your hand under my thigh."** It is obvious that this was a solemn form of taking an oath. But it is not known whether Abraham introduced it or whether he had received it from his fathers. It is true that the servant placed his hand under Abraham's thigh, but he was solemnly commanded by God, the Creator of heaven and earth. We are taught by Abraham's example that people do not sin who demand an oath for a lawful cause.

It has already been shown that the matter was of the utmost importance, since it was undertaken so that God's covenant might be ratified among Abraham's posterity.

**3.** Although this man was only a servant, yet because he was put in authority by the master of the family, his status as only a servant did not prevent him from being next in authority to his lord. Isaac himself, Abraham's heir and successor, submitted to his direction. This example should be followed by us to show that it is not right for the children of a family to arrange a marriage except with the consent of their parents.

**4.** In choosing the place, it seems that Abraham was influenced by the thought that a wife would more willingly come from there to be married to his son when she knew she was to marry one of her own race and country.

**5.** Since Moses says Isaac raised no objection to this, we may conjecture that he had total confidence in the integrity of his father's servant. We must also note the religious principles of the man, as he did not rashly take an oath. However, he wisely raised the question, **"What if the woman is unwilling to come back with me to this land? Shall I then take your son back to the country you came from?"**

**6.** If the woman was not willing to return with Abraham's servant, Isaac should not return to his country, because in this way he would deprive himself of the promised inheritance. Abraham, therefore, lived in hope as a stranger in the land of Canaan rather than living among his relatives in his native land. From this we see that in difficult situations the mind of the holy man was not deflected from carrying out God's command. This teaches us that we should follow God through every obstacle.

**7.** Using two arguments Abraham inferred that what he was deliberating concerning the marriage of his son would by God's grace have a happy ending. First, God had not led him from his own country into a foreign land in vain; and, second, God had not falsely promised to give the land, in which he was living as a stranger, to his seed. Abraham was also properly confident that he would be successful because he had undertaken this only by the authority and, as it were, under the auspices of God. For it was Abraham's exclusive regard for God that turned his mind away from the daughters of Canaan.

Abraham concluded from the past kindnesses of God that his hand would not fail him in the present undertaking. It is as if he said to the servant, "I who at God's command left my country and have experienced his continual help in my pilgrimage do not doubt that he will also guide you on your journey, for it is because you rely on God's promise that I lay on you this injunction."

Abraham then described how the servant would be helped in this task: God **"will send his angel before you."** Abraham knew that God helps his

214

servants through the ministry of angels, which he had experienced many times himself.

By calling God **"the Lord, the God of heaven,"** Abraham pointed to the divine power that was the ground of his confidence.

**10.** The servant took the **camels** with him to demonstrate that Abraham was a man of great wealth, so that he might easily obtain what he desired. For even an openhearted girl would not easily allow herself to be drawn away to a distant land unless she knew she would be provided with the necessities of life. Exile is sad enough without being accompanied by poverty. So that the girl might not be deterred by worrying about her needs being looked after but rather would be attracted by the prospect of affluence, the servant loaded up **ten of his master's camels** with presents. This would give ample proof of Abraham's opulence to the inhabitants of Chaldea.

**12. Then he prayed, "O Lord, God of my master Abraham, give me success today, and show kindness to my master Abraham."** The servant, having nobody to turn to for advice, prayed to the Lord. But he did not just ask for God's advice. He also prayed that Isaac's wife would be brought to him with a certain sign. In this way he would be able to discern if she was presented to him by the Lord.

This is clear evidence of the servant's piety and faith. In such a bewildering matter he was not perplexed, as one might have expected. He turned to prayer with a focused mind. The servant did not pray in a rash way or according to the desires of human nature, but by the secret impulse of the Spirit. His prayer can be summed up like this: "O Lord, if a girl presents herself who, on being asked to give me a drink, also kindly and courteously offers to water my camels, I will seek after her as if she is the one to be the wife for my master Isaac, as if she was delivered into my hand by you."

It should be noted that he did not look for some distant sign but for a sign from what was close to him. For if the girl revealed that she was welcoming an unknown guest, that act in itself would speak of her excellent disposition. This observation may prevent inquisitive men from using this example as a precedent for seeking all kinds of silly prognostications.

In the words of the servant's prayer note, first, that he called on the **God of his master Abraham.** This was not because he himself was unused to worshiping God, but because the matter in hand depended on the promise that had been given to Abraham. The servant only had confidence in prayer because of the covenant that God had entered into with the house of Abraham. The servant prayed as if saying, "O Lord, I will look in vain here and there, and I will not succeed as a result of my own work, labor, and industry unless you direct the work." And when he immediately added, **"and show kindness to my master Abraham,"** he implied that this undertaking only rested on the grace that God had promised to Abraham.

**15.** The events that followed amply demonstrate that the servant's wish had not been a foolish one. The speed of the answer showed God's extraordinary indulgence. He did not allow the man to be racked with anxiety for a long time, for Rebekah had left her house before he began to pray. It must be remembered that the Lord, at whose disposal are both the moments of time and the ways of man, had so arranged this that both parties would clearly see his providence. Sometimes the Lord keeps us in suspense for a long time, until we are tired from praying. But in this matter, so that his blessing might not be in doubt, God suddenly interposed.

The same thing happened to Daniel, to whom the angel appeared before he had finished his prayer (see Daniel 9:21-23). Although it often happens that on account of our sloth the Lord delays in granting our requests, it is expedient for us at such times that what we ask for should be delayed. For he has clearly proved by incontestable examples that although our prayer is not immediately granted, the prayers of God's people are never in vain. (See Isaiah 65:24.)

**21.** Abraham's servant looked at Rebekah carefully, and this shows that he had some doubt in his mind. He was silently asking himself if God had **made his journey successful.** Did he have no confidence about that divine direction about which he had received the sign or pledge? I reply that faith is never so perfect in the saints that doubts never arise. There is, therefore, nothing absurd in supposing that Abraham's servant, though committing himself generally to the providence of God, yet wavered and was agitated with so many conflicting thoughts. Faith, although it pacifies and calms the minds of the pious, so that they patiently wait for God, does not keep them from being concerned. From the hesitation of Abraham's servant we see that he was not faultless, for this flowed from a lack of faith. But it may be excused because he did not turn his eyes in any other direction. He only sought to have his faith confirmed from the event, that he might perceive God to be present with him.

**22.** Relying on the goodness of God, the servant gave Rebekah **a gold nose ring weighing a beka and two gold bracelets weighing ten shekels** as an earnest of future marriage. But it may be asked, Does God approve of ornaments of this kind, which have more to do with ostentation than with modesty? I reply that some of the things described in Scripture are not always to be imitated. Whatever the Lord commands in general terms is an inflexible rule of conduct; but to rely on particular examples is not only dangerous but even foolish and absurd. Now we know that God is displeased not only with pomp but with all kind of luxury. In order to free the heart from inner greed, he condemns immoderate splendor that contains within itself many allurements to vice. Where, indeed, is pure sincerity of heart found under sparkling ornaments? It is not, however, for us to specifically forbid every kind of ornament. However, anything beyond the frugal use of such things is tarnished to some extent with vanity. Because the greed of women is, on this point, insatiable, not only moderation but even abstinence must be cultivated as far as possible.

As far as the **gold nose ring** and **bracelets** that were given to Rebekah are concerned, as I am sure they were commonly used by the rich, they could be worn modestly. But I do not excuse this action, as I think it was flawed. This example, however, neither helps us nor alleviates our guilt if by such means we excite and continually inflame those depraved lusts that, even when all incentives are removed, it is excessively difficult to restrain. The women who desire to shine in gold seek in Rebekah a pretext for their corruption. Why, therefore, do they not conform to the same austere kind of life and rustic labor that she lived? But as I have just said, people are deceived who imagine that the examples of the saints give them a reason to oppose God's law.

It appears from the context that the ornaments were not given to Rebekah for any dishonorable purpose. They were tokens offered to the parents to facilitate the marriage contract.

**26-27.** When Abraham's servant heard that he had come across the daughter of Bethuel, his hopes rose more and more. But he did not put this down to luck or chance, as ungodly men do, but gave thanks to God. He knew that it was the result of providence that he had been led straight to the place he was looking for. He did not, therefore, boast of his good fortune, but he declared that God had shown his **kindness** and **faithfulness** to Abraham. In other words, for his own mercy's sake God had been faithful in fulfilling his promises. The language here is especially apt to describe God's character, both because he gratuitously confers favors on men and also, by never frustrating their hope, demonstrates that he is faithful and true. This thanksgiving, therefore, teaches us always to have the providence of God before our eyes, so that we may ascribe to him whatever good things happen to us.

**28-32.** It is probable that when Bethuel was told about the arrival of Abraham's servant, Laban was sent to meet the stranger.

**33.** Moses starts to show how Rebekah's parents were persuaded to give her in marriage to their nephew. That the servant, when food was set before him, should refuse to eat until he had completed his work shows his diligence and faithfulness.

The servant seemed to relate a meandering story, but there was nothing in it that did not serve his purpose. He knew it was natural for parents to be unwilling to allow their children to travel a long distance away from them. Therefore, the servant mentioned Abraham's riches, so that they might not hesitate to have their daughter married to so wealthy a husband. He then explained that Isaac was born in his mother's old age, not just to inform them that he had been miraculously given to his father,

217

from which they might infer that he had been divinely appointed to this greatness and eminence, but so additional commendation might be given because of Isaac's age. In the third place, he affirmed that Isaac would be his father's sole heir. Fourth, he related that he had been bound by an oath to seek a wife for his master Isaac from among his own people. Fifth, he stated that Abraham was totally confident that God would guide him and that Abraham had committed the whole matter to his servant. Sixth, he declared that whatever he had asked in prayer, he had obtained from the Lord, from which it appeared that the marriage of which he was about to speak was according to the will of God.

We now see the purpose behind the servant's long account about Abraham's family. First, he wanted to persuade the parents of Rebekah that he had not been sent to deceive them but had come in the fear of the Lord, as the religious obligation of marriage requires. Second, he was only seeking what would be profitable and honorable for them. And last, he wanted them to know that God had been the director of the whole undertaking.

**50. Laban and Bethuel answered, "This is from the LORD; we can say nothing to you one way or the other."** They were convinced by what the servant said that God was the Author of this marriage. They agreed that it would be wrong to oppose it in any way. They declared that the marriage came from the Lord because he had, by the clearest of signs, made his will known.

**52.** Moses repeats that Abraham's servant gave thanks to God. The acknowledgment of God's kindness is a sweet-smelling sacrifice. It is more acceptable than all other sacrifices. God is continually heaping innumerable benefits on men. Their ingratitude, therefore, is intolerable if they fail to celebrate those benefits.

**54. Then he and the men who were with him ate and drank and spent the night there. When they got up the next morning, he said, "Send me on my way to my master."** Moses emphasizes that it was **the next morning** that they left so that the servant's faithful industry in fulfilling his master's commands can be clearly seen. Although he acted as an honest and prudent servant, it should not be doubted that the Lord impelled him, for Isaac's sake, to act as he did. The Lord watches over his own people while they sleep and expedites and accomplishes their affairs in their absence.

**57. Then they said, "Let's call the girl and ask her about it."** Moses shows that Bethuel did not act in a tyrannical way over his daughter. He did not compel her to marry against her will but let her make up her own mind. In this matter the authority of parents should be sacred. But a middle way should be found so that the parties concerned decide the matter by mutual consent.

**58.** It is not right to understand that Rebekah in answering so explicitly

218

showed contempt for her parents or desired to be married too much. But since she saw that the matter had already been approved of by her father, with the consent of her mother, she also agreed.

**59.** Moses recounts that Rebekah left her home in an honorable way, accompanied by her **nurse**.

**60.** Moses adds that Rebekah's relatives **blessed** her. This means that they prayed that her life would be a happy one. We know that it is a solemn custom, in all ages and among all people, to send good wishes to all people who get married. The particular blessing that is recorded here was probably in common use because nature dictates that the propagation of offspring is the special purpose of marriage. The idea of victory over one's **enemies** is meant to indicate a prosperous life. The Lord, however, guided them into making a prophecy of which they themselves were ignorant. To **possess the gates of ... enemies** means to dominate them. For judgment was administered in the gates, and the main defense of the city was there.

**63.** Moses recounts how Isaac met his wife before she reached his home: **He went out to the field one evening to meditate, and as he looked up, he saw camels approaching.** It is probable that this was Isaac's habit, and that he sought a quiet place to pray, so that his mind, being released from all distractions, might be given over to serving God. Whether, however, he was giving his mind to meditation or to prayer, the Lord granted him a token of his own presence in that joyful meeting.

**65.** Moses says Rebekah **took her veil and covered herself** as a token of her modesty.

**67. Isaac brought her into the tent of his mother Sarah, and he married Rebekah. So she became his wife, and he loved her.** Isaac first brought Rebekah into the tent, then took her as his wife. By these words, Moses distinguishes between a correct way of marrying and barbarism. Certainly the sanctity of marriage demands that man and woman should not live together like cattle; but having pledged their mutual faith and having invoked the name of God, they may live with each other. Besides, it should be observed that Isaac was not compelled by any tyrannical command of his father to marry; but after he had made up his own mind about Rebekah, he took her freely and gladly assured her of his faithfulness to her in marriage.

**And Isaac was comforted after his mother's death.** Since Isaac's grief over the death of his mother was now assuaged, we infer how much he mourned over her, for a long time had elapsed since she died. We may also hence infer that the affection of Isaac was tender and gentle and that his love for his mother was quite unusual since he had mourned over her for so long. Knowing this stops us from imagining that the holy patriarchs were men who had barbaric habits and hearts of iron who were constantly engaged in brutality. However, care must be taken to keep grief from clouding our sight of the hope of a future resurrection.

# Genesis
# Chapter 25

**1. Abraham took another wife, whose name was Keturah.** It seems very strange that Abraham, who is said to have been as good as dead before Sarah died, should after her death marry again. Abraham acted very foolishly here. Some have conjectured that Abraham married a second wife while Sarah was still alive. Such an act is not altogether incredible. Perhaps Abraham did indulge in polygamy. Out of all the other possible explanations this seems to me the most likely. Certainly, if Abraham married a wife while Sarah was still alive (as I think most probable), his adulterous marriage was unworthy of divine benediction. But though we know not why this happened, yet God's wonderful providence is seen in this. For while many nations of considerable importance descended from his other sons, the spiritual covenant remained in the exclusive possession of Isaac.

**6. But while he was still living, he gave gifts to the sons of his concubines and sent them away from his son Isaac to the land of the east.** Moses relates that when Abraham was about to die, he planned to remove all reason for strife among his sons after his death by making Isaac his sole heir and dismissing the rest with suitable **gifts.** This dismissal was, indeed, apparently harsh and cruel. But it was in line with God's decree that the entire possession of the land might remain for the posterity of Isaac. For it was not right for Abraham to divide up the inheritance that had been granted in its entirety to Isaac. So no option was left open to Abraham but to provide for the rest of his sons in the way that is described here.

It is likely that no subsequent strife or contention took place about who should succeed Abraham. But by sending the sons of the concubines far away, **to the land of the east,** Abraham reduced this danger. In this way they would not occupy any of the land that God had assigned to the posterity of Isaac alone.

**7.** Moses now records the death of Abraham. The first thing to be noted is his age. **Altogether, Abraham lived a hundred and seventy-five years.** The number of years Abraham lived as a pilgrim is recorded.

221

Abraham deserves to be praised for his incomparable patience. For Abraham was led along by God's promise for a hundred years, through many life-threatening situations.

In addition to this, Moses shows that the Lord had fulfilled the promise he made to Abraham about his dying as an old man. For although he endured a hard battle, he had this great consolation—he knew his life was under God's protection. This looking to God sustained Abraham through all of his life, and so we must not become weary of trusting God but must rely on this support. For the Lord has promised us a happy outcome in our lives that is even more glorious than that of our father Abraham.

**8. Then Abraham breathed his last and died at a good old age, an old man and full of years.** It is wrong to suppose that this means Abraham died suddenly. It does not mean Abraham did not die as a result of a long and debilitating illness but just died without pain. Rather, Moses is saying that the father of the faithful was not exempt from the common lot of men. This should help us not languish when the outward man is perishing. At that time we should meditate on the renewal that is the object of our hope, so that with tranquil minds we can allow this frail tabernacle to be dissolved. There is, therefore, no reason why a feeble, emaciated body, failing eyes, trembling hands, and the loss of the use of all our limbs should completely dishearten us. Following the example of our father, we should look forward to death with joy.

The most important part of old age consists of a good conscience and a serene and tranquil mind. From this it follows that what God promised to Abraham can only apply to those who truly cultivate righteousness. Plato says, with both truth and wisdom, that a good hope is the nutriment of old age; and, therefore, old men who have a guilty conscience are miserably tormented and are inwardly racked with constant torture. But to this we must add something that Plato did not know: It is godliness that should accompany old age to the grave because faith produces a quiet mind.

**And he was gathered to his people.** I readily agree with those who say that the state of our future life is contained in this expression. But we should not restrict this, as some exposito rs do, to the faithful only. What it really means is that mankind is linked in death as well as in life. It may seem strange to ungodly men that David says that the reprobate are gathered together like sheep in the grave. But if we look at the expression more closely, this gathering together has no existence if their souls are annihilated. If human life vanished, and men were annihilated at death, it would not be right to speak of Abraham being **gathered to his people**. So when Scripture speaks in this way, it shows that another state of life remains after death. Leaving this world is not the destruction of the whole man.

**9.** From this it is clear that although Ishmael had been ejected long ago, he was not utterly alienated from his father, because he acted as a son in attending to Abraham's burial.

**12. This is the account of Abraham's son Ishmael, whom Sarah's maidservant, Hagar the Egyptian, bore to Abraham.** This narration is not superfluous. At the beginning of this chapter Moses alludes to what happened to the sons of Keturah. Here Moses shows how God's promise (Genesis 17:1) was fulfilled. To start with, it was a sign of God's grace that Ishmael would have twelve sons who would rule over twelve tribes. After Moses listed the towns in which the descendants of Ishmael lived, the whole people were buried in oblivion. For only spiritual descendants of Abraham will remain in the church. In addition to this, Moses, at a stroke, shows God's wonderful counsel because a region distinct from the land of Canaan is assigned to the sons of Ishmael. In this way his future is provided for and does not intrude on the inheritance of the sons of Isaac.

**19. This is the account of Abraham's son Isaac. Abraham became the father of Isaac.** What Moses has said about the Ishmaelites was incidental to the central part of his account, to which he now returns. His aim was to describe the progress of the church. He repeats that Isaac's wife was taken from Mesopotamia. He specifically calls Rebekah the **sister of Laban the Aramean** (verse 20), for Laban became the father-in-law of Jacob, concerning whom Moses had much to relate.

**21.** But it is particularly important to note that Moses says Rebekah **was barren** during the early part of her marriage. Later we will see that her barrenness lasted not for three or four years, but for twenty years. In this way when Rebekah was granted the blessing of having children, this gift was seen against the background of Rebekah's many years of despair. But nothing seems less rational than that the growth of the church should be so small and slow. But from this small and contemptible origin, even though the growth was feeble, we learn that the church was produced and increased according to God's power and grace. It did not grow through mere natural means.

**Isaac prayed to the LORD on behalf of his wife, because she was barren. The LORD answered his prayer, and his wife Rebekah became pregnant.** Isaac knew that he was deprived of children because God had not blessed him. He also knew that fruitfulness was a special gift of God. It is clear that Isaac was endued with special, persevering faith. He knew about God's covenant to him, and so he prayed earnestly, for he needed descendants so badly. But this was not the first time it had crossed his mind to pray, as he had been disappointed about this for more than twenty years. So although Moses mentions in just one sentence that **the LORD answered his prayer,** yet he had prayed for many years. The patience of this holy man is clearly seen. While it seemed that he prayed in vain into the air, he was still praying earnestly. Through this Isaac teaches us, by his example, to persevere in prayer. God also shows us here that he never turns a deaf ear to the wishes of his faithful people, although he may not answer them for a long time.

**22.** Here a new problem suddenly arises—namely, the infants struggled together in their mother's womb. This caused the mother so much grief that she wanted to die. She doubtless perceived that this conflict did not arise from natural causes but portended some dreadful and tragic end.

Moses then recounts that Rebekah asked for the Lord's help. She knew that nothing would calm her mind more than obeying God's will. In that day God made his will known by oracles. If we consider the importance of the matter, it was more appropriate that the secret should be revealed through God's mouth than by the testimony of any man. In our times a different method prevails. For God does not today reveal the future through such miracles; and the teaching of the law, the prophets, and the Gospel, which comprise all wisdom, is more than sufficient to regulate our lives.

**23. The LORD said to her, "Two nations are in your womb, and two peoples from within you will be separated; one people will be stronger than the other, and the older will serve the younger."** In the first place, God answered that the fight between the twin brothers referred to something way beyond the two people themselves. The Lord shows here that there would be discord between their two families.

When the Lord said there were **"two nations,"** the expression is emphatic. For since they were brothers and twins, and therefore of one blood, the mother did not think they would become so separate as to become the heads of two distinct nations. But God declared that the **"two peoples from within you will be separated."** He declared, second, that **"one people will be stronger than the other."** Since reprobates give way reluctantly, it follows that the children of God have to undergo many troubles because they are God's adopted children. Third, the Lord affirmed that, the order of nature being inverted, the younger, who was inferior, would be the victor. **"And the older will serve the younger."**

We must now observe what this implies. Those who restrict it to earthly riches and wealth are trifling. Undoubtedly through this word from the Lord, Isaac and Rebekah were taught that the covenant of salvation would not be for both peoples but would apply only to the posterity of Jacob.

If we look for the reason why this distinction is made, it will not be found in nature; for the origin of both nations was the same. The reason will not be found in merit because the heads of both nations were still in their mother's womb when the fight started. Moreover, God, in order to humble the pride of the flesh, determined to take away from men all reason for boasting. The preference that God gave to Jacob over his brother Esau by making him the father of the church was not given as a reward for his merits; neither did he achieve it through his own industry. It came from the sheer grace of God himself.

Faith, indeed, is what distinguishes the spiritual from the physical seed. But the question now under consideration is the *principle* on which this distinction is made, not the symbol or mark by which it is attested. God, therefore, chose the whole seed of Jacob without exception, as the Scripture in many places testifies, because he has conferred on all alike the same testimonies of his grace in the Word and sacraments. But another and special election has always flourished, which included a definite number of men, so that God might save those whom he would.

A question arises here for our consideration. While Moses speaks about the former kind of election, Paul speaks about the latter kind of election. Paul's argument is well-known. For when the Jews, inflated with the title of the church, rejected the Gospel, the faith of the simple was shaken because they thought it was improbable that Christ, and the salvation promised through him, could possibly be rejected by an elect people, a holy nation, and the genuine children of God. Therefore, Paul contends that not all who descend from Jacob, according to the flesh, are true Israelites, because God of his own good pleasure may choose whom he will as heirs of eternal salvation. Who cannot see that Paul moves from a general to a particular adoption to teach us that not all who have a place in the church are to be accounted as true members of the church?

Let it, therefore, remain as a settled point of doctrine that among men some perish and some obtain salvation; but the cause of this depends on the secret will of God. From where does it arise that those who are born of Abraham do not all possess the same privilege? The disparity of condition certainly cannot be ascribed either to the virtue of the one or to the vice of the other in this case, seeing they were not yet born. Since the common feeling of mankind rejects this doctrine, there have been found in all ages clever men who have fiercely argued against God's election. It is not my present purpose to refute or weaken their calumnies. It is sufficient for us to hold fast what we gather from Paul's interpretation—that whereas the whole human race deserves the same destruction and is bound under the same sentence of condemnation, some are delivered by gratuitous mercy, while others are justly left to their own destruction. And those whom God has chosen are not preferred to others because God foresaw they *would* be holy, but in order that they *might* be holy. But if the first origin of holiness is the election of God, we seek in vain for that difference in men that rests solely in doing the will of God.

If anyone desires a mystical interpretation of the subject, we may give the following: Whereas many hypocrites, who are for a time enclosed in the womb of the church, pride themselves on an empty title and with insolent boastings exult over the true sons of God, internal conflicts will arise as a result, which will grievously torment the mother herself.

**24.** Moses shows that the strife in Rebekah's womb continued until the twins were born. For it was not an incidental detail that Jacob caught hold of his brother by the heel and attempted to get out before him. The Lord testified by this sign that the effect of his election is not immediately apparent. Rather, the intervening path was full of troubles and conflicts. Therefore, Esau's name was allotted to him on account of his severity, which even from earliest infancy assumed a manly form; but the name Jacob signifies that this giant, vainly striving in his boasted strength, had nevertheless been vanquished.

**27.** Moses now briefly describes how the twins grew up. He does not, indeed, commend Jacob on account of those rare and excellent qualities that are especially worthy of praise and remembrance but only says he was a quiet man. In summary, the comparison implies that Moses praises Esau on account of his vigor but speaks of Jacob as being caught up in living a life of leisure. He describes the disposition of the former as indicating that he would be a courageous man, while the disposition of the latter had nothing worthy of commendation. Seeing that by a decree of heaven the honor of the firstborn would be transferred to Jacob, why did God allow him to lie down in his tent and slumber among ashes, unless he intended his election to be concealed for a time lest men should attribute something to their own actions?

**28.** So that God might more clearly show his own election to be sufficiently strong, so that it did not require any outside assistance and was powerful enough to overcome any obstacle, he allowed Esau to be preferred to his brother in the affection and good opinion of his father. In this way Jacob appeared to be a rejected person. Since, therefore, Moses clearly demonstrates by so many circumstances that the adoption of Jacob was solely founded on God's good pleasure, it is an intolerable presumption to suppose it depended on the will of man or to ascribe it, in part, to means (as they are called) and to human preparations. But how was it possible for the father, who was not ignorant of the oracle, to be thus predisposed in favor of the firstborn, whom he knew to be divinely rejected? It would have been more pious to subdue his own private affection, that he might obey God. The firstborn prefers a natural claim to the chief place in the parent's affection; but here the father was not at liberty to exalt him above his brother, for Esau had been placed in subjection by the oracle of God. Moses adds something that is still more shameful and more unworthy of the holy patriarch. Isaac had been induced to give this preference to Esau by his liking of venison. Was he so enslaved to the indulgence of his palate that, forgetting the oracle, he despised the grace of God in Jacob, while he preposterously set his affection on him whom God had rejected? Let the Jews glory in the flesh since Isaac, preferring food to the inheritance destined for his son, would pervert (as far as he had the power) the gratuitous covenant of God. For there is no room here for excuse since with a blind, or at least a most inconsiderate, love to his firstborn, he undervalued the younger.

It is unclear whether the mother was guilty of a different fault. We often find that the affections of parents are divided. If the wife sees that one of the sons is preferred by her husband, she inclines toward the other one. **Rebekah loved Jacob.** Rebekah loved her son Jacob more than she loved Esau. If in so doing she was obeying the oracle, she acted rightly; but it is possible that her love was that of a mother for her neglected son. Meanwhile, the foolish affection of the father only more fully illustrated the grace of the divine adoption.

**29.** This account hardly differs from the games children play. Jacob **was cooking some stew.** His brother returned tired from hunting and was **famished.** So he traded his birthright for food. What kind of bargain, I ask, was that? Jacob should have willingly satisfied his brother's hunger. But when asked, he refused to do so. Who would not condemn him for his inhumanity? In compelling Esau to surrender his birthright, he seemed to make an illicit and frivolous compact. God, however, exposed Esau's character in a matter of little consequence. God also showed an example of Jacob's piety, or (to speak more accurately) he brought to light what was hidden in them both.

Many people mistakenly think that Jacob's election depended on the fact that God foresaw something in him that was worthy of election. Similarly, some people are mistaken when they think Esau was made a reprobate because the ungodly acts he did later made him unworthy of the divine adoption before he was born. Paul, however, having declared election to be gratuitous, denies that the distinction is to be looked for in the individuals themselves. Paul takes it as an axiom that since mankind is ruined from its origin and devoted to destruction, all who are saved are freed from destruction in no other way than by the sheer grace of God. Some people are preferred to other people, but this is not because of their own merits. No one deserves grace. Those who are saved are those whom God, of his own good pleasure, has chosen. Paul then reasons on an even higher plain as follows: Since God is the Creator of the world, he is, by his own right, in this sense the arbiter of life and death, so that he cannot be called to account. But his own will is (so to speak) the *cause of causes.* And yet Paul does not by reasoning in this way impute tyranny to God, as the sophists allege when they refer to God's absolute power. God dwells in unapproachable light, and his judgments are deeper than the deepest abyss.

**30-32.** There was nothing wrong in Esau desiring and asking for food. But he was at fault in what he said: **"What good is the birthright to me?"** (verse 32). This is why the apostle calls him "godless" (Hebrews 12:16). But it would have been wiser to die a thousand deaths than to renounce his birthright. For his birthright was not confined to one age alone, but also to the heavenly life. So let each of us look to himself; since we all tend to live for this life alone, following nature as our guide, we too easily renounce the heavenly inheritance. Therefore, we should frequently remember the apostle's exhortation, "See that no one is. . . godless like Esau."

**33.** Jacob was not being cruel to his brother. He took nothing from him except what had been given to him by God. He had a godly motive in that he would establish for certain his own election in this way. Meanwhile, it should be noted that Esau, in the name and presence of God, did not hesitate to offer his birthright for sale. Although he had previously rushed to eat his food because he was so hungry, when an oath was exacted from him, some sense of godliness should have taken hold of him to correct his greed. But he was so given over to gluttony that he made God himself a witness of his ingratitude.

**34.** Although at first sight this statement seems to be cold and superfluous, it is very important. For in the first place Moses commends the piety of holy Jacob, who in aspiring to a heavenly life was able to bridle the appetite for food. Certainly he was not a log of wood; in preparing the food for the satisfying of his hunger, he would the more sharpen his appetite. So he had to deny himself so he could bear his hunger. But he would never have been able to subdue his flesh in this way unless a spiritual desire of a better life lived in him.

On the other hand, the remarkable indifference of his brother Esau is emphatically described in a few words. **He ate and drank, and then got up and left.** Why are these four things stated? It is so we may know what is then stated—that he counted the incomparable benefit of which he was deprived as nothing. **So Esau despised his birthright.** The cry of the Lacedaemonian captive is celebrated by the historians. The army, which had sustained a long siege, surrendered to the enemy for lack of water. After they had drunk from the river, the army commander exclaimed, "O comrades, for what little pleasure have we lost an incomparable good!" He, a miserable man, having quenched his thirst, returned to his senses and mourned his lost liberty. But Esau, having satisfied his appetite, did not consider that he had sacrificed a blessing far more valuable than a hundred lives to purchase a meal that would last less than half an hour. Anyone who acts like this is an ungodly person, alienated from the heavenly life. He does not perceive what he has lost until God thunders on him from heaven. Let us learn from this so that we will not be deceived by the allurements of the world and swerve from the right way. If we do find that we do this, we must wake ourselves from our sleep.

# Genesis
# Chapter 26

**1. Now there was a famine in the land—besides the earlier famine of Abraham's time—and Isaac went to Abimelech king of the Philistines in Gerar.** Moses recounts that Isaac was tested by a similar kind of trial as his father Abraham experienced twice. God had placed his servants as strangers and pilgrims in the land that he had promised to give them. But this was a land full of hardship and trouble. Who would not think that God had acted in a strange way since he did not even supply the needs of his own children?

**2.** I feel sure that a reason is mentioned here why Isaac went to the country of Gerar rather than to Egypt, which perhaps would have been more convenient for him. For Moses teaches that he was prevented from going to Egypt by a heavenly oracle. It may here be asked, Why does the Lord forbid Isaac from going to Egypt, where he had allowed his father to go? Although Moses does not give the reason, we may conjecture that the journey would have been more dangerous for the son. The Lord could indeed have endued the son also with the power of his Spirit, as he had done his father Abraham, so that the abundance and delicacies of Egypt would not corrupt him. But God knew that Isaac was weaker than Abraham had been, and he would have been tempted by the allurements of Egypt. God did not expose him to danger, for he is faithful and does not allow his own people to be tempted beyond what they can bear (1 Corinthians 10:13).

**"Live in the land where I tell you to live."** God commanded him to settle in the promised land, but still as a stranger. The intimation was thus given that the time had not yet arrived when he would rule over it. God kept this hope of the promised inheritance alive in him but required honor to be given to his word, so Isaac would have inner peace.

**5. "Because Abraham obeyed me."** Moses does not mean that Abraham's obedience was the reason God's promise was confirmed and ratified to Isaac. For God sometimes freely bestows on the faithful something that is beyond what they deserve and ascribes it to them. This means that Abraham, having lived his life in total obedience to God's will, walked in his service.

**7.** Moses recounts that Isaac was tested in the same way as his father Abraham had been. Isaac was undoubtedly following the example of his father so that he might be linked to him in his faith. But in this matter he should not have imitated his father's fault. Isaac's negligence here is inexcusable.

Since we are surrounded on all sides with so many dangers, we must ask the Lord to strengthen us by his Spirit, so that we do not faint from fear and trembling. If we do not do this, we will frequently become involved in worthless enterprises that we will regret after evil has been done.

**8.** God's forbearance is wonderful. He not only pardoned Isaac for his sin but stretched out his hand and protected his wife and did not make the godless king angry. Although God gives us this example of his kindness, showing that the faithful, if they fall, may confidently hope that they will find that God is gentle and propitious, yet we must bear in mind that the holy woman in this instance was the only mother of the church on earth and was kept from being dishonored as a special privilege.

**10.** The Lord did not punish Isaac as he deserved, perhaps because he did not have as much perseverance as his father had. In case it would greatly dishearten him, God mercifully prevented Isaac's wife from being taken. But so this censure would produce deep shame, God allowed a heathen to be Isaac's master and to reprove him. If God calls unbelievers to his tribunal, how dreadful a punishment awaits us if we try to obliterate by our own wickedness the knowledge that God has etched on our consciences.

**11. "Anyone who molests this man or his wife shall surely be put to death."** In proclaiming capital punishment against anyone who harmed this stranger, we may assume that Abimelech issued this edict as a special kindness toward Isaac and Rebekah. Why did the king treat Isaac in such a kind way? God helped the predicament of his servant and moved the heathen king to show him this favor.

**12.** Moses tells how Isaac reaped a fruitful harvest as a result of God's blessing. **Isaac planted crops in that land and the same year reaped a hundredfold, because the LORD blessed him.** The question may arise, How could Isaac sow seed when God had commanded him to be a pilgrim for his whole life? We find that the holy man did not stay there long but **moved away** (verse 17). But he received as a divine favor abundant fruit from his own labor.

**14. The Philistines envied him.** This teaches us that God's blessings that we receive in this earthly life are never pure and perfect but are always accompanied by troubles, in case we neglect God because we wallow in our blessings. So we must all learn not to desire great wealth. If the rich become harassed in any way, let them know that they are being awakened by the Lord, in case they fall fast asleep in the middle of their pleasures. And the poor should be comforted that their poverty is not without its benefits, for it is a great blessing to be free from envy, tumults, and strife.

**16.** It is unclear whether the king of Gerar ejected Isaac from his kingdom of his own accord or whether he told him to settle elsewhere because he saw that the people envied him. Isaac had received a large inheritance from his father, but Moses shows that Isaac had become so prosperous in a very short time so that it seemed no longer possible for the inhabitants of the land to allow him to carry on living there.

**18. He gave them the same names his father had given them.** Isaac did not give new names to the wells he **reopened** but restored the names that his father Abraham had given to them.

**22. He moved on from there and dug another well, and no one quarreled over it. He named it Rehoboth, saying, "Now the LORD has given us room and we will flourish in the land."** No matter how severely Isaac was harassed, he gave thanks to God and celebrated his goodness. In the middle of trials he kept a calm and composed mind.

**23. From there he went up to Beersheba.** Moses does not explain why Isaac moved to **Beersheba**, the ancient dwelling-place of his fathers. It might have been because the Philistines never stopped annoying him. This is indeed the probable cause when we consider the circumstances we are given in this account.

**24. That night the LORD appeared to him.** This vision prepared Isaac to listen more attentively to God and convinced him that it was God with whom he had to deal. God **appeared** to Isaac to produce confidence in and reverence toward his word. In short, visions were symbols of the divine presence, designed to remove all doubt from the minds of the holy fathers about him who was about to speak.

An objection may be raised that such evidence was open to misunderstanding, since Satan often deceives men by similar manifestations, pretending to speak for God. But we must remember that a clear and unambiguous mark was engraved on God's visions, by which the faithful might definitely distinguish them from false visions.

But God did not manifest his glory to the holy fathers but assumed a form by means of which they might understand that it was him. For as the majesty of God is infinite, it cannot be comprehended by the human mind, and by its magnitude it absorbs the whole world. Besides, it follows that men, on account of their infirmity, must not only faint but be altogether annihilated in the presence of God. Wherefore, Moses does not mean that God was seen in his true nature and greatness, but in such a way that Isaac was able to bear the sight. But what we have said—namely, that the vision was a testimony of deity, for the purpose of giving credibility to the oracle—will more fully appear from the context. For this appearance was not a mute specter, but the word immediately followed, which confirmed, in the mind of Isaac, faith in God's gratuitous adoption and salvation.

**"I am the God of your father Abraham."** This was intended as a reminder of all the promises that God had previously made. It also drew Isaac's attention to the everlasting covenant that had been made with Abraham and was to be transmitted to his posterity. The Lord, therefore, began by declaring himself to be the God who had spoken at first to Abraham, in order that Isaac might not cut this off from the previous oracles.

**"Do not be afraid, for I am with you; I will bless you and will increase the number of your descendants for the sake of my servant Abraham."** In the first place, we must observe that God thus addresses the faithful to calm their minds. For if God's word was taken away, they would become torpid because of their ignorance. From this it follows that we can receive peace from no other source than from the mouth of the Lord when he declares himself the author of our salvation. This does not free us from all fear, but our faith is enough to assuage our anxieties. The Lord gives ample proof of his love when he promises that he will bless Isaac.

**25.** From other passages we are well aware that Moses is speaking here about public worship. For an inner calling on God requires neither an altar, nor any special place. There is no doubt that the saints, wherever they lived, worshiped. But because religion ought to be a public witness to men, Isaac, having erected and consecrated an altar, professed himself a worshiper of the true and only God, and so separated himself from the polluted rites of heathens. He also **built** the **altar** not for himself alone, but for his whole family, that there, with all his household, he might offer sacrifices. Moreover, since the altar was built for the external exercises of faith, the expression **called on the name of the LORD** means the same as if Moses had said that Isaac celebrated the name of God and gave testimony of his own faith. The public worship of God also had another use—namely, that men, according to their weakness, may spiritually exercise themselves as they give reverence to God. Since we know that sacrifices were commanded, we must observe that Isaac did not rashly trifle in worshiping God but adhered to the rule of faith, that he might do nothing except according to the word of God. We must also note how preposterous and erroneous it is to imitate the fathers unless the Lord tells us to use similar means. Meanwhile, the words of Moses clearly signify that whatever exercises of piety the faithful undertake are to be directed to one end—namely, that God may be worshiped and called on in prayer. To this end, therefore, all rites and ceremonies ought to aim. Although it was the custom of the holy fathers to build an altar wherever they pitched their tent, we gather from these words that after God appeared to his servant Isaac, this **altar** was **built** by him in token of his gratitude.

**There his servants dug a well.** It is remarkable that whereas this place had already received its name from the well that had been dug in it, Isaac should have to dig a well again. This is especially the case since Abraham had purchased, for himself and his posterity, the right to the well from the king. Moreover, the digging of a well itself was difficult and laborious. So Moses' purpose in mentioning this is that throughout that whole region the inhabitants had conspired to expel the holy man. Isaac experienced a lack of water, for this well had been stopped up.

The context also shows that the first concern of the holy patriarch concerned the worship of God because Moses recounts that an altar was erected before he speaks about the well. It is important to observe what great troubles constantly fell on these holy fathers. They would never have been able to overcome or to endure unless they had been removed a long ways from living a life of luxury. How much we would have felt the loss of water, for we are often angry with God if we do have not plenty of wine. Therefore, through such examples let the faithful learn to patiently endure. If food and other necessities of life ever fail them, let them turn their eyes to Isaac, who wandered, parched with thirst, in the inheritance that had been divinely promised him.

**26.** The Lord gave Isaac a favor similar to that which he had previously shown to his father Abraham. For it was no ordinary blessing that Abimelech should voluntarily seek his friendship. Besides, Isaac would be relieved from a great deal of anxiety since his neighbors, who had harassed him in so many ways, now showed that they were afraid of him and desired to secure his friendship. Therefore, the Lord both conferred signal honor and a time of peace on his servant. There is no doubt that the king was led to act in this way by a secret divine impulse. For if he was afraid, why did he not resort to some other remedy? Why did he humble himself to ask a favor? Why did he not just send for Isaac or tell him what he must do? But God had so influenced the king that he, forgetting his regal pride, sought for peace and alliance with a man who was neither covetous, nor warlike, nor equipped with a great army. Thus we learn that the minds of men are in the hand of God, so that he makes them gentle when they had previously been full of anger.

**27.** Isaac not only now complained about the injuries he had suffered but said that in the future he could have no confidence in Abimelech and the others. This passage teaches us that it is right for the faithful to complain about their enemies so that their violence can be restrained.

**28.** By saying this they showed that they genuinely desired to make a covenant with Isaac. They acknowledged that God's favor rested on him. Their testimony contains a very useful lesson. When ungodly men acknowledge that a person has succeeded because he has been blessed by the Lord, they bear witness that God is the author of all good things, and that from him alone all prosperity flows.

**29. "And now you are blessed by the LORD."** Isaac had complained about the harm they had done to him as they expelled him out of envy. They answered that there was no reason why any shred of hatred should remain in his mind, since the Lord had treated him so kindly and exactly as he had wanted. It was as if they said, "What do you want? Are you not content with your present success? We agree that we have not been hospitable toward you; yet God's blessing on you obliterates from your memory such bad things." Perhaps through these words they asserted that they were acting toward him in good faith because he was under God's guardianship.

**31. Early the next morning the men swore an oath to each other.** Isaac did not hesitate to swear **an oath**. He did this partly so the Philistines would be easily appeased and partly so they would not suspect him of secretly being their enemy. This is the legitimate way of swearing when men mutually bind themselves to each other in order to promote peace. A simple promise should have been sufficient, but since men distrust each other so much, the Lord allows them the use of his name; so this covenant was ratified in this pious way. However, we must be careful that God's name is not profaned by rashly swearing.

**32.** From this it is clear that it took a long time to dig for water.

**34.** Moses recounts the marriages of Esau for a variety of reasons. As he mixed with the residents of the land, from whom the holy race of Abraham was separated, he became entangled with them. It also happened, by the wonderful counsel of God, that these daughters-in-law **were a source of grief to Isaac and Rebekah** (verse 35). This was so they might only gradually be favorably inclined to those reprobate people. If these people had pleased them, and if they had good and obedient daughters, Jacob might also, with his parents' consent, have taken a wife from among them. But it was not right for those to be bound together in marriage whom God planned to be permanent enemies. For how would the inheritance of the land be handed down to Abraham's descendants except by the destruction of those among whom he stayed for a time? Therefore, God cut off all inducements to these inauspicious marriages, that the disunity between the two peoples, which he had established, might remain. It appears from this how much Esau was loved by Isaac. For although the holy man justly regarded his son's wives with aversion, and his mind was exasperated by them, he never failed to act with the greatest kindness toward his son. Polygamy, this corruption of marriage, had become so widespread that the custom had acquired the sanction of law. It is not, therefore, surprising that a man addicted to the flesh indulged his appetite by taking two wives.

# Genesis
# Chapter 27

**1.** In this chapter Moses recounts, at length, a narrative that does not seem to be very useful. It amounts to this: Esau went out, at his father's command, to hunt. Jacob, in his brother's clothing, was, through the cunning of his mother, induced to obtain by stealth the blessing that belonged to the firstborn. It seems as if Jacob was playing a children's game, presenting to his father a kid instead of venison. He pretended to be a hairy person by putting on skins and in such a disguise passed himself off as his brother in order to obtain the blessing by deceit.

To learn that Moses does not recount this narrative in detail in vain, we must first observe that when Jacob received the blessing from his father, this confirmed the oracle through which the Lord chose him in preference to his brother. For the blessing referred to was no mere prayer but a legitimate sanction, divinely interposed, which showed the grace of election. God had promised to the holy fathers that he would be a God to their descendants forever. So when they were at the point of death, they passed on the favor they had received from God to their posterity, as if they were delivering it from hand to hand. So Abraham, in blessing his son Isaac, constituted him the heir of spiritual life with a solemn rite. Isaac now had the same end in view. He was worn-out with old age and thought that he was about to die, and so he wanted to bless his firstborn son, so that God's everlasting covenant would remain in his own family. The patriarchs did not do this because it was their own idea, but because it was divinely ordained. This is why the apostle declares that the "lesser person is blessed by the greater" (Hebrews 7:7). The faithful were used to blessing each other, but the Lord insisted on this special service by the patriarchs so they would transmit, as a deposit to posterity, the covenant that had been invested in them and that they had kept throughout their lives. The same command was later given to the priests, as is seen in Numbers 6:24 and similar places. Therefore Isaac, in blessing his son, did not just act as a father or a private person, for he was a prophet and an interpreter of God who constituted his son an heir of the same grace that he had received.

This is why Moses treats this subject at such length. But let us weigh each detail of the case in order. The first thing to note is that God transferred the blessing of Esau to Jacob through their father's making a mistake. Moses says that **his eyes were so weak that he could no longer see.** Jacob's sight was also very poor when he blessed his grandchildren Ephraim and Manasseh. Yet his lack of sight did not prevent him from deliberately switching his hands as he blessed them. But God allowed Isaac to be deceived, to show that it was not man's will that Jacob was raised up to the right and honor of being the heir.

**2.** There is no doubt that Isaac asked that his sons should be blessed every day throughout his life. So what happens in this narrative appears to have been an extraordinary kind of benediction. Moreover, Isaac's declaration, **"I . . . don't know the day of my death"** is as if he said that death was closing in on him every moment, for he was a decrepit man in failing health. He did not dare to think he could live any longer. Everyone, even in the prime of life, carries with him a thousand deaths. Death claims as its own the fetus in the mother's womb and accompanies it through every stage of life. But as it urges the old more acutely, so they should keep it more firmly in their sight and should live as pilgrims passing through the world or as those who already have one foot in the grave. In short, Isaac, like a person near death, wished to leave the church in the person of his son.

**4.** The faith of the holy man was mixed with a foolish and inconsiderate selfish desire. The general principle of faith flourished in his mind when, in blessing his son, he consigned to him, under the direction of the Holy Spirit, the right of the inheritance that had been divinely promised to himself. Meanwhile, he was blindly carried away by the love of his firstborn son in preference to his other son. In this way he opposed God's oracle. For he could not have been ignorant about what God had pronounced before the children were born. If anyone wants to excuse him on the grounds that he had received no command from God to change the usual order of nature by preferring the younger to the elder, this can be easily refuted. Though he knew the firstborn was rejected, he still persisted in his excessive attachment to him. Again, in neglecting to inquire respecting his duty when he had been informed of the heavenly oracle by his wife, his indolence was inexcusable. Therefore, his obstinate attachment to his son was a kind of blindness that proved a greater obstacle to him than the failing sight of his eyes. While he deserved to be rebuked for this fault, it did not deprive the holy man of the right of pronouncing a blessing. He had the authority to do this just as if God himself had spoken from heaven.

**5.** Moses now explains in detail the crafty act through which Jacob would attain the blessing. It appears to be ridiculous that an old man, deceived by the cunning of his wife, should through ignorance and error give voice to what was contrary to his wish. Rebekah's plan was not without fault. For although she could not guide her husband by counsel, yet it was not a legitimate way to behave to trick him in such a deceitful way. As a lie is in itself culpable, she also sinned in wanting to have a hand in a sacred matter by using such trickery. She knew that the decree by which Jacob had been elected and adopted was immutable. So why did she not patiently wait until God confirmed it in fact and showed that what he had once pronounced from heaven was certain? Therefore, she clouded the heavenly oracle by her lie. If we consider this matter more deeply, we must also see where this great desire to act came from. We see that it stemmed from her extraordinary faith, for she did not hesitate to turn her husband against herself or to cause implacable enmity between the brothers or to expose her beloved son Jacob to the danger of immediate death. She upset the whole family. This definitely flowed from no other source than her faith, though nevertheless she still acted wrongly.

The inheritance that God had promised was firmly fixed in her mind. She knew it was decreed to her son Jacob. Therefore, relying on God's covenant and keeping in mind the oracle received, she forgot the world. Thus we see that her faith was mixed with an unjust and immoderate zeal. This is to be carefully observed, so that we may understand that a pure and distinct knowledge does not always so illuminate the minds of the pious that all their actions are controlled by the Holy Spirit. The little light that shows them their path is enveloped in various clouds of ignorance and error, so that while they hold a right course and are traveling toward the goal, they still occasionally take a wrong turn.

Finally, both in Isaac and in his wife the principle of faith was preeminent. But each by ignorance in certain matters and by other faults stumbled along the way. Throughout all of this, God's election nevertheless stood firm. Indeed, God even carried out his plan through the deceit of a woman. Through these events praise is due to his gratuitous goodness.

**11.** Jacob did not voluntarily present himself to his father but feared that his deceit might be detected and so bring a curse on himself. Jacob did not act out of faith. When the apostle teaches that whatever does not come from faith is sin (see Romans 14:23), he teaches the children of God that they may not allow themselves to undertake anything with a doubtful and perplexed conscience. This firm conviction is the only rule of right conduct, when we, relying on the command of God, go wherever he calls us. Jacob shows that he was deficient in faith as he raised doubts about what he was doing. But by this example we are again taught that faith is not always extinguished by a particular fault. God sometimes bears with his servants and transforms what they have done perversely so that it provides for their salvation. However, we must not take this as a license to sin. It happened by the wonderful mercy of God that Jacob was not cut off from the grace of adoption. Who would not rather fear than become presumptuous? And whereas we see that his faith was obscured by his doubts, let us learn to ask the Lord for the spirit of prudence to control all our steps. Jacob made another serious error as well, for why did he not prefer to reverence God than to fear his father's anger? Why did it not rather occur to him that God's holy adoption would be stained if it seemed to owe its accomplishment to a lie? He used an incorrect means to attain a right end.

**13.** Here Rebekah sinned again, because she burned with such hasty zeal that she did not consider how much God disapproved of her evil actions. She presumptuously subjected herself to **the curse**. But where did this confidence come from? As she had no divine command, she took her own counsel. Yet no one will deny that this zeal, although preposterous, proceeded from special reverence for the word of God. For since she was informed by the heavenly oracle that Jacob was preferred in the sight of God, she disregarded whatever was visible in the world and whatever nature dictated, in favor of God's secret election. Therefore, we are taught by this example that everyone should walk modestly and cautiously according to the rule of his vocation and should not dare to go beyond what the Lord allows in his word.

**14.** Although it is probable that Jacob was not only influenced by a desire to obey his mother but was also persuaded by her arguments, he still sinned by stepping outside the bounds of his vocation. When Rebekah had taken the blame upon herself, she doubtless told him that nobody would come to any harm. After all, Jacob was not stealing another person's right but was only seeking the blessing that was decreed to him by the heavenly oracle. Therefore Jacob, instead of simply deviating from what was right in submitting to his mother, was also obeying the word of God. In the meantime (as I have said) this particular deed was not free from blame, for the truth of God is not helped by such deceitful acts.

The paternal benediction was, indeed, a seal of God's grace. But Rebekah should have waited until God brought relief from heaven by changing the mind and guiding the tongue of Isaac rather than attempting what was wrong. Therefore, on the whole, faith shone preeminently in holy Jacob; yet he was guilty of being rash as he distrusted God's providence and gained possession of his father's blessing by deceit.

**19.** At first Jacob was timid and anxious; now, having dismissed his fear, he confidently and audaciously lied. By this example we are taught that when anyone has transgressed the bounds of duty, he soon allows himself unmeasured license. So there is nothing better than for each person to keep himself within the divinely prescribed limits. In this way he will not do what is wrong and open the door to Satan.

**21.** It appears that the holy man was suspicious of being deceived and therefore hesitated. From this it might be deduced that the blessing was vain, as it did not come from faith. But it pleased God to carry out his work through Isaac's hand. However, at the time Isaac was not aware that he was furthering God's purposes. It should not be thought that it was strange that Isaac, like a blind man, should ignorantly transfer the blessing to a different person from him whom he intended. The ordinary function of pastors is similar to this. Though by God's command they reconcile men to him, yet they do not discern to whom this reconciliation comes. Thus they scatter the seed everywhere but do not know who will bear fruit. So God does not place the office and power with which he has invested them under the control of their own judgment. In this same way the ignorance of Isaac did not nullify the heavenly oracles, for God himself, although the senses of his servant failed, did not desist from carrying out his purpose. Here is a clear rebuttal of the idea that the whole force of the sacrament depends upon the intention of the man who consecrates it, as if the will of man can frustrate the design of God. Nevertheless, what I have already said must be remembered: However Isaac was deceived in the person of his son, yet he did not pronounce the blessing in vain. Faith remained in his mind and in part controlled his conduct, even though in forming his judgment from the touch, disregarding the voice, he did not act according to faith.

**26.** We know that the practice of kissing was then common and is still used by many nations today. Ungodly people, however, may say that it is ludicrous for an old man, whose mind was already obtuse and who moreover had eaten and drunk heartily, to pour forth his benedictions upon a person who was only acting a part. But whereas Moses has previously recorded the oracle of God by which the adoption was destined for the younger son, we should contemplate reverently the secret providence of God, toward which profane men pay no respect. Isaac was not so enslaved to the attractions of meat and drink that he could not with a sober mind reflect on the divine command that had been given to him. So we must not judge this blessing from its external appearance but must remember that it was a heavenly decree. If the same religion lives in us that flourished in the patriarch's heart, nothing will stop the divine power from shining forth clearly in the weakness of man.

**27.** Ambrose's allegory on this passage does not displease me. Jacob, the younger brother, was blessed under the person of the elder; the clothes that were borrowed from his brother smelled of a field and pleased his father. In the same way we are blessed, Ambrose teaches, when in the name of Christ we enter the presence of our heavenly Father. We receive from him the robe of righteousness, which by its odor procures his favor; in short, we are blessed in this way when we are put in Jacob's place.

**28. "May God give you of heaven's dew and of earth's richness— an abundance of grain and new wine."** Isaac seemed here to desire and implore nothing for his son but what was earthly; for the substance of his words was that it might be well with his son in the world—that he might have good harvests, that he might enjoy great peace and be honored more than other people. There was no mention of the heavenly kingdom; and hence it has arisen that men without learning and little exercised in true piety have imagined that these holy fathers were blessed by the Lord only in respect to this frail and transitory life. But it appears from many passages that this was not the case. As for Isaac here confining himself to the earthly favors of God, the explanation is easy: The Lord did not formerly set the hope of the future inheritance plainly before the eyes of the fathers (as he now calls and raises us directly toward heaven), but he led them as by a circuitous route. Thus he appointed the land of Canaan as a mirror and pledge to them of the heavenly inheritance. In all his acts of kindness he gave them tokens of his paternal favor, not indeed for the purpose of making them content with the present, so that they should neglect heaven or should follow a merely empty shadow, as some foolishly suppose, but so that, being assisted by such things, they might by degrees rise toward heaven. For since Christ, the firstfruits of those who rise again and the author of the eternal and incorruptible life, had not yet been manifested, his spiritual kingdom was in this way shrouded in figures only, until the fullness of the time came. As all the promises of God were involved and in a sense clothed in these symbols, so the faith of the holy fathers observed the same measure and made its advances heavenwards by means of these earthly things. Therefore, although Isaac made the temporal favors of God prominent, nothing was further from his mind than to confine the hope of his son to this world. He wanted to raise him to the same level to which he himself aspired.

**29.** These are not merely the wishes that fathers utter on behalf of their children, for the promises of God are included in them. For Isaac was appointed as God's interpreter and was used as this instrument by the Holy Spirit. Therefore, as a spokesman of God, he pronounced in an efficacious way that all those who would oppose his son's welfare would be accursed. This then is the confirmation of the promise by which God, when he receives the faithful under his protection, declares that he will be an enemy to their enemies. The whole force of the benediction turns on this point. God would prove himself to be a kind father to his servant Jacob in all things and would constitute him to be the chief and the head of a holy and elect people. God would preserve and defend him by his power and would secure his salvation in the face of enemies of every kind.

**30.** Now Moses begins to show Esau's rejection. This incident greatly strengthened the blessing that Jacob received, for if Esau had not been rejected, it might seem that he was not deprived of the honor that nature had given him. But Isaac declared (verses 33, 37) that what he had done in virtue of his patriarchal office could not but be ratified. Here it is shown again that the right of inheritance that Jacob obtained at the expense of his brother was made his by a free gift. For if we compare the deeds of both brothers, we see that Esau obeyed his father, brought him the produce of his hunting, prepared for his father the food obtained by his own labor, and spoke nothing but the truth. In summary, we find nothing in him that is not worthy of praise. But Jacob never left his home, substituted a kid for venison, insinuated himself by many lies, and did nothing that he should be commended for, but rather many things that deserved to be rebuked. Hence it must be acknowledged that the cause of this event is not to be traced to works, but that it lies hidden in the eternal counsel of God. Yet Esau was not unjustly rejected because those who are not governed by the Spirit of God can receive nothing with a right mind. It must be firmly maintained that since the condition of everyone is equal, if anyone is preferred to another, it is not because of his own merit, but because the Lord has gratuitously chosen him.

**33.** Here again the faith that had been smothered in the heart of the holy man shone out. For it is clear that his fear sprang from faith. Besides, Moses describes no ordinary fear, but that which utterly confounded the holy man. Isaac was perfectly conscious of his own vocation and therefore was persuaded that the duty of naming the heir with whom he should deposit the covenant of eternal life was divinely placed on him. As soon as he discovered his error, he was filled with fear that in an affair so great and so serious, God had allowed him to err. For unless he had thought that God had directed this action, why did he not say that he had acted in ignorance and so excuse himself? Although he was covered with shame because of the error he had committed, he nevertheless, with a collected mind, ratified the benediction that he had pronounced. I am sure that he, like a person who is waking up, began to remember the oracle to which he had not paid enough attention. Wherefore, the holy man was not ruled by ambition to be so tenacious in this action as obstinate men often are. Rather, the declaration, **"I blessed him—and indeed he will be blessed!"** was the result of a rare and precious faith. For Isaac, renouncing selfish desires, now yielded himself entirely to God and, acknowledging God as the Author of the benediction he had uttered, ascribed due glory to him and did not dare to retract it. The benefit of this teaching extends to the whole church, so that we may know for certain that whatever the heralds of the Gospel promise by God's command will be efficacious and stable, because they do not speak as private men but by the command of God himself. The infirmity of the minister does not destroy the faithfulness, power, and efficacy of God's word. He who presents himself to us charged with the offer of eternal happiness and life is subject to our common miseries and to death. Nevertheless, the promise is efficacious. He who declares our absolution from sins is himself a sinner; but because his office is given to him by God, the stability of this grace, since it rests on God's foundation, will never fail.

**34.** Esau persisted in asking for the blessing. In this he showed how desperate he was, and this is why he received no benefit—he did not enter by the gate of faith. True piety does draw out tears and great cries from the children of God. But **when Esau heard his father's words, he burst out with a loud and bitter cry and said to his father, "Bless me—me too, my father!"** But his blind incredulity was reproved by his own words; whereas one blessing only had been deposited with his father, Esau asked that another should be given to him, as if it were in his father's power indiscriminately to breathe out blessings independent of God's command. Here the admonition of the apostle may come to mind: "He could bring about no change of mind, though he sought the blessing with tears" (Hebrews 12:17). People who neglect to follow God when he calls on them later call on him in vain, when he has turned his back. So long as God addresses and invites us, the gate of the kingdom of heaven is open. This opportunity we must use if we desire to enter, according to the instruction of the prophet: "Seek the LORD while he may be found; call on him while he is near" (Isaiah 55:6). Paul interprets this passage by stating, "In the time of my favor I heard you, and in the day of salvation I helped you" (2 Corinthians 6:2). Those who allow that time to pass by may at length knock too late and without profit, because God takes revenge on their idleness. We must, therefore, fear if we allow God's voice to pass unheeded, for he will in turn become deaf to our cry.

But it may be asked, how is this rejection consistent with the promise, "But if a wicked man turns away from all his sins he has committed and keeps all my decrees and does what is just and right, he will surely live" (Ezekiel 18:21)? Moreover, it may seem at variance with the clemency of God to reject the sighs of those who, being crushed by misery, flee for refuge to his mercy. I reply that repentance, if it is true and sincere, will never be too late. The sinner who, from his soul, is displeased with himself will obtain pardon. But God punishes the contempt of his grace because those who obstinately reject it do not seriously intend to return to him. Thus it is that those who are given up to a reprobate mind are never touched with genuine penitence. Hypocrites do break out into tears, like Esau, but their heart within them will remain closed as with iron bars. Therefore, since Esau rushed forward, destitute of faith and repentance, to ask a blessing, it is no wonder that he was rejected.

**36.** The mind of Esau was in no way affected with a sense of penitence. This is clear because he now accused his brother and attached no blame to himself. But the very beginning of repentance is grief felt because of sin, together with self-condemnation. Esau ought to have looked inside himself and to have become his own judge. Having sold his birthright, he had, like a famished dog, devoured the meat and the stew. Now, as if he had done no wrong, he vented all his anger on his brother. Further, if the blessing was deemed of any value, why did he not consider that he had been repelled from it not simply by the deceit of man but by the providence of God? We see, therefore, that like a blind man feeling in the dark, he could not find his way.

**37.** Isaac now more openly confirmed what I have said before: Since God was the author of the blessing, it could not be altered, for it was permanent. Isaac did not here magnificently boast about his office but acted as a servant and denied that he was at liberty to alter anything. He considered that when one stands as God's representative, it is not right for him to do except as God's command allows him. From this Esau ought to have learned that he had fallen because of his own fault, in order that he might humble himself and join himself with his brother, in order to take part in his blessing, as his inferior. But depraved greed carried him away, so that he forgot about the kingdom of God and cared for nothing except his own private advantage.

Again we must notice Isaac's words in which he claimed a definite efficacy for his benediction. It is as if his word carried with it everything that God had promised to Abraham. For God, in requiring the faithful to depend on himself alone, nevertheless wants them to rest securely on the word, which, at his command, is declared to them by men. In this way these men are said to remit sins, but they remain only the messengers and interpreters of free forgiveness.

**38.** Esau seemed now to take courage, but he neglected his soul and turned, like a swine, to pamper his flesh. He had heard that his father had nothing left to give him; the full and entire grace of God so rested on Jacob that apart from his family there was no happiness. So if Esau sought his own welfare, he should have drawn from that fountain and subjected himself to his brother rather than to cut himself off from him. He chose, however, to be deprived of spiritual grace, wanting to possess something of his own, apart from his brother. He would not be Jacob's inferior. Yet he knew that there was only one benediction, by which his brother Jacob had been constituted the heir of the divine covenant. For Isaac would have told them every day about this great privilege that God had given to Abraham and his descendants.

**39.** In the end Esau received what he asked for. He saw that he himself was rejected as the rightful heir. So he chose to have prosperity in the world, separate from the holy people, rather than to submit to the yoke of his younger brother.

It may be thought that Isaac contradicted himself in offering a new benediction when he had before declared that he had given to his son Jacob all that was placed at his disposal. I reply that what has been before said concerning Ishmael must be noted in this place. God, though he hearkened to Abraham's prayer for Ishmael so far as concerns the present life, yet immediately restricted his promise by adding the exception implied in the declaration that in Isaac only would the seed be called. I do not, however, doubt that the holy man Isaac, when he perceived that his younger son Jacob was the divinely ordained heir of a happy life, tried to bless his firstborn, Esau, so that he might not depart from the holy and elect flock of the church. But when he saw him obstinately going in another direction, he declared what his future condition would be. Meanwhile, the spiritual blessing remained with Jacob alone. Because Esau refused to link himself to Jacob, he became a voluntary exile from the kingdom of God.

**40. "You will live by the sword and you will serve your brother. But when you grow restless, you will throw his yoke from off your neck."** We note that the events predicted here were never fulfilled in the person of Esau. Therefore, this prophecy concerns things in the far distance. God would restrict his promise, in case Esau should be too highly exalted, for nothing is more desirable than peace. Holy people are also warned that there will always be some enemies to assault them. This, however, is a very different thing from Esau's living by his own **sword**, which is as if he said that the sons of Esau, like robbers, would maintain their security by arms and violence rather than by legitimate authority. A second limitation of the promise is that though armed with the **sword**, Esau would still not escape subjection to his **brother**. And the Edomites did, at length, become subject to the chosen people.

**41. Esau held a grudge against Jacob because of the blessing his father had given him. He said to himself, "The days of mourning for my father are near; then I will kill my brother Jacob."** It is apparent that Esau's tears were not the tears of true repentance, but tears of furious anger. He was not content with secretly cherishing enmity against his brother but openly threatened him. And it is evident how deeply rooted his malice was, for he even planned to murder his brother.

A vivid picture of a hypocrite is here set before us. He pretends that the death of his father would cause him grief, and it is indeed a religious duty to mourn over a deceased father. But it was mere pretense on his part to speak of **the days of mourning** when all he longed to do was murder his brother. Anyone who abstains from wickedness merely out of the fear of man or from a sense of shame has made little progress. True piety teaches our conscience to set God before us as our witness and our judge.

**42. Moses now turns to a different topic and shows how Jacob, as a fugitive from his father's house, went into Mesopotamia.** Doubtless it was an exceedingly troublesome and severe test for the holy matron to see that, by her own deed, her son was placed in imminent danger of death. But by faith she wrestled to retain the grace she had received. For if she had been governed only by her maternal attachment for her younger son, she would have seen that the birthright was given back to Esau. Then the cause of the conflict would have been removed. That Rebekah did not do this is evidence of her extraordinary faith. She persuaded her son to go into voluntary exile and chose to be deprived of his presence rather than have him give up the blessing he had received.

**44. "Stay with him [Laban] for a while until your brother's fury subsides."** This is added to mitigate the severity of Jacob's banishment. In Hebrew the expression that is translated **for a while** literally means "one" but is written as a plural number. Rebekah meant that as soon as Jacob went away, the memory of the offense would be obliterated from Esau's mind. It is as if she said, "Only leave here for a little while, and we shall soon assuage his anger."

**45.** Why did Rebekah fear a double privation? There was no danger that Jacob, endued with such a mild and placid disposition, would rise up against his brother. Rebekah concluded that God would avenge the evil murder.

**46.** While Jacob might have fled secretly, his mother nevertheless obtained his father's permission for him to leave. For a well-ordered family should behave in a disciplined way. In giving a reason other than the true one for Jacob's departure to her husband, Rebekah may be excused from the charge of falsehood. She neither said the whole truth nor left the whole truth unsaid. No doubt it was true that she was **disgusted** at having to live among Hittite women. But she prudently concealed the real reason for Jacob's departure in case she inflicted a mortal wound on her husband. Also she did not want Esau to become even more angry. Although all of the Hittite race were disliked by Rebekah, it was due to God's wonderful providence that Jacob did not entangle himself with the future enemies of the church.

# Genesis
# Chapter 28

**1. So Isaac called for Jacob and blessed him and commanded him: "Do not marry a Canaanite woman."** It may be asked why Isaac repeated the blessing that he had previously pronounced. Did the previous one have no effect? I reply that although the blessing was in itself efficacious, yet Jacob's faith required this kind of support. In the same way, the Lord frequently reiterated the same promises. It was also of the greatest importance that Jacob should again be blessed by his father, knowingly and willingly, in case in the future a doubt might arise in Jacob's mind as he remembered his father's mistake and his own deceit. Therefore, Isaac now deliberately directed his words to his son Jacob and pronounced the blessing that was due to him by right. So it could not be thought that since he had been previously deceived, he had uttered these words in vain.

**2.** Isaac commanded Jacob to seek a wife from his maternal race. He might have sent for her by one of his servants, as Rebekah had been brought to him. But he may have decided to take this course to avoid Esau's jealousy.

**3.** Now followed a blessing that differed slightly from the previous one. Nevertheless, it expressed the same thoughts. First, Isaac desired that Jacob should be blessed by God—that is, that his own offspring should grow into a multitude of nations. It is as if he said, "Let there arise from you many tribes, who shall constitute one people." This truly was in some measure fulfilled when Moses divided the people into thirteen divisions. Isaac looked for a further result—namely, many were at length to be gathered together out of various nations to the family of his son, that in this way, from a vast and previously scattered multitude, they might be made into one group of people.

In this way Isaac made his son Jacob Abraham's heir. This is more clearly seen from verse 4, where he assigned to him the dominion over the land because it had been given to Abraham. It should be carefully noted that Jacob's faith was tested by a severe trial since the land was promised

247

to him in *word* only, while in *fact* he was cast faraway from it. He seemed to be ridiculed when he was commanded to possess the land, and yet to leave it and to say good-bye to it and depart into distant exile.

**6.** A brief account about Esau is inserted here. This is useful because we learn from it that the wicked, though they rebel against God and though, in contempt of his grace, they please themselves, are still unable to despise that grace altogether. Esau should have deeply repented, but he only tried to correct the one fault concerning his marriage. But he did this in a most absurd manner. He retained the wives his parents disliked so much and supposed that he had carried out his duty by marrying another wife (verse 9). May we tear up our sins by the roots and thoroughly devote ourselves to God!

**10.** In the course of this narrative we must especially observe how the Lord preserved his own church in the person of one man. For Isaac, on account of his age, lay like a dry trunk. Although the living root of piety was concealed within his heart, he had no hope of further offspring. Esau, like a green and flourishing branch, was full of show and splendor, but his vigor was only momentary. Jacob, like a severed twig, was taken away to a distant land. But he was not to be grafted or planted there, that he might acquire strength and greatness. Rather, being moistened with the dew of heaven, he put forth his shoots into the air itself. For the Lord wonderfully nourished him and supplied him with strength until he was brought back to his father's house.

Meanwhile, let the reader carefully observe that while God blessed the brother who was thrown into exile, the reprobate brother Esau was left in the possession of everything and ruled without a rival. So we must not be upset if the wicked parade themselves in a triumphant way, as if they had achieved all they wanted, while we remain oppressed.

**11.** Moses here, in a few words, declares how severe and arduous a journey the holy man, Jacob, endured because it was so long. Moses also adds that he lay on the ground, under the open sky, and without a companion. So if we ever think we are being treated roughly, let us remember the example of this holy man as a reproof to our selfish demands.

**12. He had a dream in which he saw a stairway resting on the earth, with its top reaching to heaven, and the angels of God were ascending and descending on it.** Moses teaches how opportunely the Lord comforted his servant. Who would not have said that holy Jacob was neglected by God since he was exposed to wild beasts and found no help or solace? But when he was thus reduced, the Lord suddenly stretched out his hand to him and wonderfully alleviated his trouble by a remarkable oracle. As, therefore, Jacob's invincible perseverance shined out, so now the Lord gave a memorable example of his paternal care toward the faithful.

Three things should be noted here. First, the Lord's appearing to Jacob in **a dream;** second, the nature of the vision as described by Moses; third, the words of the oracle. Mention of **a dream** indicates how God communicates with man. In the past the Lord often spoke to his servants in this way (see Numbers 12:6). Therefore, Jacob knew that this dream had been sent to him by God and that it was not one of his normal dreams.

Here we have the description of a vision in which form and content are closely related. God showed himself on a **stairway** [KJV, **ladder**], the ends of which touched **heaven** and **earth**. And **angels** were using it to go to and fro.

The ladder is taken by some Jewish commentators as a symbol of divine providence that includes both heaven and earth under its direction. This interpretation is not satisfactory, for God would have given a more suitable symbol. But for us who hold the truth that the covenant of God was founded on Christ and that Christ was always the same eternal image of the Father and revealed himself to the holy patriarchs, nothing in this vision is perplexing or ambiguous. Men are separated from God by sin, although his power fills and sustains all things; and we do not see the line of communication that draws us toward him. Rather, there is between us and him such a gulf that we flee from him, believing him to be hostile to us. **The angels** who are assigned the guardianship of the human race do not deal with us in a way that makes us familiar with their nearness and reveals it to our senses.

It is Christ alone who joins heaven to earth. He alone is Mediator. He it is through whom the fullness of all heavenly gifts flows down to us and through whom we on our part may ascend to God. Therefore, if we say that the ladder is a symbol of Christ, the interpretation is not forced. The metaphor of a ladder is most suited to a Mediator through whom the service of angels, righteousness, truth, and holy grace descend to us step by step. We on our part, who are firmly fixed not only upon the earth but in the abyss of the curse, climb up to God through him.

Moreover, the God of hosts stands atop the ladder because the divine fullness dwells in Christ, who therefore reaches heaven. Although all power was given by the Father to Christ's human nature, yet he would not be the support of our faith if he were not God manifest in the flesh. The fact that the body of Christ is finite in no way prevents his filling the heavens, since his grace and power is spread over all. To this Paul bears witness when he says that Christ ascended to heaven to fill all things.

Confirmation of the ladder as a symbol of Christ is found also in this consideration (and nothing has been more fully agreed upon by all): God sanctified his eternal covenant with his servant Jacob in his Son. An incalculable joy comes to us when we hear that Christ who excels all creation is joined to us. Indeed the majesty of God, plainly shown in his Son, must inspire terror so that every knee bows to Christ, all creatures pray to him and adore him, and all flesh is silent before him. Yet at the same time Christ shows himself to us as friendly and gentle, and he makes known to us by his descent that heaven is open to us and the angels are our companions; with them we have a brotherly communion because our common Head took his place on earth.

**13. "I am the Lord, the God of your father Abraham."** This is the third point that I said should be noted. For silent visions are cold; the word of the Lord is like the soul that brings them to life. **There above it stood the Lord, and he said . . .** The symbol of the ladder was inferior to God's promise. For God illustrates and adorns his word with external symbols so that greater clarity and authority may be added to it.

**"I will give you and your descendants the land on which you are lying."** We read that the land was given to Jacob's posterity, but he himself was not only a stranger in it to the end but was not even allowed to die there. From this we infer that under the pledge or earnest of the land, something better and more excellent was given, seeing that Abraham possessed the land spiritually and was content just to view it, for his sights were fixed on heaven.

**14.** This can be summarized as follows: Whatever the Lord had promised to Abraham, Jacob transmitted to his sons. Meanwhile, the holy man knew that it was right to rely on this divine testimony, to hope against hope; for though the promise was vast and magnificent, yet wherever Jacob went, he did not possess this land himself.

**"All peoples on earth will be blessed through you and your offspring."** This clause has great weight because in Jacob and in his seed, the blessing is to be restored from which the whole human race had been cut off in their first parent. Jacob will not only be an example to follow, but the fountain, cause, or foundation. Here God promises that in Jacob and his seed all nations will be blessed, because no happiness will ever be found except what comes from this source. That, however, which is special to Christ is without impropriety transferred to Jacob, in whose body Christ then was, figuratively speaking. Therefore, inasmuch as Jacob at that time represented the person of Christ, it is said that all nations are to be blessed in him; but, seeing that the manifestation of such a great benefit depended on another, the expression **and your offspring** was immediately added by way of explanation.

**15.** God now anticipated the temptation that might attack holy Jacob. For although he would be for a time thrust out into a foreign land, God declared that he would be his keeper until he brought him back again. God then extended his promise still further. God said that he would never desert Jacob until all things were fulfilled. This promise became fulfilled in two ways. First, it fixed Jacob's mind in believing in the divine covenant. Second, he learned that things would only go well if he took part in the promised inheritance.

**16.** Moses affirms that this was no ordinary dream. For when anyone wakes up, he immediately perceives that he has been dreaming; but God impressed a sign on the mind of his servant by which, when he awoke, he recognized the heavenly oracle he had heard in his sleep. Moreover, Jacob extolled the goodness of God, who deigned to present himself to one who had not sought him. Jacob thought he was there alone. But after the Lord appeared, Jacob exclaimed that he had obtained more than he could have dared hope for. It is not, however, to be doubted that Jacob had called on God and had trusted that he would be his guide on the journey; but because his faith had not persuaded him that God was close to him, he rightly extolled this act of grace. So whenever God anticipates our wishes and grants us more than our minds have conceived, let us learn from the example of this patriarch and praise God for being present with us.

**17. He was afraid and said, "How awesome is this place! This is none other than the house of God; this is the gate of heaven."** It seems surprising that Jacob should now be **afraid**, since God had just spoken to him so graciously. It may also surprise us that he should call that place **"awesome,"** as he had just been filled with incredible joy. I reply that although God exhilarates his servants, he at the same time inspires them with reverence so that they may learn and with true humility and self-denial embrace his mercy. We should not, therefore, understand that Jacob was struck with terror, as reprobates are, as soon as God showed himself; he was inspired with a reverence that produces pious submission. He also correctly called that place **"the gate of heaven"** because of the manifestation of God. For God was seen in heaven, on his royal throne. Jacob rightly declared that in seeing God, he had witnessed heaven. In this sense the preaching of the Gospel is called the kingdom of heaven, and the sacraments may be called the gates of heaven because they admit us to God's presence.

**18.** Moses recounts that the holy father was not satisfied with just giving thanks but wanted to **set up . . . a pillar** as a memorial of his gratitude to posterity. For this reason the Scripture not only commands the faithful to sing the praises of God among their brethren, but also tells them to train their children in religious duties and to encourage their descendants to worship God.

**19. He called that place Bethel, though the city used to be called Luz.** It may seem strange that Moses should speak of that place as a **city**, as he had said just before that Jacob slept there in the open air. But the difficulty is easily solved because the city had not yet been built. The place did not immediately take the name that Jacob gave it. Even when a town was later built there, no mention is made of **Bethel**, as if Jacob had never passed that way, for the inhabitants did not know what had happened there. Therefore they called the city **Luz.**

**20.** Through this **vow** Jacob showed his gratitude to God, hoping that God would show his favor to him. In the same way the Israelites offered peace-offerings under the law to testify to their gratitude. The Lord declares that vows of this nature are acceptable to him. So if we are asked if it is ever right to make vows to God, we must not be as fastidious as some people are who utterly condemn all vows in case they open the door to superstitions. Some people do make rash vows. However, we must also beware that we do not become like those who take exception to all vows. So that a vow may be right and pleasing to God, it is first necessary that it should have the correct end in sight. Next, men should never include in a vow anything that is in itself not approved of by God or that is impossible for them to carry out themselves.

When Jacob's vow is examined in detail, we see holy Jacob behaving in the way I have just outlined. In the first place, he wanted nothing but to express his gratitude to God. Second, he restricted what he was about to do to worship God in the right way. In the third place, he did not proudly promise what he did not have the power to do but gave **a tenth** (verse 22) of his goods as a sacred oblation.

**21.** In these words Jacob pledged that he would never deviate from the pure worship of the one God. But he appeared to promise what greatly exceeded his strength, for newness of life, spiritual righteousness, integrity of heart, and living a holy life were not in his power to perform. I reply that when holy men vow those things that God requires of them and that are due from them as acts of piety, they at the same time embrace what God promises concerning the remission of sins by the help of his Holy Spirit. From this it follows that they ascribe nothing to their own strength. Also, anything that falls short of complete perfection does not vitiate their worship because God mercifully and with paternal indulgence pardons them.

**22. ". . . this stone that I have set up as a pillar will be God's house, and of all that you give me I will give you a tenth."** This ceremony was an appendage to divine worship. For external rites do not make men true worshipers of God but are only aids to piety. But because the holy fathers were at liberty to erect altars wherever they pleased, Jacob poured a libation on the stone, because he had no other sacrifice to offer. He did not, however, worship God just as he liked, but he erected there **a pillar**, as he was allowed to do by the kindness and permission of God. This bore witness to the dream he had. What follows about offering **a tenth** of all that God would give him was no mere ceremony but was a charitable act. For Jacob enumerated, first, the spiritual worship of God; then the external rite, by which he both assisted his own piety and made profession of it before men; in the third place, an oblation, by which he gave friendly help to his brethren. And there is no doubt that these gifts were used in that way.

# Genesis
# Chapter 29

**1. Then Jacob continued on his journey and came to the land of the eastern peoples.** Moses now recounts Jacob's arrival in Mesopotamia and how he was received by his uncle. Moses commends the extraordinary strength of Jacob's faith when he says he **continued on his journey and came to the land of the eastern peoples.** He wants us to recognize once again God's providence. For God arranged that Jacob link up with these shepherds, who were able to bring him to the home he sought. This did not happen accidentally. He was guided by the hidden hand of God to that place; and the shepherds who guided him in this matter were brought there at precisely the same time. Therefore, whenever we may find ourselves in need of God's guidance, we must contemplate, with eyes of faith, the secret providence of God that governs us and our affairs and leads us to unexpected results.

**13. As soon as Laban heard the news about Jacob, his sister's son, he hurried to meet him. He embraced him and kissed him and brought him to his home, and there Jacob told him all these things.** Since **Laban** had previously seen one of Abraham's servants laden with great wealth, he might have viewed his nephew in a bad light, wondering why he had left home. Therefore, holy Jacob had to explain why he was no longer at home.

**14.** Although Laban did not doubt that Jacob was his nephew by his sister, he nevertheless observed him **for a whole month.** Then he arranged to pay him some wages for working for him (verse 15). From this may be inferred the uprightness of the holy man. Jacob was not idle while with his uncle but worked hard, so that he might not eat another person's bread while he did nothing in return.

**18. Jacob was in love with Rachel and said, "I'll work for you seven years in return for your younger daughter Rachel."** Laban's iniquity betrayed itself at once. For he acted in a shameful way, giving his daughter as a reward in exchange for Jacob's services. He made her the subject of a kind of barter. He should have not only given some of his property to his daughter but should have acted more generously toward his future son-in-law. Under the pretext of being a relative he defrauded Jacob of the reward of his labor, the very thing that he had previously said was not right.

We see here that although from birth men have a general understanding about right and wrong, as soon as anything that is to their own advantage presents itself to them, they do wrong, unless the Lord corrects them by his Spirit. Moses does not here relate something that is unusual but something that occurs every day. While men may not sell their daughters, their desire to earn money means they will sell their souls in the process.

**22. So Laban brought together all the people of the place and gave a feast.** Moses does not mean that a supper was prepared for all the people, but that many guests were invited, as is customary to celebrate a marriage.

**25. When morning came, there was Leah! So Jacob said to Laban, "What is this you have done to me? I served you for Rachel, didn't I? Why have you deceived me?"** Jacob rightly exploded about Laban's deceit. Laban's answer, though it is not without precedent, was no excuse for his fraud. It was indeed not the custom to give the younger daughters in marriage before the elder; an injustice would have been done to the firstborn by changing the usual order. But Laban should not, on that account, have cunningly agreed to Rachel marrying Jacob, and then substituted Leah in her place. He should have explained the situation to Jacob himself, so that Jacob could either consider Leah or refrain from marriage with either of them. We learn from this that wicked and deceitful men, as soon as they have turned away from truth, will constantly sin.

**27.** Laban now became callous in his wickedness, for he extracted another seven years from his nephew in return for allowing him to marry his other daughter. If Laban had ten more daughters, he would have been prepared to treat them all in this way! He treated his daughter as if she were a piece of merchandise. Laban, blinded by avarice, ensured that his daughters would live all their lives in a state of mutual hostility. He also perverted all the laws of nature by arranging for two sisters to be married to one man. Since Moses sets these sins before the Israelites at the start of their history, they should not be inflated by the sense of their own nobility or boast that they are descended from holy fathers.

**30. Jacob lay with Rachel also, and he loved Rachel more than Leah. And he worked for Laban another seven years.** There is no doubt that Moses wanted to expose Jacob's sins, so that we might learn to fear and to make sure that all our behavior conforms to the sole rule of God's word. For if the holy patriarch fell so badly, who among us is safe from a similar fall unless he is kept and guarded by God? This also shows us how dangerous it is to imitate the fathers while we neglect the law of the Lord. It is not right that the thoughts of any mad monk should be listened to more than all the patriarchs.

Leah was not without fault, even though she was despised by her husband. The Lord rightly punished her because she was aware of her father's deception in dishonorably obtaining possession of her sister's husband. But her fault is no excuse for Jacob's lust.

**31.** Moses here shows that Jacob's extravagant love was corrected by the Lord. The affections of the faithful, when they become inordinate, are apt to be tamed by the rod. This passage teaches us that children are a special gift from God. For the power to make someone fertile or infertile is specifically ascribed to God.

**32.** Moses recounts that Leah was not ungrateful to God. I am sure that God's gifts were more appreciated then than they are now. For a profane stupor so occupies the mind of nearly all men that, like cattle, they swallow up whatever benefits God in his kindness bestows on them. Further, Leah not only acknowledged God as the author of her fruitfulness but also said that her **misery** had been seen by the Lord, and a son had been given to her who would draw her in close affection to her husband. From this we see it is probable that when she saw herself despised she prayed, so that she might receive help from heaven. Giving thanks to God shows that people have previously prayed.

Leah gave her son a name that would remind her to offer praise to God. This passage also teaches that those who are wrongly despised by men are seen by the Lord. This is a special consolation to the faithful who, as experience shows, are most of the time despised in the world. Whenever, therefore, they are treated harshly and insolently by men, let them take refuge in the thought that God will act in a more favorable way toward them.

**33. She conceived again, and when she gave birth to a son she said, "Because the LORD heard that I am not loved, he gave me this one too." So she named him Simeon.** When Leah's second son was born, she did the same thing as she had done when her first son was born. She gave him a name that is derived from "hearing," so that she would remember that her sighs had been heard by the Lord. From this we deduce that when she was greatly afflicted, she cast her griefs on God.

**34.** Her third son she named from the word "joining" or "attached." It is as if she now said that a new link was forged so that she would be loved more by her husband.

**35.** When Leah's fourth son was born, Leah again declared her piety toward God, for she gave to him the name of "praise," as if this son had been given to her by God's special kindness. She had, indeed, previously given thanks to the Lord. But now she had even more to praise God for, and she acknowledged not only once but frequently that she had been helped by God's favor.

# Genesis
# Chapter 30

**1. When Rachel saw that she was not bearing Jacob any children, she became jealous of her sister. So she said to Jacob, "Give me children, or I'll die!"** Here Moses begins to relate that Jacob was distracted with domestic strife. Although the Lord was punishing him because he had been guilty of no light sin in marrying two wives, especially since they were sisters, his punishment was fatherly. For God, who often mercifully pardons his people, restrained his hand of judgment in this incident. But Jacob did not immediately repent but added new offenses to his previous ones.

But first we must speak of Rachel. She listened to her sister's grateful acknowledgment to God for the birth of her four sons. Nevertheless, envy inflamed her, and she would not allow Leah to be treated as a wife. We see what ambition can do. For Rachel, in seeking preeminence, did not spare even her own sister. She scarcely refrained from venting her anger against God for having honored her sister with the gift of fruitfulness. She could not bear to have a partner and an equal, even though she herself was the younger.

Moses, by exhibiting Rachel's evil, teaches us that we are all like this, so that each of us may tear up this sin by its roots. To be cured of envy we must reject pride and love of self. Paul prescribes this single remedy against strife: "Do nothing out of selfish ambition or vain conceit" (Philippians 2:3).

**2.** Jacob's tender affection made him unwilling to offend his wife. But her unworthy conduct compelled him to do this. Jacob saw that she petulantly exalted herself not only against her sister, who piously gave thanks to God for his gifts, but even against God himself, of whom it is said that the fruit of the womb is his gift (see Psalm 127:3). On this account, therefore, Jacob was angry, because his wife ascribed nothing to the providence of God and, by imagining that children are the offspring of chance, sought to deprive God of the care and government of humankind. It is probable

257

that Jacob had been already sad because of his wife's barrenness. Now he feared that her folly would provoke God even more, so that she would be punished more severely. Jacob maintained the honor due to God by holy indignation, while he corrected his wife and taught her there was good reason why she had been barren up to now. For when he affirmed that the Lord had shut her womb, he intimated that she ought to have been more humble.

**3.** Rachel did not flee to the Lord but attempted to triumph by using illicit practices. Therefore, she rushed Jacob into a third marriage. From this we infer that there is no end to sinning once the divine institution of marriage is neglected. Jacob did not repent immediately, even though God punished him. He acted in this instance at the instigation of his wife. But was his wife in the place of God, from whom alone marriage proceeds? But to please his wife, or to give way to her importunity, he did not think twice about disobeying God's command.

**5.** It is surprising that God should have deigned to honor an adulterous relationship with children. But God sometimes attempts to overcome by kindness the wickedness of men. He lavishes his favor on people who do not deserve such gifts. Moreover, he does not always punish his people as they deserve. Therefore, it was God's will that those who were born from this wrong relationship should still be regarded as legitimate children. In the same way Moses called Bilhah Jacob's wife in verse 4, when she could have more appropriately been called a prostitute.

**6.** At length Rachel began to ascribe to God what was his own. But her confession was so mixed with ambition that it had little sincerity in it. She pompously announced that her cause had been taken up by the Lord: **"God has vindicated me; he has listened to my plea and given me a son."** Rachel spoke as if she had been so injured by her sister that she deserved to be raised up by God's favor, and as if she were not to blame for being deprived of his help. We see, then, that under the pretext of praising God she attempted to make God subservient to her desires. In addition to this, she acted as hypocrites do. In adversity they rail against God with closed eyes, but in more prosperous times they indulge in vain boastings, as if God smiled on everything they did and said. Rachel, therefore, did not celebrate God's goodness but congratulated herself. Let the faithful, instructed by her example, abstain from polluting the sacred name of God by hypocrisy.

**9.** Moses returns to Leah, who, not content with four sons, devised a way by which she might always retain her superior rank. So she too substituted her maid in her place. Leah had experienced God's wonderful blessing. Now, because she stopped bearing children, she despaired about the future as if she had never taken part in God's favor. Why did she not turn to the fountain of blessing? So in obtruding her maid, she demonstrated not only her impatience but also her distrust. Both God's mercy and her own faith in God were extinguished in her heart. We know that all who rely on the Lord are so tranquil in their minds that they wait patiently for what God is about to give. When anyone stumbles through excessive haste, it is the just punishment of unbelief. We ought to beware of the attacks of the flesh if we want to maintain a right course.

**14.** This account about a boy bringing home a kind of unidentifiable fruit from the fields and presenting it to his mother, through which she bargained with her sister to have one night with her husband, seems to be of little importance. But it contains a useful instruction. We know how foolishly the Jews glory in extolling the origin of their own nation. They barely acknowledge that they have sprung from Adam and Noah with the rest of humankind. Certainly they do excel in the dignity of their ancestors, as Paul testifies (see Romans 9:5); but they do not acknowledge that this comes from God. So the Spirit deliberately aims to crush this arrogance when he recounts that they came from a people who were so lowly and abject. For he does not here erect a splendid stage on which they may exhibit themselves. Rather, he humbles them and exalts the grace of God, seeing that God had brought his church out of nothing.

**15.** Moses leaves more for his readers to reflect on than he says in these words—namely, that Jacob's house had been filled with arguments and strife. Leah spoke haughtily because her mind had been exasperated for so long that she could not speak courteously to her sister. Perhaps the sisters were not so argumentative by nature, but God allowed them to quarrel so their descendants might see that God punished their polygamy.

**17.** Moses specifically declares that **God listened to Leah** so that we may know how indulgently God dealt with that family. Who would have thought that while Leah was denying her sister the fruits gathered by her son and was using them to buy a night with her husband there would be any place for prayer? Moses, therefore, teaches us that God pardoned these faults, to prove that he would not fail to complete his work despite their great infirmity.

**21.** It is not known if Jacob had any other **daughter**, for it is not uncommon in Scripture for women to be left out of genealogies, as they do not bear their own name but lie concealed under the shadow of their husbands. However, they are mentioned if they did anything worthy of being commemorated, which was the case with **Dinah**.

**22. Then God remembered Rachel; he listened to her and opened her womb.** With God there is no before or after; everything is the present. So he is not able to be forgetful; despite the passing of time, he does not need to be reminded of what is past. But the Scripture describes the presence and memory of God from the effect it produces on us, because we imagine God to be as he appears to be in his actions.

**25.** As Jacob had been paid for his work, it might appear that he was acting in an underhanded way in desiring to leave his father-in-law. I cannot, however, doubt that the desire to return to his **own homeland** had already entered his mind. First, having experienced in many ways how unjust, and even cruel, Laban had been, it is little wonder that he should want to leave him at the earliest possible opportunity. Second, since such a long time had elapsed, Jacob hoped that his brother would be appeased, as he earnestly desired to return to his parents. But God's promise was the most powerful stimulant of all to excite his desire to return. For he had not rejected the benediction that was dearer to him than his own life. That is why he declared, **"Send me on my way so I can go back to my own homeland."** He did not use this language about Canaan just because he was born there, but because he knew it had been given to him by God.

**27. But Laban said to him, "If I have found favor in your eyes, please stay. I have learned by divination that the LORD has blessed me because of you."** It is as if Laban said that God's blessing was as clear to him as if it had been attested by prophecy or found out **by divination.** Here the insane wickedness of Laban was revealed. After he had almost worn out his nephew and son-in-law by hard and constant toil for fourteen years, he still offered him no wages for the future. In the same way the world abuses the gentleness of the pious. The more meekly the righteous behave, the more ferociously the world attacks them. But although in this world we are like sheep exposed to ravenous wolves, we must not be afraid of being wounded or killed by them, for the Heavenly Shepherd protects us.

**30. "The little you had before I came has increased greatly, and the LORD has blessed you wherever I have been. But now, when may I do something for my own household?"** It should be noted that although Jacob had worked hard, he still ascribed nothing to his own labor but imputed it entirely to God's blessing that Laban had been enriched. Although men may faithfully devote themselves to their duty, their success depends entirely on God's favor. In the same way Paul asserts that he who plants and he who waters is nothing (1 Corinthians 3:7).

Two points should be remembered about this teaching. First, whatever I attempt or whatever work I engage in, it is my duty to desire God to bless my labor, that it may not be vain and fruitless. Then if I obtain anything, my second duty is to ascribe the praise to God. Without God's blessing, it is pointless for men to get up early and work all day.

**33.** Jacob did not expect success except through his faith and integrity. It is as if he said, "If you should find with me anything **not speckled or spotted,** I am willing to be accused of being a thief. I require nothing to be given to me except the spotted lambs."

**37. Jacob, however, took fresh-cut branches from poplar, almond and plane trees and made white stripes on them by peeling the bark and exposing the white inner wood of the branches.** This part of Moses' account, at first sight, may seem absurd. He either intends to censure holy

Jacob for defrauding Laban or to praise his industry. From the context it will appear that this adroitness was not culpable. Let us then see how it should be excused. It is quite plausible to argue that Jacob was impelled to act as he did because of the numerous injuries inflicted by his father-in-law. But as far as God is concerned we should not repay a wrong with a wrong. Therefore, Jacob should not have resorted to this cunning action. Jacob should have behaved in a straightforward way unless the Lord had commanded him to act in some other way. But in this narrative there is a *hysteron proteron* (a putting of the last first), for Moses first recounts the fact and then adds that Jacob had not tried to do anything unless God had commanded it (Genesis 31).

**43. In this way the man grew exceedingly prosperous and came to own large flocks, and maidservants and menservants, and camels and donkeys.** Moses added this to show that Jacob did not become rich in this way without a miracle. From being entirely destitute, he became more wealthy than any person normally could in twenty or thirty years. To make sure that nobody should question this as being possible, Moses meets the objection by saying that the holy man was enriched in an extraordinary manner.

# Genesis
# Chapter 31

**1. Jacob heard that Laban's sons were saying, "Jacob has taken everything our father owned and has gained all this wealth from what belonged to our father."** Although Jacob ardently desired his own country and was continually thinking about returning to it, he demonstrated admirable patience about this. He delayed his return until a new opportunity presented itself. I do not, however, deny that he could have tried to hasten his return. However, God's promise always remained firmly fixed in his mind. He revealed something of his human nature in that he postponed his return for six years in order to obtain wealth. For when Laban was constantly changing his offers, Jacob could have left him.

Now, at least, he had a good reason to ask to be allowed to leave: His **wealth** upset the sons of Laban. Nevertheless, he was forced to flee secretly. Though his tardiness was to some extent excusable, it was probably linked to indolence. In the same way the faithful, when they follow God, sometimes do not do so with fervor. So whenever the indolence of the flesh slows us down, let us learn to fan the ardor of our spirits into a flame. There is no doubt that the Lord corrected the infirmity of his servant and gently spurred him on as he lived with Laban. For if Laban had been kind and pleasant to him, Jacob would have been lulled to sleep. But now he was driven away by anger. The Lord often secures the salvation of his people by subjecting them to the hatred, envy, and malevolence of the wicked rather than allowing them to be soothed with bland words. It was far more helpful for holy Jacob to have his father-in-law and his sons opposing him than to have them courteously agreeing to his wishes, for their compliance might have deprived him of God's blessing.

We too have plenty of experience with the power of earthly attractions, as they tend to make us unaware of our heavenly blessings. So we must not dislike being awakened by the Lord when we engage in conflict or receive little favor from the world. For hatred, threats, disgrace, and slanders are often more advantageous to us than the applause of all men on every side.

Moreover, we must notice the inhumanity of Laban's sons, who complained as if they had been plundered by Jacob. Greedy people labor under the false notion that they are robbed of everything with which they do not gorge themselves. For since their avarice is insatiable, it follows that the prosperity of others torments them, as if they themselves had been reduced to poverty. They did not consider whether Jacob acquired this great wealth justly or unjustly; they were angry and envious because they felt that so much had been taken from them. Laban had before stated that he had been enriched by Jacob's arrival and that he had been blessed by the Lord on account of Jacob. But now his sons murmured, and he himself was upset to find that Jacob also enjoyed the same blessing. From this we perceive the blindness of avarice, which can never be satisfied. Paul calls the love of money the root of all evil because they who want to swallow everything up must be perfidious, cruel, ungrateful, and in every way unjust. In addition to this it should be observed that the sons of Laban, in the impetuosity of their younger years, gave vent to their vexation; but the father, like a cunning old fox, was silent, though he betrayed his wickedness by his attitude.

**3. Then the LORD said to Jacob, "Go back to the land of your fathers and to your relatives, and I will be with you."** The timidity of the holy man is more plainly seen here. Perceiving that his father-in-law intended to harm him, he still did not dare to move unless he was encouraged by a new oracle. But the Lord, who had already shown him that he should no longer delay, now spoke to him again. Let us learn from this example that although the Lord may make us behave in the right way through adversity, yet we will hardly profit from this unless the stimulus of the word is added. We also see what will happen to reprobates. Either they become stupefied in their wickedness or they become furious. For directions that are given to us to benefit us, we must ask the Lord to shine upon us in his own Word. However, Moses' chief desire here is that we may know that Jacob returned to his own country under God's special guidance.

Here the land of Canaan is called **the land of your fathers**, not because they had been born there, but because it had been divinely promised to them as their inheritance. So through these words the holy man was admonished. For although Isaac had been a stranger, yet in the sight of God he was the heir and lord of that land in which he possessed nothing but a tomb.

**4.** Jacob sent for his wives in order to explain to them his plan and to exhort them to accompany him in his flight. It was his duty as a good husband to take them with him; so he had to inform them of his intention. And he was not blind to the many dangers of his plan. It was difficult to take women who had never left their father's house to a remote region by an unknown route. Moreover, they might seek to protect themselves and so betray their husband to his enemies. Jacob, therefore, behaved uprightly in choosing to expose himself to danger rather than fail to carry out his duty as a good husband and head of his family. If his wives had refused to accompany him, God's call would have compelled him to depart. But God granted him what was far more desirable—his whole family was prepared to follow him. Moreover, his wives, who had previously filled his house with the noise of their arguments, now freely consented to go with him into exile. When in good faith we carry out our plans, God enables us to succeed even in the most difficult circumstances. From the fact that Jacob called his wives to him in **the fields where his flocks were,** we infer what an anxious life he led.

**5. He said to them, "I see that your father's attitude toward me is not what it was before, but the God of my father has been with me."** These words consist of two parts. First, Jacob spoke about his own integrity and expostulated concerning the perfidy of his father-in-law. He then testified that God was the author of his prosperity, in order that Rachel and Leah might willingly accompany him.

**13. "'I am the God of Bethel, where you anointed a pillar and where you made a vow to me. Now leave this land at once and go back to your native land.'"** God, through the words of the angel, did not call himself **the God of Bethel** because he is confined to the limits of a particular place, but to make his servant remember his own promise. For holy Jacob had not yet become so perfect that the more simple rudiments of faith could be abandoned by him. Little light of true doctrine at that time prevailed, and even that was wrapped in many shadows. Nearly the whole world ran after false gods, and that region, including even his father-in-law's own house, was filled with unholy superstitions. Therefore, in the middle of so many hindrances, nothing was more difficult for Jacob than to hold his faith in the one true God.

So, in the first place he was commended for following pure religion so that, among the various errors of the world, he might obey and worship God. Second, the promise that he had previously received was repeated, so that he might always keep his mind fixed on the special covenant that God had made with Abraham and his posterity. Thus Jacob was directed to the land of Canaan, which was his own inheritance, in case the temporal blessing of God that he would have soon enjoyed should detain his heart in Mesopotamia. Since this oracle was only an appendix of the previous one, whatever benefits God afterwards bestowed belonged to his original plan.

We may also conjecture from this passage that Jacob had previously preached to his household concerning the true God and the true religion, as a pious father should. For he would have acted in a very strange way in uttering these words unless his wives had been previously instructed about that wonderful vision.

**14.** Here we see, as Paul taught, "that in all things God works for the good of those who love him, who have been called according to his purpose" (Romans 8:28). Since the wives of Jacob had been unjustly treated by their father, they were willing to follow Jacob into a distant and unknown land. "There is nothing," they said in effect, "that would make us want to remain with our father. Daughters remain loyal to their fathers because they are esteemed members of his family; but he has not only passed us off without a dowry but has set us up for sale and has devoured the price for which he sold us."

**16.** There is also no doubt, seeing they were persuaded that Jacob was a faithful prophet of God, that they freely embraced the heavenly oracle from him, for they ended their reply by saying, **"So do whatever God has told you."** They thus showed that they did not so much yield to his wish as to the command of God.

**19. When Laban had gone to shear his sheep, Rachel stole her father's household gods.** From this we see that the human mind has a great inclination to idolatry. In all ages this evil has prevailed, as men seek visible representations of God. Holy Jacob had not been silent during the past twenty years but had endeavored, by counsel and admonition, to correct these gross vices. But that was all in vain because superstition prevailed. Even Rachel was contaminated by this disease. She had often heard her husband speaking about the true and genuine worship of God. But she was so addicted to the corruptions that she had imbibed from her childhood that she was ready to infect God's chosen land with them. She imagined that, with her husband, she was following God as her leader and yet took with her the idols by which she would undermine his worship. It is even possible that by the excessive indulgence of his beloved wife, Jacob might give too much encouragement to such superstitions. Pious fathers must learn to use their utmost diligence to make sure no stain of evil remains in their wives or children.

**29. "I have the power to harm you; but last night the God of your father said to me, 'Be careful not to say anything to Jacob, either good or bad.'"** Laban is speaking here. Pride always accompanies unbelief. So unbelievers, even when they are defeated, continue to rebel against God. They add to their sins and complain that God is oppressing them.

**"'The God of your father.'"** Why did Laban not also acknowledge God as his own God, unless Satan had corrupted his mind already, so that he preferred to wander in darkness rather than turn to the light? Willingly or unwillingly, he was compelled to yield to the God of Abraham.

**30.** We learn from this that no one can live in the world without sometimes bearing undeserved reproach. Whenever this happens to us, let the precious promise sustain us that the Lord, in his own time, will bring forth our innocence as the morning light (Psalm 37:6).

**32. "But if you find anyone who has your gods, he shall not live. In the presence of our relatives, see for yourself whether there is anything of yours here with me; and if so, take it." Now Jacob did not know that Rachel had stolen the gods.** Moses recounts how Rachel concealed her theft (verses 33-35). Did she do this through shame or obstinacy? It was disgraceful to be caught in the act of theft. She also dreaded the severe sentence of her husband. Yet to me it appears probable that fear did not so much influence her as the obstinate love of idolatry. For we know how superstition infatuates the mind. Therefore, as if she had obtained an incomparable treasure, she thought that she must do anything rather than allow herself to be deprived of it. Moreover, she chose rather to incur the displeasure of her father and her husband than to relinquish the object of her superstition. She not only stole the gods—she lied about her theft and so deserved great censure.

**36.** Jacob again acted in a wrong way in contending with Laban about something that he did not know enough about.

**42. "If the God of my father, the God of Abraham and the Fear of Isaac, had not been with me, you would surely have sent me away empty-handed. But God has seen my hardship and the toil of my hands, and last night he rebuked you."** Jacob said that it was due to God's favor that he was not about to return home entirely empty. He therefore denied that he had been made rich by the kindness of his father-in-law. It is as if he said, "I do not owe any of my possessions to you but to God, who has looked after me." Since God is not the defender of unfaithfulness, and since he does not help the wicked, Jacob's integrity may be seen from the fact that God stepped in to vindicate him.

It should also be noted that by deliberately distinguishing between the God of Abraham and all fictitious gods, Jacob declared that there is no other true God. In this way he also showed that he himself was a pious worshiper of God.

**44. "Come now, let's make a covenant, you and I, and let it serve as a witness between us."** Laban now acted like a guilty man who wanted to protect himself in case Jacob decided to take revenge on him. Moses had previously given a similar example of this when Abimelech made a covenant with Isaac. So we must take great care, if we want to have tranquil minds, to be sincere to our neighbors and never to harm them. Meanwhile, Moses shows how placable Jacob was. He had endured many wrongs but now forgot them all. He freely stretched out the hand of kindness. He did not defend himself. He set up a pillar (verse 45).

It becomes the children of God not only to embrace peace quickly but to search for it ardently, as we are commanded in Psalm 34:14. As for the **stones** (verse 46), they were used as a sign that a covenant had been made.

A pillar (verse 45) was set up so future generations could be reminded of it.

**47. Laban called it Jegar Sahadutha, and Jacob called it Galeed.** Each person gave this **pillar** a name. Moses, in using the name of **Galeed**, does it proleptically; since he was writing for his own times, he did not worry about giving it the generally accepted name.

**49.** By these words Laban means that God will avenge every wickedness, even when no human judge is there to make a pronouncement.

**53. "May the God of Abraham and the God of Nahor, the God of their father, judge between us." So Jacob took an oath in the name of the Fear of his father Isaac.** It was indeed right for Laban to adjure Jacob by the name of God, for this confirmed the covenants. Both parties appealed to God to not allow a betrayal of trust to pass unpunished. But Laban, by mentioning **the God of Nahor**, mixed in idols with the true God, between whom there is nothing in common.

**55. Early the next morning Laban kissed his grandchildren and his daughters and blessed them. Then he left and returned home.** Note how Laban's character is portrayed in this verse. Laban, who had lapsed from true piety, who behaved in ungodly ways, still kept the habit of giving his blessing. This teaches us that certain principles of divine knowledge remain in the hearts of the wicked, and so they are left with no excuse and cannot claim to be ignorant about God. The practice of pronouncing a blessing arose because men were certain that God alone is the author of all good things. Although they proudly arrogate what they please to themselves, yet when they return to their right mind, they are compelled, whether they like it or not, to acknowledge that all good proceeds from God alone.

# Genesis
## Chapter 32

**1. Jacob also went on his way, and the angels of God met him.** After Jacob escaped from the hands of his father-in-law—that is, from the danger of death—he went on his way to meet with his brother, who was just as cruel. For it was on account of his brother's threats that he had been driven out of his country.

Jacob therefore proceeded with trepidation, like one going to the slaughter. Seeing, however, it was scarcely possible but that he should be overcome with fear, the Lord gave him timely comfort. The Lord prepared Jacob for this conflict as well as for others in such a way that he could stand as a brave and invincible champion in them all.

So that Jacob might know that God protected him, **angels** were sent to meet him. There are two purposes in this vision. First, since the holy man was very anxious about the future, the Lord planned to remove the cause of his fear, or at least to offer him some alleviation from it, so that he would not collapse under the trial. Second, God designed to plant the memory of this divine favor in Jacob's mind so that it would never be forgotten. We know how prone men are to forget God's favors. Even while God is stretching out his hand to help them, scarcely one out of a hundred raises his eyes toward heaven. Therefore, it was necessary that the visible protection of God should be placed before the eyes of the holy man. In this way, like a splendid theater, Jacob would see that he had not been recently delivered by chance from the hand of Laban. He would realize that **the angels of God** had been fighting for him. This gave him hope that their help would still be with him to protect him from his brother. After the danger had passed, he would also remember that they had protected him, and not his own schemes.

From this we should learn to note the invisible presence of God in his manifested favors. Chiefly, however, it was necessary that the holy man should be furnished with new weapons to endure the approaching contest. He did not know whether his brother Esau had been changed for the

269

better or for the worse. But he suspected that he would be hostile toward him. Therefore, the angels came to strengthen his faith, so that in the future he would recall God's favors that had been lavished on him.

**3.** It happened, by the providence of God, that Esau, having left his father, had gone to **Seir** of his own accord. Since he had in this way left the land of promise, it could be claimed for the posterity of Jacob without any fighting among the brothers.

The question now arises, how did Jacob know that his brother lived in that region? Though I assert nothing with certainty, I think it is probable that he had been informed of it by his mother. Among the large number of her servants, there would be a faithful messenger. It is easy to see from the words of Moses that Jacob, before he entered the land, knew where his brother now lived. And we know that many things like this were omitted by Moses, which may be deduced by the reader.

**4. He instructed them: "This is what you are to say to my master Esau: 'Your servant Jacob says, I have been staying with Laban and have remained there till now.'"** Moses recounts how anxious Jacob was to appease his brother. It seems, however, absurd that he handed over to his brother what he had risked his life for. I reply that although he gave up oversight temporarily, he did not give up his right to the secret benediction. He knew that the effect of the divine promise was still suspended. He was, therefore, content with the hope of the future inheritance; so he did not hesitate, at present, to give deference to his brother and say that he was his brother's **servant.**

**5.** Jacob declared that he had not come to consume his father's substance, nor to be rich at his brother's expense. It is if he said, "Your earthly inheritance is safe. Your claim will not be harmed by me. Just allow me to live." By this example we are taught how to cultivate peace with the wicked. The Lord does not forbid us to defend ourselves, but we must not insist on our own rights if that causes a fight.

**6.** Esau came to meet his brother in a friendly way. But Jacob, reflecting on his cruel ferocity and savage threats, did not expect this. The Lord willed that his servant should be oppressed with this anxiety for a time so that he might be more prayerful. In order to stir up our faith, God often allows us to fear things that are not terrible in themselves. God does not promise that he will be present with us so that all danger is taken away from us, but so that fear may not overwhelm us. Moreover, our faith is never so strong at every point that we are able to repel wicked doubts and sinful fears as we would wish.

**7.** Moses recounts that Jacob made his plans to meet what he considered to be the present situation. He divided his family into **two groups.** This action stemmed from Jacob's faith. He separated his family into two sections so that if one part was destroyed, the whole seed of the church would not perish. In this way the survivors would receive the promised inheritance.

**9.** Having arranged his affairs, Jacob now prayed. His prayer shows that he was not so oppressed with fear that his faith was stopped from being victorious. He cast his cares and his troubles on his heavenly Father.

**10.** Jacob confessed that God's great mercies had been heaped on him in a way that he had not dared to hope for. So he knew he was **unworthy** to ask God for anything on account of any merit in himself.

**"I had only my staff."** Jacob did not list all of God's mercies but in mentioning just one of them, he included all of them. He had crossed over the River Jordan a poor, solitary traveler; but now he returned with an abundance of possessions. The antithesis between **only my staff** and **two groups** should be noted, and by this he compared his former solitude and poverty with his present affluence.

**11.** After he declared that he had received so many of God's benefits that he could not boast of his own merits, he mentioned his own necessities. It is as if he said, "O Lord, unless you decide to reduce so many excellent gifts to nothing, now is the moment for you to help me and to avert the destruction with which my brother threatens me."

**"Also the mothers with their children."** I think this was a proverbial saying among the Jews that meant to leave nothing. It is a metaphor taken from birds, when hawks seize the young with their mothers and empty the whole nest.

**13.** In his attempt to appease his brother with presents, Jacob was showing that he was distrusting God, as if he doubted whether he would be safe under his protection. It is a common fault among men that when they have prayed to God, they then forget God and trust in their own devices. But the point of prayer is to wait for the Lord in silence and quietness.

**22. That night Jacob got up and took his two wives, his two maidservants and his eleven sons and crossed the ford of the Jabbok.** After he had prayed to the Lord and arranged his plans, he took courage and went out to meet the danger. This example teaches the faithful that whenever any danger approaches, the following things should be observed. First, resort directly to the Lord; second, use whatever help is at hand; and third, be like people who are prepared for any eventuality, and proceed with resolution and courage wherever the Lord leads you.

**24. So Jacob was left alone, and a man wrestled with him till daybreak.** This vision was particularly useful to Jacob. It taught, ahead of the many conflicts that awaited him, that he would be able to conquer them all. But this vision also teaches us. So it is right to keep in mind the purpose of the vision, which represents all God's servants in this world as wrestlers. For the Lord tests them with various kinds of conflicts. Moreover, it is not said that Satan or any mortal man wrestled with Jacob; it was God himself. This teaches us that our faith is tried by God, and whenever we are tested, he descends into the arena to try our strength. At first sight this seems to be absurd. But experience and reason teach us that it is true. For as all prosperity flows from God's goodness, so adversity is either the rod with which he corrects our sins or a test of our faith and patience. And since there is no kind of test in which God does not try his faithful people, the comparison with a wrestler is a good one, as it represents God in hand-to-hand combat with us. So what was once seen in visible form by our father Jacob is daily experienced by individual members of the church. For in our tests we have to wrestle with God.

The question now arises, who is able to stand against an Antagonist, at whose breath alone all flesh perishes and vanishes away, at whose look the mountains melt, at whose word or call the whole world is shaken to pieces? To attempt any kind of contest with him would be reckless contempt. But it is easy to untie this knot, for we do not fight against him except by his own power and with his own weapons. For God, having challenged us to this contest, at the same time furnishes us with the means to resist, so that he both fights *against* us and *for* us. In short, he arranges the conflict in such a way that while he attacks us with one hand, he defends us with the other. He supplies us with more strength to resist than he uses to attack us. We may rightly say that he fights *against* us with his left hand and *for* us with his right hand. For while he opposes us in a gentle way, he gives us invincible strength so we can overcome. It is true he remains in perfect unity with himself; but the double way in which he deals with us cannot be expressed in any other way.

**25. When the man saw that he could not overpower him . . .** Here is described the victory of Jacob, which, however, was not gained without a wound. In saying that the wrestling angel—God—wished to retire from the contest because he saw he could not prevail, Moses speaks in a human way. For we know that God, when he descends to us from his majesty, transfers the properties of human nature to himself. The Lord knew the outcome of the contest before he came down to engage in it. He had already determined what he would do.

**. . . he touched the socket of Jacob's hip so that his hip was wrenched as he wrestled with the man.** Though Jacob was victorious, the angel struck him on the thigh, making him lame for the rest of his life. Moreover, by this sign it is made manifest to all the faithful that they can be conquerors in their trials, even though they are injured and wounded in the conflict. For we know that God's strength is made perfect in our weakness, in order that our exaltation may be linked with humility. For if our own strength remained intact and we never suffered any injury or dislocation, the flesh would immediately become haughty, and we would forget that we had conquered with God's help. But the wound received and the weakness that follows it compel us to be modest.

**26. But Jacob replied, "I will not let you go unless you bless me."**

From this it appears that at length the holy man knew the identity of his antagonist. For this prayer, in which he asked to be blessed, was no ordinary prayer. The inferior was blessed by the greater. It is in God's nature alone to bless us. In this way Jacob's father had blessed him, by divine command, as one who represented God. A similar office also was imposed on the priests under the law, so that as ministers and expositors of divine grace they might bless the people. Jacob knew, then, that the combatant with whom he had wrestled was God, because he desired a blessing from him. For it is not right to ask such a blessing from mortal man.

Moreover, this passage teaches us to always expect God's blessing, even if we have experienced his presence to be harsh and grievous, or even if our limbs are put out of joint. It is far better for the sons of God to be blessed, though mutilated and half destroyed, than to desire that peace in which they fall asleep or to withdraw themselves from the presence of God, so as to disobey him and join in the activities of the wicked.

**28. Then the man said, "Your name will no longer be Jacob, but Israel, because you have struggled with God and with men and have overcome."** Jacob, as we have seen, received his name when he was born because he seized the heel of his brother's foot and attempted to hold him back. God now gave him a new and more honorable name. This did not obliterate his other name, which remained a token of God's grace. But his new name testified to even more of God's grace. Therefore, of the two names, the second is preferred to the former, as it is more honorable.

**29.** This verse seems to contradict what has just been stated—that when Jacob sought a blessing, it was a token of his submission. Why, therefore, as if he had doubts, did he now inquire the name of him whom he had before acknowledged to be God? The solution is easy. While Jacob did acknowledge God, yet, not content with an obscure view or a partial knowledge, he wished to ascend higher. And it is not surprising that the holy man, to whom God had manifested himself under so many veils and coverings, and who had not yet received any clear knowledge of him, should now express this wish. **"Please tell me your name."** It is certain that all the saints, under the law, were on fire with this desire. In summary, we can say that although Jacob's wish was a pious one, the Lord did not grant it, because the time for full revelation had not yet arrived. For the fathers, in the beginning, were required to walk in the twilight of morning; and the Lord manifested himself to them by degrees until at length Christ, the Sun of Righteousness, arose, in whom perfect brightness shines forth. This is the reason he showed himself in a more conspicuous way to Moses, who nevertheless was only allowed to see his glory from behind. But because he held a place between patriarchs and apostles, he is said, in comparison with them, to have seen face to face him who had been hidden from the fathers. But now, since God has come closer to us, our ingratitude is most impious and detestable if we do not run with ardent desire to obtain such great grace. This is why Peter admonishes us as he does in the first chapter of his first epistle (see verses 12-13).

It should be noted that although Jacob piously desired to know God more fully, yet, because he was carried beyond the bounds prescribed to the age in which he lived, he was refused. For the Lord commanded him to be content with his own blessing.

**30. So Jacob called the place Peniel, saying, "It is because I saw God face to face, and yet my life was spared."** The gratitude of our father Jacob is again commended because he took diligent care that God's grace should be forever remembered. He, therefore, left a monument to posterity, from which they might know that God had appeared there. For this was not a private vision but was meant for the whole church.

Moreover, Jacob not only declared that he had seen the **face** of God but also gave thanks that he had been snatched from death. This language frequently occurs in the Scriptures and was common among the ancient people. There was a very good reason for this. For if the earth trembles at the presence of God, if the mountains melt, if darkness overspreads the heavens, what must happen to miserable men! The immense majesty of God cannot be comprehended even by angels but rather absorbs them. Were his glory to shine on us, it would destroy us and reduce us to nothing unless he sustained and protected us. So long as we do not perceive God to be present, we proudly please ourselves; and this is the imaginary life that the flesh foolishly arrogates to itself when it inclines toward the earth. But the faithful, when God reveals himself to them, feel themselves to be more like a vapor than any smoke.

Finally, if we want to defeat the pride of the flesh, we must draw near to God. So Jacob confessed that, by God's special indulgence, he had been rescued from destruction when he saw God. It may, however, be asked, "Why, when he had obtained so slight a taste of God's glory, should he boast that he had seen him **face to face?**" I answer, it is in no way absurd that Jacob celebrated this vision above all others, in which the Lord had not so plainly appeared to him. For if it is compared with the splendor of the Gospel, or even of the law, it will appear like a spark or an obscure ray. The simple meaning is that he saw God in an extraordinary way. Now, if Jacob so greatly exulted and congratulated himself in that slender measure of knowledge, what ought we to do today? For Christ, the living image of God, is clearly set before us, as in a mirror, in the Gospels.

**32.** Moses recounts that **the Israelites do not eat the tendon attached to the socket of the hip.** But this was not done out of superstition. For that age, as we know, was the beginning of the church. So the Lord kept the faithful who then lived under the teaching of the schoolmaster. Since the coming of Christ, we are more free; yet the memory of this event should remain among us, for God disciplined his ancient people through this external happening.

# Genesis
# Chapter 33

**1. Jacob looked up and there was Esau, coming with his four hundred men; so he divided the children among Leah, Rachel and the two maidservants.** We have said how much Jacob feared his brother. But now when Esau himself approached, Jacob's terror was not only renewed but increased. For although he went out like a courageous combatant to this contest, he was not exempt from a sense of danger. From this it follows that he was not free either from anxiety or fear, for his cruel brother still had the same reason to hate him. Jacob divided up his wives and **children** so that if Esau should attempt anything hostile, the whole seed might not perish, but some would have the opportunity to escape.

**3.** Jacob may have **bowed down** before **his brother** in this way to show that he was giving honor to him, for we know that the people of the east are given to far more ceremonies than we are. To me, however, it seems more probable that Jacob did not pay this honor simply to his brother, but that he worshiped God. He did this partly to give him thanks and partly to implore him to make his brother well disposed toward him. For he is said to have bowed down **seven times** as he approached his brother.

**4. But Esau ran to meet Jacob and embraced him; he threw his arms around his neck and kissed him. And they wept.** Esau met his brother with unexpected benevolence and kindness. This was the result of the special favor of God. Therefore, in this way God showed that he has the hearts of men in his hands. He can soften their hardness and mitigate their cruelty whenever he pleases. In short, he tames them as wild beasts are tamed. So whenever the threats of enemies alarm us, let us learn to resort to this sacred anchor. God, indeed, works in various ways and does not always incline cruel minds to humanity; but while they rage, he restrains them from doing harm by his own power. And if he considers that it is right, he can as just as easily make them friendly toward us, as we see here that Esau approached his brother Jacob in a friendly way.

**5.** Moses recounts the conversation between the brothers. As Esau had shown his brotherly affection by tears and embraces, there is no doubt that he inquired about **the women and children** in a spirit of congratulation. Jacob's answer breathed piety as well as modesty. **"They are the children God has graciously given your servant."** Jacob acknowledged that children are not just produced by nature, but are rewards and gifts from God. Let parents learn from this and celebrate God's special kindness in providing them with children. In a modest way Jacob called himself his brother's **servant.** Here again it is right to remember that the holy man did not boast about his birthright, as the hidden grace of God was more than sufficient for him. Jacob knew that God would manifest this at his appointed time. It becomes us to follow his example while we live in this world, to depend upon the word of the Lord, that we may not deem it wearisome to be wrapped in the shadow of death until our real life is manifested. For although apparently our condition is miserable and accursed, yet the Lord blesses us with his word and on this account only pronounces us happy because he owns us as sons.

**6.** Jacob's wives, having left their country, had come as exiles into a distant land. Now as they arrived, they were met by a fear of death. When they prostrated themselves before Esau, they did not know if they were paying homage to their executioner. This trial was very severe for them and greatly upset the holy man. But it was right that his obedience should be tried in this way, so that he might become an example to us all. Moreover, the Holy Spirit here places a mirror before us, in which we may contemplate the state of the church as it appears in the world. For though many tokens of divine favor were manifest in the family of Jacob, nevertheless we see that he was not held in any special honor in the presence of an ungodly man. Jacob thought that he would be well treated if he was allowed by his brother, as a favor, to live in the land of which he was the heir and lord. Therefore, let us bear it patiently if today also the glory of the church is an object of derision to the wicked.

**8.** Esau did not ask about **all these droves** as if he were entirely ignorant, as he had heard from the servants that oxen and camels and donkeys and other cattle were sent to him as a present. He asked about them so he could refuse the gift that was being offered to him. Jacob, however, did not stop pressing his brother to receive the gift, for it was a pledge of reconciliation. Further, in order to persuade his brother, he declared that it would be taken as a great kindness not to refuse what was given. For we do not willingly receive anything but what we certainly know to be offered to us freely. Jacob said that he rejoiced at the sight of his brother as if he had seen **God** (verse 10). By this he meant that he not only really loved his brother, but also that he held him in high esteem.

It may seem that he was wrong to compare God with a reprobate man and that he spoke falsely because, had the choice been given him, he would have avoided this meeting with his brother. Both these knots are easily untied. It is a customary way of speaking among the Jews to call whatever is excellent divine. So it was right for Jacob to say that he had been exhilarated by that friendly and fraternal reception as if he had seen God. It was as if God had given some sign of his presence. And Jacob did not speak deceitfully. He himself was totally free of all hatred and, more than anything else, wanted to act in a brotherly way toward Esau, so long as Esau did the same.

12. Although Esau was showing kindness, Jacob still distrusted him. A proud and ferocious man is easily upset over a small matter. Although the holy man had good reason to be fearful, I do not deny that his anxiety was excessive. He suspected the liberality of Esau, but did he not know that God, who was watching over his salvation, was standing between them? How can one account for such an incredible change of mind in Esau unless he had been divinely transformed from a wolf into a lamb? Let us then learn from this example to restrain our anxieties, lest when God has provided for us, we tremble and doubt his divine favor.

17. **Jacob, however, went to Succoth, where he built a place for himself and made shelters for his livestock. That is why the place is called Succoth.** In the word **Succoth** there is a prolepsis. It is probable that Jacob rested there for some days, to rest his family and his flocks after the toil of a long journey, for he had found no quiet resting-place until he arrived there. Therefore he named the place **Succoth** or "Tents."

20. **There he set up an altar.** As soon as Jacob found a place in which he might provide for his family, he set up a place for the solemn worship of God, in the same way that Abraham and Isaac had done. Although in every place they gave themselves up to the pure worship of God in private prayers and other acts of devotion, they did not neglect the public worship of God whenever the Lord allowed them to settle down anywhere. Whenever we read that an altar was built by them, we must consider what its purpose was. They did it to offer sacrifices and to call on the name of God, so that in this way their religion and faith would become known. I say this lest anyone should think that they rashly trifled with the worship of God. For they worshiped God according to the divinely prescribed rule that was handed down to them from Noah and Shem. So under the word *altar*, let the reader understand, by synecdoche, the external testimony of piety. Moreover, from this it may be clearly seen how important worshiping God was to the holy man. Although he was surrounded by various troubles, Jacob nevertheless did not forget to erect **an altar**. He not only worshiped privately, but he worshiped God in the ceremonies that are useful and commanded by God. For he knew that men need help as long as they are in the body, and that sacrifices were not instituted without reason. He also had another purpose—namely, so his whole family would worship God with the same sense of piety. A pious father must ensure that he has no profane house, but rather that God should reign

there as in a sanctuary. Besides, since the people of that region had fallen into many superstitions and had corrupted the true worship of God, Jacob wanted to be distinctive from them. The Shechemites and other neighboring nations certainly had altars of their own. Jacob, by establishing a different method of worship for his household, thus declared that he had a God who was special to him and had not ignored the holy fathers, from whom the perfect and genuine religion had been passed down. This action would mean that he would be reproached, because the Shechemites and other inhabitants would feel they were despised. But the holy man thought that anything was preferable to mixing with idolaters.

. . . **and called it El Elohe Israel.** This name does not seem to be an appropriate one for the **altar,** for it sounds as if a heap of stones or turf formed a visible statue of God. But the holy man meant something different. Because the **altar** was a memorial and a pledge of all the visions and promises of God, he honored it with this title, so that as often he looked at the altar, he would remember God.

# Genesis
# Chapter 34

**1. Now Dinah, the daughter Leah had borne to Jacob, went out to visit the women of the land.** This chapter records a severe trial in which God again tested his servant. We may readily conjecture from the uprightness of Jacob's whole life how precious the chastity of his **daughter** would be to him. When, therefore, he heard that she had been violated (verse 2), this disgrace inflicted the deepest sadness on him. But his grief was multiplied when he heard that his sons, out of revenge, committed a most dreadful deed.

**Dinah . . . went out to visit the women of the land.** Dinah was ravished because, having left her father's house, she wandered around more freely than she should have. She should have remained quietly at home. Therefore, fathers are taught by this to keep their daughters under control if they want to keep them from being dishonored. For if a vain curiosity was so severely punished in the daughter of holy Jacob, ever greater danger hangs over weak virgins today if they go boldly in public places and excite the passions of youth toward themselves. It is clear that Moses apportions part of the blame of the offense on Dinah herself when he says that she **went out to visit the women of the land**, when she should have remained under her mother's eyes in the tent.

**3.** Moses intimates that Dinah was not violated by force, and that Shechem after violating her did not treat her with contempt, as is usual with prostitutes. Rather, **he loved the girl and spoke tenderly to her.** He loved her as a wife and did not even object to being circumcised so that he might have her (verses 17-18); but lust had so prevailed that he first subjected her to disgrace. Therefore, although he embraced Dinah with real and sincere attachment, yet in his lack of self-control he sinned greatly.

**4.** Here it is more clearly stated that Shechem desired to have Dinah for his **wife.** For his lust was not so unbridled that when he had defiled Dinah, he despised her. Besides, a laudable modesty was shown since he

paid deference to his father's will. For he did not attempt to form a contract of marriage by himself but left this to his father's authority.

**5.** Moses inserts just one verse about the silent sorrow of Jacob.

**7.** Moses begins to relate the tragic events that followed. Shechem had
acted wickedly and impiously, but it was far more atrocious and wicked
that the sons of Jacob should murder a whole group of people to take
revenge in this way for the fault of one man. It was not fitting to seek
cruel compensation for the rashness of one youth by slaughtering so
many men. Therefore, we must beware in case, after we have severely
condemned the faults of others, we then proceed to act in an even more
evil way ourselves. We must refrain from violent remedies that surpass
the evil we desire to correct.

**8.** Although the sons of Jacob were justly incensed, their indignation
should have been appeased or at least somewhat mitigated by the great
courtesy of Hamor. And if the humanity of Hamor could not reconcile
the sons of Jacob to Shechem, the old man himself was at least worthy of
a kind reception.

**13-17.** Since the Shechemites had no strength to resist the sons of Jacob,
they were cruelly butchered (verse 25). This increased the wickedness of
Jacob's sons, who cared for nothing so long as they could gratify their
rage.

They used circumcision as a pretext to carry out their wicked plan.
They wickedly severed the sign from the truth that it represents, as if
anyone just by being circumcised could immediately become a member of
the church of God. In this way they polluted the spiritual symbol of life,
admitting foreigners indiscriminately into their fellowship.

We must note that the sons of Jacob said it would be disgraceful for
them to give their sister to an uncircumcised man. This was true, if those
who said the words had been sincere. For since they bore the mark of
God in their flesh, it was wrong for them to marry unbelievers. So also at
the present time our baptism separates us from the ungodly, so that whoever mixes himself with them fixes a mark of infamy upon himself.

**25. Three days later, while all of them were still in pain, two of
Jacob's sons, Simeon and Levi, Dinah's brothers, took their swords
and attacked the unsuspecting city, killing every male.** Because Moses
says that the slaughter took place on the third day, the Jews think that at
that time the pain of the wound was most severe. This is not the case, but
that is hardly important. Although Moses names only two people as being
responsible for the slaughter, **Simeon and Levi, Dinah's brothers**, it does
not appear to me probable that they came alone, but that they were the
leaders of a troop. Jacob had a large family, and they probably called some
of their brothers to join them. But because the matter was conducted by
their counsel and direction, it is ascribed to them, just as Cartage is said
to have been destroyed by Scipio. Moses calls them **Dinah's brothers**

because they had the same mother. Dinah was the daughter of Leah, and so Simeon and Levi, whose sister she was by both parents, were the more enraged at the violation of her chastity. They were therefore impelled, not so much by the common reproach brought upon the holy and elect race, as they had recently said, as from a sense of shame that this brought on them. However, there is no reader who does not readily perceive how dreadful and detestable this crime was. Only one man had sinned, and he had tried to compensate for the injury by many acts of kindness. But the cruelty of Simeon and Levi could only be satiated by the destruction of the whole city; so under the pretext of a covenant, they hatched a plot against friends and hospitable people in a time of peace that would not have been tolerated against enemies in a time of war.

From this we see how mercifully God dealt with that people, seeing that from the descendants of a bloodthirsty man, who was also a wicked robber, he raised up a priesthood for himself. Let the Jews now go and be proud of their noble origin! The Lord declared his gratuitous mercy in so many ways that the ingratitude of man cannot be hidden. Moreover, we learn from this that Moses did not speak as an ordinary person but was the instrument of the Holy Spirit and the herald of the celestial Judge. For although he was a Levite, he did not excuse his own race. He did not hesitate to brand the father of his tribe with perpetual infamy. And it is clear that the Lord purposely intended to stop the mouths of impure and profane men, such as the Lucianists who confess that Moses was a very great man and of rare excellence, but that he procured for himself, by craft and subtlety, authority over a great people, as if indeed an intelligent man would not have known that by this single act of wickedness the honor of his race would be greatly tarnished. He had, however, no other intention but to extol the goodness of God toward his people.

As far as the Shechemites are concerned, although in the sight of God they were not innocent, seeing they preferred their own advantage to a religion that they thought lawful, yet it was not the Lord's will that they should be so grievously punished for their fault; but he allowed this signal punishment to follow the violation of one unmarried girl so that he might testify to all ages his great abhorrence of lust. Furthermore, seeing that the iniquity had arisen from a ruler of the city, the punishment was in a sense rightly extended to all the people. Since God never commits evil rulers to govern except in righteous judgment, it is hardly surprising that when they sin, they involve their subjects with them in the same condemnation. Moreover, from this example let us learn that if at any time fornication is tolerated, God will at length exact even more severe punishments. For if the violation of one unmarried girl was avenged by the horrible massacre of a whole city, God will not sleep or be quiet if a whole people indulge in a common license of fornication and on all sides indulge each other's iniquity. The sons of Jacob indeed acted wickedly, but we must observe that fornication was in this manner divinely condemned.

**28. They seized their flocks and herds and donkeys and everything else of theirs in the city and out in the fields.** Moses shows that, not content with simple revenge, they grabbed all the spoil they could lay their hands on. They may have been blinded with anger as they shed blood, but what right did they have to sack the city? This certainly cannot be ascribed to anger; these are the ordinary fruits of human intemperance. Anyone who gives himself over to one wickedness soon moves on to commit another. Thus the sons of Jacob, from being murderers, also become robbers, and the guilt of avarice was added to that of cruelty.

So we should be all the more careful to bridle our desires, so they do not ignite each other. We must beware of using force that brings with it many perverse and brutal assaults. Moses says that the sons of Jacob did this because the Shechemites had defiled their sister; but the whole city was not guilty. Moses, however, only states how the instigators of the slaughter were affected. For although they wanted to appear to be just avengers of the injury, yet they paid no respect to what was right for them to do and made no attempt to control their depraved affections and consequently set no bounds to their wickedness.

**30. Then Jacob said to Simeon and Levi, "You have brought trouble on me by making me a stench to the Canaanites and Perizzites, the people living in this land. We are few in number, and if they join forces against me and attack me, I and my household will be destroyed."** Moses declares that the crime was condemned by the holy man, so that no one would think he had participated in their counsel. He also expostulated with his sons because they had made him **a stench** among the inhabitants of the land. They had made him so odious that no one would be able to bear him. If then the neighboring nations should conspire among themselves, he would be unable to resist them, seeing that his people were **few in number** in comparison with their great number.

He also expressly mentions **the Canaanites and Perizzites,** who, though they had not been wronged, were prone to inflict injury. But Jacob seemed to act preposterously in overlooking the offense committed against God and in considering only his own danger. Why was he not rather angry at their cruelty? Why was he not offended at their treachery? Why did he not reprove their rapaciousness? It is, however, probable that when he saw them terror-stricken by their recent crime, he chose his words to suit their state of mind. For he acted as if he were complaining that he, rather than the Shechemites, was slain by them. We know that men are seldom, if ever, drawn to repentance except by the fear of punishment. This is especially so when they have any specious pretext to cover over their fault. Besides, Moses may have selected this as just one part from a long expostulation, to make his readers understand that the fury of

Simeon and Levi was so outrageous that they were more insensible than brute beasts, to their own destruction and that of their whole family. This is clear from their own answer: **"Should he have treated our sister like a prostitute?"** (verse 31), which not only breathes a barbarous ferocity but shows that they had no feeling. It was barbarous, first, because they excused themselves for having destroyed a whole people and plundered their city on account of the injury done by one man; second, because they answered their father so shortly and rebelliously; third, because they obstinately defended the revenge that they had rashly exacted. Moreover, their insensibility was enormous because they were not affected by the thought of their own death and that of their parents, wives, and children, which seemed at hand.

Thus we are taught how intemperate anger deprives men of their senses. We are also admonished that it is not enough for us to be able to lay blame on our opponents—we must always see how far it is right for us to proceed.

# Genesis
# Chapter 35

**1. Then God said to Jacob, "Go up to Bethel and settle there, and build an altar there to God, who appeared to you when you were fleeing from your brother Esau."** Moses recounts that when Jacob had been reduced to the last extremity, God came to his help at the right time and at the critical juncture. And thus he shows in the person of one man that God never deserts his church, which he has embraced, but will procure its salvation. We must, however, observe the order in which this takes place. For God did not immediately appear to his servant but allowed him first to be tormented by grief and excessive cares, so that he might learn patience. Certainly Jacob's condition was then most miserable. For all on every side were enraged against him, and he was not unaware of his danger. God allowed the holy man to be tossed with cares and tormented with troubles until, by a kind of resurrection, he restored him as one who was half-dead. Whenever we read this and similar passages, let us reflect that the providence of God watches for our salvation, even when it most seems to sleep. Moses does not say how long Jacob was kept in anxiety, but we may infer from the context that he had been very greatly perplexed when the Lord revived him in this way.

Moreover, we must observe that the principal medicine by which Jacob was restored was contained in the expression, **Then God said.** Why did God not by a miracle transfer him to some other place and thus immediately remove him from all danger? Why did he not even, without a word, stretch out his hand over him, so that no one could attempt to hurt him? But Moses does not insist upon this point in vain, for by this we are taught where we should look for our greatest consolation in our afflictions. It is the principal business of our life to depend on the word of God, as those who are fully convinced that when God has promised salvation, he will deal well with us, so that we need not hesitate to walk through all the dangers in which we are set. Another reason for the vision was so that Jacob might not only truly perceive that God was his

285

deliverer, but, being forewarned by his word, might learn to ascribe to God whatever then followed. For seeing that we are slow and dull, bare experience is by no means enough to attest God's favor for us unless faith, coming from the word, is added.

"Go up to Bethel." Although it was God's design to raise his servant from death to life, he might appear to be ridiculing him here. For the following objection could be made: "You, O Lord, commanded me to go up, but all the routes are closed; for my sons have raised such antagonism against me that I cannot remain safe in any hiding-place. I hardly dare move a finger. What, therefore, will become of me if with a great multitude I start to move my camp? Will this not provoke new hostility against me because of my movements?" But in this way Jacob's faith was most fully proved, for now he knew that God was the leader and guardian of his journey. So he set off, relying on God's favor.

Moreover, the Lord did not simply command what had to be done but encouraged his servant by adding a promise. For in reminding Jacob that he was the same God who had previously appeared to him as he fled in terror from his brother, a promise was included.

The word **altar** refers to the same point. For since an altar was a divinely appointed token of thanksgiving, it followed that Jacob would arrive at **Bethel** safely, so that he might give thanks for the grace of God. God chose and assigned **Bethel**, rather than any other place, for his sanctuary because the very sight of it would take away Jacob's fear when he remembered that there the glory of the Lord had been seen by him. Further, since God exhorted his servant to be grateful, he showed that he is kind to the faithful, so that they in return may realize that they are indebted for everything to his grace and may give thanks to God in public for this.

**2.** The prompt obedience of Jacob is described here. For when he heard the voice of God, he neither doubted nor questioned within himself about what had to be done. Rather, as he was commanded, he quickly prepared himself for his journey. But to show that he obeyed God, he not only collected his goods but also purified his house from idols. **"Get rid of the foreign gods you have with you."** If we want God's blessing, all such hindrances must be removed, so that they in no way separate him from us. From this we also see what Rachel's theft encouraged. She had not wanted her father to take away from her this superstitious way of life. And she did not keep this poison to herself but spread it through the whole family. Thus was that sacred house infected with the worst possible disease. From this we see how humankind has a great propensity to indulge in godless worship. We must boldly resist the beginning of any evil, so that true religion is not harmed by the sloth and silence of the pastors.

**". . . and purify yourselves and change your clothes."** This was an exhortation to demonstrate penitence in an external way. Jacob wanted his **household,** who had polluted themselves, to testify to their renewed purification by a change of clothes. With the same aim in mind, the people, after they had made the golden calves, were commanded by Moses to take off their ornaments.

**4. So they gave Jacob all the foreign gods they had and the rings in their ears, and Jacob buried them under the oak at Shechem.** Everyone obeyed Jacob and threw away their idols. But I think their own fear of danger made them do this. From this we infer how important it is for us to be aroused from slumber by suffering, for we know how pertinacious and rebellious superstition is. If in a peaceful and joyous state of affairs Jacob had given any such command, most of his family would have concealed their idols. Some people might have refused to hand them over. But now the hand of God urged them, and with ready minds they quickly repented.

It is also probable that, according to the circumstances of the time, Jacob preached to them about the righteous judgment of God, to move them with fear. When he commanded them to cleanse themselves, it is as if he said, "Until now you have been defiled before the Lord. So, seeing that he has looked on us so mercifully, wash out this filth, so that he does not again turn away from us."

It seems, however, absurd that Jacob should have **buried** the idols **under the oak,** rather than breaking them in pieces and burning them in the fire, as we read that Moses did with the golden calves (see Exodus 32:20) and Hezekiah did with the bronze serpent (see 2 Kings 18:4). But Jacob's action is not mentioned for no reason. Here the infirmity of the patriarch is touched on, because he was not sufficiently far-sighted. Perhaps the Lord punished his previous excessive connivance and lack of firmness by depriving him of prudence or courage. Yet God also accepted his obedience, as he knew that the holy man's purpose was to remove idols from his family and to bury them in the earth as a sign that he detested them. The earrings were doubtless part of this superstition.

**5. Then they set out, and the terror of God fell upon the towns all around them so that no one pursued them.** It is now abundantly clear how necessary God's promise to the holy man about deliverance was. Although they lived in the middle of so many hostile swords, they left in safety. As a result of the destruction of the Shechemites, all the neighboring people were against a single family. But no one moved to take vengeance. The reason is given by Moses: **the terror of God fell upon the towns all around them.**

From this we learn that the hearts of men are in the hands of God. God can strengthen those who in themselves are weak. He can also soften the hard-hearted when he pleases. So whenever we see the wicked bent on our destruction, so that our hearts will not fail us, let us remember this terror of God by which the rage, however furious, of the whole world may be easily subdued.

**7. There he built an altar, and he called the place El Bethel, because it was there that God revealed himself to him when he was fleeing from his brother.** Now we know why the holy fathers had to have their own altar, distinct from those of other nations. It was to bear witness that they worshiped not the various gods who were recognized everywhere in the world, but a God of their own. For although God is worshiped in the heart, yet external confession is the inseparable accompaniment of faith. And there is no one who does not know how helpful it is to us to be roused to the worship of God by external aids.

If anyone objects that this **altar** looked no different from the others, I answer that the actual difference was very great. Others built altars, rashly and with thoughtless zeal, to unknown gods. Jacob bound himself always to the word of God. No altar is legitimate unless it is consecrated by God's word. Jacob's worship excelled that of others simply because he did nothing without the command of God.

In calling the place **El Bethel**, he may seem to be too bold; and yet the faith of the holy man is praiseworthy at this point also, since he keeps himself within the limits set by God. People are stupid when they claim to honor humility by exhibiting dull moderation. Humility deserves praise truly when it does not seek to know more than the Lord permits. But when he descends to us, adapting himself to us and chattering to us, he wishes us also to chatter back to him. True wisdom is to embrace God exactly as he adapts himself to our little measure. Thus Jacob did not dispute with learned arguments about God's essence, but according to the oracle he had received, he drew near to God and made himself accessible to him. Because he opened his mind to the revelation, his prattling and his simplicity were pleasing to God.

Today when the knowledge of God shines clearer, and when God in the Gospel has undertaken the role of nurse, let us learn to yield our minds to him. Let us remember that he came down to us to raise us up to him. He did not adopt an earthly way of speaking to keep us at a distance from heaven but rather as a means of raising us up to heaven.

Since the **altar** was commanded by a heavenly oracle, the building of it was truly a work of faith. Where the living voice of God does not sound, pomp and ceremony, however elaborately observed, are like empty phantoms.

**8.** Here is inserted a short narrative about the death of **Deborah**, whom we may conclude was a holy matron, and whom the family of Jacob venerated as a mother. For the name given in perpetuity to the place, **Allon Bacuth**, testifies that she was buried with special honor and much mourning.

**9. After Jacob returned from Paddan Aram, God appeared to him**

**again and blessed him.** Moses, having said a few words about the death of Deborah, records a second vision, through which Jacob was strengthened after his return to Bethel. Once before in this place God had appeared to him, when he was on his way into Mesopotamia. In the meantime God had testified in various ways that he would be present with him throughout his journey. Now Jacob was brought back to that very place where a most memorable oracle had been given to him, so that he might again have his faith renewed. The blessing of God here means nothing other than his promise. While men pray for blessings on each other, God declares himself to be the sole dispenser of perfect happiness. Jacob did not hear anything new on this occasion, as the same promise was repeated to him. He must, as one who had returned from captivity to his own country and had gathered new strength for his faith, carry out with greater courage all that remained to be accomplished in his life.

10. **God said to him, "Your name is Jacob, but you will no longer be called Jacob; your name will be Israel." So he named him Israel.** The first name was not abolished, but the honor of the second name, which he was given later, was preferred. He was called **Jacob** from his birth because he had wrestled with his brother. Later he was called **Israel** because he fought with God and obtained the victory. In this he had not prevailed by his own power (for he had received courage and strength from God alone), but because it was the Lord's will freely to confer upon him this honor. The Lord therefore made a comparison between the two names. The name **Jacob** was obscure and ignoble when compared with the name **Israel.** Two names were given to the holy man, one of which was by far the most excellent. We see that the prophets often combine them both, thus marking the constancy of God's grace from the beginning to the end.

11. Here, as elsewhere, God proclaimed his own might so that Jacob would rely on his faithfulness. He then promised that he would make Jacob multiply, not only into one nation, but into a multitude of **nations.**

**"Kings will come from your body."** This, in my judgment, refers to David and his posterity. God did not approve of the kingdom of Saul, and therefore it did not last. The kingdom of Israel was but a corruption of the legitimate kingdom.

12. Jacob was made the lord of **the land,** as the sole heir of his grandfather **Abraham** and of his father **Isaac.** The Lord clearly excluded Esau from the holy family when he transferred the land, by right of inheritance, to the posterity of Jacob alone.

13. God's ascent is like his descent. For God who fills heaven and earth does not change location. He is said to come down to us when he shows us a sign of his presence suited to our littleness. He ascended from Jacob when he disappeared from his sight or when the vision ended.

By this way of speaking, God shows us the value of his word, which is always near us as a witness to his grace. Because of the great distance between us and his heavenly glory, he himself came down to us through the word. This he did wholly and finally in the person of Christ; and Christ by his ascent into heaven has so elevated our faith that by the power of his Spirit he dwells always with us.

17. We know that the ancients longed to have children, especially a son. Since Rachel, therefore, did not accept by way of consolation the words, **"Don't be afraid, for you have another son,"** we infer that she was completely oppressed with pain. She, therefore, died in agony, thinking of nothing but her sad childbirth and her own sorrows. In this sad state she gave the name for her son [**Ben-Oni**, meaning "son of my trouble"], but Jacob later corrected this mistake (verse 18).

19. **So Rachel died and was buried on the way to Ephrath (that is, Bethlehem).** Rachel's burial is here mentioned. The holy fathers could not have given such religious care to this if it were not for their hope of the future resurrection. Whenever, therefore, we read about them burying their dead, let us remember that was no foolish ceremony but a living symbol of the future resurrection.

22. A sad and even tragic event is now related about the incestuous intercourse of **Reuben** with **his father's concubine Bilhah**. If even a stranger had defiled the wife of the holy man, it would have been a great disgrace. So it was even more atrocious that Jacob should suffer such an indignity from his own son. And how great and detestable was the dishonor, that the mother of two tribes should not only contaminate herself with adultery in this situation but even with incest, a crime that is so abhorrent to nature that not even among the Gentiles has it ever been allowed. By the dreadful scheme of Satan this great obscenity entered the holy house, so that God's election seemed to be of no avail. Satan tries, by whatever means he can, to pervert the grace of God in the elect. But because he cannot achieve this, he either covers it with infamy or at least obscures it. This is why there are such disgraceful examples of evil behavior in the church. In this way the Lord allows his own people to be humbled, that they may not stumble and that they may give more attention to prayer and may learn to depend on God's mercy.

Moses only recounts that **Israel heard of** this crime. But Moses conceals the patriarch's grief, not because Jacob had no feelings, but because his grief was too great to be expressed. Here Moses seems to be like the painter who, in representing the sacrifice of Iphigenia, put a veil over her father's face because he could not sufficiently express his grief. In addition to this eternal disgrace of the family, there were other reasons why anxiety filled this holy man. All of his happiness rested in his offspring, from which the salvation of the whole world would come. Already two of his sons had been bloodthirsty robbers. Now the firstborn is even more wicked than both of them. But here the gratuitous election of God is seen to be even greater because it was not on account of their worthiness that he preferred the sons of Jacob to the rest of the world. Even when they fell in such a terrible way, their election remained firm and efficacious. Warned by such examples, let us strengthen ourselves against those dreadful scandals through which Satan tries to disturb us.

Everyone should also use this example to strengthen his own faith. For sometimes even good men slide into sin, as if they had fallen from grace. This would end in desperation if the Lord did not offer us the hope of pardon. Reuben is a remarkable instance of this. After this extreme act of iniquity, he still remained a patriarch in the church. We must, however, remain watchful, so that temptation does not take us by surprise. For the Holy Spirit did not give us this example of vile lust so that everyone might rush into incestuous relationships, but rather to expose this depraved act.

This passage also refutes the error of Novatus. Reuben had been correctly taught. He carried on his body, from early infancy, the symbol of the divine covenant. He was even born again by the Spirit of God. We see, therefore, from what a deep abyss he was raised by the incredible mercy of God. The Novatians, therefore, and similar false teachers have no right to cut off the hope of pardon from the lapsed. For we do not honor Christ if we suppose that the grace of God was restricted in such a way by his coming.

**Jacob had twelve sons.** Moses again lists the **sons** of **Jacob** (verse 23). **Reuben** is put at the top of the list. He is not put there because he was the most honorable, but so that great reproach may be heaped on him. For the greater the honor anyone receives from the Lord, the more severely is he blamed if he later makes himself the slave of Satan and deserts his post. Moses seems to insert this list before the account of the death of Isaac in order to make a clear distinction between the progeny of Jacob and the Edomites, whom he is about to mention in 36:1. For upon the death of Isaac the fountain of the holy race became divided, as into two streams. But since God only adopted one branch, it was necessary to distinguish it from the other.

**29.** When it is said that Isaac was **old and full of years**, it means that, having finished his life, he died an old man, and this is ascribed to the blessing of God. Nevertheless, I refer these words not merely to the duration of his life, but also to the state of his feelings, implying that Isaac, being satisfied with life, willingly and placidly left this world. We may see certain decrepit old men who still long for life as when they were in the prime of life. Even though they have one foot in the grave, they still fear death. Although long life is thought to be one of the blessings of God, it not enough for men just to become old, unless they feel they are satisfied with the favor of God and in that frame of mind prepare themselves for death.

**And his sons Esau and Jacob buried him.** Moses adds that Isaac was buried by his two **sons**. Since at that time the resurrection had not been clearly revealed and its firstfruits had not yet appeared, the holy fathers paid much more attention to the significance of these ceremonies, so that they might correct the impression produced by the apparent destruction that is seen in death. The fact that Esau is put first again indicates that the fruit of the paternal benediction was not received by Jacob in his lifetime, for the firstborn was still subjected to the other after his father's death.

# Genesis
# Chapter 36

**1. This is the account of Esau (that is, Edom).** Although Esau was an alien from the church in the sight of God, yet since he was a son of Isaac, he was favored with a temporal blessing. So Moses gives details about his family. This commemoration, however, resembles an honorable tomb. For although Esau, with his posterity, took precedence over Jacob in his lifetime, his status, like a bubble, burst as soon as he died. Along with other ungodly nations, Esau was exalted as if he were on a stage. But since everything outside the kingdom of God is temporary, the splendor attributed to Esau was like a vanishing vapor, and all of his pomp disappeared like the closing of a scene onstage. The Holy Spirit planned to bear witness to the prophecy that Isaac gave about Esau. But no sooner does he show its effect than he turns our attention away from it, as if throwing a veil over it, so that we may concentrate on Jacob and his family.

Esau had children by three wives, in whom God's blessing shone out. But this does not mean that polygamy is being approved of, or that the impure lust of man should be excused. We should note that the goodness of God, contrary to the order of nature, brought a good result out of an evil beginning.

**6.** Moses does not mean that Esau left in order to give way to his brother. For Esau was so proud and ferocious that he would never have allowed himself to appear to be inferior to his brother. But Moses, disregarding Esau's motives, commends the secret providence of God, by which Esau was driven into exile so that the possession of the land might remain free for Jacob alone. Esau moved to Mount Seir in order to profit from such a move, as is stated in verses 8-9 and elsewhere. Nothing was further from his mind than to provide for his brother's welfare. But God directed the blind man by his own providential hand, that Esau might not live in the part of the land that God had appointed for his own servant. Thus it often happens that the wicked do good to the elect children of God, contrary to their own intention. While the wicked in their greed run after present advantages, they promote the eternal salvation of those whose destruction they have sometimes desired. Let us, then, learn from the passage before us to view, with the eyes of faith, both in accidental circumstances (as they are called) and in the evil desires of men, that secret providence of God that directs all events to a result predetermined by himself. For when Esau went forth that he might live more spaciously apart from his father's family, he **moved to a land some distance from his brother Jacob** because the Lord planned this.

**9.** To make it clear that God had bestowed his favor on Esau for the sake of his father Isaac, Moses specifically states that he became the father of a famous people. Therefore, he traces the fulfillment of this prophecy in the progeny of Esau. If God's promise flourished so strongly toward a stranger, how much more powerfully would it flourish in his own children, who through adoption inherited his grace?

**31. These were the kings who reigned in Edom before any Israelite king reigned.** We must remember that reprobates are suddenly exalted that they may immediately fall, like herbs on the roofs that are devoid of roots and start to grow but quickly wither. The two sons of Isaac had been promised that kings would spring from them. The Edomites reigned first, and so the position of Israel seemed to be inferior to them. But the Edomites soon vanished. There is, therefore, no reason for the faithful, who slowly pursue their way, to envy the children of this world or their rapid rise to success. For the happiness that the Lord promises them is far more secure. As it is expressed in the Psalm, "The children of your servants will live in your presence; their descendants will be established before you" (Psalm 102:28).

# Genesis
## Chapter 37

**1. Jacob lived in the land where his father had stayed, the land of Canaan.** Moses confirms what he had previously declared: When Esau left the land, it was left vacant for holy Jacob who took sole charge of it. While that patriarch may not have obtained a single clod from it, he was content with the sight of the land as he exercised his faith. Moses specifically compares him with **his father,** who had been a stranger in that land all his life. Therefore, though by the removal of his brother Jacob gained a lot, it was still the Lord's will that this advantage should be hidden from his eyes, so that he might depend entirely on God's promise.

**2. This is the account of Jacob. Joseph, a young man of seventeen, was tending the flocks with his brothers, the sons of Bilhah and the sons of Zilpah, his father's wives, and he brought their father a bad report about them.** Moses does not now list all the sons and grandsons but explains why Joseph's brothers were jealous of him and why they made a wicked conspiracy against him and sold him as a slave. It is as if Moses said, "Having briefly summed up the genealogy of Esau, I now revert to the main plot and to what happened to the family of Jacob."

**3.** As Moses is about to speak of the abominable wickedness of Jacob's sons, he begins with the statement that **Israel loved Joseph more than any of his other sons, because he had been born to him in his old age.** It was not surprising that the boy was a great favorite with his elderly father, for this often happens. No just grounds are given here for envy. Moses, however, states that this was the reason for the brothers' jealousy. If they did not want to share in this love for their brother, why did they not excuse it in their father? From this we perceive their malignant and perverse disposition (see verse 4).

**He [Israel] made a richly ornamented robe for him [Joseph].** That a many-colored coat and similar trifles drove Joseph's brothers to plot his murder proves their detestable cruelty.

**6. He said to them, "Listen to this dream I had."** Moses shows that

Joseph had been elected, by the wonderful purpose of God, to great things. Joseph had learned about this in a **dream.** But it caused his brothers to be outraged. God, however, revealed in dreams what he would do, so that later it would be known that nothing had happened by chance. In this way it was seen that what had been fixed by a heavenly decree, at length, in its proper time, occurred through a circuitous route until it was completed. It had been predicted to Abraham that his seed would wander from the land of Canaan. God arranged that this should happen and for Jacob to go down to Egypt, by making Joseph rule over Egypt in a time of famine. In this way he brought his father there, along with his whole family, and supplied them with food. But from the initial facts no one could have forecast such a result. The sons of Jacob conspired to put to death the very person without whom they could not be preserved. He who was ordained to be the minister of their salvation was thrown into a well and was with difficulty rescued from the jaws of death. Driven along by various misfortunes, he seemed to be an alien from his father's house. Later he was thrown into prison, as into another tomb, where he languished for a long time. Nothing, therefore, was less probable than that the family of Jacob should be preserved in this way. For Joseph had been cut off from it and carried far away and not even reckoned to be alive. Nor did he have any hope of freedom, especially after he was neglected by the chief butler. It looked as if he had been condemned to imprisonment forever and that he had been left there to rot. God, however, by such complicated methods accomplished what he had planned.

So in this account we have not only a most beautiful example of divine providence, but also two other points that are especially noteworthy. First, the Lord performs his work through wonderful and unusual ways; and, second, he brings about the salvation of his church not from magnificent splendor, but from death and the grave. In addition to this, in the person of Joseph a living image of Christ is presented.

God, out of his sheer grace, conferred special honor on the boy, who was the last but one among twelve brothers. What merit did he possess that he should rule over his brothers? From the **dream** we learn that it was God's free gift, which in no way depended upon Joseph's beneficence. Rather, he was ordained to be chief by God's good pleasure, so that he might show kindness to his brethren.

**7. "We were binding sheaves of grain out in the field when suddenly my sheaf rose and stood upright, while your sheaves gathered around mine and bowed down to it."** The Lord at that time revealed his secrets in two ways, by visions and by dreams, and one of these methods occurs here. Joseph doubtless had often dreamed in the normal way. But Moses now shows that a dream was sent to him by God that had the power of an oracle. We know that dreams are often produced by our daily thoughts. Sometimes they are indications of an unhealthy state of the body. But whenever God intends to make known his counsel by dreams, he engraves on them certain marks that distinguish them from passing and frivolous imaginations, so that their credibility and authority are beyond doubt. Thus Joseph was certain that he had not been deluded by an empty idea, and so he courageously announced that his dream was a heavenly oracle. Although dominion was promised to him in the form of a rural symbol, it was one that did not seem ideal to teach the sons of Jacob, for they were shepherds, not farmers. Since they had no harvest they could gather in, it seems hardly congruous that homage should be paid to Joseph's **sheaf**. But perhaps God purposely chose this symbol to show that this prophecy was not dependent on Joseph's present fortunes, and that his dominion would not be made up of those things that were at hand but would be a future benefit that would be sought for in a place other than their home.

**8.** Here we see clearly the paternal favor of God toward the elect. When the sons of Jacob heard they were fighting in vain against God, their unjust hatred ought, by such means, to have been corrected. For it was as if God would crush their anger by saying, "All your ungodly conspiracies will be fruitless. Although you boast, I have appointed the man, whose ruin your wicked envy seeks to destroy, to be your leader." Perhaps, also, through this consoling dream God intended to alleviate the trouble faced by the holy youth. Yet the obstinacy of Joseph's brothers only increased.

Let us then learn not to be upset if at any time people become jealous because God's grace is shining on us. The sons of Jacob understood the meaning of the dream; but they derided it as a fable, for it was repugnant to their wishes. It often happens that those who are not well disposed toward God are nevertheless quick to perceive God's will. But because they have no reverence for God himself, they despise his will.

**9. Then he had another dream, and he told it to his brothers. "Listen," he said, "I had another dream, and this time the sun and moon and eleven stars were bowing down to me."** The scope of this dream was the same as the previous one. The only difference was that God, to inspire greater confidence in the oracle, used things from the heavens. Joseph's brothers had despised what was said about the sheaves. The Lord now called on them to look toward heaven, where his august majesty shines forth. It may, however, be asked how this dream can be reconciled with the fact that his mother, who was now dead, could come and bow down to him. The solution to this is simple. In the dream the **sun** and **moon** stood for each side of the head of the family. Joseph saw himself honored by his whole family.

**10.** If Israel thought the dream originated in vain ambition, he was right to rebuke his son. But if he knew that God had sent the dream, he should not have expostulated with him. The fact that he did know this may be inferred because he went on to give it serious consideration. For

Moses, making a distinction between him and his sons says, **His brothers were jealous of him, but his father kept the matter in mind** (verse 11). So why did Jacob rebuke his son? This did not give honor to God and to his word. Israel should have realized that although Joseph was under his authority, he still had the character of a prophet. It is probable that when he saw that his sons were so malevolent, he wanted to avert a problem and so rebuked his son Joseph. For he did not want his other sons to take offense because of the dream. I am sure that he only reproved his son from a desire to appease the anger of Joseph's brothers. Nevertheless, this way of pretending to be against the truth when we are endeavoring to appease the anger of those who rage against it is not approved of by God. Israel should have told his sons not to "kick against the pricks." Or at least he should have said, "If this is an ordinary dream, let it be treated with ridicule rather than with anger; but if it has come from God, it is wrong to speak against it." It is even possible that the old man had thought that what the dream predicted could never take place.

**12.** Before Moses mentions the terrible incident of fratricide, he describes Joseph's journey and so emphasizes the atrocity of the crime. Their brother approached them as a result of orders from his father in order to find out how they were. He searched for them, and although they had moved he found them. Therefore, their cruelty was even worse than madness, for they did not shrink from plotting the death of a brother who acted in such a humane way toward them. We now see why Moses mentions that Joseph had to look for his brothers and how he met someone who told him that they had gone to Dothan (verses 15-17). Joseph had searched for them with an indefatigable spirit. So the brothers were even more guilty for repaying such kindness in the way they did.

**18. But they saw him in the distance, and before he reached them, they plotted to kill him.** Here again Moses does not praise his own people by adulation but brands them with a mark of eternal infamy. He exposes their evil so that all nations can mock them. If at any time among heathen nations a brother murdered his brother, such impiety was treated with the utmost severity. It was never held up as an example that should be imitated. But in profane history no such thing is found to compare with this evil. For there is no instance of nine brothers conspiring to kill an innocent youth and, like wild beasts, pouncing on him with bloody hands. Therefore, a horrible and even diabolical fury possessed the sons of Jacob when, having cast aside all natural feelings, they were prepared to vent their anger on their own blood.

**19. "Here comes that dreamer!" they said to each other.** In addition to the wickedness we have already discussed, Moses condemns their impious contempt of God. They said contemptuously, **"Here comes that dreamer!"** They insulted the unhappy youth because he had been called by the heavenly oracle to an unexpected honor. They attacked their brother on account of his dreams, as if this were an unforgivable offense. If they were so indignant over his dreams, why did they not rather attack God? For Joseph received as a precious gift what had been divinely revealed to him. But because they did not dare to attack God himself, they wrapped themselves in clouds and lost sight of God, so that they might vent their fury against their brother.

If such blindness afflicted the patriarchs, what will become of reprobates who are driven along by obstinate malice, so that they do not hesitate to resist God to the end? We see that as often as they are offended by God's punishments, they rise up against his ministers and seek to take revenge against them. The same thing would happen to us all unless God bridled us and made us submissive to him.

**20.** Before they murdered him, they figured out a way to conceal their crime. Meanwhile, it never entered their mind that what is hidden from men cannot escape the eyes of God. Hypocrisy is so stupid that while it flees from the disgrace of the world, it is careless about the judgment of God. But it is a disease deeply rooted in the human mind to make up some excuse for every extreme act of iniquity. For although an inner judge convicts the guilty, they still want to hide their disgrace from others.

**"Then we'll see what comes of his dreams."** It is as if the truth of God could be altered by the death of one man. They boasted that they would succeed in their plan when they killed their brother, since his dreams would then come to nothing. This was not, indeed, their stated aim, but their turbulent envy drove them headlong to fight against God. But whatever they planned in fighting against God would not succeed, for God always finds a way through the deepest abyss to accomplish what he has decreed. If, then, unbelievers provoke us by their reproaches and proudly boast that our faith will never benefit us, we must not let their insolence discourage or weaken us. Rather, let us confidently proceed.

**21. When Reuben heard this, he tried to rescue him from their hands. "Let's not take his life," he said.** It is good to observe that while others were making plans to kill Joseph, one person acted in a way that saved him. Reuben, without doubt, in one respect, was the most wicked of them all when he earlier defiled his father's concubine. That unbridled lust was the sign of a depraved nature. But now he alone wanted to rescue Joseph from the ungodly conspiracy. Moses declares that it was Reuben's intention to restore the boy safely to his father (verse 22). So it is possible that he thought that saving his brother's life would be enough to reconcile him to his father. However this may be, the humanity that he showed in attempting to free his brother shows that he was not totally given over to every kind of wickedness. And perhaps God, by this testimony of his penitence, planned to reduce his former disgrace. From this we are taught that men's characters should not be judged by a single act, however atrocious that deed might be, so that they are thought to be beyond salvation.

**22.** The godly trick that Reuben was reduced to proves how vehemently his brothers attacked Joseph. For Reuben did not dare to openly oppose them and did not attempt to dissuade them from their crime. For he saw that no reason would soften them.

**23.** We see that these men were full of lies. They callously stripped their brother **of his robe.** They had no compunction about throwing him with their own hands into **the cistern** (verse 24), where hunger, which was worse than ten swords, would kill him. They hoped their crime would be concealed, and so they took home his clothes. Their father would believe Joseph had been torn apart by a wild beast. In this way Satan infatuates wicked minds, so that they entangle themselves by frivolous evasions. Conscience is indeed the fountain of modesty; but Satan so soothes by his allurements those whom he has entangled in his snares that conscience itself, which ought to cite them as guilty before God, only hardens them.

**25.** This shows how they behaved like barbarians. They could quietly feast while, in intention, they were guilty of their brother's death. Had there been one drop of humanity in their souls, they would at least have felt some inner compunction. Indeed it is normal for the very worst of men to be afraid after they have committed a crime. Since the brothers had no such feelings, let us learn from their example, so that no lethargy dims our senses.

Meanwhile, it is right to consider the progress God's counsel was making. Joseph was, beyond all expectation, now rescued from the grave. For it was a death sentence to be sold as a slave to foreigners; but this was a secret plan by which God had determined to raise him up. And at length this event shows how much better it was that Joseph should be led far away from his own family than that he should remain in safety at home.

**27.** Judah's words, by which he persuaded his brothers to **sell** Joseph, appeared to be more reasonable. For he confessed that they would be guilty of homicide if they allowed Joseph to perish in the cistern. **"What will we gain if we kill our brother and cover up his blood?"** (verse 26). By this time their anger had cooled a little; so they listened to more humane counsel. Although it was outrageous to sell their brother to strangers, yet he would at least be kept alive as a slave. We see, therefore, that the diabolical rage of madness was abating when they acknowledged that they would not benefit by hiding their crime from the eyes of men, as their homicide would be known to God. At first they absolved themselves from guilt, as if no judge sat in heaven. But now their natural senses, which the cruelty of hatred had previously numbed, began to exert themselves. Those who can be healed and whom the Lord leads to repentance differ from reprobates in this way. While the latter obstinately conceal the knowledge of their crimes, the former gradually return from the indulgence of sin to obey the voice of reason. Moreover, what Judah here declared concerning his brother, the Lord, through the prophet, extends to the whole human race. Whenever, therefore, depraved desires lead to violence or any other injury, let us remember this sacred bond by which the whole of society is bound together, so that it may restrain us from doing evil. For a man cannot injure men without becoming an enemy to his own flesh and violating and perverting the whole order of nature.

**30. When Reuben returned to the cistern and saw that Joseph was not there, he tore his clothes.** We may surmise that Reuben, pretending to attend to some other business, left his brothers so that, unknown to them, he might take Joseph out of the cistern and restore him to his father. So he was not present when Joseph was sold. But now Reuben, having lost all hope, told his brothers of his intention, which previously he had not dared to mention, in case the boy was immediately murdered.

**31-34.** They now returned to their first scheme. So that their father would have no suspicion of their crime, they sent the bloodstained coat, from which Jacob would conclude that Joseph had been torn to pieces by some wild animal. To escape the consequences of one fault, they added sin to sin.

It is rather surprising that after Jacob had been tried in so many ways and had always come out as a conqueror he should now sink under grief. It is strange that the death of his son caused him greater sorrow than the incestuous pollution of his wife, the slaughter of the Shechemites, and the defilement of his daughter. Where was that invincible strength by which he had even prevailed over the angel? Where were the many lessons of patience with which God had tested him, so that he might never fail? This tendency to mourn teaches us that no one is endued with such heroic virtues as to be exempt from that weakness of the body that betrays itself sometimes even in little things. It also happens that those who have been used to bearing a cross for a long time and who like veteran soldiers ought bravely to bear up against every kind of attack fall like young recruits in a new skirmish. Who then among us may not fear for himself when we see holy Jacob faint after having given so many proofs of patience?

**35. All his sons and daughters came to comfort him, but he refused to be comforted. "No," he said, "in mourning will I go down to the grave to my son." So his father wept for him.** The burden of his grief was more clearly expressed when all **his sons and daughters** met together **to comfort him.** The sons of Jacob assumed a character that they did not possess. They pretended to be godly, though that was a foreign way of life to them. If they had respect for God, they would have acknowledged their fault; and though no remedy might have been found for their evil, repentance would have yielded some fruit. But as it was, they were satisfied with a vanity that is as empty as the wind.

From this example we are taught how much we ought to avoid being deceitful, which continually implicates men in new snares.

**But he refused to be comforted.** It may be wondered if Jacob was now

301

completely devoid of perseverance. This is what these words seem to say. Besides, he sinned even more because he deliberately indulged in his grief. But I think that his refusal **to be comforted** only applies to man-made comfort. For nothing is more unreasonable than that a holy man who all his life has borne God's yoke so meekly should now, like an unbroken horse, bite his bridle. I am, therefore, sure that he was now willing to submit himself to the Lord, even though he rejected human consolation.

If the angelic minds of holy men were darkened by sadness, how much deeper gloom will rest on us unless God, by the shining of his Word and Spirit, should scatter it. The principal comfort in sorrow is the consolation of the future life. Anyone who focuses on this need not worry that he will be absorbed by excessive grief.

Jacob's inordinate sorrow should not be approved of, but Moses' special purpose was to underline the hard-heartedness that cruelly reigned in his sons. They saw that their father was already dying through their wickedness. If they were not able to heal the wound, why, at least, did they not attempt to alleviate his pain? They were exceedingly cruel. They did not care enough for their father's life to do what was in their power to do.

**36. Meanwhile, the Midianites sold Joseph in Egypt to Potiphar, one of Pharaoh's officials, the captain of the guard.** It was a sad spectacle that Joseph should be handed over from one person to another in this way. It was an additional indignity to his former suffering that he was now sold as a slave. The Lord, however, did not stop caring for him. He even allowed him to be transferred from hand to hand, so that at length it might be beyond question that he had come by heavenly guidance to that very position that had been promised him in his dreams.

# Genesis
# Chapter 38

**1.** Before Moses continues to record what happened to Joseph, he inserts Judah's genealogy. He does this in some detail because the Redeemer came from his line. The complete history of that tribe from which salvation came had to be recorded. But instead of its glory being celebrated, its great disgrace was exposed. What Moses recounts here, so far from boosting the minds of the sons of Judah, should cover them with shame.

At first sight Christ's honor seems to be tarnished by these events. But we do Christ a disservice if we forget that he alone can blot out any ignominy that arises from the evil behavior of his forebears. So unbelievers should not take any offense from this. Second, we know that the riches of God's grace shine in that Christ clothed himself in our flesh in order to make himself of no reputation.

Meanwhile, let us remember that Christ derives no glory from his ancestors, and that he himself has no glory in the flesh, but that his chief and most illustrious triumph was on the cross. Moreover, that we may not be offended at the stains with which his ancestry was defiled, let us know that by his infinite purity they were all cleansed.

**2.** It was wrong for Judah to entangle himself in a forbidden relationship. The Lord cursed the offspring from this marriage. Judah's sin only increased the burden on Jacob. Now a wicked grandson was born to him through Judah, of whose sin he was not ignorant.

**7. But Er, Judah's firstborn, was wicked in the LORD's sight; so the LORD put him to death.** We know that long life is rightly thought to be one of God's gifts. It follows from this that when the wicked die prematurely, they are being punished. Let us, therefore, learn that as long as God keeps us in the world, we should meditate on his benefits. Then everyone will praise God for the life he has given them. Even today sudden death should be thought of as one of God's scourges since the teaching of the psalmist remains true: "But you, O God, will bring down the wicked into the pit of corruption; bloodthirsty and deceitful men will not live out half their days" (55:23). But this judgment was carried out more extensively under the law, when the knowledge of a future life was comparatively obscure. Now, since the resurrection is clearly revealed to us in Christ, it is not right that death should be so dreaded so much. Nevertheless, it can never be said that it is a general rule that those who lived a long life demonstrated in this way that they were pleasing and acceptable to the Lord, for God sometimes prolonged the life of reprobates as a form of punishment. We know that Cain survived his brother Abel for many centuries. But God's vengeance was unmistakable in Er's death so that it would be clearly seen that the earth had been purged, as if it had been filthy.

**8. Then Judah said to Onan, "Lie with your brother's wife and fulfill your duty to her as a brother-in-law to produce offspring for your brother."** No law had yet been prescribed concerning the marriage of a brother's widow; so the surviving brother could raise up seed to one who was dead. It is wonderful that through instinct men have been inclined to do this. For since each man is born for the preservation of the whole race, if anyone dies without children, there seems to be some defect in nature. It was deemed, therefore, an act of humanity to acquire some name for the dead, through whom it could be said that they lived. The only reason the children born to the surviving brother should be reckoned to him who had died was that there might be no dry branch in the family. In this way the stigma attached to barrenness was removed. Besides, since the woman was given as a help to the man, when any woman married into a family, she was in a certain sense given over to the name of that family.

**9. But Onan knew that the offspring would not be his; so whenever he lay with his brother's wife, he spilled his semen on the ground to keep from producing offspring for his brother.** According to this way of thinking, Tamar was not altogether free but was under an obligation to the house of Judah to have some children. Although this does not stem from any godly rule, yet the Lord had impressed it on the hearts of men as a duty of humanity. From this we infer Onan's animosity; he was jealous of his brother because he knew that any child would give his brother honor. So **he spilled his semen on the ground to keep from producing offspring for his brother.** Many people give their own sons to their friends so they can be adopted. It was, therefore, an outrageous act to deny to his own brother what is given even to strangers.

**10.** It is a horrible thing to deliberately avoid childbirth in this way. For this means that one quenches the hope of his family and kills the son that could be expected, even before he is born. This wickedness is here severely condemned by the Spirit through Moses. **What he did was wicked in the Lord's sight; so he put him to death also.**

**11.** Moses intimates that Tamar was not free to marry into another family, so long as Judah wanted to keep her under his own authority. It is possible that she voluntarily submitted herself to the will of her father-in-law when she might have refused. But these words seem to mean that this was the usual practice. Tamar could not just go over to another family unless her father-in-law agreed, as long as there was a successor who might have children through her. However this may be, Judah acted wrongly in keeping one bound whom he intended to defraud. For there was no reason why he should be unwilling to allow her to leave his house.

Let us then learn from this example that whenever anything adverse happens to us, we should not blame anyone else but should attend to our own sins.

**13.** Moses recounts how Tamar avenged herself for the injury that had been inflicted on her. She did not at first perceive the fraud but discovered it after a long time. When **Shelah** (verse 11) had grown up, Tamar realized that she had been deceived and so turned her thoughts to revenge. She had doubtless spent a long time hatching her plot, for the message bringing her news about Judah's journey was not brought to her by accident. Because she intended to carry out her plan, she had set spies who would bring her news about Judah's movements.

Although she had this evil plan in mind, which was hardly worthy of any modest woman, yet it can be said in her favor that she did not seek Judah except while she was celibate. Nevertheless, she rushed into a sin that is no less detestable than adultery. For by adultery a marriage is violated; but Tamar's incestuous intercourse undermined the whole dignity of nature. It must be carefully observed that those who are injured should not rush to take unlawful remedies. It was not lust that impelled Tamar to prostitute herself. She was greatly upset because she had been forbidden to marry, that she might remain barren at home. But she had no other reason in mind than to reproach her father-in-law for the fraud by which he had deceived her. So we see that she committed an atrocious crime.

**15.** It was disgraceful that Judah desired sexual intercourse with an unknown woman. He was now old, and therefore age alone, even in a lascivious man, ought to have restrained the fervor of intemperance. Lust was ignited within him as a stallion neighs when it smells a mare. The fear of God or a regard for justice cannot have flourished greatly in the heart of one who indulgences his passions in this way.

He is, therefore, set before us as an example, that we may learn how easily the lust of the flesh overwhelms us unless the Lord restrains it. Knowing that we have this weakness, let us ask the Lord for a spirit of continence and moderation. But in case the same self-confidence sweeps over us that caused Judah to indulge in fornication, let us note the dishonor that resulted from Judah's incest. This was a divine punishment inflicted on him. Who then will indulge in a such an evil act when he sees from this dreadful vengeance how much God hates it?

**16.** Tamar did not want to make any money from acting as a prostitute.

But she did ask for a pledge, so that she might boast about the revenge she had taken for the injury she had sustained. God doubtless blinded Judah, as he deserved, for how else could he not have recognized the daughter-in-law's voice he had known for so long? Besides, if a pledge had to be given for the promised kid, how foolish it was to hand over his **seal** and its **cord** (verse 18). It appears, therefore, that he was devoid of all judgment. These things are written by Moses to teach us that Judah's miserable mind was darkened by the just judgment of God, because by heaping sin upon sin he had quenched the light of the Spirit.

**20. Judah sent the young goat by his friend the Adullamite in order to get his pledge back from the woman,** so that he would not reveal his ignominy to a stranger. This is also why he did not dare to complain about the lost pledges, in case he exposed himself to ridicule for having been so credulous. But he was mainly afraid of the disgrace arising from his fornication. Here we see that men who are not governed by the Spirit of God are always more solicitous about the opinion of the world than about God's judgment. For why, when the lust of the flesh excited him, did he not remember, "Behold, now I shall become vile in the sight of God and of angels"? Why, at least, after his lust had cooled did he not blush at the secret knowledge of his sin? But he thought he would be safe if he could protect himself from public infamy.

**24. About three months later Judah was told, "Your daughter-in-law Tamar is guilty of prostitution, and as a result she is now pregnant." Judah said, "Bring her out and have her burned to death!"** Tamar could have revealed her evil action earlier, but she waited until she could incur capital punishment. For then she would have stronger grounds to help her win her case. Judah subjected his daughter-in-law to such a severe punishment because he deemed her guilty of adultery. For what the Lord later confirmed by his law appears to have been the normal practice. Once a girl was married, she had to be strictly faithful to her husband. God's law commands adulterers to be stoned. Before punishment was sanctioned by a written law, the adulterous woman was **burned to death.**

**26. Judah recognized them and said, "She is more righteous than I, since I wouldn't give her to my son Shelah." And he did not sleep with her again.** Tamar took her revenge with this open reproach. Judah immediately acknowledged his fault and so showed that he was being honest. But while he confessed his fault, he was silent about punishment.

From this we see that those who are rigid in censuring others are much more pliant in forgiving themselves. But in this we should imitate him—that without rack or torture, truth should so far prevail with us that we should not be ashamed to confess before the whole world those sins of which God accuses us. This account also teaches us about the importance of not condemning anyone who has not been given the opportunity of presenting his side of the case. This is not just because it is better that the innocent should be absolved than that a guilty person should perish, but also because a defense brings many things to light and so changes the verdict.

**"She is more righteous than I."** This expression is not meant to convey that Tamar's conduct was approved of but speaks in a comparative way. It is as if he said that he had been, unjustly and without cause, angry against a woman by whom he himself should have been accused.

**27.** Although Judah received pardon for his error, and Tamar for her wicked contrivance, the Lord caused something extraordinary to take place at the birth in order to humble them. Something similar had happened before in the case of Jacob and Esau, but for a different reason. We know that prodigies are sometimes omens for good, and sometimes for evil. Here, however, there is no doubt that the twins, in their very birth, brought with them marks of their parents' infamy. This was beneficial to them, so they were reminded of their shame, and also served as a public example that such a crime should be branded with eternal disgrace.

# Genesis
# Chapter 39

1. **Now Joseph had been taken down to Egypt. Potiphar, an Egyptian who was one of Pharaoh's officials, the captain of the guard, bought him from the Ishmaelites who had taken him there.** Moses briefly recaps his account of Joseph. Joseph had been sold to **Potiphar, an Egyptian**.

2. Moses then adds, **The LORD was with Joseph and he prospered.** Although it often happens that things go well with wicked men, whom God nevertheless does not bless with his favor, it remains true that it never really is well with men except insofar as the Lord shows himself to be gracious to them. For he gives his blessing, for a time, even to reprobates with whom he is justly angry, so that he may gently invite and even allure them to repentance. If they remain obstinate, they are made even more inexcusable. Whenever God deprives men of his blessing, whether they are strangers or whether they belong to his own family, they will fall. For no good flows except from God who is the fountain. The world makes a goddess out of fortune, and each person adores his own industry. But Scripture draws us away from this depraved imagination and declares that adversity is a sign of God's absence, while prosperity is a sign of his presence. There is not the least doubt that the special and extraordinary favor of God came to Joseph, so that he was clearly known to be blessed by God.

Moses then adds that Joseph **lived in the house of his Egyptian master** to teach us that he was not at once elevated to an honorable condition. Nothing is more desirable than freedom, but Joseph was a slave. Let us then learn, even in the middle of our sufferings, to perceive God's grace.

3. The grace of God shone on Joseph in an exceptional way. For it became clear to a man who was a heathen, and in this respect blind, **that the LORD was with him [Joseph] and that the LORD gave him success in everything he did.** If we do not give God credit for every good thing that happens to us, we are showing great ingratitude. For Scripture often

teaches us that nothing that comes from men will be of any benefit to them unless God gives his blessing.

**The LORD gave him success in everything he did.** All the blessing by which the Lord was pleased to testify his paternal love toward Joseph benefited the Egyptians. For since Joseph neither sowed nor reaped for himself, he was not at all enriched by his labor. But in this way a proud man, who otherwise might have treated Joseph harshly as a slave, treated him humanely and generously. We here see how abundantly the grace of God is poured out on the faithful, since part of his kindness flows from them even to reprobates.

**6.** Joseph reaped the fruit of God's love and kindness toward him, so that he had some relief from his slavery, at least for a short time. But a new temptation soon assailed him. For the favor that he had received was not only wiped out but became the cause of a great misfortune. Joseph was governor over the whole house of Potiphar. From that honorable position he was thrown into prison, which was like a death sentence. He must have thought that he was abandoned by God as he was constantly exposed to new dangers. He might even have imagined that God had declared himself to be his enemy.

This teaches us that the pious need special discernment to view events with the eyes of faith. We need to reflect on God's blessings, which mitigate the severity of the crosses we have to bear. God meets with us in our difficulties so that, with renewed strength, we are more prepared for other conflicts.

**7. After a while his master's wife took notice of Joseph and said, "Come to bed with me!"** Moses only summarizes these events. There is no doubt that this impure woman endeavored by various means to allure the pious youth. While this demonstrates her lust, Joseph remains an example of faithfulness for us.

**10.** Joseph repelled one attack after another and conquered every temptation. We know how easy it is to fall when Satan tempts us through another person, for then we seem to be free from blame. Holy Joseph, therefore, must have been endowed with the power of the Spirit since he stood invincible to the last against all the allurements of that impious woman.

We see here what evils people indulge in when propriety is replaced by carnal intemperance. So we must ask the Lord to not allow the light of his Spirit to be quenched within us.

**11.** The Spirit of God gives us this example in a young man. So what excuse is left for older men and women if they voluntarily give way to a light temptation? To this, therefore, we must bend all our efforts—that regard for God alone may subdue all carnal affections. We must make sure that we value a good and upright conscience more than the plaudits of the whole world. For no one will prove that he loves virtue except the person who is content to have God as his only witness and who does not hesitate to submit to any disgrace rather than be deflected from his duty. Therefore we must banish vain pretexts such as, "I wish to avoid offense" or "I am afraid in case men wrongly interpret what I have done," because God is not really honored unless we ignore our own reputation and follow him wherever he calls us. God does not want us to be indifferent about our own reputation, but he does not want us to place it above his will. So let the faithful endeavor to edify their neighbors by the example of an upright life. To this end, let them prudently guard against every mark of evil. But if it be necessary to endure the infamy of the world, let them follow their divine vocation.

**14. She [Potiphar's wife] called her household servants. "Look," she said to them, "this Hebrew has been brought to us to make sport of us! He came in here to sleep with me, but I screamed."** Here we see the results of the desperation of Potiphar's wife. For the wicked woman changed from love to fury. From this it is easy to see what brutal impulses lust brings with it when its reins are let loose. Once Satan has gained power over miserable men, he never leaves them alone until he drives them into mad actions. We see also how he hardens the reprobate, whom he holds in his power.

**20. Joseph's master took him and put him in prison, the place where the king's prisoners were confined.** Although Moses does not state how severe Joseph's imprisonment was, we can assume that he was not allowed any freedom but was thrown into some obscure dungeon. The authority of Potiphar was paramount. He had the keeper of the prison under his power and at his disposal. What clemency could be hoped for from a man who was jealous and carried away with the vehemence of his anger? What a reward for an innocent person!

**20-21. But while Joseph was there in the prison, the LORD was with him; he showed him kindness and granted him favor in the eyes of the prison warden.** It appears from the testimony of the psalmist that Joseph's extreme sufferings were not immediately alleviated: "They bruised his feet with shackles, his neck was put in irons, till what he foretold came to pass" (Psalm 105:18-19). The Lord purposely allowed him to be reduced to extremity, that he might bring him back as from the grave. We know that as the light of the sun is most clearly seen when we are looking from a dark place, so in the darkness of our miseries, the grace of God shines more brightly when, beyond expectation, he comforts us.

Moreover, Moses says, **the LORD was with him** because he extended the grace of mercy toward him. From this we may learn that God, even when he delivers us from unjust violence or when he assists us in a good cause, does so on account of his own goodness. Since we are unworthy of his helping us, the reason for God doing so must be in himself, since he is merciful.

How God showed his kindness to Joseph is mentioned—namely, **he showed him kindness and granted him favor in the eyes of the prison warden**. The official laid aside his cruelty and acted in a kind and gentle way because God changed his heart to follow God's will. But it is a wonder that the keeper of the prison did not fear that he might incur Potiphar's wrath. It is clear that his cruelty had been divinely restrained. But it is also probable that Potiphar had suspected and at length found evidence about his wife's subtle scheme. Yet while Potiphar might be appeased toward holy Joseph, he was unwilling to acquit him and so suffer dishonor himself.

Meanwhile, Joseph's remarkable integrity was seen in that he did not attempt to escape from prison but waited for his freedom to be given to him.

# Genesis
# Chapter 40

**1. Some time later, the cupbearer and the baker of the king of Egypt offended their master, the king of Egypt.** We have already seen that when Joseph was in prison, God cared for him. Therefore, before God freed his servant from prison, he met him there and strengthened him. Then Joseph was not just freed from prison but was given the highest possible honor. In the meantime, God's providence led the holy man through most intricate paths. The king's **cupbearer** and **baker** were thrown into the prison. Joseph interpreted their dreams. The cupbearer was told that he would be restored to his office. Joseph was hopeful about being released from prison, for the cupbearer agreed to speak to the king on Joseph's behalf. But this hope was short-lived as the cupbearer did not say a word to the king about the miserable prisoner. Joseph must have thought he was buried in perpetual oblivion, until the Lord again suddenly rekindled the light that had been smothered and almost extinguished. Thus, when God might have delivered the holy man from prison immediately, he chose to lead him by a circuitous route to test his patience and to show by the way he was set free that God's wonderful ways of working are hidden from our view. God does this so that we may learn not to think about the salvation that he has promised us in any human way.

**5. . . . each of the two men—the cupbearer and the baker of the king of Egypt, who were being held in prison—had a dream the same night, and each dream had a meaning of its own.** Many of our dreams are of no value and are best forgotten. Some, however, are like prophecies. These two dreams belong to the second category, in which God reveals the future. For if the dreams had not appeared to be heavenly oracles, **the cupbearer and the baker** would not have been so upset.

**8. "We both had dreams," they answered, "but there is no one to interpret them." Then Joseph said to them, "Do not interpretations belong to God? Tell me your dreams."**

Joseph offered his services in accordance with his vocation. This should be noted, to stop any of us from unconsciously taking on himself anything other than what he knows God has allowed him to do. Paul carefully warns us that the gifts of the Spirit are given in such a way that a different role is given to each one of us, and so no one should grab a gift that has been given to someone else. Each individual should rather confine himself to his own vocation and its prescribed limits. Unless such modesty prevails, everything is confused; for God's truth is rashly torn apart by the stupidity of many. Peace and concord are disturbed, and in the end no kind of order will be safe. We know that Joseph was later correct in promising to interpret Pharaoh's dream because he knew he was taught and ordained for this manifestation of God's grace. That is why he had been given the gift of interpreting dreams. But he did not try to go beyond these limits. He did not say that he could interpret Pharaoh's dreams but that God could (see 41:15-16). The case of Daniel was different. Daniel was given the spirit of being able to interpret dreams to such an extent that he could interpret the king's dream even when the king had forgotten what he had dreamed about. Thus we see that Joseph, who was given only half as much as Daniel, kept himself within proper bounds.

Moreover, Joseph was not only careful not to be presumptuous but also declared that what he had was the gift of God. He said that of himself he possessed nothing. He did not boast that he was clever but wished only to be known as God's minister. Our vanity must be controlled, not only so God alone may be glorified, but so that the prophets and others who excel in heavenly gifts may humbly submit themselves to the direction of the Spirit.

**12. "This is what it means," Joseph said to him. "The three branches are three days."** Joseph did not say what he thought might be the case, but he asserted, by the revelation of the Spirit, the meaning of the dream. For why did he say that **the three branches** stood for **three *days*** rather than years unless the Spirit of God had suggested it? That is how Joseph interpreted the dream. The cupbearer was so struck by the interpretation that he acted as if he had already been restored to his position. It is as if he said, "I am convinced that what you have heard about me has come from God." In this way he showed that he thought about God's oracles in an honorable way. He spoke of their future effect with as much confidence as if it had already taken place.

**16. When the chief baker saw that Joseph had given a favorable interpretation, he said to Joseph, "I too had a dream: On my head were three baskets of bread."** The chief baker did not care about Joseph's skill and faithfulness as an interpreter. But because Joseph had brought good news to his companion, he wanted to receive a similar interpretation. In a similar way many people with ardor and alacrity desire the word of God, not because they simply wish to be governed by the Lord and to know what is right, but because they just want something for themselves. When, however, the teaching does not correspond with their wishes, they leave sad and wounded.

Although the explanation of the dream was about to prove unpleasant and severe, Joseph faithfully carried out his divinely given office and stated, without ambiguity, what had been revealed to him. This freedom must be maintained by prophets and teachers, that they may not hesitate by their teaching to inflict a wound on those whom God has sentenced to death. All love to be flattered. Hence the majority of teachers, in desiring to yield to the corrupt wishes of the world, adulterate the word of God. Wherefore, no one is a sincere minister of God's word except the person who despises reproach and yet teaches according to the command of God. Joseph would, indeed, have preferred to predict something pleasant for them both. But because it was not in his power to give a fortune to anyone, nothing remained for him but frankly to pronounce whatever he had received from the Lord.

**23. The chief cupbearer, however, did not remember Joseph; he forgot him.** This was the most severe trial of Joseph's patience, as we have before intimated. For since he had obtained an advocate who without trouble was able to extricate him from prison, especially as the opportunity of doing so had been given to him by God, he felt certain that he would be delivered and eagerly waited for this every hour. But when he was kept in prison for a second year (41:1), not only did this hope vanish, but he sank into great despair.

Joseph teaches us that nothing is more improper than to prescribe the time when God will help us. For he deliberately, sometimes for a long time, keeps his people in anxious suspense, so that they may know for certain how to trust in God. Besides, in this way God planned to publicly bring glory to himself when Joseph was set free from prison. For if Joseph had gained his freedom as a result of the entreaty of the cupbearer, it would have been generally believed that he had gained it as a result of the actions of a man and not those of God. Moreover, when Moses says that the cupbearer **forgot him,** we should understand that he did not dare to mention Joseph in case he upset the king.

# Genesis
# Chapter 41

**1. When two full years had passed.** We can imagine how anxious the holy man became during this time. The Lord tried his servant not only by a long delay, but also by another kind of trial, because he removed all human grounds of hope from him. We must note the winding route of divine providence by which Joseph was led until he came to the notice of the king.

**Pharaoh had a dream.** Regarding the king's dream, it should first of all be observed that God sometimes deigns to give his oracles even to unbelieving and profane men. It was certainly a singular honor to be told about an event that would happen fourteen years later. For the will of God was manifested to Pharaoh just as if he had been taught by the word, except that its interpretation had to be sought elsewhere. Although God designs his word especially for the church, it should not be thought strange that he sometimes allows strangers into his school. The teaching that leads to the hope of eternal life belongs to the church, while the children of this world are only taught incidentally concerning the state of the present life. If we observe this distinction, we shall not be surprised that some oracles are given to ungodly people, although the church possesses the spiritual doctrine of life as the treasure of its own inheritance.

**5. He fell asleep again and had a second dream.** A second dream was given for two reasons. God wanted to stir Pharaoh to urgently seek their meaning. God also gave more light to an obscure vision when he added the second dream.

**8. In the morning his mind was troubled, so he sent for all the magicians and wise men of Egypt.** Pharaoh's heart had been moved by these dreams, so that he would know he had to deal with God. **His mind was troubled**—an inward seal of the Spirit of God, to give authenticity to the dream. However, Pharaoh deserved to be deprived of the advantage of this revelation because he resorted to **the magicians and wise men of Egypt,** who often turned the truth of God into a lie. Pharaoh was convinced by a secret impulse that the dream sent by God meant that something important was about to happen.

**Pharaoh told them his dreams, but no one could interpret them for him.** In this way God ensured that the dream would not fail to achieve its purpose. We know what an impudent race of men these **magicians** were and how extravagantly they boasted. Why did they give the king no answer? They could have made up any story, and he would have believed them. The Lord made those deceitful people so dumb that they could not even find a plausible explanation of the dreams. Moreover, in this way the anxiety of the king heightened. He thought that what had escaped the wisdom of the magicians must be very important.

**9.** Although the Lord took pity on Egypt, he did not do it for the sake of the king or of the country, but so that Joseph might at length be brought out of prison; and further, so that, in the time of famine, food might be supplied to the church. For although the produce was stored to provide for the kingdom of Egypt, God cared for his church, which he valued more than ten worlds. Therefore **the chief cupbearer,** who had resolved to be silent about Joseph, was constrained to speak up for the holy man so that he might be set free.

**14. So Pharaoh sent for Joseph, and he was quickly brought from the dungeon. When he had shaved and changed his clothes, he came before Pharaoh.** We see in the person of a proud king, as in a mirror, what can take place when people are forced to act out of necessity. People who live in happy and prosperous circumstances will rarely condescend to listen to those who they think are true prophets, let alone to foreigners. So Pharaoh's obstinacy had to be broken, so that he might send for Joseph and accept him as his teacher. The same kind of preparation is also necessary even for the elect, because they never become docile until their pride is beaten down. So whenever, therefore, we are pitched into terrible troubles, which keep us in a state of anxiety, we must remember that God is using them to make us obey him.

Moses recounts that Joseph, before he came into the presence of the king, **shaved and changed his clothes.** From this we learn that God's servant was kept in terrible conditions until the day of his release.

**15. Pharaoh said to Joseph, "I had a dream, and no one can interpret it. But I have heard it said of you that when you hear a dream you can interpret it."** We see that Pharaoh was prepared to learn from Joseph, as he had been persuaded by the chief cupbearer that Joseph was a prophet from God. This was indeed a humble act, but it is recorded so that when the opportunity to learn presents itself, we may not refuse it but reverently honor the gifts of the Spirit.

Joseph referred Pharaoh to God (verse 16). Joseph knew he was talking with a heathen person who was given over to superstitions. So Joseph, above everything else, ascribed to God the glory that was due to him. It is as if he said, "I am able to say nothing about this dream, nor will I offer anything as from myself; God alone will be the interpreter of his own secret."

**16. "God will give Pharaoh the answer he desires."** Joseph added this out of the kindness of his heart, for he did not yet know what the oracle said. Therefore, what is said here to the king about him having the answer he wants is a prayer rather than a prophecy.

**17.** By this **dream** God was saying that the famine would be so great that people would go hungry (see verse 27).

**25. Then Joseph said to Pharaoh, "The dreams of Pharaoh are one and the same."** Joseph simply meant that the same thing was shown to Pharaoh in two ways. But before Joseph started his interpretation, he stated that this was no mere passing dream but a divine oracle. For if the vision had not come from God, it would have been foolish to inquire so anxiously about its meaning. Pharaoh, therefore, did not in vain seek to know about God's counsel.

Joseph's precise words should be noticed: **"God has revealed to Pharaoh what he is about to do."** Joseph did not just say that God would declare what might happen as a result of somebody else's action, but what he himself was about to do. From this we infer that God does not indolently contemplate the fortuitous outcome of things, as most philosophers do, but that he determines, through his own will, what will happen.

**32. "The reason the dream was given to Pharaoh in two forms is that the matter has been firmly decided by God, and God will do it soon."** God wanted Pharaoh to be certain that this event he had revealed would take place. Since God pronounces nothing but from his own fixed and steadfast purpose, it is enough that he only says it once. But our dullness and inconstancy make him repeat the same thing, so that what he has certainly decreed may be fixed in our hearts.

Moreover, Joseph also declared that what God has determined to do, **God will do . . . soon.** There was no time for Pharaoh to ignore his dream. Although we confess that the judgments of God are always hanging over our heads, unless we think they are near, we are not affected by them.

**33.** Joseph did more than he had been asked to do. He not only interpreted the dream, but, fulfilling the role of a prophet, added instruction and counsel. We know that God's genuine prophets do not just predict what will happen in the future but propose remedies concerning the impending evils. Therefore Joseph, after he had prophesied what would happen in fourteen years, now told Pharaoh what he should do. One of the marks of a genuine prophet was that he had the power to teach and exhort, so that he would not predict future events in an empty way. So here it is as if Joseph said, "Do not be upset by this revelation. Use it so that your kingdom will benefit from it." However, there is no doubt that God guided Joseph's words so that Pharaoh would entrust him with this work. For Joseph did not insinuate himself into the king's favor, nor did he abuse this gift of revelation for his private gain. Rather, what had been divinely ordained was brought about without him knowing about it—namely, that the starving house of Jacob would find unexpected sustenance.

**39.** Observe that Pharaoh, although he had been infatuated by his magicians, nevertheless honored the gifts of the Spirit in Joseph. For God never allows man to become so brutalized that he does not feel his power, even in their darkness. This kind of knowledge often enlightens profane men, but it does not make them repent.

**40-45.** Not only was Joseph made governor of Egypt, but he was given the insignia of royalty, so that everyone would respect and obey him. The royal **signet ring** was put on his finger to confirm everything he said. He was clothed in **robes of fine linen**, which were then a luxury. He had **a gold chain** hung around his neck and rode in **a chariot**. It may, however, be asked whether it was right for the holy man to go around with such great pomp. I reply that every kind of splendor that kings and other rulers possess should not be condemned, so long as they are not displayed in an ostentatious way. Moderation should always be cultivated. But since it was not in Joseph's power to choose how he would be invested with regal power, he was free to accept more than he himself would have thought necessary. While God's servants have to accommodate themselves to a public custom, they must beware of all ostentation and vanity.

**46. Joseph was thirty years old when he entered the service of Pharaoh king of Egypt. And Joseph went out from Pharaoh's presence and traveled throughout Egypt.** Moses records Joseph's age when he came to govern the kingdom for two reasons. First, because it is rare that old men allow themselves to be governed by a younger man. From this it may be inferred that it was through God's special providence that Joseph governed without being envied, and that reverence and majesty were given him beyond his years. For if there was a danger that Timothy's youth should make him be held in contempt, Joseph would have been equally exposed to scorn unless divine authority had been given to him.

A second reason for noting his age is so the reader may reflect on how long he suffered. However humane his treatment might have been, thirteen years of exile, which had prevented him from returning to his father's house, would have been a terrible trial. But added to that, he suffered as a slave and from being cruelly imprisoned.

**53. The seven years of abundance in Egypt came to an end.** The unparalleled harvests, which Joseph had prophesied, meant that he was held in high esteem by the Egyptians. Nevertheless, it is surprising that such a proud people should have allowed a foreigner to rule over them in the time of prosperity.

**54.** When Moses says that **there was famine in all the other lands, but**

**in the whole land of Egypt there was food,** Joseph's skill and prudence are seen. Egypt would not have been provided for unless Joseph had arranged for the harvests to be carefully stored.

**55. When all Egypt began to feel the famine, the people cried to Pharaoh for food. Then Pharaoh told all the Egyptians, "Go to Joseph and do what he tells you."** It is not unusual for kings, while their subjects are oppressed by extreme suffering, to indulge themselves in pleasure. But Moses does not mean that here. For Pharaoh did not exonerate himself from the trouble of distributing corn because he wanted to have a trouble-free life, but because he had such confidence in holy Joseph. So Pharaoh happily left everything to Joseph and did not allow him to be disturbed in carrying out the work he had undertaken.

# Genesis
## Chapter 42

**1. When Jacob learned that there was grain in Egypt, he said to his sons, "Why do you just keep looking at each other?"** In this chapter Moses begins to explain how Jacob, with his whole family, was drawn to Egypt. There is hardly any more illustrious example of divine providence to be found anywhere than in this account. Pious readers should carefully meditate on it, so that they may acknowledge that those things that appear to be fortuitous are directed by the hand of God.

**"Why do you just keep looking at each other?"** Jacob censured this inactivity of his sons because none of them tried to provide for the present necessity.

**2-4.** Moses says that they went into Egypt at their father's command and that he told them to go without Benjamin.

**5.** Moses also adds that they were part of a great crowd of people. This enhanced the fame of Joseph. He supplied food for all of Egypt and dispensed it until the drought ended. He also helped neighboring nations with the supplies.

**6. Now Joseph was the governor of the land, the one who sold grain to all its people. So when Joseph's brothers arrived, they bowed down to him with their faces to the ground.** Moses links the honor of Joseph with his faithfulness and diligence. Note that the grain was **sold** by Joseph. However, it was not measured out with his own hands, and he himself did not collect the money for it, for he organized the sale of the grain throughout the different parts of the kingdom, and he could scarcely have just stayed in one single storehouse. All the storehouses were under his control and management.

**7.** It may be asked why Joseph **spoke harshly** to his brothers. If he was motivated because of the harm they had done him, he must have been taking revenge. It is, however, probable that he was not controlled either by anger or a desire to enact revenge but acted as he did for the following two good reasons. First, he wanted Benjamin to come with all his other brothers. Second, he wanted to find out whether they had repented or not. In short, Joseph wanted to learn how they had been living since he had last seen them. If he had made himself known at this first meeting, Joseph feared they might hide this from their father, wanting to throw a veil over their detestable wickedness. In this way they would have only committed another evil act.

Joseph also suspected that they might harm Benjamin in some way. It was, therefore, important that they should be more thoroughly tested. That Joseph feigned something other than the truth should never be used by us as a pretext for behaving in the same way.

**9. Then he remembered his dreams about them and said to them, "You are spies! You have come to see where our land is unprotected."** When as a boy Joseph had spoken about receiving obeisance, it seemed so absurd that his brothers hatched a wicked plot to kill him. Now, although they bowed down to him without knowing him, there was nothing better for them to do. Indeed, their only way of being safe was to prostrate themselves at Joseph's feet. Meanwhile, their conspiracy, by which they attempted to subvert the celestial decree lest they should have to bear the yoke, came to nothing. The Lord restrains the obstinate, just as wild horses are treated more severely, the more they kick.

It may, however, seem absurd that Joseph should at this time have **remembered** his dreams, as if he had forgotten them through all these years. This could not have been the case, as he could not have forgotten them unless he had lost sight of the promises of God. I reply that there is nothing recorded here that does not frequently happen to us. Although the word of God may be dwelling in our hearts, yet it does not constantly fill our minds but is sometimes so smothered that it may seem to be extinct. This particularly happens when faith is oppressed by dark clouds of affliction. God had moved Joseph by these dreams to hope that he would be given great authority. He was, however, thrown into a well that resembled a grave. From there he was sold as a slave and carted off to a distant land. And as if slavery was not a severe enough punishment, he was locked up in prison. Although his misery was a little alleviated when he was released from his iron chains, there was little, if any, prospect of being delivered from prison. But I do not think that the hope he entertained was entirely destroyed. It was as if a cloud had passed over it, so that he was deprived of the light of comfort.

**17. And he put them all in custody for three days.** Now, with more than mere words, Joseph acted in a harsh way toward his brothers and then shut them up in prison, as if he were about to punish them. During the **three days** the brothers would have been tormented with fear.

**18. On the third day, Joseph said to them, "Do this and you will live, for I fear God."** In case they became so afraid that they decided not to return, Joseph promised to act with good faith toward them. To convince them of this Joseph said, **"I fear God."** This expression deserves to be carefully noted. Doubtless he spoke from the inner feeling of his heart when he declared that he would treat them fairly because he feared God. Therefore the fountain of a good and honest conscience, by which we cultivate faithfulness and fairness toward men, is the fear of God. For anybody who thinks that he need never give an account to God for the way he has lived has no reason to stop living an entirely self-centered life.

**21. They said to one another, "Surely we are being punished because of our brother. We saw how distressed he was when he pleaded with us for his life, but we would not listen; that's why this distress has come upon us."** This is a remarkable verse, for it shows that the sons of Jacob, when put under the most severe pressure, called to mind a fratricide they had committed thirteen years earlier. From this we see that in adversity God searches and tries men. This kind of examination is very necessary for us.

So Joseph brought about some good when he forced his brothers to acknowledge their sin. The Lord had compassion on them and took away their deceitful covering, under which they had hidden for so long. In the same way, when God daily chastises us by the hand of man, he draws us, as guilty people, to his tribunal. It would hardly benefit anyone to be tried by adversity unless his heart was touched. For we see how few reflect on their sins even when they are admonished by the most severe punishments. So there is no doubt that God, in order to lead the sons of Jacob to repentance, impelled them, by both the secret instinct of his Spirit and by outward chastisement, to become conscious of the sin that had been concealed for too long.

Let the reader also observe that the sons of Jacob not only fixed their minds on something that was close at hand but considered that divine punishments were inflicted in various ways on sinners. And doubtless, in order to understand the divine judgments, we must look far and wide. Sometimes by inflicting present punishment on sinners, God puts them, as it were, on the stage of a theater so that everyone can observe them. But God often takes vengeance on our sins unexpectedly and from an unseen quarter. If the sons of Jacob had merely looked for some present cause for their sufferings, they could have only loudly complained that they had been injured, and at length despair would have followed. But while considering how far and wide the providence of God extends, looking beyond their present circumstances, they reflected on a more distant reason.

**"We saw how distressed he was when he pleaded with us for his life, but we would not listen."** They acknowledged that it was by the just judgment of God that they obtained nothing through their entreaties because they themselves had acted so cruelly toward their brother. Christ had not yet uttered the sentence, "For in the same way you judge others, you will be judged, and with the measure you use, it will be measured to you" (Matthew 7:2), but it was a law of nature that those who had been cruel to others were not worthy of receiving mercy. We should take great care not to be deaf to the many warnings of Scripture. Therefore, while we have time, let us learn to sympathize with the miserable and to stretch out our hand to help them.

"Our brother," they said in essence, "entreated us when he was desperate. But we rejected his cries. Therefore, it is because of divine retribution that we can now obtain nothing." With these words they bore witness that the hearts of men under God's rule can be hardened. Moreover, God hated their cruelty because since his goodness is diffused through heaven and earth, nothing is more contrary to his nature than that we should cruelly reject those who beg us to protect them.

**22-26.** Because he had attempted to rescue Joseph out of the hands of his brothers in order to restore him in safety to his father, Reuben underlined their fault in not having at that time listened to any prudent counsel. His words conveyed a reproof for their repentance that had come too late. Joseph was not yet satisfied with this confession and so kept Simeon in prison and dismissed the rest. This was not done out of malevolence, but because he was not certain about the safety of his brother Benjamin. For he rightly feared that when they found that their wicked plan to put their brother to death had been discovered, they might again attempt some horrible crime, as desperate men are inclined to do. Or they might desert their father and flee to some other country.

Nevertheless, Joseph's action should not be taken as a precedent because it is not always right to be so severe. Therefore, we must seek the spirit of discretion from heaven, which will so control us that we do nothing out of rash impetuosity or immoderate severity. It should also be borne in mind that under Joseph's stern countenance was concealed not only a mild and placid disposition, but the most tender affection.

**27.** Why Joseph had ordered that the price paid for the corn should be secretly deposited in the sacks of his brothers can be easily deduced. He feared that his father, already being impoverished, would not be able to buy provisions again. But the brothers, having found their money, were baffled by the discovery. They became afraid and saw that the hand of God was against them.

**29-34.** The events that have just taken place are deliberately repeated. Moses wanted to show how anxious the brothers were as they made their excuses to their father for having left Simeon in chains and related how strenuously they had pleaded with the Egyptian governor, trying to gain Simeon's freedom, so Israel would allow them to take their brother Benjamin. This was their objective.

We know how terrible hunger is. Yet, although the only way to relieve this was to go to Egypt for corn, Jacob preferred that he and his family perish rather than allow Benjamin to accompany the rest of the brothers. Although their declaration that Joseph had been torn apart by a wild beast was possible, there still remained in the heart of the holy patriarch a secret wound, arising from suspicion. He was fully aware of their fierce and cruel hatred of the innocent youth. It is clear from this what a miserable condition the holy man had lived in for the past thirteen years. But the worst part of this burden was that the promise of God might prove illusory and vain. For he had no hope except from the promised seed. But he seemed to be bringing up devils at home, from whom a blessing was no more to be expected than life from death. He thought that Joseph was dead. He only had Benjamin left, who had not been corrupted. How could the salvation of the world come from such a vicious offspring? He must, therefore, have been endowed with great perseverance, seeing he did not stop relying on God. He was convinced that he cherished the church in his house even though there was scarcely any sign of this.

Let the faithful now apply this example to themselves, so that they do not give way to the horrible devastation that is in view almost everywhere.

**35. As they were emptying their sacks, there in each man's sack was his pouch of silver! When they and their father saw the money pouches, they were frightened.** This shows how upset they had been on their journey since each of them had not at least examined his sack after money had been found in one. But these things are written to show that as soon as men are smitten with fear, they have no particle of wisdom and soundness of mind until God calms them down. Moreover, Joseph did not act with enough consideration, in that he brought about very great grief for his father, whose poverty he really intended to relieve. Whence we learn that even the most prudent are not always right in what they do.

**36.** Jacob did not openly accuse his sons of the crime of their brother's murder; yet he was angry as if, two of his sons being already taken away, they were rushing to destroy the third. He implied that all these evils were falling on him alone. He did not think they were affected as they should have been. They did not share in his grief with him but were making light of the destruction of their brothers, as if they had no interest in their lives.

**38.** We see, as in a living picture, what sorrow had oppressed holy Jacob. He saw his whole family starving, but he preferred to die rather than allow his son Benjamin to be taken from him. From this we do not conclude that he was hard-hearted. His patience deserves more praise than that. He was overcome with excessive grief when he complained to his sons in essence, "You are too cruel to your father in taking away from me a third son after I have been deprived of first one and then another."

# Genesis
# Chapter 43

**1. Now the famine was still severe in the land.** This chapter records the second journey of the sons of Jacob into Egypt, after the previous supply of provisions had been exhausted. It may, however, here be asked how Jacob could have supported his family, even for a few days, with so small a quantity of corn. Even if you grant that several donkeys were brought by each of the brothers, what was this to sustain 300 people? It seems to me that they lived on acorns, herbs, and roots. For we know that the Orientals, especially when any necessity impinges on them, are content with meager and dry food. Surely, in the scarcity of wheat there was a supply of other food. I suppose, therefore, that no more corn had been bought than would suffice to furnish a frugal and restricted measure of food for Jacob himself and for his children and grandchildren. There is, indeed, no doubt that the whole region had been compelled to resort to acorns and fruits and that bread made from wheat was a luxury that belonged only to the rich.

This was, indeed, a severe trial. Holy Jacob, whom God had promised to take care of, almost perished, with his family, through hunger. The land of which he was the lord denied him bread as if he were a stranger. He probably thus seriously doubted what was the meaning of that remarkable promise, "I am God Almighty. Grow and multiply; I will bless you." It is profitable for us to know these conflicts of the holy fathers, that, fighting with the same weapons with which they conquered, we also may stand invincible, even if God should seem to withhold his help.

**3. But Judah said to him, "The man warned us solemnly, 'You will not see my face again unless your brother is with you.'"** Judah seemed to be deceitful in order to extract from his father what he knew he would not freely give; but it is probable that many discourses were given by Judah that have not been recorded. Since Joseph so ardently desired to see his brother Benjamin, it is not surprising that Judah should have labored in every possible way to obtain this. It deserves to be noticed that Moses recounts the long conversation that Jacob had with his sons, so that we may know with what difficulty he allowed his son Benjamin to be torn away from him. Though hunger was pressing, he nevertheless tried to retain him, as if he were striving for the salvation of his whole family. From this we again may conjecture that he suspected his sons of a wicked conspiracy. On this account Judah offered himself as a surety. He did not promise anything, but for the sake of clearing himself and his brothers, he took Benjamin under his care, promising that if any injury should be done to Benjamin, he would bear the punishment and the blame. From Jacob's example let us learn patient endurance, should the Lord compel us, by pressure of circumstances, to do many things contrary to the inclination of our own minds. Jacob sent away his son as if he were handing him over to death.

**11. Then their father Israel said to them, "If it must be, then do this: Put some of the best products of the land in your bags and take them down to the man as a gift—a little balm and a little honey, some spices and myrrh, some pistachio nuts and almonds."** Though the fruits that Moses lists were, for the most part, not very precious, because the condition of holy Jacob was not such that he could send any royal present, according to his slender ability he wished to appease Joseph. Besides, we know that fruits are not always judged according to their cost.

And then (verse 14), having commanded his sons to do what he thought was necessary, he prayed that God would give them favor with the governor of Egypt. We must note both these points whenever we are perplexed by anything. We must not omit any of those things that are expedient or that may seem to be useful; and yet we must place our reliance on God. For the tranquillity of faith has no affinity with laziness. He who longs for a prosperous outcome of his affairs from the Lord will at the same time look closely to the means that are in his power and will apply them to the matter in hand.

Meanwhile, let the faithful observe this moderation—that when they have tried all means, they still ascribe nothing to their own industry. At the same time, let them be certainly convinced that all their endeavors will be in vain unless the Lord blesses them.

It is to be observed, also, in the form of his supplication that Jacob regarded the hearts of men as subject to the will of God. When we have to deal with men, we too often stop looking to the Lord because we do not sufficiently acknowledge him as the secret ruler of their hearts.

So Jacob, although his sons had found an austere severity in Joseph, yet trusted that Joseph's heart would be in the hand of God, so that it would be generous. Therefore, as we must hope in the Lord when men deal unjustly with us and must pray that they may be changed for the better, so, on the other hand, we must remember that, when they act with severity toward us, it is not done without God's counsel.

**13. "Take your brother also and go back to the man at once."** Jacob may seem to be inconsistent here. For if the prayer that Moses has just related was grounded in faith, he should have been more calm. He should at least have allowed for the manifestation of the grace of God. But he appeared to cut himself off from every ground of confidence when he supposed that nothing was left for him but bereavement. This is like the speech of a man in despair: "I shall remain bereaved as I am." It was as if he had prayed in vain or had deceitfully professed that the remedy was in the hand of God.

If, however, we observe to whom his speech was directed, the solution is easy. It is clear that he stood firmly on the promise that had been given to him, and therefore he would hope for some fruit of his prayers. But he wished deeply to affect his sons, so they would take greater care of their brother. It was as if he said, "I see what my condition is—I am a most wretched old man. My house, which recently was filled with people, I find almost deserted." So in general terms he was deploring the loss of all his sons and was not speaking of only one of them. Moreover, he wanted his sons to attend to their duty with greater fidelity and diligence.

**16. When Joseph saw Benjamin with them, he said to the steward of his house, "Take these men to my house, slaughter an animal and prepare dinner; they are to eat with me at noon."** Here we perceive the fraternal disposition of Joseph, though it is uncertain whether he was perfectly reconciled. It is probable that the crime that the brothers had committed against Joseph came into their minds and that this fear came from a guilty conscience. For unless the judgment of God had tormented them, there was no reason why they should suspect a betrayal (verse 18). It may seem odd that strangers should be welcomed to a feast by a prince of the highest dignity. But why not rather incline to a different conjecture—namely, that the governor of Egypt had done this for the purpose of exhibiting to his friends the new spectacle of eleven brothers sitting at one table? It, indeed, sometimes happens that similar anxiety to that felt by Joseph's brothers invades even the best of men; but I would rather ascribe it to the judgment of God that the sons of Jacob, whose conscience accused them of having inhumanely treated their brother, suspected that they would be dealt with in the same manner.

**23. "It's all right [KJV: Peace be to you]," he said. "Don't be afraid. Your God, the God of your father, has given you treasure in your sacks; I received your silver."** Then he brought Simeon out to them. Because the Hebrew word *shalom* signifies not only **peace** but any prosperous and desirable condition, as well as any joyful event, this passage may be expounded in two ways—either that the ruler of Joseph's house commanded them to be of a peaceful and secure mind, or that he pronounced it to be well and happy with them. The sum of his answer, however, amounted to this: There was no reason for fear because their affairs were in a prosperous state. And since, after the manner of men, it was not possible that they should have paid the money for the corn that was found in their sacks, he ascribed it to God's favor.

**25. They prepared their gifts for Joseph's arrival at noon, because they had heard that they were to eat there.** It was also more honorable, according to ancient custom, that a portion of food should be sent to each from Joseph rather than that it should be distributed by the cook.

**33. The men had been seated before him in the order of their ages, from the firstborn to the youngest; and they looked at each other in astonishment.** Although of the sons of Jacob four were born of bondwomen, yet, since they were older, they had precedence over their younger brothers, who had descended from freeborn mothers; whence it appears that they had been accustomed by their father to keep this order. What, then, someone may say, becomes of the declaration, "The slave woman's son will never share in the inheritance with the free woman's son" (Galatians 4:30)? Truly, I think, since Ishmael was rejected by the divine oracle proceeding from the mouth of Sarah, as Esau was afterwards, Jacob was fully taught that he had as many heirs as he had sons. Hence arose that equality that caused each to keep his place—first, middle, or last—according to his age. But the design of Moses was to show that although Benjamin was the youngest, yet he was preferred to all the rest in honor (verse 34); Joseph could not refrain from giving him the principal token of his love. It was, indeed, Joseph's intention to remain unknown. But he suddenly broke out into a declaration of his affection.

**34. When portions were served to them from Joseph's table, Benjamin's portion was five times as much as anyone else's. So they feasted and drank freely with him.** From the end of the chapter we conclude that there was a sumptuous banquet at which they indulged themselves more freely and hilariously than was usual. The verb *shakar* **(drank freely)**, which is often translated "be drunk," indicates either that they were not accustomed to drinking wine or that an unusual amount was drunk at this banquet given in their honor. But the word does not necessarily mean drinking to excess (as riotous men interpret it in order to excuse their own dissipation by the example of the patriarchs), but rather drinking with honest and free enjoyment. I admit that the word is ambiguous and is often used in a bad sense, as in Genesis 9:21 and similar passages, but in this place Moses' meaning is clear.

If anyone raises the objection that a frugal use of food and drink is sufficient for the nourishment of the body, I answer: Although food is proper provision for our bodily need, yet the legitimate use of it goes beyond mere sustenance. Good flavors were not added to food value without a purpose, but because our heavenly Father wishes to give us pleasure with the delicacies he provides. It is not by accident that Psalm 104:15 praises his kindness in creating wine to cheer man's heart.

But the more kindly God treats us, the more it becomes our duty to be careful to control ourselves and to use his gifts temperately. For we know how unrestrained our appetite is; in abundance it always overindulges itself, and it is always impatient during scarcity. In fact, we must keep Paul's rule (Philippians 4:12) and know both how to be in want and how to abound. This means to be on our guard when large quantities are at hand so that we are not tempted to indulge in extravagance; and again we must see to it that we endure privation calmly. Someone will perhaps say that the flesh is much too clever at camouflaging extravagance, and therefore nothing beyond actual necessities should be allowed it. I certainly agree that Paul's requirement (Romans 13:14) must be observed, and we must not serve our lusts. But what is most important for religious people is to receive their food from God's hand with a quiet conscience. And to do this, we must determine how far the enjoyment of food and wine is allowable.

# Genesis
# Chapter 44

**1. Now Joseph gave these instructions to the steward of his house:
"Fill the men's sacks with as much food as they can carry, and put
each man's silver in the mouth of his sack."** Here Moses recounts how
skillfully Joseph had contrived to test the dispositions of his brothers.
Whereas God has commanded us to cultivate candor without pretense,
we are not to take this and similar examples as affording license to turn
aside to indirect and crafty arts. For it may have been that Joseph was
impelled by a special influence of the Spirit to act in this way. He also had
a special reason to inquire how his brothers had been affected. Charity
is not suspicious. Why, then, did he so distrust his brothers? And why
could he not suppose that they had anything good unless he first subjected them to the most rigorous examination? Truly, since he had found
them to be exceedingly cruel and unfaithful, it was an excusable suspicion
if he did not believe them to be changed for the better until he had seen
their penitence for himself.

It may, however, be asked, "If the sons of Jacob had been easily
induced to betray the safety of Benjamin, what would Joseph himself
have done?" We may readily conjecture that he examined their fidelity
so that, if he should find them dishonest, he might retain Benjamin and
drive them with shame from his presence. But by pursuing this method
his father would have been deserted, and the church of God ruined. And
certainly it was not without risk to himself that he thus terrified them;
he could scarcely have avoided the necessity of denouncing some more
grievous and severe punishment against them if they had again relapsed.
It was, therefore, due to the special favor of God that they proved that
this had changed.

**2. "Then put my cup, the silver one, in the mouth of the youngest
one's sack, along with the silver for his grain." And he did as Joseph
said.** Joseph ordered the cup to be enclosed in Benjamin's sack, so that
he might claim him as his own when convicted of the theft and might

send the rest away. However, he accused all alike, as if he knew not who among them had committed the crime. First he reproved their ingratitude because they did not reciprocate the welcome they received. Next he contended that the crime was unappeasable because they had stolen what was most valuable to him—the **cup** in which he was accustomed both to drink and to divine. He made this charge through his steward. From this I infer that the steward was not altogether ignorant of his master's design.

**5. "'Isn't this the cup my master drinks from and also uses for divination? This is a wicked thing you have done.'"** This clause seems to mean this: Joseph had used the cup for divinations and for magical arts, which, however, he feigned for the sake of aggravating the charge brought against them. But the question arises, how does Joseph allow himself to resort to such an expedient? Besides it being sinful to indulge in augury, he would thus vainly and unworthily transfer to imaginary deities the honor due only to divine grace. On a former occasion he had declared that he was unable to interpret dreams except so far as God would suggest the truth to him; now he obscured this entire ascription of praise to divine grace. And what is worse, by boasting that he was a magician rather than proclaiming himself a prophet of God, he impiously profaned the gift of the Holy Spirit. Doubtless, in this dissimulation it is not to be denied that he sinned grievously. Yet I think that at first he had endeavored by all means in his power to give to God his due honor; and it was not his fault that the whole kingdom of Egypt was ignorant of the fact that he excelled in skill not by magical arts, but by a heavenly gift.

**7. But they said to him, "Why does my lord say such things? Far be it from your servants to do anything like that!"** The sons of Jacob boldly excused themselves because a good conscience gave them confidence. They also argued from the greater to the lesser, contending that their voluntarily bringing back the money earlier, which they might with impunity have kept and used, proved their honesty. They, therefore, declared themselves ready to submit to any punishment if they were found guilty of the theft. When Moses states that the cup was discovered in Benjamin's sack, he does not relate any of their complaints but only declares that they manifested the most bitter grief by tearing their clothes.

Therefore, when they came into the presence of Joseph, they confessed the offense, not because they acknowledged that the crime had been committed by them, but because excuses would be of no avail. It is as if they said, "It is of no use to deny a thing that is manifest in itself." In this sense they said that their iniquity had been found out by God; although they had some secret suspicion of fraud, thinking this had been a contrivance for the purpose of bringing an unjust charge against them, they chose rather to trace the cause of their punishment to the secret judgment of God.

**16. "What can we say to my lord?" Judah replied. "What can we say? How can we prove our innocence? God has uncovered your ser-**

vants' guilt. We are now my lord's slaves—we ourselves and the one who was found to have the cup." They had previously called themselves servants through modesty; now they consigned themselves over to him as slaves. But in the case of Benjamin they pled for a mitigation of the severity of the punishment.

17. But Joseph said, "Far be it from me to do such a thing! Only the man who was found to have the cup will become my slave. The rest of you, go back to your father in peace." If Joseph intended to retain Benjamin alone and to dismiss the others, he would have done his utmost to tear the church of God apart. But his purpose was nothing other than to pierce their hearts more deeply. He must have anticipated great mischief if he had perceived that they did not care for their brother. But the Lord provided against this danger by causing the earnest apology of Judah not only to soften Joseph's mind, but even to draw forth tears and weeping in profusion.

18. Then Judah went up to him and said: "Please, my lord, let your servant speak a word to my lord. Do not be angry with your servant, though you are equal to Pharaoh himself." Judah asked to speak with Joseph. He began by declaring that he was not ignorant of the great honor that Joseph had received in Egypt, for the purpose of showing that he was becoming bold, not through impertinence, but through necessity. Later he recalled how he and his brothers had left their father. He said that he had bound himself by covenant to bring the youth back.

# Genesis
# Chapter 45

**1. Then Joseph could no longer control himself before all his atten-
dants, and he cried out, "Have everyone leave my presence!" So there
was no one with Joseph when he made himself known to his brothers.**
Moses recounts in this chapter the manner in which Joseph **made himself
known to his brothers.** In the first place, he declares that Joseph suppressed his feelings as long as he presented to them an austere and harsh
countenance. But at length the strong fraternal affection poured itself
forth with abundant force. From this it appears that nothing severe or
cruel had before been harbored in his mind. And whereas this softness or
tenderness burst forth in tears, it was more deserving of praise than if he
had maintained an equable disposition.

The stoics speak foolishly when they say it is heroic not to be moved
by compassion. Had Joseph remained inflexible, who would not have
pronounced him to be a stupid or ironhearted man? But now by the
vehemence of his feelings he manifested a noble magnanimity as well as a
divine moderation, so superior both to anger and to hatred. He ardently
loved those who had wickedly conspired to ruin him, though they had
received no injury from him.

Joseph ordered all men to leave his presence, not because he was
ashamed of his kindred, but because he was considerate about his brothers' possible fear that he might make their detestable crime known to
many witnesses. And it was not the smallest part of his clemency to
desire that their disgrace should be wholly buried in oblivion. We see,
therefore, that witnesses were removed for no other reason than that he
might more freely comfort his brothers; for he not only spared them by
not exposing their crime, but when shut up alone with them, he abstained
from all bitterness of language and gladly administered to them friendly
consolation.

**3. Joseph said to his brothers, "I am Joseph! Is my father still liv-
ing?" But his brothers were not able to answer him, because they were**

**terrified at his presence.** Although he had given them the clearest token of his mildness and his love, yet when he told them his name, they were terrified, as if he had thundered against them. For while they pondered in their minds what they deserved, the power of Joseph seemed so formidable to them that they anticipated nothing for themselves but death. When, however, he saw them overcome with fear, he uttered no reproach but sought only to calm them down.

By this example we are taught to take heed lest sadness should overwhelm those who are truly and seriously humbled from a sense of shame. So long as the offender is deaf to reproofs or excuses himself by hypocrisy, he should be treated severely. But rigor should have its bounds, and as soon as the offender lies prostrate and trembles under the sense of his sin, moderation should immediately follow. Therefore, so that our severity may be rightly and duly tempered, we must cultivate this inner affection that Joseph possessed, so that it will become evident at the right time.

**4. Then Joseph said to his brothers, "Come close to me." When they had done so, he said, "I am your brother Joseph, the one you sold into Egypt!"** This was more efficacious than any mere words. He kindly invited them to embrace him. Yet he also tried to remove their fear by using courteous language. He would go on to tell them that God had **sent** him ahead of them to preserve them (verses 4, 7, 8). In short, he had not been **sent** into Egypt by them but had been led there by God's hand.

**8. "So then, it was not you who sent me here, but God. He made me father to Pharaoh, lord of his entire household and ruler of all Egypt."** This is an especially significant passage, for it teaches us that the true course of events is never disturbed by the wickedness and malice of men. On the contrary, God directs men's confused and turbulent movements to a good end. Also it shows us how we ought to think of God's providence and how we are to profit from it. When the inquisitive talk about this, they not only muddle and pervert everything by ignoring its purpose, but also concoct whatever absurdities they can to insult God's justice. Their effrontery even makes some pious and modest men wish they could bury this part of our doctrine. For as soon as it is proclaimed that God controls the government of the whole world and that nothing is done without his assent and command, those who feel too little reverence for the mysteries of God burst out with various questions that are not only frivolous but also pernicious.

However, in our desire to stop such profane intemperance, we should be very careful not to be satisfied with crass ignorance of truths that are not only revealed by the Word of God but are also very useful for us to know. Good men are ashamed to confess that nothing that men undertake is accomplished unless God wills it, in case unbridled tongues clamor either that God is the author of sin or that no blame is incurred by impious men since they are only following God's purpose. Although there is no way of refuting this sacrilegious madness, we should be content to detest it and meanwhile hold firmly to the clear witness of Scripture, whatever men may invent. In the middle of all the shoutings of men, God directs men's plans and efforts from heaven, and he finally accomplishes by their hands what he himself has decreed.

Good men who fear to expose the justice of God to the slanders of the impious take refuge in the distinction that God wills some things to be done and only permits other things to take place. As if without his will any freedom of action would be possible for men! If he had merely permitted Joseph to be carried to Egypt, he would not have ordained him as the instrument for saving the lives of his father Jacob and his sons; and this is what is explicitly said here. A statement like our text would be meaningless if evil things that God afterwards turns to a good end were done only by his permission and not by his intention and will.

We must hold that God's action is distinct from man's, so that his providence is free from all iniquity and his decrees have no affinity with the wrongdoings of men. A most beautiful illustration of this truth is seen in this story. Joseph was sold by his brothers for no other reason than that they wanted him out of the way. The same act is ascribed to God, but with a very different purpose. God did this in order to provide the house of Jacob with food in time of famine. Hence it is clear that although God at first seems to act in the same way as wicked men, in the end their crime is a far cry from his wonderful justice.

I ask you to note how often God not only resists the malice of those who desire to harm us but also turns their evil efforts to our good! Thus he mitigates the afflictions of our flesh and gives us a calm spirit and greater peace.

**9. "Now hurry back to my father and say to him, 'This is what your son Joseph says: God has made me lord of all Egypt. Come down to me; don't delay.'"** In giving this command, he showed that he spoke about his power to inspire his father with stronger confidence. We know how slow to respond old men are; and, besides, it was difficult to tear holy Jacob away from the inheritance that was divinely promised to him. Therefore Joseph, having pointed out the necessity of the step, declared what relief the Lord had offered.

**16. When the news reached Pharaoh's palace that Joseph's brothers had come, Pharaoh and all his officials were pleased.** Before Joseph sent for his father, the report of the coming of his brothers had reached the palace. And Joseph would not have so confidently promised a home to his brothers in Egypt without the king's permission. What, therefore, Moses had before briefly alluded to, he now explains more fully—namely, that the king, with a ready and cheerful mind, declared his high esteem for Joseph in freely offering to his father and brothers the most fertile part of Egypt for them to live in. From another statement of Moses it appears that as long as Joseph lived, the Israelites were treated with clemency and kindness. For in Exodus 1:8 the commencement of the tyranny and cruelty is said to have been made by his successor, to whom Joseph was unknown.

**22. To each of them he gave new clothing, but to Benjamin he gave three hundred shekels of silver and five sets of clothes.** It is not surprising that Joseph furnished his brothers with supplies for their journey. But why did he load them up with money and garments, seeing they would return so soon? I do not doubt that he did it on account of his father and the wives of his brothers, so that they might leave the land of Canaan less reluctantly. For he knew that his message would scarcely be believed unless some clear tokens of its truth were presented.

**24. Then he sent his brothers away, and as they were leaving he said to them, "Don't quarrel on the way!"** Joseph had made peace with his brothers. He now admonished them not to stir up any strife among themselves. We ought to imitate Joseph's kindness. We must prevent quarrels from taking place as much as we can. For Christ requires his disciples not only to love peace but also to be peacemakers. We know that what Joseph taught his brothers is commanded by God's Spirit and applies to us all. We should not be angry with each other.

**26. They told him, "Joseph is still alive! In fact, he is ruler of all Egypt." Jacob was stunned; he did not believe them.** We know that some people have fainted with sudden and unexpected joy. Therefore, certain interpreters suppose that the heart of Jacob was in a sense suffocated, as if seized by a kind of ecstatic stupor. But Moses gives a different reason—namely, not having confidence in his sons, he was torn between hope and fear. It was not, therefore, a simple affection of joy but a troubled mind that shook Jacob. Therefore, Moses says a little later that his spirit **revived** when he, having returned to himself and being composed in mind, believed that what he had heard was true (verses 27-28). And he showed that his love toward Joseph had not languished through the years, for he now set no value on his own life. He just wanted to see Joseph. He had been resigned to endless days of sorrow until the day he died. But now he declared that he would have a joyful death.

# Genesis
# Chapter 46

**1. So Israel set out with all that was his, and when he reached Beersheba, he offered sacrifices to the God of his father Isaac.** Because the holy man was compelled to leave the land of Canaan, he offered a sacrifice to the Lord. He wanted to testify that the covenant that God had made with his fathers was confirmed and ratified to him. There was also a special reason for his sacrifice. He was about to be deprived of the inheritance promised to him. For the sight of that land was the type and the pledge of the heavenly country. By renewing the divine covenant, Israel strengthened his faith, so that it would not fail him.

For this reason he offered a sacrifice on the very boundaries of that land, and so we may know that it was very special. And he presented this worship to the God of his fathers, to testify that although he was departing from that land into which Abraham had been called, yet he did not thereby cut himself off from the God in whose worship he had been brought up.

It was proof of his constancy that when he was driven by famine into another land, he yet retained the hope of his secret right. By offering a sacrifice, he both increased his own strength and witnessed to his faith. Although piety is not bound up with external symbols, Jacob would not neglect those helps that he had found to be by no means superfluous.

**2. And God spoke to Israel in a vision at night and said, "Jacob! Jacob!" "Here I am," he replied.** In this way God proved that Jacob's sacrifice was accepted by him. He stretched out his hand again and ratified his covenant. The night vision gave greater dignity to the oracle. Jacob obeyed God and did not need to be frightened into submitting to God. Yet, because he was clothed in human frailty, it helped him to see God's glory. This helpful word penetrated more effectually into his heart. No living image of God can exist without the word of God. Note this link between a vision and the word. For a vision that gives greater dignity to the word came first. Then the word followed immediately, as if it were the soul of the vision. There is no question that this was an appearance of the visible glory of God, which removed Jacob's doubt. It firmly sustained the patriarch, so that he confidently embraced the oracle.

**3. "I am God, the God of your father," he said. "Do not be afraid to go down to Egypt, for I will make you into a great nation there."** The purpose of the repetition was to make Jacob more attentive. For by addressing him in this way, God gently insinuated himself into his mind, just as in the Scripture he kindly allures us, that he may prepare us to become his disciples. The docility of the holy man is seen in that as soon as he was persuaded that God spoke, he replied that he was ready to receive with reverence whatever was spoken, to follow wheresoever he may be called, and to carry out whatever may be commanded. Later a promise was added, by which God confirmed and revived the faith of his servant. For Jacob, to travel to Egypt was a sad event. So he was told to have a cheerful mind, for the Lord would always be his keeper.

**28. Now Jacob sent Judah ahead of him to Joseph to get directions to Goshen. When they arrived in the region of Goshen . . .** Because **Goshen** had been selected by Joseph as the place for his father and his brothers to live in, Jacob now desired that, on his coming, he might find the place prepared for him. The expression that Moses uses in verse 34 (**to settle in the region of Goshen**) implies not that he required a house to be built and furnished for him, but only that he may be allowed to pitch his tent without being molested. For it was necessary that some unoccupied place should be assigned to him.

**31. Then Joseph said to his brothers and to his father's household, "I will go up and speak to Pharaoh and will say to him, 'My brothers and my father's household, who were living in the land of Canaan, have come to me.'"** After Joseph had gone out to meet his father in order to honor him, he also provided what would be useful for him. On this account, he advised Jacob to declare that he and all his family looked after livestock, so that Jacob might obtain from the king somewhere to live. Seeing that the land of Goshen was fertile and celebrated for its rich pastures, he wanted his father to live there. Keeping the richness of the land out of Pharaoh's mind, he gave another reason—namely, that Jacob with his sons were detested by the Egyptians, and that therefore he was seeking a place of seclusion in which they might dwell apart from the Egyptians. The king knew all about the fertility of the land of Goshen, yet of his own accord had offered them, unsolicited, the best and choicest place in the kingdom. Therefore, this bounty of his was not elicited from him by a cunning plan, because he was free to form his own judgment about what he would give. It would have been inconsiderate for men who were strangers to desire the best and most convenient place for themselves, as if they possessed a right to choose for themselves. Joseph knew that the Egyptians detested shepherds. So he explained to the king that Goshen would be a suitable retreat for his brothers. For had the Israelites mixed with the Egyptians, they might have been scattered far and wide. But now, seeing that they were thought to be unworthy of being admitted to Egyptian society, they learned, in this state of separation, to cherish more fervently their union among themselves. In this way the body of the church, which God had set apart from the whole world, was not dispersed. The Lord often allows us to be despised or rejected by the world, so that we may be freed and cleansed from its pollution and may cultivate holiness. Finally, he does not allow us to be chained to the earth, so that we may be borne upward to heaven.

# Genesis
# Chapter 47

**1. Joseph went and told Pharaoh, "My father and brothers, with their flocks and herds and everything they own, have come from the land of Canaan and are now in Goshen."** Joseph intimated to the king his desire to obtain a place for his brothers in the land of **Goshen**. Pharaoh immediately gave this to him. We gather from this that what he gave, he did not give in ignorance. He was not unacquainted with Joseph's wish.

**3. Pharaoh asked the brothers, "What is your occupation?" "Your servants are shepherds," they replied to Pharaoh, "just as our fathers were."** This was a humiliating admission for the sons of Jacob, and especially for Joseph. For among the Egyptians being a shepherd was thought to be a disgraceful way of life. Why, then, did Joseph not describe his brothers as people engaged in agriculture or any other honest and creditable way of living? Why did Joseph deliberately expose his brothers to such an ignominy, which would bring dishonor also on himself, unless he was not very anxious to escape from worldly contempt? To live in splendor among the Egyptians would have been very appealing, but his family would have been placed in a dangerous position. Now, however, their mean and contemptible way of living became a wall of separation between them and the Egyptians.

Joseph seemed to deliberately throw off, in a moment, the nobility he had acquired, so that his own posterity might not be swallowed up by all the Egyptians. If, however, this consideration did not enter their minds, there is no doubt that the Lord directed their tongues, so that the body of the church might be kept pure and distinct. This passage also teaches us that it is much better to possess a remote corner in the courts of the Lord than to dwell in the middle of palaces beyond the precincts of the church. God's purpose was to keep the sons of Jacob in a lowly position until he restored them to the land of Canaan. So, to preserve their unity until the promised deliverance took place, they did not conceal the fact that they were shepherds. We must beware, therefore, lest the desire of empty honor should elate us, whereas the Lord reveals no other way of salvation than by bringing us under his discipline.

**5. Pharaoh said to Joseph, "Your father and your brothers have come to you."** It was a sign of God's favor that Pharaoh was not offended when they asked for a separate place to live. In asking to be admitted as guests and strangers, they took the precaution that Pharaoh would not hold them in the chains of servitude. A passage from Sophocles says:

> *Who refuge seeks within a tyrant's door,*
> *When once he enters there, is free no more.*

It was, therefore, important for the sons of Jacob to say on what condition they wished to live in Egypt. Therefore the law of hospitality was wickedly violated when the Israelites were later oppressed as slaves and when they were not allowed to return to their own country. Faithfulness and humanity should have been extended to them by the king since they had been welcomed by an earlier Pharaoh and lived under his protection. It appears, therefore, that the children of Israel guarded themselves, for in the presence of God they had just grounds for complaint against the Egyptians. But seeing that the pledge given them by the king did not prove to be of any advantage to them according to the flesh, let the faithful learn from their example to train themselves to be patient. For it often happens that the person who enters the court of a tyrant is necessarily forfeiting his freedom.

**6. ". . . and the land of Egypt is before you; settle your father and your brothers in the best part of the land. Let them live in Goshen. And if you know of any among them with special ability, put them in charge of my own livestock."** This is recorded not only to show that Jacob was courteously received but also that nothing was given to him by Joseph except at the king's command. Although Joseph, with the king's permission, placed his family in the middle of the best pastures, yet he did not avail himself of the other part of the royal beneficence—to make his brothers keepers of the king's cattle. For this privilege would have made the Egyptians jealous. Also he did not want to be entangled in such a snare.

**7. Then Joseph brought his father Jacob in and presented him before Pharaoh. After Jacob blessed Pharaoh . . .** Jacob is said to have **blessed Pharaoh.** By this term Moses does not mean a common and profane salutation, but the pious and holy prayer of a servant of God. For the children of this world greet kings and princes for the sake of honor, but not to in any way raise their thoughts to God. Jacob acted differently from this. For he added to civil reverence that pious affection that made him commend the safety of the king to God. In the same way Jeremiah prescribed the rule to the Jews that they should pray for the peace of

Babylon as long as they were in exile, because in the peace of that land and empire their own peace would be involved (Jeremiah 29:7).

If this duty was enjoined on miserable captives, forcibly deprived of their liberty and torn from their own country, how much more did Jacob owe it to a king so humane and beneficent? But whatever character they may be who rule over us, we are commanded to offer up public prayers for them (1 Timothy 2:1-2). Therefore, the same subjection to authority is required from each of us.

**8. Pharaoh asked him, "How old are you?"** This personal question proved that Jacob was received courteously and without ceremony. But the answer is of far greater importance, as Jacob declared that he had been on his pilgrimage for 130 years (verse 9). The apostle, in his epistle to the Hebrews (11:13-16), gathers from this the memorable doctrine that God was not ashamed to be called the God of the patriarchs because they confessed themselves to be "strangers" and pilgrims on the earth. As they were not ashamed to wander for all their lives and to be called foreigners and strangers wherever they went, so God gave them the incomparable dignity of being heirs of heaven.

But no one ever had a more special and hereditary possession in the world than the holy fathers had in the land of Canaan. In what spirit, then, should we live in a world where no permanent place to live has been promised to us? Therefore, whether one remains in his own country or is compelled continually to move, let him diligently meditate on the fact that he is on a journey for a short time on earth, until he moves on to the heavenly country.

**9. And Jacob said to Pharaoh, "The years of my pilgrimage are a hundred and thirty. My years have been few and difficult, and they do not equal the years of the pilgrimage of my fathers."** Jacob here seemed to complain that he had lived but a little while, and that in this short space of time he had endured many afflictions. Why did he not rather recount the great favors of God that abundantly compensated for every kind of evil? Besides, his complaint about the brevity of life seemed unworthy of him. For why did he not think that 100 years and an additional thirty years were enough for him?

But if anyone will rightly weigh Jacob's words, they will see that he is really expressing his own gratitude, celebrating the goodness of God toward his fathers. For he did not so much deplore his own decrepitude but rather extolled the vigor divinely given to his fathers. It is as if he said, "I indeed have reached the age that is deemed by others to be mature old age. But the Lord so prolonged the life of my fathers that they far exceeded this limit." He mentioned that his years had been **difficult** to show that he was not so much infirm due to old age, but had been burdened by labors and troubles. It was as if he said, "My senses might yet have flourished in their prime if my strength had not been exhausted by continual labors, by excessive cares, and by severe sufferings." We now see that nothing was further from the mind of the holy man than to expostulate with God.

**12. Joseph also provided his father and his brothers and all his father's household with food, according to the number of their children.** This means that Joseph fed everyone, from the greatest to the least. Therefore, there was enough bread for the whole family of Jacob because, through Joseph's care, even **their children** were **provided** for. In this way Moses commemorates both the clemency of God and the piety of Joseph; for it was an instance of uncommon attention that these hungry shepherds, who had not a grain of corn, were entirely fed at his expense.

**13. There was no food, however, in the whole region because the famine was severe; both Egypt and Canaan wasted away because of the famine.** It was a memorable judgment of God that the most fertile regions, which were accustomed to supply provisions for distant nations, were reduced to such poverty. Therefore, those who cultivate fertile lands are not to trust in their abundance; rather, let them acknowledge that a large supply of provision does not so much spring from the earth but rather flows from heaven by God's hidden blessing. For there is no wealth that is so great that it is not soon exchanged for bankruptcy when God sprinkles it with salt instead of rain. Meanwhile, it is right to turn our eyes to that special kindness of God by which he nourishes his own people in the middle of famine, as is said in Psalm 37:19.

If, however, God is pleased to try us with famine, we must pray that he would prepare us to endure hunger with a meek mind, lest we should rage like fierce, ravenous wild beasts. Although it is possible that grievous commotions were raised during the protracted scarcity, yet the more straightforward meaning of the passage seems to me to be that the Egyptians and Canaanites had sunk under the famine and were lying prostrate, at the point of death.

Moreover, Moses pursues the history of the famine to show that Joseph's prediction was proved to be true in this event. Also, by his skill and industry, the greatest dangers were so well and skillfully provided against that Egypt justly acknowledged him as the agent of their deliverance.

**14. Joseph collected all the money that was to be found in Egypt and Canaan in payment for the grain they were buying, and he brought it to Pharaoh's palace.** Moses first declares that the Egyptian king had acted well and wisely in committing the work of providing corn to the sole care and authority of Joseph. He then commends the sincere and faithful administration of Joseph himself. We know how few people can handle the money of kings without becoming defiled. Such great sums of money provide opportunity for dishonest, personal gain. But Moses says that whatever money Joseph **collected**, he brought to the house of the king. It is a rare and unparalleled integrity to keep one's hands pure in the middle of such heaps of gold. Joseph would not have been able to conduct himself with such moderation unless his divine calling had been like a bridle holding him back.

**15. When the money of the people of Egypt and Canaan was gone, all Egypt came to Joseph and said, "Give us food. Why should we die before your eyes? Our money is used up."** Moses does not mean that all the money in Egypt had been brought into the royal treasury; for many of the nobles of the court were free from the effects of the famine. What Moses means is that nearly everyone had been exhausted by the famine, and that now the ordinary people did not have enough money to buy corn. So the Egyptians had to employ a second solution to the problem, which Moses goes on to relate.

Many people in similar circumstances would have rebelled against Joseph. Yet the context shows that nothing was farther from their minds than to upset by their rash behavior the man whose compassion might provide more food for them.

Therefore they asked, **"Why should we die before your eyes?"** This means that they felt they were at their wits' end. They could only beg for him to have mercy on them and to bring relief to their plight.

**16. "Then bring your livestock," said Joseph. "I will sell you food in exchange for your livestock, since your money is gone."** It was a miserable spectacle, and one that might have softened hearts of iron, to see rich farmers who previously had stored provisions in their granaries for others now reduced to begging for food. Therefore, Joseph might be thought to be cruel because he did not freely give bread to those who were poor and exhausted but robbed them of all their cattle, sheep, and donkeys.

Seeing, however, that Joseph was acting on behalf of someone other than himself, I do not dare accuse him of being cruel. If during the seven fruitful years he had extorted corn by force from an unwilling people, he would now have acted in a tyrannical way by seizing their flocks and herds. But seeing that they had the freedom to accumulate in their private stores what they had sold to the king, they now paid the just penalty of their negligence. Joseph also perceived that they were deprived of their possessions by a divine interposition, so that the king alone might be enriched by these spoils from them all. Besides, since it was lawful for him to offer corn for sale, it was also lawful for him to exchange it for cattle. Truly, the corn belonged to the king; why then should he not demand payment from those who bought it?

**18. When that year was over, they came to him the following year and said, "We cannot hide from our lord the fact that since our money is gone and our livestock belongs to you, there is nothing left for our lord except our bodies and our land."** Moses does not calculate **the following year** from the date of the famine, but from the time when the money had failed. But since they knew from the oracle that the end of the dearth was in sight, they did not just want corn for food, but also for seed. From this it is clear that they had become wise too late and had neglected God's helpful admonition and had not provided for their future when they had the opportunity. Moreover, when they declared that their **money** and **livestock** had failed, they did so not in order to argue with Joseph, as if they had been unjustly deprived of these things by him, but to show that the only thing they had left with which to purchase food and seed was their **bodies** and their **land**. There was no other way they would survive if Joseph would not enter into this deal with them. For it would have been impudent to offer nothing in exchange for the food that they so desperately needed. So they began by saying that they had nothing in their hands to offer in exchange for food and that, therefore, their lives would be lost unless Joseph was willing to buy their lands.

**22. However, he did not buy the land of the priests, because they received a regular allotment from Pharaoh and had food enough from the allotment Pharaoh gave them. That is why they did not sell their land.** The priests were exempt from the common law because the king provided for them. Moses wanted to point out that a heathen king paid particular attention to divine worship in freely supporting the priests so that their lands and their property were spared. Truly this is set before us like a mirror, in which we may discern that a desire for piety, which men cannot wholly efface, was implanted in their minds. These priests only spread wicked superstitions; yet they were in one sense worthy of commendation. At least Pharaoh did not allow the worship of God to be totally neglected, which in a short time would have happened if the priests had perished in the famine.

From this we infer how much we ought to be on our guard, and that we should never undertake anything with misplaced zeal. For nothing is easier, as human nature is so corrupt, than for religion to degenerate into frivolous trifles. Nevertheless, because this inconsiderate devotion (as it may be called) flowed from a right principle, how should our rulers behave who desire to be deemed Christians? If Pharaoh was so solicitous about his priests, what a sacrilege it is for Christian rulers to neglect the ministry of holy things.

But it may be asked whether it was lawful for holy Joseph to undertake this work, for in doing this, did he not use his labor to cherish impious superstitions? Though I can readily grant that in such great, arduous, and varied offices of trust, it was easy for him to slide into various faults, yet I dare not absolutely condemn this act. Nor can I, however, deny that he may have erred in not resisting these superstitions with sufficient boldness. But since he was required by no law to destroy the priests by hunger and was not allowed to dispense the king's corn as he may have desired, if the king wished that food should be gratuitously supplied to the priests, Joseph was no more at liberty to deny it to them than to the nobles at court. Therefore, though he did not willingly take charge of such dependents, yet when the king imposed the duty upon him, he could not refuse it, though he knew they were not worthy of being fed like oxen.

**23. Joseph said to the people, "Now that I have bought you and your land today for Pharaoh, here is seed for you so you can plant the ground."** Here Moses describes Joseph's remarkable humanity. The men who were entirely destitute, and in a sense exiles, Joseph reinstated, on the most reasonable condition that they should pay one fifth of their harvest to the king (verse 24). It is well-known that in various places kings have demanded by law the payment of one tenth of a person's harvest. But in the time of war they doubled this tax. Therefore, what harm can we say was done to the Egyptians when Joseph exacted the payment of one fifth of the harvest for the king?

**27. Now the Israelites settled in Egypt in the region of Goshen. They acquired property there and were fruitful and increased greatly in number.** Moses does not mean that Jacob and his sons were proprietors of that land in which Pharaoh had allowed them to live in the same way in which the other parts of Egypt were given to the inhabitants for a perpetual possession. But they lived there for a time and were provided for. Hence they quickly grew in number. Therefore, what Moses says here summarizes what happened over many years in the future. Moses now returns to the proper thread of his narrative, in which he set out to show how God protected his church from many deaths; and not that only, but God wonderfully exalted it by his own hidden power.

**28. Jacob lived in Egypt seventeen years, and the years of his life were a hundred and forty-seven.** It was no ordinary temptation for the holy old man to be an exile from the land of Canaan for so many years. But on account of the famine, he was compelled to go to Egypt. Why could he not return when the fifth year had passed? He did not lie there in a state of torpor, but he remained quiet because he was not allowed to leave. In this respect, God did not lightly exercise his patience. For however sweet the delights of Egypt might be, Jacob was sad to be deprived of the sight of that land that was the living proof of his heavenly country. With the men of this world, earthly advantage would have prevailed; but such was the piety of the holy man that the profit of the flesh weighed nothing against the loss of spiritual good. But he was more deeply wounded when he saw his death approaching because not only was he himself deprived of the inheritance promised to him, but he was leaving his sons, of doubtful or at least feeble faith, buried in Egypt as in a tomb. Moreover, his example is given to us, that our minds may not languish by the weariness of a protracted warfare. The more Satan attempts to weigh us down with earthly concerns, the more we must fervently look to and soar toward heaven.

**29. When the time drew near for Israel to die, he called for his son Joseph and said to him, "If I have found favor in your eyes, put your**

hand under my thigh and promise that you will show me kindness and faithfulness. Do not bury me in Egypt." From this we infer not only the anxiety of Jacob, but his invincible magnanimity. It demonstrates his great courage that none of the wealth or the pleasures of Egypt could so allure him that he stopped longing for the land of Canaan, in which he had always lived a painful and laborious life.

But the constancy of his faith is seen even more clearly when he ordered that his dead body should be carried back to Canaan. This encouraged his sons to have hope about their eventual deliverance from Egypt. In this way, although he was dead, he animated those who were alive and remained, as if he were a trumpet sounding in their ears. Why else should Jacob take such trouble about where he would be buried? Clearly he did this so that God's promise might be confirmed to his posterity. Therefore, though his faith was tossed about by turbulent waves, he was far from suffering shipwreck. He even managed to guide others into the haven.

"Put your hand under my thigh and promise that you will show me kindness and faithfulness." Moreover, Jacob's insistence that his son Joseph should take an oath about this showed that it was a matter of the greatest consequence. Certainly Joseph would not take God's name in vain by swearing in a lighthearted manner. For the more sacred and solemn the promise was, the more all Jacob's sons would remember that it was most important that his body be carried to the tomb of his fathers.

It is also probable that Jacob prudently thought of alleviating any enmity that might be brought against his son Joseph. For he knew that this choice of his tomb would not be popular with the Egyptians, as it appeared to be a rejection of their whole nation. "This stranger, as if he could find no fit place for his body in this splendid and noble country, wishes to be buried in the land of Canaan." Therefore, so that Joseph might dare to ask this favor from the king, Jacob bound him by an oath. Later Joseph used this as a pretext, to avoid giving offense. Jacob also asked Joseph to do this because it involved all the brothers.

30. "But when I rest with my fathers, carry me out of Egypt and bury me where they are buried." "I will do as you say," he said. It appears from this passage that the word rest, whenever it is used instead of the word die, does not refer to the soul but to the body. For what did it matter to him to be buried with his fathers unless it bore witness that he was associated with them after death? And what bound them together except that not even death itself could extinguish the power of their faith? From the same tomb this voice would seem to speak. Such is our common inheritance.

31. "Swear to me," he said. Then Joseph swore to him, and Israel worshiped as he leaned on the top of his staff. By this expression, he leaned on the top of his staff, Moses again affirms that Jacob thought it a special kindness that his son should promise to do what he asked for con-

cerning his burial. He exerted his weak body inasmuch as he was able in order to give thanks to God, as if he had obtained something most desirable. He is said to have **worshiped** toward the head of his bed because, seeing he was quite unable to rise from the bed on which he lay, he yet composed himself with a solemn air as one who was praying. The same is recorded of David (1 Kings 1:47) when, having obtained his last wish, he celebrated the grace of God. The Greeks have translated this part of the verse as **the top of his staff.** The apostle repeats this in the epistle to the Hebrews (11:21). Let it suffice for us to remember that by this ceremony Jacob openly manifested the greatness of his joy.

# Genesis
# Chapter 48

**1. Some time later Joseph was told, "Your father is ill." So he took his two sons Manasseh and Ephraim along with him.** Moses now passes to the last event in Jacob's life, which, as we shall see, was especially worthy of being remembered. For since he knew that he had been given a special task by God in being made the father of the fathers of the church, he fulfilled, in the immediate prospect of death, the prophetic office about the future state of the church. Most people arrange their domestic affairs through their last will, but this holy man used a very different way because God had established his covenant with him that had to continue with his descendants.

But before I continue with this subject, two things must be observed. First of all, Moses briefly alludes to the fact that as soon as Joseph was told about his father's sickness, he immediately went to see him. Second, Jacob, when he learned of Joseph's arrival, **sat up on the bed** (verse 2), as his way of honoring his son. Joseph counted it much more important to carry out his duties toward his own family than to preside over a hundred kingdoms. For in bringing **his two sons** with him, he behaved as if he would emancipate them from the country in which they had been born and restore them to their own family. For they could not be thought of as belonging to the progeny of Abraham unless they were detested by the Egyptians. Nevertheless, Joseph preferred that reproach for them to every kind of wealth and glory, if they would but become one with the sacred body of the church.

**3-4. Jacob said to Joseph, "God Almighty appeared to me at Luz in the land of Canaan, and there he blessed me and said to me, 'I am going to make you fruitful and will increase your numbers. I will make you a community of peoples, and I will give this land as an everlasting possession to your descendants after you.'"** The holy man's aim was to withdraw his son from the wealth and honors of Egypt and to reunite him to the holy race, from which he had been for a little while separated.

Moreover, he did not either proudly boast of his own excellence, nor of his present riches, nor of his power for the sake of inducing his son to comply with his wishes, but simply set before him God's covenant. So it is also right that the grace of adoption, as soon as it is offered to us, should, by filling our thoughts, extinguish our desire for everything splendid and costly in the world.

This is a remarkable passage. Joseph was held in the highest honor in Egypt. But in place of all the riches and honors of Egypt, Jacob placed the vision in which God had adopted himself and his race as his own people. Whenever, therefore, Satan tries to entangle us with the allurements of the world, that he may draw us away from heaven, let us remember to what we are called. In comparison with the inestimable treasure of eternal life, all that the flesh can offer should be considered as nothing. For if holy Joseph held an obscure vision in such esteem that for this sole object, forgetting Egypt, he gladly passed over to the despised flock of the church, how shameful it would be for us today if we are not moved as much as he was, since our heavenly Father has opened the gate of his kingdom and invites us to himself.

At the same time, however, we must observe that holy Jacob did not impose vain imaginations in order to allure his son. He placed before him the sure promise of God, on which he could safely rely. From this we are taught that our faith is not rightly founded on anything except the sole word of God. We are further taught that this is a sufficiently firm support for our faith, to prevent it from ever being shaken or overthrown by any kind of devices. Wherefore, whenever Satan attempts to draw us here or there through his enticements, let us learn to turn our minds to the Word of God. We must rely on it so firmly that we may spurn those things that the flesh now sees and touches. Jacob said that God appeared to him in the land of **Canaan**, so that Joseph, aspiring after that land, might become alienated in his heart from the kingdom of Egypt.

5. **"Now then, your two sons born to you in Egypt before I came to you here will be reckoned as mine; Ephraim and Manasseh will be mine, just as Reuben and Simeon are mine."** Jacob conferred on his son a special privilege. He made Joseph's two sons succeed to an equal right with their uncles, as if they had been heirs in the first place. What is this? Here is a decrepit old man assigning to his grandchildren, as a royal patrimony, a sixth part of the land that he had entered as a stranger and from which he was now an exile! Who would not have said that he was dealing in fables? It is a common proverb that no one can give what he has not. How could Joseph benefit in any way from his father? But from this it is clear how strong a faith the holy fathers had as they relied on the word of the Lord. Joseph chose to rely on what Jacob said rather than seek an inheritance in the land in which he lived.

Jacob was dying an exile in Egypt. He summoned the governor of

Egypt and called him to exchange his great wealth and status and become an exile. But Joseph was happy about this because he acknowledged that his father was God's prophet.

Jacob also commanded Joseph's other sons (if there should be any) to be reckoned in the families of these two brothers (verse 6). It is as if he directed them to be adopted by the two whom he himself now adopted.

**7. "As I was returning from Paddan, to my sorrow Rachel died in the land of Canaan while we were still on the way, a little distance from Ephrath. So I buried her there beside the road to Ephrath"** (that is, Bethlehem). Jacob mentioned the death and burial of his wife Rachel, so that the name of Joseph's mother might stay in his mind.

**8. When Israel saw the sons of Joseph, he asked, "Who are these?"** I have no doubt that Israel asked who the youths were before he called them to be his heirs. In Joseph's answer we observe that the fruit of the womb is not born by chance but is to be reckoned as a precious gift from God. Everyone is quite prepared to agree with this. But few people heartily acknowledge that their children have been given to them by God. And so a large proportion of man's offspring becomes continually more and more degenerate. For the ingratitude of the world makes it unable to perceive the effect of God's blessings.

**9-11. "They are the sons God has given me here," Joseph said to his father. Then Israel said, "Bring them to me so I may bless them." Now Israel's eyes were failing because of old age, and he could hardly see. So Joseph brought his sons close to him, and his father kissed them and embraced them. Israel said to Joseph, "I never expected to see your face again, and now God has allowed me to see your children too."** We must briefly consider Moses' purpose here. He shows that a solemn symbol was given through which the adoption might be ratified. Jacob put his hands upon his grandsons (verse 13). Jacob did this to demonstrate that he gave them a place among his sons. He ordered them to be brought close to him, that he might confer on them a new honor, as if he had been appointed to dispense this from the Lord himself.

**12. Then Joseph removed them from Israel's knees and bowed down with his face to the ground.** Moses explains more fully what he had touched upon in a single word. Joseph knew that his sons were going to receive a blessing from God's prophet. He knew for certain that holy Jacob did not want to embrace his grandsons in the normal way, because he was going to pass on God's blessing to them. In this way they would be two of the patriarchs of the church and would hold an honorable preeminence in the spiritual kingdom of God.

**14. But Israel reached out his right hand and put it on Ephraim's head, though he was the younger, and crossing his arms, he put his left hand on Manasseh's head, even though Manasseh was the firstborn.** So we see that **Israel** deliberately crossed his arms. He wanted to place **his**

**right hand . . . on Ephraim, who was the younger.** He wanted to place **his left hand** on **the firstborn.** We gather that the Holy Spirit directed this action. The Spirit irradiated the mind of the holy man and through this symbolic act made him see more correctly than those who could see most clearly.

**15. Then he blessed Joseph and said, "May the God before whom my fathers Abraham and Isaac walked, the God who has been my shepherd all my life to this day . . ."** Although Jacob knew that a dispensation of the grace of God was committed to him, so that he might effectually bless his grandchildren, yet he arrogated nothing to himself but suppliantly resorted to prayer, lest he should in the smallest way detract from the glory of God. As he was the legitimate administrator of the blessing, so he had to acknowledge that God was its sole Author.

From this we deduce something that all the ministers and pastors of the church should observe carefully. For although they are not only called witnesses of God's heavenly grace but are also entrusted with the dispensation of spiritual gifts, yet when they are compared with God, they are nothing. For God alone contains all things within himself. Wherefore let them learn to willingly keep their own place, lest they should obscure God's name.

**16. ". . . the Angel who has delivered me from all harm—may he bless these boys. May they be called by my name and the names of my fathers Abraham and Isaac, and may they increase greatly upon the earth."** Jacob linked the angel to God as if he were an equal. He worshiped him and asked from him the same things he praised God for in verse 15. If you take this verse as a reference to an ordinary angel, the words are absurd. These words must be understood to refer to Christ, who is intentionally given the title of **Angel** because he has been and is the perpetual Mediator.

Christ had not yet been sent by the Father to put on our flesh, that he might come nearer to us; but he was always the link joining men to God, and God did not reveal himself in any other way than through him. Therefore, he is rightly called an angel or messenger. For there has always been such a gap between God and man that there could be no communication without a Mediator.

But although Christ has appeared in the form of an angel, we must hold to what is said in Hebrews 2:16—that Christ did not put on the nature of an angel and become one of the angels—he became a man. When the angels are clothed with a human body, they do not become men.

Moreover, we are taught by these words that the true gift of Christ to us is that he guards us and rescues us from all evils. And we must, therefore, take heed that our faithless forgetfulness does not bury this gift, which has been shown to us more clearly than it was formerly to the saints under the law. For Christ proclaimed openly that the faithful are brought into his protection and that none of them will perish.

His help is, indeed, especially necessary for us today. For if we think over all the dangers that surround us, we can scarcely find a day in which we were not rescued from a thousand deaths. And how does this happen unless we are under the care of God's Son, who took us from his Father's hand to watch over us?

**"May they be called by my name."** This is a mark of their adoption. He put his name on them so that they would obtain a place among the patriarchs. Indeed, the Hebrew phrase signifies nothing other than to be reckoned among the family of Jacob. Thus the wife is called by the name of the husband (Isaiah 4:1) because the wife borrows the name from the head to which she is subject. In summary, we can say that the Lord would complete in them what he had promised to the patriarchs.

**17. When Joseph saw his father placing his right hand on Ephraim's head he was displeased; so he took hold of his father's hand to move it from Ephraim's head to Manasseh's head.** By crossing his arms, Jacob had placed his hands so that his left hand was on the head of the firstborn. Joseph wanted to correct this as if his father had made a mistake. He thought he had done this because of his poor sight. But his father had followed the Spirit of God as his secret guide, so that he might transfer the title of honor, which nature had conferred upon the elder, to the younger. As he did not rashly assume the office of conveying the blessing, so it was not right for him to attempt anything from himself and according to his own will. And at length it was evident by the event that whatever he had done had been dictated to him from heaven.

**19. But his father refused and said, "I know, my son, I know. He too will become a people, and he too will become great. Nevertheless, his younger brother will be greater than he, and his descendants will become a group of nations."** Jacob did not dispute which of the youths would be the more worthy. He only pronounced what God had decreed about each of them. Jacob simply said that Ephraim would have more descendants than Manasseh. Meanwhile, sinful emulation was forbidden when he commanded Manasseh to be content with his lot. Scripture defines in one word that the people who are called to salvation are the ones whom God has chosen (Romans 8:29), and that the primary source of election is his free good pleasure.

**21. Then Israel said to Joseph, "I am about to die, but God will be with you and take you back to the land of your fathers."** Jacob repeated what he had already said. And truly all his sons, and especially Joseph and his sons, required something more than one simple confirmation, so that they might not live forever in Egypt but might dwell, in their minds, in the land of Canaan. Jacob mentioned his own death to teach them that the eternal truth of God by no means depends on the life of men. It is as if he said, "My life, since it is short and fading, passes away; but God's promise, which has no limit, will flourish when I am dead."

No vision had been seen by his sons, but God had ordained the holy old man to be the one to convey the promises of the covenant. He, therefore, told them that their faith would not be shaken by his death. So when the Lord delivers his word to the world by mortal men, although they die, having finished their course of life according to the flesh, yet the voice of God is not snuffed out in them but brings us life, even to this present day. Therefore, Peter writes that even after he had died, the church would recall the teaching that had been committed to him (2 Peter 1:15).

22. **"And to you, as one who is over your brothers, I give the ridge of land I took from the Amorites with my sword and my bow."** In order to increase the confidence of his son Joseph, Jacob here bequeathed him a special piece of land. Jacob wanted to testify that he had taken nothing by means of his two sons Simeon and Levi, who behaved like robbers. When Jacob stripped them of their empty title, he transferred this right of victory to himself, as being divinely given to him. For though he always detested their wickedness, yet because they had armed his whole household, they fought as under his auspices. Gladly would he have preserved the citizens of Shechem, a design that he was not able to accomplish. Yet he appropriated to himself the land left empty and deserted by their destruction because for his sake God had spared the murderers.

# Genesis
## Chapter 49

**1. Then Jacob called for his sons and said: "Gather around so I can tell you what will happen to you in days to come."** In the previous chapter, the blessing on Ephraim and Manasseh was related because, before Jacob spoke about the whole nation that was about to spring from him, it was right that these two grandsons should be added to the number of his sons. Now, as if carried above the heavens, he announced, not like any human being, but as from the mouth of God, what would happen to each of his sons in the future.

It is right to note that as Jacob had then thirteen sons, he mentioned the same number of nations or tribes. In this Jacob's strong faith shone brightly for all to see. For since he had often heard from the Lord that his descendants would so increase that they would become a multitude of people, this oracle was to him like a sublime mirror, in which he could perceive things deeply hidden from human senses.

Moreover, this was not a simple confession of faith by which Jacob testified that he hoped for whatever had been promised him by the Lord. Jacob was superior to men, for he was God's interpreter and ambassador, through whom future regulations about the church were given. Some interpreters who saw how noble and magnificent this prophecy is have added new mysteries to it. In this way they have tried to extract profound allegories from it; but in doing so, they have departed from the genuine meaning of the words. But so we do not depreciate the literal sense of these verses, let us note the purpose of the Holy Spirit.

In the first place, the sons of Jacob were informed beforehand of their future fortune that they might know themselves to be objects of God's special care. Although the whole world is governed by God's providence, they are preferred to other nations, as members of his own household. It seems apparently a mean and contemptible thing that a region productive of vines that would yield an abundance of choice wine, an area rich in pastures that would supply milk, was promised to the tribe of Judah. But if anyone will consider that the Lord is here giving an illustrious demonstration of his own election in descending like the father of a family, caring for their food, and also showing in minute things that he was united by the sacred bond of a covenant to the children of Abraham, he will look for no deeper mystery.

In the second place, the hope of the promised inheritance was again renewed to them. Therefore, Jacob, as if he would put them in possession of the land by his own hand, expounded what kind of place each person would live in. Can the confirmation of a matter so serious appear contemptible to sane and prudent readers? It is, however, the principal purpose of Jacob to point out from where a king would come from among them.

**"Gather around so I can tell you what will happen to you in days to come."** Jacob began by inviting them to pay attention to him (see verse 2). He started by speaking seriously and claimed for himself the authority of a prophet, in order to teach his sons that he was by no means making a statement about their family affairs. He told them about those oracles that had been entrusted to him. For he did not command them simply to listen to his own wishes, but gathered them together so they could hear what would happen to them in the future. Moreover, I do not doubt that he contrasted this future period about which he spoke with their exile in Egypt.

Now, from the above remarks it may be easily inferred that this prophecy referred to the whole period from the departure out of Egypt to the reign of Christ. Jacob did not enumerate every event, but in the summary of things on which he briefly touched, he arranged a settled order and course until Christ appears.

**3. "Reuben, you are my firstborn, my might, the first sign of my strength, excelling in honor, excelling in power."** He began with the firstborn, not to confirm him in his rank, but so that he might be completely humble. For Reuben is here (verses 3-4) cast down from his primogeniture because he had polluted his father's bed by incestuous intercourse with his mother-in-law. These words mean: "You are indeed, by nature, the firstborn, and you should have excelled. But since you flowed away like water, you have no grounds for boasting. For from the day you committed incest, the status that you received on the day of your birth has vanished." Nothing wounds us more than when we compare the favors that God bestows on us with the punishments that we bring on ourselves.

**4. "Turbulent as the waters, you will no longer excel, for you went up onto your father's bed, onto my couch and defiled it."** Jacob showed that Reuben was not strong but evanescent, and so he rejected him from the inheritance that had belonged to him as the oldest brother. Jacob gave Reuben the reason for this in case his son should complain that he was being punished though he was innocent. For it was most important that he should be convinced of his fault, in case he did not benefit from his punishment. We now see Jacob, who has put all earthly affection to one side, doing the work of a prophet with vigor and magnanimity. This judgment should not be attributed to his anger, as if the father desired to take private revenge on his son. Rather, it proceeded from the Spirit of God as Jacob kept in mind the burden imposed on him.

**5. "Simeon and Levi are brothers—their swords are weapons of violence."** Jacob condemned the massacre of the city of Shechem by his two sons Simeon and Levi. From this we learn how much God hates cruelty, since man's blood is precious in his sight. It is as if he judged these two men when they thought they had already escaped being punished.

It may, however, be asked if pardon had not been granted to them long ago. If God had already forgiven them, why does Jacob call them to account again? It was necessary that this slaughter should not remain unpunished, even though the two men might have already been forgiven. Therefore the Lord, partly to humble them and partly to make them an example for all ages, inflicted on them the punishment of perpetual ignominy.

**7. "Cursed be their anger, so fierce, and their fury, so cruel! I will scatter them in Jacob and disperse them in Israel."** We are divinely admonished by the mouth of the holy prophet, so that we will keep away from all wicked counsels. Jacob pronounced a woe upon their **anger**. Why is this, unless others may learn to restrain themselves and to be on their guard against such cruelty? However, it is not enough to keep our hands pure, unless we do not associate at all with crime.

**"I will scatter them in Jacob and disperse them in Israel."** It may seem a strange way to proceed that Jacob, while designating his sons patriarchs of the church and calling them heirs of the divine covenant, should pronounce a curse on them instead of a blessing. Nevertheless, it was necessary for him to begin with the chastisement, as this would prepare the way for the manifestation of God's grace. But God mitigates the punishment by giving them an honorable name in the church.

God, who in the beginning produced light out of darkness, found another reason why the Levites should be dispersed among the people, and this reason was not only free from disgrace but was highly honorable. God made sure that no corner of the land did not have competent instructors. Further, God made them overseers and governors, in his name, over every part of the land, as if he wanted to scatter the seed of eternal salvation everywhere, and so he sent out ministers of his grace. From this we conclude how much better it was for Levi to be punished at the time, for his own good, than to be left to perish in consequence of present impunity in sin.

**8. "Judah, your brothers will praise you; your hand will be on the neck of your enemies; your father's sons will bow down to you."** In the word **praise** there is an allusion to the name of Judah. He had been given this name by his mother because his birth had been an occasion for praising God.

"**Your hand will be on the neck of your enemies.**" By these words Moses shows that Judah would not be free from enemies. While many of them would trouble him and attempt to deprive him of his right, Jacob promised Judah victory. This did not mean that the sons of David would always prevail against their enemies, for their ingratitude interfered with the constant grace of God. But in this respect at least, Judah had the upper hand because in his tribe stood the royal throne that God approved and that was founded on his word. Although the kingdom of Israel was more wealthy and had a bigger population, because it rejected God it never became the object of God's favor. Nor was it right that its tarnished splendor should eclipse the glory of the divine election that was engraved on the tribe of Judah. In David, therefore, the force and effect of this prophecy plainly appeared. It appeared again in Solomon's reign. In this way the children of Judah imposed their yoke **on the neck of** their enemies. When defection carried away ten tribes that would not bow their knees to the sons of David, the legitimate government was disturbed and lawless confusion introduced. Yet nothing could violate God's decree, by which the right to govern remained with the tribe of Judah.

9. "**You are a lion's cub, O Judah; you return from the prey, my son. Like a lion he crouches and lies down, like a lioness—who dares to rouse him?**" This metaphor confirms the preceding verse's assertion that Judah would be formidable to his enemies. Yet Jacob seemed to allude to that diminution that took place when most of the people rebelled in Jeroboam's day. At that time the king of Judah looked like a sleeping **lion,** for he did not shake his mane to diffuse his terror far and wide but, as it were, lay down in his den. Yet God's secret power lay hidden under that slumber, and those who most longed for his destruction and who were most able to harm him did not dare to disturb him. Therefore, after Jacob had transferred the supreme authority over his brothers to Judah alone, he added by way of correction that though his power should happen to be diminished, he would nevertheless be feared by his enemies, like a **lion** who lies down in his lair.

10. "**The scepter will not depart from Judah, nor the ruler's staff from between his feet, until he comes to whom it belongs and the obedience of the nations is his.**" Although this passage is obscure, it would not have been very difficult to elicit its genuine meaning if the Jews had not endeavored to envelop it in clouds. It is certain that the Messiah, who was to spring from the tribe of Judah, was promised here. But whereas the Jews should have willingly run to embrace him, many purposely use every possible means to lead themselves and others astray. It is no wonder, then, that the spirit of bitterness and obstinacy and the lust of contention have so blinded them that, in the clearest light, they have perpetually stumbled.

Christians also, in a pious attempt to set forth the glory of Christ, have nevertheless been excessively fervent. When they lay too much stress on certain words, they only manage to ridicule the Jews.

Warned by these examples, let us seek, without contention, the true meaning of the passage. In the first place, we must keep in mind the true purpose of the Holy Spirit, which until now has not been fully considered or expounded with sufficient care. After he had invested the tribe of Judah with supreme authority, Jacob immediately declared that God would show his care for the people by preserving the state of the kingdom. For the dignity of Judah was upheld in order to show that its proposed end was the common salvation of all people. The blessing promised to the seed of Abraham could not be firm unless it flowed from one head. Jacob now testified the same thing—namely, that a King would come, under whom the promised happiness would be complete in all its parts. Even the Jews will not deny that while a lower blessing rested on the tribe of Judah, the hope of a better and more excellent condition is set out here. They also freely grant another point—that the Messiah is the sole Author of full and solid happiness and glory. We now add a third point—that the kingdom that began from David was a kind of prelude, a shadowy representation of that greater grace that was delayed and held in suspense until the coming of the Messiah. They have indeed no relish for a spiritual kingdom; and therefore they rather imagine for themselves wealth and power and prefer sweet repose and earthly pleasures to righteousness and newness of life with free forgiveness of sins. They acknowledge, nevertheless, that the felicity that was to be expected under the Messiah was hinted at in their ancient kingdom. I now return to the words of Jacob.

The words **the scepter will not depart from Judah** refer to dominion. In short, the kingdom of the tribe of Judah will be no ordinary kingdom because from it, at length, will come the fullness of the promised blessing. To us also it is no less useful for the confirmation of our faith to know that Christ has been not only promised, but that his origin had been pointed out, as with a finger, 2,000 years before he appeared.

11. "**He will tether his donkey to a vine, his colt to the choicest branch; he will wash his garments in wine, his robes in the blood of grapes.**" He now spoke about the territory that fell by lot to the sons of Judah and intimated that the abundance of vines would be so great, they would be everywhere, just as brambles or unfruitful shrubs grow everywhere. Donkeys were usually tied to hedges, and he here reduced vines to this mundane use. The hyperbolic forms of speech that followed should be applied in the same way. Judah will **wash his garments in wine**. He meant that **wine** would be so abundant that it would be poured out to wash with, like water, at no great expense. It may seem to be wrong that intemperance or extravagance should be thought of as a blessing. I reply that although fertility and affluence are described here, this does not mean

they are sanctioned. If the Lord deals very bountifully with us, he may still, as a general rule, expect us to use his gifts with purity and frugality. But in this verse Jacob did not state what is lawful but just extolled the abundance of the **wine.** We should be amazed at the thought that Moses, who had never seen the land of Canaan, should mention its different areas so accurately, as if he had cultivated them with his own hand. If we suppose that he had heard about the existence of vines in the land in a general way, he still could not have assigned to Judah abundant vineyards, nor could he have assigned to him rich pastures by saying that **his teeth** would be **whiter than milk** (verse 12) unless he had been guided by the Spirit.

13. **"Zebulun will live by the seashore and become a haven for ships; his border will extend toward Sidon."** Although this blessing contains nothing rare or precious, as is the case with some of the others that follow, we should notice that it was just as if God were stretching out his hand from heaven for the deliverance of the children of Israel and to distribute to each his own dwelling-place. It is said that Zebulun's portion would not only be on the **seashore** but would also have havens; for Jacob placed this tribe's boundary next to the country of **Sidon,** where we know there were commodious and noble havens. God, by this prophecy, would not only stimulate the sons of Zebulun to prepare themselves to enter the land but would also assure them it was the home that had been ordained for them by God.

14-15. **"Issachar is a rawboned donkey lying down between two saddlebags. When he sees how good is his resting place and how pleasant is his land, he will bend his shoulder to the burden and submit to forced labor."** The inheritance is mentioned here, and an indication is given about the future condition of this tribe. Although he is called **a rawboned donkey** on account of his strength, at the same time his laziness is indicated; for it is added a little later that he would have a servile disposition. This means that the sons of Issachar, although they were very strong, were quiet rather than courageous and could bear burdens like mules do as they submit their backs to the packsaddle and the load. The reason for this is that, being content with their fertile and pleasant country, they did not refuse to pay tribute to their neighbors, provided they could enjoy rest there. Although this submissiveness is not publicly mentioned either to their praise or their condemnation, it is probable that their indolence is censured, because their lack of energy hindered them from keeping possession of the freedom that God had given them.

16-17. **"Dan will provide justice for his people as one of the tribes of Israel. Dan will be a serpent by the roadside, a viper along the path that bites the horse's heels so that its rider tumbles backward."** Jacob now gave a new meaning to Dan's name; namely, the sons of Dan would have a significant part in ruling the people. The Jews foolishly restrict this to Samson because he alone presided over the whole people, whereas the language rather applies to the perpetual condition of the tribe. Jacob therefore meant that although Dan was born from a concubine, he would still be one of the judges of Israel. Not only would his offspring govern, but that tribe would be appointed the standard-bearer to lead the fourth division of the camp of Israel.

In the second place, his subtle disposition is described. For Jacob compared this people to serpents who rise out of their lurking-places by stealth against the unwary whom they want to injure. The sense, then, is that he shall not be so courageous to earnestly and boldly engage in open conflict but would fight with cunning and make use of snares. In the meantime, Jacob showed that Dan would be superior to his enemies, whom he does not dare to approach with collected forces, just as serpents, by their secret bite, throw down the horse and his rider. In this place also no statement is specifically made as to whether this subtlety of Dan—that instead of presenting himself in open conflict with his enemies, he would only fight them secretly—was to be deemed worthy of praise or of censure. But conjecture rather inclines us to place it among his faults, or at least his disadvantages.

**18. "I look for your deliverance, O Lord."** It may be asked, in the first place, what occasion induced the holy man to interrupt his discourse and suddenly introduce this expression. He had recently predicted the coming of the Messiah, and the mention of **deliverance** would have seemed more appropriate in that place. I think, indeed, that when he perceived, as from a lofty watchtower, the condition of his offspring continually exposed to various changes, and even to being tossed by storms that would almost overwhelm them, he was moved with concern and fear; for he had not so put off all paternal affection as to be entirely without care for those who were of his own blood. He, therefore, foreseeing many troubles, many dangers, many assaults, and even many slaughters that threatened his seed with destruction, could not but be troubled at the sight. But so that he might rise against every kind of temptation with victorious constancy of mind, he committed himself to the Lord, who had promised to be the guardian of his people. Unless this circumstance is observed, I do not see why Jacob exclaimed here, rather than at the beginning or the end of his discourse, that he waited for the salvation of the Lord. When this sad confusion of things presented itself to him, which was not only sufficiently violent to shake his faith but was more than sufficiently burdensome entirely to overwhelm his mind, his best solution was to present this shield against such an attack.

I doubt not also that he would advise his sons to rise with him with the same confidence. Moreover, because he could not be the author of his own salvation, it was necessary for him to rest on God's promise. In the same way also, we today must hope for the salvation of the church; for although it seems to be tossed on a turbulent sea and almost sunk in the waves, and though still greater storms are to be feared in the future, yet in the middle of manifold destructions, salvation is to be hoped for, in the deliverance that the Lord has promised. It is even possible that Jacob, foreseeing by the Spirit how great would be the ingratitude, perfidy, and wickedness of his posterity, by which the grace of God might be smothered, was battling against these temptations. But although he expected salvation not for himself alone, but for all his posterity, it deserves to be specially noted that he exhibited the life-giving covenant of God to many generations, to prove his own confidence that after his death God would be faithful to his promise.

From this it also follows that with his last breath and as if in the midst of death, he laid hold on eternal life. If he, in the middle of obscure shadows, relying on a redemption seen afar off, boldly went forth to meet death, what ought we do on whom the clear day has shined? What excuse remains for us if our minds fail amidst similar agitations?

**19. "Gad will be attacked by a band of raiders, but he will attack them at their heels."** Jacob also alluded to the name Gad. He had been so called because Jacob had obtained a numerous offspring by his mother Leah. His father now admonished him that though his name implied *a multitude*, he would yet have to deal with a great number of enemies, by whom, for a time, he would be oppressed. Jacob predicted this event, not so his posterity would depend on their own strength and become proud, but so they might prepare themselves to endure the suffering by which the Lord intended and now decreed to humble them. Yet, as he here exhorted them to patient endurance, so he presently raised and animated them with the special consolation that, at length, they would emerge from oppression and would triumph over those enemies by whom they had been vanquished and routed.

Moreover, this prophecy may be applied to the whole church, which is assailed not for one day only, but is perpetually crushed by fresh attacks, until at length God shall exalt it to honor.

**20. "Asher's food will be rich; he will provide delicacies fit for a king."** The inheritance of Asher is only alluded to. Jacob declared that Asher would be fruitful in the best and finest wheat, so that he would need no foreign supply of food since he had plenty of his own. By **delicacies fit for a king**, Jacob meant exquisite food. Should anyone object that it is no great thing to be fed with nutritious and pleasant bread, I reply that we must consider the purpose of this statement, which was so that they might know they were fed by God's paternal care.

**21. "Naphtali is a doe set free that bears beautiful fawns [KJV: he giveth goodly words]."** Some think that in the tribe of Naphtali fleetness is commended; I prefer another meaning—namely, that it would guard and defend itself by eloquence and suavity of words rather than by force of arms. It is an admirable virtue to soothe ferocious minds and to appease excited anger by calm and gentle discourse, or if any offense has been stirred up, to allay it by a similar ingenuity. He therefore assigned this praise to the sons of Naphtali—that they would rather study to fortify themselves by humanity, by sweet words, and by peace than by the defense of arms. He compared them to **a doe set free**, which, having been taken in hunting, is not put to death but is rather cherished with delicacies.

**22-24. "Joseph is a fruitful vine, a fruitful vine near a spring, whose branches climb over a wall. With bitterness archers attacked him; they shot at him with hostility. But his bow remained steady, his strong arms stayed limber, because of the hand of the Mighty One of Jacob, because of the Shepherd, the Rock of Israel."** The meaning of this figure is that Joseph was born to grow like a tree planted near a spring, so that by its beauty and lofty stature it might surmount the obstacles around it. His branches are said to **climb over a wall** when they spread themselves far and wide. Jacob's discourse did not relate simply to the whole tribe, nor was it a mere prophecy of future times; the personal history of Joseph was blended with that of his descendants. Thus some things are peculiar to himself, and others belong to the two tribes of Ephraim and Manasseh.

Whereas Jacob had compared him to a tree, he called both Joseph's brothers and Potiphar, with his wife, **archers**. Afterwards, however, he changed the figure by making Joseph himself like a strenuous archer whose **bow** is strong and whose arms do not relax. By these expressions he predicted the invincible fortitude of Joseph, because he had yielded to no blows no matter how hard and severe they were. At the same time we are taught that he stood, not by the power of his own arm, but was strengthened by the hand of God, whom Jacob gives the special title of **the Mighty One of Jacob**, who designed his power to be conspicuous and to shine most brightly in the church. He declared that Joseph received help from God, who had chosen that family for himself. The holy fathers were extremely eager that the gratuitous covenant of God should be remembered by themselves and by their children, whenever any benefit was granted to them. And truly it is a mark of shameful negligence not to inquire from what spring we drink water. In the meantime he tacitly censured the impious and ungodly fury of his ten sons because by attempting the murder of their brother, they, like the giants, had carried on war against God. He also admonished them because in the future they would not choose to be protected by God rather than to make him their enemy, though he wished to help them all. The sons of Jacob, therefore, needed to take care lest they, by confiding in their own strength, ruin themselves. Rather, they must bear themselves nobly and triumphantly in the Lord.

**25-26 ". . . because of your father's God, who helps you, because of the Almighty, who blesses you with blessings of the heavens above, blessings of the deep that lies below, blessings of the breast and womb.**

Your father's blessings are greater than the blessings of the ancient mountains, than the bounty of the age-old hills. Let all these rest on the head of Joseph, on the brow of the prince among his brothers." Again Jacob more fully affirmed that Joseph had been delivered from death and was exalted to such great dignity not by his own industry, but by God's favor. There is not the least doubt that he commended to all the pious the sheer goodness of God, in case they should arrogate anything to themselves, whether they may have escaped from dangers or whether they may have risen to any rank of honor.

It is as if he said, "Joseph, although you have proved the paternal care of God in his helping you, I want you to ascribe this to the covenant that God has made with me." After he declared that Joseph would be blessed in every way, both in respect to his own life and in respect to the number and preservation of his posterity, he affirmed that the effect of this blessing was near and almost present by saying that God blessed Joseph more efficaciously than Jacob himself had been blessed by his fathers. Although from the beginning God had been true to his promises, yet he frequently postponed the effect of them, as if he had been feeding Abraham, Isaac, and Jacob with nothing but words. For to what extent were the patriarchs multiplied in Egypt? Where was that immense seed that would equal the sands of the seashore and the stars of heaven? Therefore, not without reason, Jacob declared that the full time had arrived in which the result of his benediction, which had laid concealed, would emerge as from the deep. This comparison ought to inspire us with much greater alacrity at the present time, for the abundant riches of the grace of God that have flowed to us in Christ exceed a hundredfold any blessings that Joseph received and felt.

27. "Benjamin is a ravenous wolf; in the morning he devours the prey, in the evening he divides the plunder." Some of the Jews think the Benjamites are here condemned because, when they had allowed lusts to prevail like lawless robbers among them, they were at length cut down and almost destroyed by a terrible slaughter for having defiled the Levite's wife. Others regard it as an honorable encomium by which Saul or Mordecai was adorned, who were both of the tribe of Benjamin. The interpreters of our own age most inaptly apply it to the apostle Paul, who was changed from a wolf into a preacher of the Gospel. Nothing seems to me more probable than that the disposition and habits of the whole tribe is here delineated—namely, that they would live by plunder. "In the morning he devours the prey, in the evening he divides the plunder." By these words Jacob describes their diligence in looting.

28. All these are the twelve tribes of Israel, and this is what their father said to them when he blessed them, giving each the blessing appropriate to him. Moses teaches us by these words that his predictions did not apply only to the sons of Jacob but extended to their whole race. We have shown that the expressions relate not to these people only; this

verse was added so that the readers might more clearly perceive the heavenly majesty of the Spirit. Jacob beheld his twelve sons. Let us grant that at that time the number of his offspring, down to his great grandchildren, had increased a hundredfold. Jacob did not, however, merely declare what the condition of 600 or 1,000 men would be but included regions and nations. Nor did Jacob put himself rashly forward, since it is seen afterwards, by the event that God had certainly made known to him [i.e., the Exodus of the tribes of Israel from Egypt], what God had himself decreed to execute.

Moreover, seeing that Jacob beheld with the eyes of faith things that were not only very remote but altogether hidden from human sense, woe betide us if we close our eyes to the very accomplishment of the prediction in which the truth conspicuously appears.

But it may seem contrary to reason that Jacob is said to have blessed his posterity. For in deposing Reuben from the primogeniture, he pronounced nothing joyous or prosperous about him; he also declared his abhorrence of Simeon and Levi. I reconcile these things with each other like this: The temporal punishments with which Jacob mildly and paternally corrected his sons would not subvert the covenant of grace on which the benediction was founded. Rather, by obliterating their stains it would restore them to the original degree of honor from which they had fallen, so that at least they would be patriarchs among the people of God. And the Lord daily proves in his own people that the punishments he lays upon them, although they occasion shame and disgrace, are so far from opposing their happiness that they rather promote it. Unless they were purified in this way, it was feared that they might become more and more hardened in their vices. We see how freely the flesh indulges itself, even when God rouses us by the tokens of his anger. What then do we suppose would take place if he should always ignore transgression? But when we, after having been reproved for our sins, repent, the result not only absorbs the curse that was felt at the beginning but also proves that the Lord blesses us more by punishing us than he would have by sparing us. Hence it follows that diseases, poverty, famine, nakedness, and even death itself, insofar as they promote our salvation, may rightly be thought of as blessings.

When it is added at the end of the verse, **giving each the blessing appropriate to him**, Moses again affirms that Jacob not only implored a blessing on his sons, from a paternal desire for their welfare, but pronounced what God had put into his mouth, because at length the event proved that the prophecies were efficacious.

**29-32. Then he gave them these instructions: "I am about to be gathered to my people. Bury me with my fathers in the cave in the field of Ephron the Hittite, the cave in the field of Machpelah, near Mamre in Canaan, which Abraham bought as a burial place from**

Ephron the Hittite, along with the field. There Abraham and his wife Sarah were buried, there Isaac and his wife Rebekah were buried, and there I buried Leah. The field and the cave in it were bought from the Hittites." We have seen before that Jacob specifically ordered his son Joseph to make sure that his body was buried in the land of Canaan. Moses now repeats that the same command was given to all Jacob's sons, so that they might go to that country together and might help each other in this task. We have stated elsewhere why he made such a point about this tomb. We must always remember this, in case the example of the holy man should be drawn injudiciously into a precedent for superstition. He did not want to be carried into the land of Canaan, as if he would be nearer heaven by being buried there. Rather, once he was dead, he could in a sense claim possession of a land that he had held during his life, but only by a precarious tenure. Not that any advantage would hence accrue to him privately, seeing he had already fulfilled his course; but it was profitable for the memory of the promise to be renewed by this symbol among his surviving sons, so that they might aspire to it. Meanwhile, we gather that he did not cling to the earth because unless he had been an heir of heaven, he would never have hoped that God, for the sake of one who was dead, would prove so bountiful toward his children.

To give greater weight to his command, Jacob declared that this thing had not come first into his own mind, but that he had been thus taught by his forefathers. Abraham, he said, bought that sepulcher for himself and his family. He was saying, "Up to this point we have sacredly kept the law delivered to us by Abraham. You must, therefore, take care not to violate it, so that after my death also some token of God's favor may continue with us."

33. **When Jacob had finished giving instructions to his sons, he drew his feet up into the bed, breathed his last and was gathered to his people.** The expression **he drew his feet up into the bed** is not superfluous. Moses wanted to describe the placid death of this holy man. It is as if he said that the aged saint gave directions about the disposal of his body as easily as healthy and vigorous men compose themselves for sleep. And it is not to be doubted that such efficacy of the Holy Spirit manifested itself in him as served to produce in his sons confidence in and reverence for his prophecies. At the same time, it is proper to observe that it is the effect of a good conscience to be able to leave the world without fear. For since death is by nature formidable, great torments agitate the wicked when they perceive that they are summoned to the tribunal of God. Moreover, so that a good conscience may lead us peacefully and quietly to the grave, it is necessary to rely on the resurrection of Christ; for we go willingly to God when we have confidence in a better life. We shall not deem it grievous to leave this failing tabernacle when we reflect on the everlasting abode that is prepared for us.

# Genesis
# Chapter 50

**1. Joseph threw himself upon his father and wept over him and kissed him.** In this chapter, what happened after the death of Jacob is briefly related. Moses, however, states that Jacob's death was honored with a double mourning—natural (so to speak) and ceremonial. That Joseph **threw himself upon his father and wept over him and kissed him** flowed from true and pure affection; that the Egyptians mourned for him for seventy days, in order to honor him and in accordance with their custom, is more from ostentation and vain pomp than from true grief. And yet the dead are generally mourned over in this manner, that the last debt due to them may be discharged. From this practice the proverb originated that the mourning of the heir is laughter under a mask. Although sometimes minds are full of real grief, yet something is added to it by the affectation of making a show of pious sorrow, so that they indulge largely in tears in the presence of others but would weep more sparingly if there were no witnesses of their grief. But Joseph is not here reproved because he manifested his grief by weeping; his filial piety is rather commended. We, however, need to be careful that intemperate grief does not lead us to complain against God, for excessive grief always leads to such rebellion. Moreover, the mitigation of sorrow is chiefly to be sought for in the hope of a future life, according to the doctrine of Paul.

**2. Then Joseph directed the physicians in his service to embalm his father Israel. So the physicians embalmed him.** In former days more labor was expended on funerals, even without superstition, than has been deemed right subsequent to the proof given of the resurrection exhibited by Christ. Yet we know that among the Egyptians there was greater pomp given to funerals than among the Jews. Even the ancient historians record this among the most memorable customs of that nation. Indeed, it is not to be doubted that the sacred rite of burial descended from the holy fathers, to be a kind of mirror of the future resurrection. But as hypocrites are always more diligent in the performance of ceremonies than they are who possess the solid substance of things, it happens that those who have declined from the true faith assume a far more ostentatious appearance than the faithful, who pertain the truth and the right use of the symbol. If we compare the Jews with ourselves, these shadowy ceremonies in which God required them to be occupied would at this time appear intolerable. But when they are compared with those of other nations, they were moderate and could easily be borne. But the heathen hardly knew why they incurred so much labor and expense. Hence we infer how empty and trivial a matter it is to attend only to external signs when the pure doctrine that exhibits their true origin and their legitimate end does not flourish.

It is an act of piety to bury the dead. To embalm corpses with aromatic spices was in former times no fault, inasmuch as it was done as a public symbol of future incorruption. For it is not possible but that the sight of a dead man should grievously affect us, as if one common end, without distinction, awaited both us and the beasts that perish. But today the resurrection of Christ sufficiently supports us from yielding to this temptation. But the ancients, on whom the full light of day had not yet shone, were aided by figures. They, however, whose minds were not raised to the hope of a better life did nothing but trifle and foolishly imitate the holy fathers.

Finally, where faith has not so breathed its odor as to make men know that something remains for them after death, all embalming will be vapid. If death is to them the eternal destruction of the body, it would be an impious profanation of a sacred and useful ceremony to attempt to place what had perished under such costly custody. It is probable that Joseph, in conforming himself to the Egyptians, whose superfluous care was not free from absurdity, acted rather from fear than from judgment or approval of their method. Perhaps he improperly imitated the Egyptians lest the condition of his father might be worse than that of other men. But it would have been better had he confined himself to the frugal practice of his fathers. Nevertheless, although he might be excused, the same practice is not now lawful for us. For unless we wish to subvert the glory of Christ, we must cultivate greater sobriety.

3. . . . taking a full forty days, for that was the time required for embalming. And the Egyptians mourned for him seventy days. We have shown already that Moses is speaking about a ceremonial mourning. Therefore he does not prescribe this as a law or produce it as an example for us to follow. The seventy days that Moses says were set apart for solemn mourning, Herodotus, in his second book, assigns to the embalming. But Diodorus writes that the seasoning of the body was completed in thirty days. Both authors diligently describe the method of embalming. Though I will not deny that in the course of time the skill and industry in practicing this art increased, yet it appears to me probable that this was handed down from the fathers.

**4-5. When the days of mourning had passed, Joseph said to Pharaoh's court, "If I have found favor in your eyes, speak to Pharaoh for me. Tell him, 'My father made me swear an oath and said, "I am about to die; bury me in the tomb I dug for myself in the land of Canaan." Now let me go up and bury my father; then I will return.'"** A brief narration is here inserted about Joseph obtaining permission to leave Egypt and bury his father. Joseph said that it was not his choice to bury his father in a different land, but that he was asked to do this under oath. Wherefore we see that he was oppressed by servile fear, so that he did not dare frankly and boldly to profess his own faith, since he was compelled to act a part in order to transfer to the deceased whatever odium might attend the transaction. Whereas a more simple and upright confession of faith is required of the sons of God, let none of us seek refuge under such pretexts; rather let us learn to ask from the Lord the spirit of fortitude and constancy that enables us to witness to true religion. Seeing that Joseph did not dare to move his foot except with the king's permission, we infer that he was bound by his splendid fortune as by golden chains. This is the condition of all who are honored and favored in royal courts. So there is nothing better for men of sane mind than to be content with their own private condition. Joseph also mitigated the offense that he feared he was giving by another circumstance when he said that the desire to be buried in the land of Canaan was not one that had recently entered his father's mind, because he had dug his grave there long before. So it follows that he had not been induced to do so because of anything he found in the land of Egypt.

**6. Pharaoh said, "Go up and bury your father, as he made you swear to do."** We have seen that Joseph adopted a middle course. He was not willing utterly to fail in his duty; yet by using his father's wish as a pretext, he did not conduct himself with sufficient firmness. It is possible that Pharaoh was inclined by the modesty of his manner more easily to assent to his requests. Yet this cowardice is not on this account so sanctioned that the sons of God are free to indulge themselves in it. For if they intrepidly follow where duty calls, the Lord will give the result that is desired, beyond all expectation. For although humanly speaking Joseph's bland submission succeeded, it is nevertheless certain that the proud mind of the king was influenced by God to concede to his wishes. It is also to be observed in what high esteem blind unbelievers held an oath. For though Pharaoh himself had not sworn, he still deemed it unlawful for him to violate by his own authority the pledge given by another. But today reverence for God has become so rare that men commonly regard it a mere trifle to deceive anyone in the name of God. But such unbridled license, which even Pharaoh himself denounced, shall not escape God's judgment with impunity.

**7-13. So Joseph went up to bury his father. All Pharaoh's officials**

accompanied him—the dignitaries of his court and all the dignitaries of Egypt—besides all the members of Joseph's household and his brothers and those belonging to his father's household. Only their children and their flocks and herds were left in Goshen. Chariots and horsemen also went up with him. It was a very large company. When they reached the threshing floor of Atad, near the Jordan, they lamented loudly and bitterly; and there Joseph observed a seven-day period of mourning for his father. When the Canaanites who lived there saw the mourning at the threshing floor of Atad, they said, "The Egyptians are holding a solemn ceremony of mourning." That is why that place near the Jordan is called Abel Mizraim. So Jacob's sons did as he had commanded them: They carried him to the land of Canaan and buried him in the cave in the field of Machpelah, near Mamre, which Abraham had bought as a burial place from Ephron the Hittite, along with the field. Moses gives a full account of the burial. What he recounts concerning the renewed mourning of Joseph and his brothers, as well as of the Egyptians, should not become the norm for us. For we know that since our flesh has no self-government, men commonly exceed bounds both in sorrowing and in rejoicing. The tumultuous glamour, which the inhabitants of the place admired, cannot be excused. And although Joseph had a right end in view when he fixed the mourning to last through seven successive days, yet this excess was not free from blame. Nevertheless, it was not without reason that the Lord allowed this funeral to be honorably celebrated in this way. For it was of great consequence that a kind of sublime trophy should be raised that might transmit to posterity the memory of Jacob's faith. If he had been buried privately and in the usual way, his fame would have quickly been forgotten. But now, unless men deliberately close their eyes, they have continually before them this noble example, which may cherish the hope of the promised inheritance.

Wherefore, we are not here to consider the honor of the deceased so much as the benefit of the living. Even the Egyptians, not knowing what they did, bore a torch before the Israelites to teach them to keep the course of their divine calling. The Canaanites did the same when they honored the place with a new name. In this way it came to pass that the knowledge of the covenant of the Lord flourished afresh.

14. After burying his father, Joseph returned to Egypt, together with his brothers and all the others who had gone with him to bury his father. Although Joseph and the rest had left so many pledges in Egypt that it would be necessary for them to return, it is yet probable that they were rather drawn back thither by the oracle of God. For God never allowed them to choose where they should live. As he had before led Abraham, Isaac, and Jacob in their journeying, so he held their sons enclosed in the land of Goshen as within barriers. They returned, therefore, into Egypt not only because they were compelled by present neces-

sity, but because it was not lawful for them to shake off the yoke that God had put on their necks. If the Lord does not hold all men by voluntary obedience to himself, he nevertheless holds their minds by his hidden power, that they may not withdraw themselves from his government. Nor can we form any other conjecture than that they were restrained by his fear, so that even when admonished concerning the tyrannical oppression that was coming upon them, they did not attempt to make their escape. We know that their disposition was not so mild as to prevent them from rebelling against lighter burdens. Wherefore, on this point a special sense of religious obligation subdued them, so that they prepared themselves quietly and silently to endure the hardest servitude.

**15. When Joseph's brothers saw that their father was dead, they said, "What if Joseph holds a grudge against us and pays us back for all the wrongs we did to him?"** Moses here recounts that the sons of Jacob, after the death of their father, were apprehensive in case Joseph should take revenge for the harm they had done to him. They did not attribute his being placable to true piety toward God, nor did they account it a special gift of the Spirit; rather, they imagined that out of respect for his father alone, he had so far only postponed his revenge. But by such perverse judgment, they did a great injury to one who by the liberality of his treatment had borne them witness that his mind was free from all hatred and malevolence. Part of their harmful surmise reflected badly even on God, whose special grace had shone out in Joseph's moderation. We gather from this that guilty consciences are so disturbed by blind and unreasonable fears that they stumble in broad daylight. Joseph had forgiven his brothers for the crime they had committed against him; but they were so agitated by guilty compunctions that they became their own tormentors. And they had not themselves to thank that they did not bring down upon themselves the very punishment that had been remitted, because the mind of Joseph might well have been wounded by their distrust. For what could they mean by still malignantly suspecting him to whose compassion they had again and again owed their lives? I do not doubt that long ago they had repented of their wickedness. But, perhaps because they had not yet been sufficiently purified, the Lord suffered them to be tortured with anxiety and trouble—first, to make them an example to others that an evil conscience is its own tormentor, and then to humble them under a renewed sense of their own guilt. For when they saw themselves as obnoxious in their brother's judgment, they could not forget, unless they were worse than senseless, God's heavenly tribunal.

**16. So they sent word to Joseph, saying, "Your father left these instructions before he died . . ."** Because they were ashamed to speak themselves, they sent messengers of peace, in whom Joseph might have greater confidence. But here also we perceive that those who have an accusing conscience are devoid of counsel and reason. For if Jacob had been fearful on this point, why did he not effect reconciliation between the son who was so obedient to himself and his brothers? Besides, for what reason would they attempt to do through mediators what they could do so much better themselves? The Lord, therefore, allowed them to act like children, that we, being instructed by their example, might look for no advantage from the use of frivolous inventions.

**17-18. "'This is what you are to say to Joseph: I ask you to forgive your brothers the sins and the wrongs they committed in treating you so badly.' Now please forgive the sins of the servants of the God of your father." When their message came to him, Joseph wept. His brothers then came and threw themselves down before him. "We are your slaves," they said.** They did not dissemble the fact that they had grievously sinned; and they did not excuse themselves about the wrong they had done. They did not, therefore, ask that pardon should be granted them as if the offense were light. Their confession would have been worthy of commendation, had they proceeded directly and without tortuous contrivances to appease their brother. Now, since they had drawn from the spring of piety the instruction that it is right for sin to be remitted to the servants of God, we may receive it as a common exhortation that if we have been injured by the members of the church, we must not be too rigid and immovable in pardoning the offense. And we must observe that they specifically mentioned **"the God of your father."** The special faith and worship by which they were distinguished from the rest of the nations was to unite them with each other in a closer bond. It was as if God, who had adopted that family, stood forth in the middle of them and produced this reconciliation.

**19. But Joseph said to them, "Don't be afraid. Am I in the place of God?"** Some think that in these words he was rejecting the honor paid him, as if he would say that it was unjustly offered to him because it was due to God alone. But this interpretation is not probable since he often allowed himself to be addressed in this manner and knew that the minds of his brothers were utterly averse to transferring the worship of God to mortal man. I equally disapprove another meaning given to the passage, which makes Joseph refuse to exact punishment because he was not God. For he did not restrain himself from retaliating in the hope that God would prove to be his avenger. Others adduce a third interpretation—namely, that the whole affair was conducted by the counsel of God, and not by Joseph's own. I do not entirely reject this view because it approaches the truth; yet I do not embrace the interpretation as true.

But as to the sum of the matter, there is no ambiguity. For seeing that Joseph considered the design of divine providence, he bridled his feelings in case he was carried away by them. He was indeed of a mild and humane disposition; but he knew that nothing was better or more suitable to assuage his anger than to submit himself to God's rule. When, therefore, the desire to take revenge overtakes us, let all our feelings be subjected to the same authority. Moreover, he desired his brothers to be tranquil and secure, due to the consideration that he, ascribing due honor to God, willingly submitted to obey the divine command. Let us learn thus that it is to our advantage to deal with men of moderation, who set God before them as their leader and who not only submit to his will but also cheerfully obey him. For if anyone is carried away by the lusts of the flesh, we must fear a thousand deaths from him, unless God should forcibly break his fury.

**20. "You intended to harm me, but God intended it for good to accomplish what is now being done, the saving of many lives."** Joseph considered God's providence, and so not only pardoned his brothers but also acted positively on their behalf. We must notice the difference in his language. Whereas in the previous passage Joseph, wanting to soothe their grief and to alleviate the fear of his brothers, wanted to cover their wickedness by every means that ingenuity could suggest, he now corrected them a little more openly and freely, perhaps because he was offended with their disingenuousness. Yet he held to the same principle as before. Seeing that by the secret counsel of God he had been led into Egypt for the purpose of preserving the lives of his brothers, he now felt he must devote himself to that object, in case he should resist God. He said by his action, "Since God has deposited your life with me, I would be rebelling against him if I were not faithful in giving you the grace that he has committed to me."

Meanwhile, he skillfully distinguished between the wicked counsels of men and the admirable justice of God by so ascribing the government of everything to God, so as to preserve the divine administration free from contracting any stain from the vices of men. The selling of Joseph was a detestable act because of its cruelty and perfidy; yet he was not sold except by the decree of heaven. Thus we may say with truth and propriety that Joseph was sold by the wicked consent of his brothers *and* by the secret providence of God. Yet it was not a work common to both in such a sense that God sanctioned anything connected with or relating to their wicked cupidity. For while they were contriving the destruction of their brother, God was effecting their deliverance from on high. From this also we conclude that there are various ways in which God rules the world. It truly must be generally agreed that nothing is done without his will, because he both governs the counsels of men and sways their wills and turns their actions to his pleasure and regulates all events. But if men undertake anything right and just, God so moves them inwardly by his Spirit that whatever is good in them may justly be said to be received from him. But if Satan and ungodly men rage, he acts by their hands in such an inexpressible manner that the wickedness of the deed belongs to them, and the blame for it is imputed to them. For they are not induced to sin, as the faithful are to act aright, by the impulse of the Spirit, but they are responsible for their own evil and follow Satan as their leader. Thus we see that the justice of God shines brightly in the midst of the darkness of our iniquity.

**"The saving of many lives."** Joseph made his office subservient to God's providence. This sobriety is always to be cultivated, that everyone may behold, by faith, God from on high holding the helm of the government of the world and may keep himself within the bounds of his vocation, and even, being admonished by the secret judgments of God, may exhort himself to the discharge of his duty. What Joseph said about his being divinely chosen to save many lives, some extend to the Egyptians. Without condemning such an extension, I would rather restrict the application of the words to the family of Jacob; for Joseph amplifies the goodness of God by this circumstance—that the seed of the church would be rescued from destruction by his labor. And truly from these few men, whose seed would otherwise have been extinct before their descendants had been multiplied, that vast multitude sprang into being that God soon raised up.

**21. "So then, don't be afraid. I will provide for you and your children." And he reassured them and spoke kindly to them.** It was a token of a solid and not a feigned reconciliation not only to abstain from malice and injury, but also to overcome evil with good, as Paul teaches (Romans 12:21). Anyone who fails in his duty when he has the power to help and when the occasion demands his assistance shows by this very course that he is not forgetful of injury. This must be carefully observed because, commonly, the greater part weakly conclude that they forgive offenses if they do not retaliate. We act as if we are not taking revenge when we withdraw our hands from giving help. You would assist your brother if you thought him worthy. He implores your aid in necessity, but you desert him because he has done you some unkindness. What hinders you from helping him but hatred? Therefore, we shall only prove our minds to be free from malevolence when we treat with kindness those enemies by whom we have been ill treated. Joseph is said to have spoken **kindly** to his brothers. By addressing them with grace and kindness, he removed all their scruples.

**22-23. Joseph stayed in Egypt, along with all his father's family. He lived a hundred and ten years and saw the third generation of Ephraim's children. Also the children of Makir son of Manasseh were placed at birth on Joseph's knees.** It is not without reason that Moses recounts how long Joseph lived, because the length of his life shows more clearly God's unfailing constancy. Although he was raised to great honor and power among the Egyptians, he still was closely united with his father's house. Hence it is easy to conjecture that he gradually took his leave of the treasures of the court, because he thought there was nothing better for him to do than to hold them in contempt, in case earthly dignity should separate him from the kingdom of God. He had before spurned all the allurements that might have occupied his mind in Egypt. He now thought that it was necessary to proceed further, that, laying his honor to one side, he might descend to an ignoble condition and wean his own sons from the hope of succeeding to his worldly rank. We know how anxiously others labor, both so they themselves may not be reduced in circumstances and so they may leave their complete fortune to their posterity. But Joseph for sixty years used all his efforts to bring himself and his children into a state of submission, lest his earthly greatness should alienate them from the little flock of the Lord. In short, he imitated serpents, who throw off their skin that, being stripped of their old age, they may gather new strength.

**24. Then Joseph said to his brothers, "I am about to die. But God will surely come to your aid and take you up out of this land to the land he promised on oath to Abraham, Isaac and Jacob."** It is uncertain whether Joseph died first or last of the brothers, or whether just some of them survived him. Here indeed Moses includes, under the name of **brothers**, not only those who were actually brothers but other relatives as well. I think, however, that certain of the chiefs of each family were called at his command, from whom the whole of the people might receive information. Although it is probable that the other patriarchs gave the same command respecting themselves (verse 25), since their the bones were all in a similar way conveyed to the land of Canaan, special mention is made of Joseph for two reasons. First, since the eyes of everyone were fixed on him on account of his high authority, it was his duty to give the lead and cautiously to beware in case the splendor of his dignity should be a stumbling block for any of them. Second, it was of great consequence as an example that it should be known to all the people that he who held the second place in the kingdom of Egypt, regardless of so great an honor, was contented with his own situation, which was only that of the heir of a bare promise.

**"I am about to die."** This expression was like a command to his brothers to be of good courage after his death, because the truth of God is immortal. He did not want them to depend on his life or on the life of anyone else in such a way as to limit God's power. Rather, he wanted them to patiently rest until the suitable time arrived. But from where did he gain this great certainty that he would be a witness and a surety of future redemption unless he had been taught this by his father? For we do not read that God had appeared to him, or that an oracle had been brought to him by an angel from heaven. But because he was fully convinced that Jacob was a teacher and prophet divinely appointed to transmit to his sons the covenant of salvation deposited with him, Joseph relied on his testimony as if some vision had been given to him or as if he had seen angels descending to him from heaven. For unless the hearing of the word is sufficient for our faith, we do not deserve that God, whom we then rob of his honor, should condescend to deal with us. It is not that faith relies on human authority; rather, it hears God speaking through the mouth of men and through their external voice is drawn upward to God. For what God pronounces through men, he seals on our hearts by his Spirit. Thus faith is built on no other foundation than God himself; and yet the preaching of men is not lacking in its claim of authority and reverence. This restraint is put on the rash curiosity of those who eagerly desire visions and who despise the ordinary ministry of the church. They act as if it is absurd that God, who previously showed himself to the fathers out of heaven, should send out his voice from the earth. But if they would reflect how gloriously God once descended to us in the person of his only-begotten Son, they would not so importunately desire that heaven should daily be opened to them. When the brothers saw that Joseph, who in this respect was inferior to his fathers, having been partaker of no oracle, had been imbued by them with the doctrine of piety, so that he contended with a faith similar to theirs, they would at once be most ungrateful and malignant if they rejected the participation of his grace.

**25-26. And Joseph made the sons of Israel swear an oath and said, "God will surely come to your aid, and then you must carry my bones up from this place." So Joseph died at the age of a hundred and ten. And after they embalmed him, he was placed in a coffin in Egypt.** By these words he intimated that they would be buried as in oblivion so long as they remained in Egypt. Truly that exile was as if God had turned his back on them for a season. Nevertheless, Joseph did not cease to fix his eyes on God; as it is written in the prophet, "I will wait for the LORD, who is hiding his face from the house of Jacob" (Isaiah 8:17).

This passage in Genesis also clearly teaches the purpose behind his careful choice of his tomb—namely, that it might be a seal of redemption. For after he had asserted that God was faithful and would in his own time grant what he had promised, he immediately ordered his brothers to transport his bones. These were useful reminders, the sight of which plainly signified that by the death of men, the eternal covenant in which Joseph commanded his posterity safely to rest had by no means become extinct. For he deemed it sufficient to adduce the oath of God to remove all their doubts concerning their deliverance.